LIBRARIES:
GLOBAL REACH—
LOCAL TOUCH

Edited by
Kathleen de la Peña McCook
Barbara J. Ford
and
Kate Lippincott

AMERICAN LIBRARY ASSOCIATION
Chicago and London
1998

The paper used in this publication meets the minimum requirements of the American National Standard for Information Sciences—Permanence of Paper for Printed Library Materials, ANSI Z39.48-1992.

Library of Congress Cataloging-in-Publication Data
Libraries: global reach, local touch / edited by Kathleen de la Peña McCook, Barbara J. Ford, and Kate Lippincott.
      p.   c.m.
  Includes bibliographic references (p.)
  ISBN 0-8389-0738-5
  1. Libraries. 2. Libraries and readers. I. McCook, Kathleen de la Peña. II. Ford, Barbara J. III. Lippincott, Kate.
Z721.L6 1998   98-4397
027—dc21

02 01 00 99 98   5 4 3 2 1

Contents

Preface   v

Librarians as Culture Keepers and Information Providers
Kathleen de la Peña McCook   1

1. Inaugural Remarks
Barbara J. Ford   3

2. A Global Perspective
Robert Wedgeworth   6

3. From *Amoxcallis* to Electronic Libraries
Daniel Mattes   12

4. Improving University Libraries in El Salvador
William V. Jackson   24

5. Academic Libraries in Colombia
Charlotte E. Ford and Luz M. Quiroga   31

6. Discovering Treasures in Ecuador
Patricia A. Wand   39

7. When Literacy and Oracy Meet
Philip J. Calvert   44

8. Developing Library and Information Services in Micronesia
Arlene Cohen, Joanne Tarpley Crotts, and Irene Lovas   50

9. Libraries and Information Services in Malaysia
Diljit Singh   60

10. Libraries and Information Centres in India
T. N. Kamala   70

11. Libraries in Azerbaijan
Muzhgan Nazarova   82

12. Touching Turkey
Jordan M. Scepanski   90

13. Post-Soviet Russian Librarianship in Transition
Michael Neubert and Irina L. Klim   98

14. Estonia
Eric A. Johnson and Aira Lepik   104

15. Romanian Libraries
Stephen R. Amery   110

16. Genesis of a Library in the Czech Republic
Norma J. Hervey   124

17. Polish Libraries and Librarianship
    in a Time of Challenge and Change
    George S. Bobinski and Maria Kocojowa   139

18. Slavic Book and Serial Exchanges
    Bradley L. Schaffner   144

19. African Librarianship
    Kingo J. Mchombu   150

20. Dreams and Realities
    Peter G. Underwood and Mary Nassimbeni   157

21. Queens Library
    Gary E. Strong   165

22. Global Relevance through Sustained Achievement
    Ken Haycock   173

23. Quality Library Services to Children and Young Adults
    for Changing Needs
    Barbara Immroth   181

24. International Library Women
    Suzanne Hildenbrand and Mary Biblo   187

25. The Influence of Information Technology Infrastructure
    and Policies on Library Services in Developing Countries
    Donald E. Riggs   195

26. Freedom of Expression
    Matthew B. Barrett and Beverly P. Lynch   202

27. The Ethics of Naming and the Discourse of Globalization
    Hope A. Olson   210

28. Family Literacy
    Rebecca Knuth   219

29. Going Global via the Literature
    Alma Dawson   234

Contributors   249

Preface

I am not an Athenian or a Greek, but a citizen of the world
— Socrates

Global Reach, Local Touch," Barbara Ford's theme for her 1997–98 American Library Association presidency, provides a focus for this compilation on international issues in librarianship and descriptions of library services in specific countries.

Ford's theme echoes efforts by other groups to "think globally and act locally." Increasingly, many issues, such as those involving the environment, health, the economy, population growth, and poverty, are global in scope. By acting locally, however, each proactive step that individuals and groups take in their own communities helps to address the challenges that cross national boundaries. Individually, we might be able to influence only a small area, but collectively these individual actions have a much wider ripple.

Why a book on global librarianship? Coping with many global issues is based in large part on understanding and using accurate, up-to-date information. Access to information and freedom of expression are taken for granted in the United States, but are not available elsewhere in many places. Yet information is perhaps the most powerful tool available to people around the world for solving problems.

The ever expanding information technology makes the world seem smaller every day. There is controversy, however, on whether the technology is creating wider gaps between the rich and the poor or whether it can be a tool to help developing countries "leapfrog" into the twenty-first century and become a source of empowerment for individuals, organizations and nations.

As Ford has suggested in various forums, we can help shape the global information infrastructure by addressing issues of information equity, funding, copyright, and more. The new communications technology can help bridge the geographical, social and economic gaps that currently exist in the availability and access to information.

In her inaugural address to the ALA, Ford said, however, there are still many who cannot read. This is nearly a billion people. In addition, some 130 million children are denied the right to primary education. Without basic literacy and education for all, the information technologies cannot reach their potential in providing an international network to converse, teach, learn, hold meetings, send and receive information.

What can we as librarians do? Certainly, we can serve our ethnic communities and students better if we can provide collections that make the library more relevant to community members from different cultures and help all citizens understand our increasingly diverse society.

As librarians in the global village, we can participate in partnership and exchanges of staff and materials with libraries in the other countries. We can become more active in international professional associations and in the development of international standards. We can help rebuild libraries in war-torn countries or those recovering from natural disasters. We can provide book donations and share skills with those in developing countries.

As we broaden contacts internationally through networking, sharing, and communicating (whether in person or through cyberspace), we learn and grow as individuals and we broaden our horizons and those of our institutions. We indeed become citizens of the world.

Margaret Myers, Peace Corps Volunteer, 1997
Palapye, Botswana

Librarians as Culture Keepers and Information Providers

Introductory Notes to *Libraries: Global Reach—Local Touch*

Kathleen de la Peña McCook

Librarians who activate their philosophical and intellectual commitment to literacy, preservation, life-long learning and information provision will protect the rights of individuals and the heterogeneity of cultures during this time of accelerated "globalization." Globalization is not a new phenomenon. Every foray of explorers, conquerors and traders from the earliest times to the present has embodied an expansion of territory at a cost to the cultures in the area of expansion. The result of voyages of discovery was conquest and subjugation, pillaging of resources and forced labor to produce commodities for sale. These earlier forms of globalization "produced a world economic and political structure through which corporate interests in the imperial centers benefited from the exploitation of labor in the peripheral areas."[1]

The current manifestation of globalization is a move toward a "global monoculture, the homogenization of culture, lifestyle and level of technological immersion, with the correspondent dismantlement of local traditions and self-sufficient economies."[2] The protection of local culture, historic traditions, and valuation of difference becomes a charge to librarians and archivists who work to preserve the unique aspects of clans, tribes and nations.

As the global marketplace grows and financial markets are deregulated, it is more important than ever to "elevate the rights of the workers to the same importance as the protection of property in trade agreements."[3] This can only be done if librarians hold as central the tenet that information provision imbues individuals with the power to understand and guard against cultural destruction. New sources of identity must be strengthened as old sources are disrupted by processes of economic modernization.[4]

Multinational corporations and media conglomerates control increasingly large proportions of intellectual production. The long-term capacity of these entities to overpower cultural identities leads to "McWorld"—"pressing nations into one homogeneous global theme park."[5] Never before has the role of librarians been more crucial to the retention of the traditions and rituals of individual nations, traditions, and rituals.

The essays that follow were selected to demonstrate how libraries and librarians have made use of the power of the new technologies to protect and ensure continuation of local cultures. The "call for papers" for this book was conducted through postings on dozens of listservs and webpages with a request that authors consider the theme of American Library Association President, Barbara J. Ford.

Margaret Myers, a librarian and Peace Corps volunteer in Botswana, prefaces the book with a pure declaration of what it means to be a citizen of the world. Barbara J. Ford's inaugural remarks as ALA President sweep across hemispheres to establish a tone of idealism and commitment. Robert Wedgeworth, Past President of the International Federation of Library Associations, establishes a broad global perspective.

The essays then move south to Mexico, El Salvador, Colombia, and Ecuador, then west to the South Pacific, Micronesia, Malaysia, and India, north to Azerbaijan, Turkey, Russia, Estonia, Romania, the Czech Republic, Poland. The Slavic Book exchange, African librarianship and South Africa are discussed, and finally the essay returns to the U.S. where the Queens Library stands for a microcosm of world cultures. After these local essays, the role of the International Association of School Librarians and of two of IFLA units are presented. The essays conclude with four cross-cutting papers on technology, infrastructure, freedom of expression, the ethics of naming and family literacy. The final contribution is a selective guide to the literature of international and global librarianship by Dr. Alma Dawson, faculty member and former LIS bibliographer at Louisiana State University.

The work of a President of the American Library Association is to develop a thematic approach to a presidential year that enables the U.S. library community to examine its values. During Barbara J. Ford's year of service as ALA President she has ensured that all U.S. librarians have an opportunity to participate in an assessment of the impact of globalization. At the 1998 Midwinter Meeting her "President's Program" brought together four prominent world citizens to discuss the impact of the emergent information age libraries: Stephney Ferguson, Head of the Department of Library and Information Studies at the University of the West Indies; Josef Jarab, Senator of the Czech Republic and Rector of Central European University in Budapest; P. B. Mangla, Head of the Department of Library and Information Science at the University of Delhi; and Robert Wedgeworth, University Librarian and professor at the University of Illinois at Urbana–Champaign.

The issues discussed at President Ford's 1998 Conference programs, archived at the Global ALA website (http://www.ala.org/GoGlobal) and analyzed in this volume, provide librarians with a foundation for a renewed global orientation. But we must remember the local counterpoint. Even in a nation as wealthy as the U.S. appears to be on the brink of this new millennium, there is poverty and information deprivation. One solution in which librarians can play a consistent role in the amelioration of poverty in the U.S., or in the nations in which they serve, is to embrace the ideals of radical humanism. These principles are described with passion in Earl Shorris's book, *New American Blues: A Journey through Poverty to Democracy*.[6] It all begins with understanding. Librarians will open this door and will ensure the preservation of individual cultures.

Notes

1. David Broad, "Globalization Versus Labor," *Monthly Review* 47 (December 1995).
2. Jerry Mander, "The Dark Side of Globalization," *The Nation* 263 (July 15, 1996).
3. John Sweeney, et al., "Containing Globalization," *New Perspectives Quarterly* 14 (Spring 1997).
4. Samuel Huntington, *The Clash of Civilizations and the Remaking of World Order* (New York: Simon and Schuster, 1996).
5. Benjamin Barber, *Jihad vs. McWorld* (New York: Time Books, 1995).
6. Earl Shorris, *New American Blues: A Journey through Poverty to Democracy* (New York: W. W. Norton, 1997).

1. Inaugural Remarks

Barbara J. Ford
President, American Library Association
July 1, 1997

Libraries: Global Reach—Local Touch

Ours is a small world—and getting smaller all the time. All you have to do is look around to see, hear, and taste the influence of world cultures. One of the biggest hits now on stage—*River Dance*—is a performance of traditional Irish dance.

Radios play Latin music. Restaurants offer not just pizza and chow mein—but pad thai, tira misu, tabouleh, and empanadas.

Intricate braids and pierced noses may look new to our eyes, but they are old news in Africa and the Middle East!

The same multicultural forces at work in art, music, and fashion are reshaping the way we do business.

Today's *Wall Street Journal* reports as much on corporate expansion into global markets as U.S. operations. Businesses—and even countries—are being restructured to reflect the global context in which we now live, work, and govern.

I have always believed in the power of information to build bridges and promote understanding among diverse cultures. One of the first things I did after graduating from college was to join the Peace Corps, where I served in Panama and Nicaragua. It remains one of my most valued experiences—one that has infused my life with a deeper understanding and appreciation of intercultural exchange.

Of course, back then, I had no idea that I would one day be president of the oldest and largest library association in the world! Thank you all for this great honor.

During my year as American Library Association (ALA) president, I will focus on an area of great personal and professional concern—the role of libraries and librarians in the global village.

The theme I have selected is simple and to the point: "Libraries: Global Reach—Local Touch." It focuses on a unique, exciting, and invaluable aspect of what today's libraries offer: access to worldwide information resources and local accessibility.

Tonight, I would like to focus briefly on just a few of the opportunities, responsibilities, and challenges we face as a profession and nation—and invite you to join me in "going global."

James Madison once said, "Information is the currency of democracy." The value of that currency is skyrocketing in the new global economy. No one understands this better than librarians.

ALA Goal 2000 says that all people must be able to participate intellectually in an information society. To achieve this, there are three key areas that demand our attention.

The first is literacy. One of 1996-1997 ALA President Mary Somerville's favorite statements was "Kids who aren't logged on and literate will be lost in the next century." This is true. Our children must know how to use computers to succeed in the next century. We must also remember, however, that without basic literacy skills, technology has no relevance.

The number of people in the world who cannot read is staggering. The number of adults in the United States who lack basic reading skills is estimated to be as high as one-third. Librarians have always been leaders in promoting literacy. This role is more important than ever as we face the new millennium. The Clinton administration's focus on preschool learning provides an opportunity for us to showcase our work in promoting literacy at the earliest level. If your library does not already have a "Born to Read" program, there is no better time to start one. This program, initiated by ALA's Association for Library Service to Children, reaches out to new parents and teaches them to raise children who are healthy and ready to read. It is an excellent model of the kind of leadership we, as librarians, can exercise both in our own country and around the world.

The second critical area is equity of access. Our profession was among the first to recognize the growing importance of electronic information, and 1995–1996 ALA President Betty Turock was instrumental in bringing equity issues to the attention of policymakers and the public. With support from its expanded Washington Office and new Office for Information Technology Policy, ALA has enjoyed noteworthy successes, including passage of the new Library Services and Technology Act and significant discounts on telecommunications services for libraries. But the goal of connecting every school, public, college, and university library to the Internet remains to be achieved. It is up to each of us to take an active role in advocating funding and other legislative support needed to keep information free and open in the twenty-first century. If you lack the knowledge or confidence to speak out, I encourage you to take advantage of ALA's library advocacy training.

The third key area—and the one that I will focus on—is international cooperation and communication. The digital age has released us from geographic limitations as the basis for friendship, collaboration, commerce, and community.

As librarians, we have a responsibility to facilitate the flow of communication. We understand how to organize and present information and how people use information once they have it.

International cooperation will further transform the library's role from warehouses for books to electronic information delivery centers. Imagine the possibilities when scholars, diplomats, and school children around the world can do extensive research without leaving their universities, offices, or classrooms. That day is not far off.

Just as information easily crosses borders, our challenge now is to take a larger role on the world stage. ALA's participation in the Geneva copyright negotiations is a good example of how we can act on a larger stage to ensure a balanced and fair information doctrine.

As president of the American Library Association, I will lead our association in addressing literacy, equity of access, copyright, and other critical issues that will shape the global information infrastructure. I will also urge members of the public and policymakers to use and support libraries as multicultural institutions that connect even the smallest and most remote communities to global resources.

A year from now, when we meet in Washington, D.C., I will host an International Literacy Fair that will showcase model literacy programs in the United States and around the world. I look forward to having you join me there. I also urge you to start planning for the new millennium by marking your calendars for the conference of

International Federation of Library Associations and Institutions that will be held in Boston in the summer of 2001.

But you don't have to wait until 2001 or even the next conference to "go global." There are things that each of us can begin doing immediately when we go back to our libraries. The "Going Global" tip sheet in your folders will help you think globally and act locally. I encourage you to put it to good use.

I started tonight by saying the world is becoming a smaller place—often in ways we can scarcely imagine.

The American Library Association has received countless letters about how libraries make a difference in the lives of real people. I'd like to share the story of one of those people—Kathleen Vereeren, of Pitman, New Jersey—whose life was touched by events far from home. Kathleen wrote: "In our small, comfortable town, it seemed that we would be untouched by the war in Bosnia. But that was not the case."

Kathleen and her family had hosted a teenage girl named Aida from the former Yugoslavia as an exchange student. The family and girl initially stayed in touch, but Aida's letters became fewer and fewer. Then telephone calls stopped going through, and mail service no longer reached her town. The family received a message from Aida via the Red Cross begging them to help her escape from her town that had been besieged for four months.

After numerous phone calls and letters, Aida was again accepted as a foreign student. Back safely in Pitman, Aida was starved for reading but her English was weak. Bookstores were not able to help. Finally, the local library was able to obtain books in her language from another library. Not only that, it located a lifeline in the form of a librarian fluent in Serbo Croatian.

Kathleen concluded her letter by saying "As small as my town and library are, they were able to give Aida an important connection to her world across the ocean."

I would like to close by reminding all of us that as important and exciting as new technology is, it is the local touch that sets our libraries apart and will ensure their future as treasured institutions in the next century and beyond.

2. A Global Perspective

Robert Wedgeworth

From the beginning of my career as a librarian in 1961 I have had an international perspective on libraries and librarianship. This started with my early involvement with the acquisition of library materials from other countries and continued through my active efforts to expand the international activities of the American Library Association (ALA) when I was its Executive Director. This perspective was limited by the small number of countries with which I could have meaningful contact through visits, and the few foreign librarians I came to know through correspondence and conferences.

It was not until 1980 when I created the *World Encyclopedia of Library and Information Services* (3d edition 1993) that I came to realize that a global perspective on the field was indeed possible for me. The concepts, events, individuals, and institutions that have shaped the field, along with reports on 162 countries, formed the basis for this publication. But it was the contact with the correspondents from across the globe who, in addition to submitting the specified material, shared their pride, their hopes and their frustrations with the local library situation that allowed me to begin to feel part of a global library world.

Since 1985 I have been a member of the Executive Board of the International Federation of Library Associations and Institutions (IFLA), and president from 1991 until September 1997. That experience has given me an even broader understanding of the word "global" as applied to libraries and librarianship. For library and information services, there is both a context and a capability that appears to be shared internationally.

International or Global?

North American librarians (U.S. and Canada) have a long tradition of international involvement not only with each other but also with other nations through their foreign memberships, foreign conference guests and activities with colleagues in other nations.

North American librarians have also benefited from the liberal education in international relations presented by their contacts with the international book trade. Booksellers like Richard Blackwell (Blackwell's), Marcel Blancheteau (*Aux Amateurs des Livres*), and Richard Dorn (Otto Harrassowitz) revived the trans-Atlantic book trade following the disruption caused by World War II by visits to mostly academic institutions across North America that lasted months at a time. A Council on Library Resources, Inc., Fellowship allowed me to study the operations of these firms in depth in the late 1960s. As a result of their effective business and social relationships, these and other trusted firms helped broaden our understanding of the economic, political and cultural dimensions of western Europe. Some of the sons and daughters of the above continue these relationships, traveling mostly by air rather than via ship, rail and auto.

While these contacts have been important in advancing international interests, their sporadic and limited nature obscure a broader, more global perspective on librarianship.

Government or Non-government?

By their very nature all library activities among individuals, institutions or organizations that cross national borders operate either implicitly or explicitly under the auspices of national governments. International travel, correspondence and other communications across national borders are authorized by bi-national or multi-national agreements.

Some international activities are conducted directly by government-to-government relationships. Examples of these are Fulbright exchanges, relations between national libraries or consultative visits sponsored by government agencies.

Other government-sponsored international activities are carried out through inter-governmental agencies established by national governments for that purpose. Examples of these include the United Nations and its subsidiaries, UNESCO, World Health Organization and the Food and Agriculture Organization. All of these entities sponsor general or specialized library and information service programs aimed primarily at developing countries. Participants in these organizations are designated by government agencies which comprise the members.

A third pattern for the sponsorship of international library activities is through non-governmental organizations like the International Federation of Library Associations and Institutions (IFLA), International Council of Archives (ICA) and International Federation of Documentation (FID). These are the principal international organizations representing professional librarians, archivists, and scientific and technical information specialists. Participants in these organizations come from a variety of institutions and organizations.

In a small academic or professional field, activities of non-governmental organizations are essential supplements to those sponsored by government. For this reason IFLA has become a principal way to advance international library and information service activities. Its size and scope give it a breadth and depth that exceed that of any other international library organization.

IFLA Milestones

Until 1985 the United States and Canada had not been exceptionally influential in IFLA. They had hosted IFLA conferences in 1974 (Washington), 1982 (Montreal) and 1985 (Chicago), but had never had more than one of its members serve on the Executive Board at any given time. In 1985 I joined Henriette Avram on the IFLA Executive Board. While there was no active collusion to advance a specific program, we shared an understanding of the role and function of associations that distinguishes North American librarianship from the rest of the world. Some distinguishing characteristics are that our major institutions tend to exert leadership through active support and participation in associations. Associations tend to be larger and more influential than in other countries. There also tends to be more active participation by commercial entities as exhibitors and as contributors to the program of activities.

These are areas in which IFLA began to focus more attention after 1985. The fall of the Berlin Wall in 1989 and the subsequent political and social turmoil of central and eastern Europe posed both a challenge and an opportunity for IFLA. Socialist governments that had regularly paid dues for participation in IFLA were overthrown, leaving librarians and other information specialists without the financial means to participate in IFLA. However, participation now opened up to representatives other than those officially sanctioned by their governments. By 1991 the dues problem threatened to become a major crisis for IFLA, whose finances were quite precarious. On August 18,

1991, I was elected president of IFLA in Moscow. On the following day there was an attempted coup d'etat and the conference was disrupted for almost three days. Some delegates left immediately. There were calls to close the conference. However, the conference provided the only protection for those delegates who had to stay due to air ticket restrictions.

This experience of watching our Russian colleagues come to work each day at the conference not knowing what was happening to their families, friends and neighbors during the conference day gave many of us a ground-level view of the end of the Cold War. We left Moscow with a renewed sense of the importance of libraries and librarians in the work of building world peace through understanding.

The 1993 IFLA conference in Barcelona represented a major turning point for IFLA as a worldwide organization. Building on the strong representation of Asian participants in New Delhi the previous year, the Barcelona organizers mounted an impressive effort through the Spanish government to reach professional delegates in all parts of the world. They put together a splendid social program and provided the largest professional exhibition ever shown at an IFLA conference. It attracted record attendance, especially from Spanish-speaking countries, as this was the first conference in such a country since Spanish became an official language of IFLA in 1987.

The 1994 IFLA conference in Havana was the first in Latin America and the Caribbean region. That year IFLA launched its electronic network, IFLANET, with a new strategy to connect librarians and information specialists all over the world. Within one year individuals in institutions in more than seventy countries were actively communicating with each other via IFLANET.

The 1995 IFLA conference in Istanbul brought IFLA face-to-face with conflict over information policies. A substantial number of delegates came to that conference with concerns about Turkey's human rights record and similar concerns about past and future conference site selections that did not appear to be sensitive to human rights issues. Recognizing that these issues are perceived differently in different parts of the world, a Committee on Access to Information and Freedom of Expression (CAIFE) was created in Istanbul to address these issues and advise IFLA not later than 1997.

The Chinese government used all of its influence to bring libraries and librarianship center stage during the 1996 IFLA conference in Beijing. Earlier in the year the government had promulgated a new national program to bring libraries to every Chinese village and town by the year 2010. Conference activities were on national television morning and evening. Chinese librarians made substantial contributions to the professional program and the cultural tours were well-attended. Perhaps no western delegate attending that conference will ever forget the seventy-bus caravan that carried the IFLA conference participants from the suburban conference site across central Beijing to the Great Hall of the People with policemen at every intersection stopping rush hour traffic while the IFLA buses passed.

The 1997 IFLA conference in Copenhagen brought to a head all of the progress IFLA has made since its first conference outside Europe and North America held in Manila in 1980. A special DANIDA grant from the Danish Foreign Ministry brought 141 delegates from 81 developing countries which helped set a new record for IFLA conference attendance of 2,976 delegates from 141 countries. One hundred eighty-five professional and commercial exhibits provided a wide range of products and services marketed worldwide to libraries. A record number of new members joined IFLA and its budget was balanced for the fourth consecutive year.

This record of growth, strength and stability enabled IFLA to launch two new policy initiatives that reinforce the emerging global reach of libraries. A permanent Committee on Access to Information and Freedom of Expression (CAIFE) was established and based in Denmark. A second permanent Committee on Copyright and other Legal Matters was also established for the first time. These two initiatives recognize new global forces that are likely to exert influence on the theory and practice of librarianship in the future. IFLA's leadership in establishing these bodies gives it a bold new profile on the global scene.

Global Forces

A global perspective on libraries and librarianship would suggest that there are a set of global forces that are influencing the field. With a few exceptions, times have not been good for libraries economically in recent years. Nevertheless, new tools and techniques have transformed libraries as institutions and the services they provide. A larger and more diverse group of users demand increasingly more services. Cultural issues increasingly result in conflict over the contents and services of libraries.

Economics

The most common manifestation of global library economics is flat or declining budgets in the face of increases in the number, variety and the cost of library materials. Following a long period of relative stability in foreign exchange in North America, we have now joined the rest of the world experiencing a weak currency and hyperinflation in the 1970s and periodic volatility in the 1980s and 1990s. These factors have put imported library materials virtually out of reach of libraries in most developing countries.

Technological hardware and software associated with integrated library management systems are no longer optional purchases by libraries connected via the Internet. These represent new costs that must be added to traditional budgets. New and renovated library facilities occur less and less frequently due to costs. Salaries for librarians and other library workers are a constant source of complaint within the field.

Technology

New technologies have been a driving force in the development of libraries since the introduction of computers and photocopying machines in the 1960s. Until the 1980s it was rare to see a modern library technical services department in developing nations. In 1994 China had no academic library network. By 1996 it was up and functioning in many parts of the country. IFLA's electronic strategy for global library development has stimulated enormous growth in Internet connections in every region of the world with the exception of sub-Saharan Africa. However, achieving greater connectivity and providing technical training to library personnel are still fundamental barriers to the globalization of librarianship.

Demographics and Culture

Population growth, emigration and changes in the roles of women and children are exerting significant influence on libraries and librarianship. In the 1980s when the democratic government came to power in Argentina, 60,000 new students enrolled in the University of Buenos Aires. More students at every level of education are in need of library services around the world. Fully one-quarter of children under eighteen in the United States are from single-parent homes compared to 17 percent in the United Kingdom or 12 percent in France and Germany.

Waves of immigrants seeking better economic opportunities generate an unprecedented need for multi-cultural library services in North America and Europe. International norms for the roles of women and children increase their numbers in the work force and in schools, respectively.

Cultural differences related to language, religion and life-styles add to the complexity and the cost of serving multi-cultural populations. The concept of global access to information is greatly inhibited by the limitations of these factors. Dominant languages common to library materials from developed nations limit their use in developing nations. Religious differences restrict access to information and, perhaps, the Internet itself. Films and television promote life-styles that have a global impact on culture and education.

Toward a Global Library Agenda

My vision of a global library community is one that is asynchronous, multi-lingual, multi-cultural, geographically diverse, Internet-enabled and technically competent. Achieving this vision will require concerted efforts on a number of fronts simultaneously.

The global library agenda will require the stimulation of information policies with special attention to intellectual property rights and censorship issues. Global access to information cannot be achieved without international adherence to Article 19 of the Universal Declaration of Human Rights, which guarantees the right of access to information. New technical standards will need to be promulgated that will permit ease of transition from one information to another and ease of transfer of networked information sources. Currently, large amounts of digitized data are being created with little or no attention to common standards for data storage, retrieval and transfer.

Libraries will continue to be in demand worldwide given the growth of both traditional and innovative information sources. New roles for libraries can be effective and economical. One example of innovative thinking about libraries is the Finnish government policy of linking its communities via the Internet with public libraries as a principal point of access. This policy originated with the Ministry of Finance and has not only been effective, but also quite popular.

The education and training of librarians and other information specialists is a daunting agenda item given the number of individuals who will need retraining. One model for this effort can be seen in the Walter C. and Gerda B. Mortenson Center at the University of Illinois. Since its inception in 1988 it has trained more than three hundred librarians from more than sixty countries. Under the leadership of Professor Marianna Tax Choldin, its Director, the Center provides opportunities for librarians and those engaged in library-related activities to come to the University of Illinois for short or extended periods of training. The training emphasizes modern tools and techniques of librarianship with special attention to new technologies. A major focus of the program is to provide training skills so that participants can share their expertise with colleagues and library users when they return home. Programs like this, in cooperation with formal degree or certificate programs, will be necessary to achieve the retraining necessary to prepare librarians for a global role. Other partners in the overall effort to create a global library community will include governmental and non-governmental organizations, library and information societies and associations, and scholarly and scientific societies as well as technology companies.

Navigating a global route to the future of library and information services will be difficult and sometimes risky. Unstable economies and dramatic technological developments are likely to cause occasional course changes. Widespread access to information will generate expertise in unexpected locations that can contribute to the process. Competing professional and commercial forces will require libraries and librarians to fight for their proper role in the global information infrastructure. The global library community will need to pave its own way into the future based on its competence and experience. Remaining focused on the objectives of broadening access to information and facilitating the use of information will reward us with many opportunities to be of service.

References

Borgman, Christine. "Will the Global Infrastructure Be the Library of the Future? Central and Eastern Europe as a Case Example." *IFLA Journal* 22 (1996): 121-127.

Chen, Ching-chih, ed. *Planning Global Information Infrastructure*. Norwood, N.J.: Ablex, 1995.

Keller, George. "The Impact of Demographic and Social Changes on Higher Education and the Creation of Knowledge." *ACLS Occasional Paper*, no. 26, American Council of Learned Societies (1994): 1-6.

Martin, William J. *The Global Information Society*. 2d rev. ed. London and Brookfield, Vt.: ASLIB Gower, 1996.

Speh, Marcus. "Enabling a Global Community of Knowledge." *ASLIB Proceedings* 48, no. 9 (September 1998): 199-203.

3. From *Amoxcallis* to Electronic Libraries: Libraries and Librarianship in Mexico

Daniel Mattes

Libraries in Mexico have a long and convoluted history dating back to before the Spanish Conquest of 1521 when the Aztecs and other Mesoamerican civilizations controlled different parts of present-day Mexico. Many of the country's most important libraries have been privately owned, or based on what were previously private collections, but the outcry for public access to libraries has been loud and constant since at least the mid-nineteenth century. Today Mexico boasts a host of public, medical, special and academic libraries, as well as a National Library, a National Periodicals Library and a Library of Congress. These libraries vary greatly in terms of the size of their collections, the professionalization of their staffs and their use of new technologies. While some school and public libraries consist of collections of a few hundred books housed in one room, there are university libraries with holdings of hundreds of thousands of volumes where the latest in technology is being used and special projects to meet local and regional needs have been on-going for a number of years. All of these libraries face important economic and political realities that will shape their future as well as public access to information in general. Librarians receive professional education at a small number of public institutions. Their interests are promoted by a number of professional associations, both general and specialized. Formal library literature in and on Mexico is scarce, but we will use conference papers and other documents to shed light on these different aspects of Mexican librarianship to piece together the story of Mexican library development.

Early Library History

Upon arriving in Mexico, the Spanish *conquistadores* were surprised to find libraries with large collections of books on religious beliefs and ceremonies, history, economics and finances, and other topics. Scribes or *tlacuilos* painted hieroglyphs on amate paper, strips of venison hide and rolls of cotton.[1] These materials had wooden covers which gave them something of the appearance of books. These documents, known as *amoxtli* or codexes, were housed in *amoxcallis,* or "houses of books," which were located in temples, tribunals, tribute centers, markets and palaces, depending upon their subject matter.[2] The scribes lived in the *amoxcallis,* where they dedicated all of their time preparing manuscripts on topics relating to their individual specialization and reading them to those who sought information.[3] Unfortunately, all but a very few of these manuscripts were destroyed either when the Spanish soldiers took the buildings where they were housed by force, or by priests who destroyed them since they were considered to be "works of the devil."[4] (Juan Ángel Vázquez provides an interesting study of the important social role of Aztec scribes, manuscripts and libraries in his recent study, *La Función Social del Tlacuilo, los Amoxtlis y los Amoxcallis*.[5]) Ironically, a few years later Spanish priests who witnessed the rapid disappearance of the indigenous cultures would commission native scribes to try to reconstruct these lost manuscripts in the form of codexes or chronicles and became the first foreign experts on Mesoamerican cultures.[6] This activity extended on throughout the early years of Mexico's colonial period.

Mexico or "New Spain" was the queen of Spain's colonies and became an important cultural center in its own right. Here the first printing press in the New World was set up in 1539 and the first university in the Americas was established in 1553, the Real y Pontificia Universidad de México (Royal and Pontifical University of Mexico).[7] Not surprisingly, then, the first library in the New World was also established in Mexico; it was founded at the cathedral by Fray Juan de Zumárraga, Bishop of Mexico.[8]

Many libraries were established in the colonial period. Generally they were to be found at religious institutions and their collections specialized in philosophy and theology.[9] Some of these libraries also housed valuable codexes and chronicles which dealt with the history and culture of the Aztecs, Mayans, Mixtecs and Zapotecs. In the nineteenth century, the conflict between Liberals and Conservatives in newly independent Mexico (1821) resulted in a complete rupture between the Church and the State, which in turn led to the expropriation of ecclesiastical properties and their libraries. Unfortunately, the tug of war for control of the goverment by the Liberals and Conservatives, invasions by both the United States and France, and the Mexican American War made nineteenth-century Mexico a very chaotic place indeed, and many of the books and manuscripts previously held by ecclesiastical libraries either disappeared or were bought by wealthy collectors in Mexico, Europe and the United States, thus greatly impoverishing Mexican libraries and representing a loss for Mexico's cultural heritage in general.

Public Libraries

As in other parts of the world, the Mexican people have long valued public libraries as a means to personal fulfillment and improvement through self-teaching. It is worth mentioning that the first public library in Mexico was founded in 1788; the priests Luis and Cayetano Antonio Torres donated their own books, as well as those of their uncle, Luis Antonio Torres, to establish it. So it is that the "Turriana" library was established with 19,295 volumes, a huge collection for its time, which would continue to grow due to donations made by many important citizens of the day.[10] (Ten other public libraries were established after Independence in Oaxaca (1826), Chihuahua (1829), Toluca (1830) and Zacatecas (1831)). In 1905, during the waning years of the dictatorship of Porfirio Díaz, the Secretaría de Instrucción Pública y Bellas Artes (Ministry of Public Instruction and Fine Arts) was established. Among other functions, it was given the responsibility of establishing libraries; unfortunately, few attempts were made to comply with this commitment.

In spite of these different efforts to provide public library service, it was not until after the Mexican Revolution (1910-1917) that public libraries began to have much of an impact on a nationwide scale. In 1921 President Álvaro Obregón created the

Departmento de Bibliotecas (Department of Libraries) as part of the newly-established Secretaría de Educación Pública or SEP (Ministry of Public Education). One of Mexico's great intellectuals, José Vasconcelos, was put in charge of the SEP. During his administration some 1,661 public libraries were set up around the country with total holdings of around 218,224 volumes.[11] Small library collections were organized to meet the needs of peasants, workers and children and were housed in hospitals, labor union offices, agrarian communities and wherever else a need was detected. Unfortunately, after Vasconcelos left the SEP, support for public libraries disminished and by 1935 only thirty-one public libraries remained.[12]

During the administration of President Lázaro Cárdenas (1934-1940) interest in public libraries reappeared with a strong focus on providing service to rural communities. Small rural libraries numbered 1,136 with collections of from fifty to one hundred books.[13]

At the end of the Cárdenas administration, even limited support for public libraries disappeared. One exception to this trend was the establishment of the country's largest public library, the Biblioteca México, in Mexico City by Vasconcelos. It had an original collection of some 40,000 volumes when the library opened in 1946 and currently has well over 250,000 volumes.[14] Much of the library's growth has been due to the donation and purchase of a number of private collections, including those of some of Mexico's most important intellectuals. The Biblioteca Mexico is thus a rather special library, since it is visited not only by crowds of students of all ages, but also by serious researchers.

In general, then, the public library movement virtually disappeared from the Mexican scene until 1983 when President Miguel de la Madrid established the Red Nacional de Bibliotecas Públicas (National Network of Public Libraries) with the goal of providing public library service in every community that had a middle school. At the beginning of this ambitious program there were only 351 public libraries to serve the entire country.[15] The important goal of providing equal opportunity to all Mexicans to free reading material has revolutionized the Mexican library scene, since the country presently boasts some 6,000 public libraries.

As part of this national program, larger public libraries have been established in state capitals and major urban areas within each state. Besides having larger library collections (minimum 10,000 volumes) and more space for library patrons (250 simultaneous library users), the libraries located in state capitals often offer special services, such as services for the blind, meeting rooms, space for exhibitions and computer workshops for children.[16] Both the libraries located in state capitals and those found in major urban areas within the same state provide assistance to the libraries located in smaller communities. This work is overseen by a state committee whose work is in turn supervised by the Dirección General de Bibliotecas (General Directorate of Libraries), which works under the auspices of the Consejo Nacional para la Cultura y las Artes (National Commission on Culture and the Arts).[17]

At the local level, municipal public libraries have collections which include reference works, works of general interest on a variety of topics, serials and books for children. Some libraries also have audiovisual collections and special collections (usually rare books). Service is free of charge and includes the following: in-house loans, home loans, reference and reader advisory, as well as general orientation services.

One of the public library's most important programs is aimed at promoting reading. The philosophy that underlies this program is that the library should be open to all kinds of artistic and cultural expressions that promote a closer relationship between the library user and the book. To promote reading, library staff organize a wide variety of activities, including plays, reading discussion groups, conferences and workshops for housewives. Special emphasis is placed on promoting reading by children. Story hours, science workshops and special summer reading programs are designed to make reading and libraries fun.[18]

Two other special programs are worth noting: free computer workshops for children and the loan of videos relating to a wide variety of cultural topics. In the computer workshops, children learn not only the basic concepts relating to computers but also practical applications which can be of everyday use, such as the operation of data bases and word processing programs. Home loan of videos is designed to allow adults and children alike to view classic Mexican and foreign films as well as documentaries relating to science, Mexican culture and other topics of general interest.[19] In all of these activities, the Dirección General de Bibliotecas (DGB) plays a central role. Staff from the DGB select materials, provide technical processes, train staff and prepare rules and regulations that must be followed in all public libraries. They also conduct research with the aim of providing better library service in the future.[20]

While existing public libraries are far from providing all the services and resources needed, the continued support of the National Network of Public Libraries even during times of economic crisis speaks well of Mexico's commitment to serve its people's educational and recreational reading needs. Currently public libraries' principal users are school-age children, since school libraries tend to be very poor. It is to be hoped that in the future the Dirección General de Bibliotecas not only continues to establish more libraries, but also continues to look for ways to expand and improve the services offered by already existing public libraries.

Medical Libraries

Adequate health care service is a basic human need, but different governments have responded to this necessity in a variety of ways. In the case of Mexico, many people cannot afford private health care. As a result the Mexican government has created an extensive public health care system which includes facilities run by the Secretaría de Salud or SSA (Ministry of Health), the Instituto Mexicano de Seguro Social or IMSS (Mexican Institute of Social Security), the Instituto de Seguridad y Servicio Social para los Trabajadores del Estado or ISSSTE (State Workers' Social Security Institute) and the Desarrollo Integral de la Familia or DIF (Family Integral Development Organization). Together, these agencies cover approximately 90 percent of the population.[21] Mexico also has nine National Institutes of Health specializing in pediatrics, cardiology, nutrition, oncology, neurology and neurosurgery, pneumology, perinatology, psychiatry and public health.

Special mention should be made of the IMSS due to the fact that it serves the largest sector of the population and has more resources than other agencies. Access to up-to-date information is essential to providing quality health care. The IMSS funds 165 information centers as well as a central library and information center, the Centro Nacional de Investigación Documental en Salud or CENAIDS-IMSS (National Center for Documental Research in Health), whose holdings include 10,000 specialized texts and subscriptions to 1,331 serial titles.[22] Unfortunately, a recent study by Dr. César A. Macías-Chapula of ninety-two IMSS hospital libraries indicates the existence of important deficiencies in furniture and equipment, services and library staff in the hospital libraries studied.[23]

Another important source of information in the life sciences is run by the Secretaría de Salud (Ministry of Health). The Centro de Documentación Institucional or CDI (Institutional Documentation Center) was created in 1986 to organize and provide access to the Ministry's internal documents and archives.[24] Among other projects, the CDI has prepared data bases relating to documents on health (*Documentos en Salud, DOCSAL*), tables of contents of Mexican medical journals (*Revistas en Salud, REVSA*), health legislation (*Legislación en Salud, LEGISA*) and pamphlets and other ephemera (*Catálogos de material gráfico, CATMAT*). The CDI is also in charge of the Health Ministry's historical archives, which contain information on public health from the sixteenth century to the present; since 1994 the CDI's staff has been working to provide access to this rich source of information by creating another important data base, the *Archivo Histórico de la Secretaría de Salud* or AHSSA (Historial Archives of the Ministry of Health).[25]

In spite of these important efforts made by different government agencies to provide medical practitioners and researchers with up-to-date information, it became obvious that individual libraries and information centers could often provide the citations to relevant publications but could not so often actually provide the publication itself. In response to the imperative to provide actual documents to health care professionals, in 1975 the Ministry of Health created the Centro Nacional de Información y Documentación sobre Salud or CENIDS (National Center for Information and Documentation on Health). One of the first important achievements of the CENIDS took place in 1976 when it signed an agreement with the U.S. National Library of Medicine to provide on-line access in Mexico to MEDLARS (Medical Literature on Line). At first, access to these services was relatively limited, but in 1986 the CENIDS assumed the commitment of providing access to MEDLARS by way of nineteen Centros Regionales de Información y Documentación en Salud or CRIDS (Regional Centers for Information and Documentation on Health).[26] It should also be mentioned that the staff of the CENIDS analyzes the articles published in forty-one Mexican medical journals and provides this information to the Biblioteca Regional de Medicina or BIREME (Regional Medical Library) in São Paulo, Brazil for inclusion in the LILACS data base *(Literatura Latinoamericana en Ciencias de Salud*, Latin American Literature on Health Sciences).[27]

Besides providing access to data bases and training physicians and researchers in their use, the CENIDS has also promoted network building to share information on a national basis. As a part of this effort, the CENIDS along with the Mexican Institute of Social Security (IMSS) and four state universities pooled their efforts to form the Red Nacional de Colaboración en Información y Documentación en Salud or RENCIS (National Cooperative Network on Information and Documentation on Health). RENCIS now includes Mexico's twenty-two most important institutions in the area of the life sciences and allows physicians and researchers alike to fulfill their needs for journal articles and other documents on a national level 90 percent of the time.[28] RENCIS has produced data bases on CD-ROM which are updated annually; *ARTEMISA (Artículos Editados en México sobre Información en Salud*, Articles Published in Mexico on Health Information) indexes and contains the full text of twenty-eight Mexican medical journals. RENCIS has also produced on CD-ROM its *Catálogo Colectivo de Publicaciones Seriadas* (Union Catalog of Serials), which lists the holdings of Mexico's sixty-three best biomedical libraries that between them have subscriptions to 5,041 serial titles.[29]

More information on Mexican health services and sources of information in the life sciences can be found at the following Internet site: http://www.ssa.gob.mx.

Special Libraries

There is no question that during the last two decades Mexican academic and special libraries have developed the most, due to their access to more resources of all kinds.[30] Unfortunately, very little has been published on these important libraries and information centers. Many of them are a part of Mexico's public universities, especially the Universidad Nacional Autónoma de México or UNAM (National Autonomous University of Mexico); others are run by the private sector with varying degrees of financial support from the government and still others are supported wholly by the private sector. In the case of the UNAM, on whose campus can be found a number of special libraries, we might mention the libraries of the Centro Universitario de Investigaciones Bibliotecológicas or CUIB (University Center for Research in Library Science) and the Instituto Nacional de Energía Nuclear or INEN (National Atomic Energy Institute). Another important library supported by the government is the Biblioteca Nacional de Antropología e Historia (National Library of Anthropology and History). Other important special libraries can be found in the different Ministries that make up the Mexican federal government's Cabinet. Additional major special libraries include those of the Instituto Mexicano del Petróleo (Mexican Oil Institute), the Instituto de Investigaciones Eléctricas (Institute for Research on Electricity), the Banco de México (Bank of Mexico) and the Universidad Autónoma Chapingo (Mexico's most important agriculture school).

Sadly, the dearth of publications on special libraries allows us to merely mention a few of the most well known. It is to be hoped that more research will be published on these important libraries in the future.

Academic Libraries

Mexico's public and private universities have some of the largest and most technologically up-to-date libraries in the country. Public universities generally have a central library and departmental libraries for each of their schools and research institutes. This apparently centralized organization is only partial.[31] In more than one case the so-called "central library" only has materials that were unwanted by the departmental libraries and has little or no say on library practices in the departmental libraries.

When speaking about Mexican academic libraries, it is only logical to begin with the Universidad Nacional Autónoma de México or UNAM (National Autonomous University of Mexico), since it has the country's largest library system that is dedicated to the support of research and higher education.[32] The UNAM's Dirección General de Bibliotecas or DGB (General Directorate of Libraries) coordinates a system of 170 libraries, including a Biblioteca Central (Central Library) which has some 294,228 volumes of books. These libraries provide service to approximately 275,000 students and 25,000 professors and researchers.[33] The system includes libraries, both large and small, found in affiliated high schools as well as university schools and research centers.

The Dirección General de Bibliotecas (General Directorate of Libraries) has taken a leading role in implementing modern technology. Some of its most important projects include the construction of large data bases based principally but not exclusively on the holdings of the UNAM's own collection of books (LIBRUNAM), serials (SERIUNAM) and undergraduate and graduate theses (TESISUNAM). The DGB offers training for its own librarians as well as those of other institutions, often in coordination with the UNAM's Centro Universitario de Investigaciones Bibliotecológicas or CUIB (University Center for Research in Library Science).

Another major public university is also located in Mexico City, the Universidad Autónoma Metropolitana or UAM. The UAM has three campuses, each with its own libraries. Library holdings at the Azcapotzalco campus include some 195,000 volumes; the Iztapalapa campus has over 180,000 volumes of books and the Xochimilco campus has library holding in excess of 150,000 volumes.[34]

El Colegio de México is one of the country's premier research centers, which offers both research and teaching programs in history, international relations, political science, economics, demography, linguistics, literature and sociology. The Biblioteca "Daniel Cosío Villegas" boasts a collection of approximately 550,000 volumes.[35] The Colegio de México has an ambitious publication program and has produced a data base in CD-ROM based on the library's holding on the Far East.

Some of Mexico City's other private universities also have large library collections, including the Universidad Iberoamericana (162,846 vols.), the Universidad Anáhuac (113,336 vols.) and the Universidad La Salle (112,036 vols).[36] The library at the Instituto Tecnológico Autónomo de México (ITAM) also has a strong collection, especially in the fields of business administration and economics.

There are also major private universities located outside of the Mexico City metropolitan area. One is the Universidad de las Américas, located in Cholula in the State of Puebla. The Instituto Tecnológico y de Estudios Superiores de Monterrey (ITESM) has a large library at its main campus in the northern city of Monterrey and smaller libraries at its other twenty-eight campuses. It goes without saying that a number of public universities located outside of Mexico City also have major library collections. The Universidad de Colima is particularly important for its development of the SIABUC automated library system (used by 450 libraries) and the production of some 160 data bases in CD-ROM, as well as hosting the biannual Coloquio sobre Automatización de Bibliotecas (Colloquium on Library Automation) since 1984.

As can be seen by looking at just these few examples, library holdings at Mexico's largest and most prestigious centers of learning tend to be somewhat small. Nevertheless, there is hope for the future, since university libraries in general have received strong support during the last two decades.

The National Library

The Biblioteca Nacional (National Library) has had a particularly complicated history with many ups and downs. Efforts were made to establish a National Library based on confiscated ecclesiastical libraries and to provide library services to the public on several occasions in the nineteenth century, but internal strife between Liberals and Conservatives, the Mexican American War, and invasions by both the United States and France never allowed this project to proceed far. The law which was to finally lead to the establishment of the Biblioteca Nacional was signed by President Benito Juárez on November 30, 1867. This same law ratified previous laws promulgated in 1833, 1846 and 1857. It obliged Mexican publishers to provide two copies of all books published in legal deposit to the Biblioteca Nacional. It also stipulated that the holdings of the ecclesiastical libraries and of the Biblioteca de la Catedral would serve as the basis of the Biblioteca Nacional, which would be established at the site of what had been the church of San Agustín. Nevertheless, the Biblioteca Nacional was not to be formally inaugurated until April 2, 1884.[37]

Despite efforts by a number of dedicated directors, the Biblioteca Nacional continued to suffer from a series of problems. On the one hand, the period of the Mexican

Revolution (1910-1917) and its aftermath was a period of strife and chaos in which libraries were plundered and received at best moral support from the government. On the other hand, numerous changes in goverment led to constant changes of the library's directors. Even in the best of times, the government was hard-pressed to find the funds required to rennovate the inadequate installations found at the ex-church of San Agustín, where the Biblioteca Nacional had been installed. Changes central to the library's administration persisted. The Biblioteca Nacional originally was part of the Secretaría de Instrucción Pública y Bellas Artes (Ministry of Public Instruction and Fine Arts). On April 15, 1914, however, the Biblioteca Nacional became a dependency of the Universidad Nacional de México (National University of Mexico), which was in turn part of the Ministry already mentioned. In 1917, the Biblioteca Nacional would become a dependency of the Dirección General de Bellas Artes (General Directorate of Fine Arts) and later, during the administration of Álvaro Obregón, a dependency of the Departmento de Bibliotecas (Department of Libraries), which was part of the newly-created Secretaría de Educación Pública (Ministry of Public Education). The Biblioteca Nacional would later be considered one of the National University's research institutes. Throughout all of these years, books and serials were located in different rooms in the installations of the Biblioteca Nacional. So it was that in December of 1967, when the Instituto de Investigaciones Bibliográficas (Institute of Bibliographic Research) was created, it had two principal sections: the Biblioteca Nacional and the Hemeroteca Nacional (National Periodicals Library). The inadequacy of these installations and the lack of space which prohibited the organization and processing of materials finally led to the construction of new buildings to house the Biblioteca Nacional and the Hemeroteca Nacional in 1979 and 1993.[38]

Although the Biblioteca Nacional has suffered greatly since its creation, it boasts unique collections dating from Mexico's colonial past to the present. Besides its collection of rare books, the library also has important collections of photographs, maps and printed and recorded music. The Biblioteca Nacional's collection of approximately 2,106,914 volumes makes it Mexico's largest library.[39] Its resources are consulted by school children, university students, researchers and the general public.

Besides the Biblioteca Nacional, Mexico also has a Biblioteca del Congreso de la Unión (Library of Congress). It was inaugurated in 1936 and like the Biblioteca Nacional enjoys legal depository privileges.

Library Science Education

In 1915 Agustín Loera and Ezequiel A. Chávez established the country's first school for librarians and archivists. It only lasted for two years "due to the lack of an economic future for the profession." [40] Another attempt was made to set up a school for librarians in 1925, this time by the Departmento de Bibliotecas (Department of Libraries), but the school closed within a year. In 1945 the Departmento de Bibliotecas of the Ministry of Education established the Escuela Nacional de Bibliotecarios y Archivistas or ENBA (National School of Librarians and Archivists). The ENBA is still preparing librarians and archivists, now under the name of the Escuela Nacional de Bibliteconomía y Archivonomía (National School of Library and Archival Sciences). It is Latin America's oldest functioning library school. Degrees are offered at technical and undergraduate levels. (A master's degree is not required of librarians in Mexico and, in fact, the vast majority of librarians only have an undergraduate degree.) The UNAM began its own programs in library and archival sciences in 1956.

Presently, undergraduate library science programs are offered at the ENBA (Mexico City), the UNAM (Mexico City), the Universidad Autónoma de San Luis Potosí (San Luis Potosí) and the Universidad Autónoma de Nuevo León (Monterrey). Only the UNAM and the Universidad Autónoma de Nuevo León offer master's degree programs. There is no doctoral program in library science in Mexico.

All of these schools have small enrollments, especially at the graduate level. As the head of the undergraduate program at the UNAM points out, "the task of educating library science professionals has still not been recognized as being a primary necessity for the country." [41]

Professional Associations

Despite the relatively small number of professional librarians in Mexico, there are a number of general and specialized library associations. Attempts were made to form a professional association under the name of the Asociación de Bibliotecarios Mexicanos (Association of Mexican Librarians) in 1924, 1927 and 1933, but the association never lasted for long.[42]   Finally, it was reorganized yet again in 1954 as the Asociación Mexicana de Bibliotecarios, Asociación Civil or AMBAC (Mexican Association of Librarians) and exists today as the country's largest library association with some 416 dues-paying members. (Many librarians attend AMBAC meetings without ever becoming official members.) Semi-autonomous chapters have been set up in the states of Jalisco, Michoacán, Morelos, Nuevo León and Sonora, and other groups are being formed in the Estado de México and the state of Oaxaca.[43] One of the AMBAC's major goals for the future is to form a more unified national organization, since the parent association is sometimes viewed as principally an association for librarians from Mexico City. (For more information on the history of the AMBAC, see Rosa María Fernández de Zamora's *La Asociación Mexicana de Bibliotecarios, A.C.: notas para su historia*.[44])

Whether this criticism is valid or not is often a subject for heated debate. What cannot be denied is that the AMBAC has had a very important impact on the profession. One reason for this is that the AMBAC organizes the country's most important library conference, *the Jornadas Mexicanas de Biblioteconomía* (Mexican Library Conferences). The first *Jornadas* were held in 1957 (Mexico City), 1959 (San Luis Potosí), 1960 (Mexico City), 1965 (Jalapa), 1969 (Mexico City) and 1974 (Guanajuato). In recent years, the *Jornadas* have been held anually in different parts of the country.

Other library associations and the year that they were founded include the following: Asociación de Bibliotecarios de Instituciones de Enseñanza Superior e Investigación or ABIESI in 1957 (Association of Librarians from Institutes for Research and Higher Education); Bibliotecarios de Biomedicina or BIBAC in 1977 (Biomedical Librarians); Asociación de Bibliotecarios de Instituciones Gubernamentales de México, A.C. or ABIGMAC in 1978 (Association of Librarians from Mexican Governmental Institutions); El Colegio Nacional de Bibliotecarios, A.C. or CNB in 1979 (the National College of Librarians, the professional association which legally has the role of advising the government on matters affecting libraries and librarians); Documentación en Educación Superior e Investigación Educativa or DESIE in 1980 (Documentation in Higher Education and Educational Research) and the Asociación Nacional de Bibliotecarios Agropecuarios, A.C. or ANBAGRO in 1983 (National Association of Agricultural Librarians). As one author points out, this division of a small number of librarians in several professional groups far from benefitting Mexican librarians actually works against them and "does not permit group efforts or an authentic union which could translate to a real force for the defense of our interests." [45]

Prospects for the Future

In this article we have seen how libraries have sprung up, often in spite of obstacles of all kinds, to meet the needs of different sectors of the Mexican population. Political conflicts and economic crises continue to plague Mexico, yet its libraries continue to improve and make more and more use of technologies used by libraries in all parts of the world to better serve their patrons.

In terms of the implementation of modern technology, Mexico is advancing rapidly. Major data bases have been created by the UNAM, the medical library community and the Universidad de Colima, to mention just a few examples. More libraries of all types have automated, using some of the same systems used in modern libraries all over the world. The libraries belonging to the system of the Instituto Tecnológico y de Estudios Superiores de Monterrey, the ITESM or "Monterrey Tec," are all migrating to Ameritech's Horizon system. On the other hand, such major libraries as those of the UNAM, El Colegio de México and the Universidad Iberoamericana are migrating to the Israeli system "Aleph." The library of the Universidad Anáhuac, formerly a Dynix site, is in the process of migrating to Aleph, too.

It is becoming more and more common for libraries, especially academic libraries, to offer their users access to the Internet and to a wide variety of data bases—either in CD-ROMs or via the Internet. Reference and Bibliographic Instruction are being taken more seriously, without undermining the traditionally central role of the librarians in the Technical Processes departments. More and more sophisticated Web pages are being designed for libraries—with or without the help of specialists in computer science.

In terms of library cooperation, important advances are being made both in the national and international spheres. The "Grupo Amigos" has provided international interlibrary loan services since 1989 and is looking for ways to expand the scope of library cooperation. The "Foro Transnational ILL Pilot Project" is allowing smaller Mexican libraries and those located outside of the Mexico City metropolitan area to provide modern ILL services via fax and Ariel to their patrons. Different library networks are being formed, either because member libraries use the same automation system (Dynix, Horizon or Aleph) or share a common institutional framework (ITESM, Universidad Anáhuac). These individual efforts will surely promote more interlibrary cooperation at the national level. The Transborder Library Forums or "FORO" are promoting interlibrary cooperation between Mexico, the United States and Canada. Robert Seal discusses these different forms of cooperation in which Mexico is participating in detail in a recent article that appeared in *Advances in Librarianship*.[46]

What does all this mean? It seems to mean that libraries have become an essential part of Mexico's plans to offer a better life to its citizens. The Mexican people value libraries and are demanding better collections and services. Mexican librarians are taking seriously the important social role of their profession and working hard to offer more resources and quality services to library users, sometimes relying on technology and sometimes relying on more institutionalized relationships, which are taking the place of previous informal relationships based primarily on interpersonal relations between individual library directors.

There is still a lot to be done. But the Mexican people are demanding better library services, and library professionals are rising to meet the challenge.

Notes

1. Joaquín Galarza, "Los Códices Mexicanos," *Arqueología Mexicana* 4, no. 23 (enero-febrero 1997): 79.
2. Ibid., 78.
3. Ibid.
4. Ibid., 80.
5. Juan Ángel Vázquez Martínez, *La función social del tlacuilo, los amoxtlis y los amoxcallis* (México, D.F.: Secretaría de Educación Pública, 1995).
6. Miguel León-Portilla, "Grandes momentos en la historia de los códices," *Arqueología Mexicana* 4, no. 23 (enero-febrero 1997): 18-19.
7. Rosa María Fernández de Zamora, "Mexico, Libraries," in *Encyclopedia of Library and Information Science*, vol. 18 (New York: Marcel Dekker, 1976), 4.
8. Ibid., 4-5.
9. Ibid., 5.
10. Ibid., 8.
11. Ibid., 12.
12. Ibid.
13. Ibid.
14. Ibid., 14.
15. Ana María Magaloni de Bustamante, "Red Nacional de Bibliotecas Públicas: Desarrollo, Servicios y Resultados," in *La bibliotecología en el México actual y sus tendencias : libro conmemorativo de los 25 años de la Dirección General de Bibliotecas* (México, D.F.: Universidad Nacional Autónoma de México, 1992), 73.
16. México, Consejo Nacional para la Cultura y las Artes, Dirección General de Bibliotecas, *La Red Nacional de Bibliotecas Públicas* (México, D.F.: Consejo Nacional para la Cultura y las Artes, 1991), 24-25.
17. Ibid., 29-34.
18. Magaloni de Bustamante, 75-76.
19. Ibid., 76-79.
20. México, Consejo Nacional para la Cultura y las Artes, 11-20.
21. César A. Macías-Chapula, "A Descriptive Study of Ninety-Two Hospital Libraries in Mexico," *Bulletin of the Medical Library Association* 83, no. 1 (January 1995): 67.
22. "Los centros de documentación del IMSS: un apoyo para la educación e investigación médicas," *Revista CONAMED* 1, no. 3. (1997): 32-33.
23. Macías-Chapula, 66-70.
24. "Centro de Documentación Institucional, Centro Nacional de Información y Documentación sobre Salud: alternativas de consulta y actualización médica," *Revista CONAMED* 1, no. 2 (1997) : 40.
25. Ibid., 41.
26. César A. Macías-Chapula, "Información científica sobre salud en México," *Ciencia y Desarrollo* 117 (julio/agosto de 1994): 10.
27. "Centro de Documentación Institucional, Centro Nacional de Información y Documentación sobre Salud," 42.
28. Ibid., 42-43.
29. Gladys Faba Beaumont, "CENIDS: el poder de la información en salud al alcance de todos," *Investigación Bibliotecológica* 8, no. 16 (enero/junio 1994): 27.
30. Guadalupe Carrión Rodríguez, "Las bibliotecas especializadas en México," in *La bibliotecología en*

el México actual y sus tendencias: libro conmemorativo de los 25 años de la Dirección General de Bibliotecas (México, D.F.: Universidad Nacional Autónoma de México, 1992), 59.

31. Fernández de Zamora (1976), 18.

32. Adolfo Rodríguez Gallardo, "El sistema bibliotecario de la UNAM," in *La bibliotecología en el México actual y sus tendencias: libro conmemorativo de los 25 años de la Dirección General de Bibliotecas* (México, D.F.: Universidad Nacional Autónoma de México, 1992), 15.

33. Ibid., 20.

34. Rosa María Fernández de Zamora, "Mapa bibliotecario y de servicios de información de la ciudad de México," in *XXVIII Jornadas Mexicanas de Biblioteconomía. Memoria* (México, D.F.: Asociación Mexicana de Bibliotecarios, A.C., 1997), 223.

35. Ibid.

36. Ibid.

37. Ignacio Osorio Romero and Boris Berenzon Gorn, "Biblioteca Nacional de México," in *Historia de las Bibliotecas Nacionales de Iberoamérica* (México, D.F.: Universidad Nacional Autónoma de México, 1995), 327-334.

38. Ibid., 336-340.

39. Fernández de Zamora (1997), 223.

40. Fernández de Zamora (1976), 14.

41. Hugo Alberto Figueroa Alcántara, "Algunas notas sobre la educación bibliotecológica en México," in *La bibliotecología en el México actual y sus tendencias: libro conmemorativo de los 25 años de la Dirección General de Bibliotecas* (México, D.F.: Universidad Nacional Autónoma de México, 1992), 186.

42. Rosa María Fernández de Zamora (1976), 15.

43. Linda Sametz, e-mail dated December 2, 1997.

44. Rosa María Fernández de Zamora, *La Asociación Mexicana de Bibliotecarios, A.C.: Notas para su historia* (México, D.F.: Asociación Mexicana de Bibliotecarios, A.C., 1995).

45. José Alfredo Verdugo Sánchez, "La función social de las asociaciones de bibliotecarios en México: un particular punto de vista," in *La Bibliotecología en el México actual y sus tendencias: libro conmemorativo de los 25 años de la Dirección General de Bibliotecas* (México, D.F.: Universidad Nacional Autónoma de México, 1992), 292.

46. Robert A. Seal, "Mexican and U.S. Library Relations," *Advances in Librarianship* 20 (1996): 69-121.

4. Improving University Libraries in El Salvador

William V. Jackson

Although El Salvador is a small country (8,124 square miles, about the size of Massachusetts) with a population approaching six million, it attracted worldwide attention during twelve years of civil war (ending in the peace agreement of January 1992). During the past five years of rapid economic recovery and institutional rebuilding, policymakers have given a great deal of attention to improving the country's educational system at all levels—primary, secondary and higher.

The development of universities in this small nation has been somewhat unusual. Although the national university (Universidad de El Salvador, UES) dates back to 1841, the first private institutions did not appear until 120 years later, when the Central American University (Universidad Centroamericana José Simeón Cañas, UCA) was established in 1965, followed by Universidad Albert Einstein and Universidad Dr. Matías Delgado in 1977. In the past decade or so, a veritable explosion in the establishment of new private universities has taken place, due in part to the fact that the national university (UES) was closed during much of the civil war and the government tacitly encouraged the opening of new institutions. The pent-up demand for advanced study was another factor; as a result, higher education became, in some respects, a business, with some new institutions operating almost like "for profit" groups (through a corporation which obtains quarters and leases them to the university, buys and resells to it supplies, etc.). Under these circumstances, it is not surprising that in some cases this has led to a "shoestring" type of operation.[1]

By 1997 there were thirty-nine institutions of higher education in El Salvador, with an enrollment of 90,807 in degree programs and an additional 19,457 in other types of study. Faculty numbers 7,473 (most part time).[2] However, the fifteen largest institutions account for 87 percent of the students (Table 1), with only 12,233 (13 percent) in the remaining twenty-four. As expected, the national university (UES) has the largest student body (27 percent of the total), leaving 73 percent distributed among the thirty-eight private institutions. In the fifteen large institutions, the average student body is 5,238, but if we exclude UES it falls to 3,824. The twenty-four smallest institutions have an average student body of only 510; one wonders how viable they may be in the long run.

Another important development has occurred in recent years. The government's Directorate of Higher Education (Dirección de Educación Superior), concerned with questions of financing higher education and of quality, has embarked upon a program of accreditation, which includes both self-study and visitation. Although this first attempt gives perhaps too much attention to quantitative norms, its long-range implications are positive. First results are scheduled to appear in the spring of 1998, and it is quite possible that some small and poorly funded institutions may not survive this process.

It is against this background that this paper presents a picture of the current state of

TABLE 1
Universities with Largest Enrollments, 1997

University	Students in Degree Programs
de El Salvador (UES)	24,897
Tecnológica de Comercio y Administración de Empresas (UTEC)	12,818
Centroamericana José Simeón Cañas (UCA)	6,734
Francisco Gavidia	5,328
Modular Abierta	4,944
Dr. José Matías Delgado	3,724
de Oriente (UNIVO)	3,025
Salvadoreña Alberto Masferrer	2,990
Dr. Andrés Bello	2,933
Albert Einstein	2,353
Evangélica de El Salvador	2,254
Capitán General Gerardo Barrios	2,062
Politécnica de El Salvador	1,754
Don Bosco	1,382
Católica de Occidente (UNICO)	1,376
Total	78,574

Source: El Salvador, Dirección Nacional de Educación Superior, *Resultados Finales de la Primera Calificación a las Instituciones de Educación Superior en El Salvador* ([San Salvador, 1997?]).

university libraries in El Salvador, with emphasis on recent improvements. Chief factors which compose library and information service (administration and finance, collections and their organization, reader services, personnel, quarters, and interlibrary cooperation) are examined. This paper is neither a history of these libraries nor a statistical summary, but an overview with emphasis on "the better institutions." It draws primarily on extensive field work conducted from 1994 through 1997, but also utilizes the limited documentation presently available.

Administration and Finance

Of the thirty-nine universities in El Salvador at only one, UES, had library service developed along the lines of older universities in Latin America: a separate library in each faculty, operating under the dean, with nearly complete independence and no coordination among them.[3] Efforts to form a library system took place in the 1960s and 1970s, but early success did not continue during the civil war. The administrative structure remains complicated, with a Central Library, nine faculty libraries, and three at satellite campuses operating outside the capital. Recent plans call for a library system on the main campus consisting of three units: the present Central Library (for the humanities and social sciences), a health sciences library and an engineering library. Many of the steps necessary to implement this plan are, however, "on hold," due to problems facing the Central Library after its move to a new building in 1994. In contrast, the Universidad Centroamericana (UCA) has long had centralized library services, although several research institutes possess small documentary collections.

General administration at all of the libraries, even UES and UCA, is remarkably simple. The librarian reports to either the rector, the vice rector for academic affairs, or the general secretary, through whose office come the budget, approval for book purchases and other expenditures, negotiations for staff, etc. Librarians certainly have less latitude in financial matters than their U.S. counterparts.

In recent years rectors have shown a growing concern for libraries and the role they should play in academic programs. Dr. Fabio Castillo, twice rector of UES, demonstrated an unusual interest and support for the library during both of his terms. To encourage greater library awareness, in March 1997 the U.S. Information Service (USIS) sponsored a meeting for rectors on the role of the library. It had considerable success in making the rectors more "library minded" and some immediate increases in budgets resulted.

Collections and Organization of Materials

Collections obviously represent the most important element in library service, but it must be admitted that progress here has been slow. Both UES and UCA have total holdings in excess of 100,000 volumes—not large in view of the number of faculties and research institutes found at each.

The library at UES suffered serious losses of material during the civil war and from the 1986 earthquake. In 1994, a UNESCO expert was secured not only to plan and implement improved service in a new building, but also to re-incorporate older materials into the collection, to increase book and journal resources, and to secure access to data bases and to the Internet. For several years information technology received more emphasis than collections, but by 1997 there was a growing realization that an adequate infrastructure of traditional materials would need to be in place, e.g., journal subscriptions were increased, with selection based on faculty recommendation.

Since the library at UCA suffered no such losses, its resources have continued to grow. The most important development here occurred in 1993, when UCA received a grant of $335,000 "toward the development of its library" from the Mellon Foundation.[4] It was reported that a substantial portion of these funds would be spent on reference and bibliographical resources, and the expanded and updated holdings have become the country's best reference collection.

No other universities approach these two in size of collections; even such important institutions as Don Bosco, Evangélica, Matías Delgado and UTEC have fewer than 50,000 volumes in their libraries, and libraries in smaller universities may not exceed a few thousand volumes. Holdings are even less useful than these figures would suggest, because they include multiple copies of textbooks and works containing required supplementary reading. Too many institutions have failed to recognize the distinction between a library and a textbook collection; maintenance of the latter is *not* a library function. Moreover, few libraries have formed a collection of general cultural titles (e.g., classics of Spanish and Latin American literature), even though many are available in relatively inexpensive editions, such as the "Colección Austral." The USIS book program has, for more than twenty-five years, donated useful books to universities (and to other libraries as well)—usually translations of U.S. titles in the social sciences, but this help can only supplement institutional efforts.

Although low budgets bear most of the blame for these weaknesses in collections, librarians must share responsibility because they have not formulated policies for collection building; this probably also accounts for the failure to exploit gift and exchange as a means of enhancing holdings, although it is true that most Salvadoran universities (with the exception of UCA) have only modest publication programs (or none at all). The need, in the 1990s, for audiovisual and electronic resources only puts more pressure on limited acquisition funds. Improvement has come slowly but surely as rectors, deans and others recognize that larger budgets for library materials are essential. One university has steadily increased its acquisition budget, which now stands at 200,000 *colones* (about $23,000) per semester.

Cataloging and classification have traditionally received much attention in Latin American libraries, and El Salvador is no exception. The AACR2 rules and Dewey Decimal Classification are generally used; recently, many universities have created on-line catalogs, which unfortunately often include only recent publications, so that readers face the inconvenience of consulting two tools to access holdings.

Reader Services

Although very few collections are open-shelf, circulation is available to students, faculty, and staff; in some libraries circulation has been automated. Photocopy machines are ubiquitous, and prices are usually quite low.

Reference services and bibliographical assistance remain limited for two reasons: the lack of trained staff and the inadequacy of the reference collection. Latin American university libraries do not have a long tradition of reference service, so improvements come slowly.

Hours of service are long, often from 8:00 A.M. to 8:00 P.M. Since most students are part-time, libraries receive heaviest use during late afternoon and evening hours; much of this relates, however, to using texts and other books on reserve.

Staff

The staff at university libraries ranges from two or three persons to twenty-four at the Central Library at UES. Most of these persons have had little formal training in library and information science, because the three-year program at the Faculty of Sciences and Humanities at UES has never attracted many students.[5] In recent years, the most important step toward professionalization of staff came when twenty persons were sent (under a grant from AID) to the University of Puerto Rico's library school for a year-long special program.[6] They returned to El Salvador in July 1996, and several now work in university libraries. One person received a scholarship from AID to do graduate study in the United States and completed the master's degree at Dominican University in December 1995.

To improve the quality of staff the Pan American University (Universidad Panamericana, UP), with encouragement from the Committee on Library Cooperation (CCBES), began a new program for practicing librarians in July 1997. It consists of three semesters of course work (given all day Saturday) leading to a diploma.[7] Since the first group will not complete the program until 1998, it is too early to judge the effect it will have upon the staffing of university libraries.

TABLE 2
New University Library Buildings

Date Completed	University	Approximate Size (sq. m)
Feb. 1992	Don Bosco	*
Mar. 1994	de El Salvador: Central Library	*
Dec. 1995	Matías Delgado	450
Dec. 1997**	Tecnológica (UTEC)***	800**
Dec. 1997**	Evangélica***	*
Dec. 1997**	del Oriente (UNIVO)***	200
July 1998**	de Santa Ana (UNASA)	160
1998**	de El Salvador: Engineering	*

* Not available

** Estimate

*** Library within administration or classroom building

Source: Figures furnished by institutions, Fall 1997

Buildings

Until the end of the civil war only two universities (UES and UCA) had separate library buildings; the first new construction took place at Don Bosco, followed by seven other facilities (several scheduled for completion at the end of 1997 or in 1998). This is a remarkable accomplishment considering not only the pressing needs for classroom space, but also the difficulty of financing buildings for higher education in El Salvador. State funds are scarce and donations rare, so that private institutions must divert tuition income or, more generally, depend on bank loans at annual interest rates sometimes exceeding 20 percent. Since libraries do not help a university's income stream, as do classrooms which allow increased numbers of tuition-paying students, the reluctance to undertake large facilities is understandable; moreover, it is difficult to calculate the number of seats needed, when the majority of students are part-time and make minimal use of the library.

Table 2 shows the eight new facilities constructed in recent years. The Rafael Meza Ayau Library at Don Bosco was the gift of the Foundation of the same name, while the largest, the Central Library at UES, was financed by the Spanish international development agency (Agencia Española de Cooperación Internacional) as a replacement for the previous central library (damaged beyond use by the 1986 earthquake). This three-story facility provides several reading rooms, space for collections and for technical service (some books continue to be stored in the basement of the old library). Of the remaining libraries, three are in separate buildings, while three are housed within administration or classroom buildings. Given the above financial constraints, it is not surprising to find most facilities almost starkly functional in design, with the exception of Don Bosco—a very attractive building affording a panoramic view of parts of San Salvador from the top floor. The Hugo Lindo Library at Matías Delgado is small, but the adjacent site is reserved for expansion.

Interiors for the most part reflect a desire to safeguard the collection against losses, so the stacks are closed.[8] At several institutions (Evangélica, UNIVO and UNASA) there is now a movement toward the "open shelves, exit control" philosophy. (Despite having a traditional building, UCA began to allow stack access in 1996.) Reader accommodations are changing, too, with a considerable number of individual tables and chairs and some provision for group study.

Interlibrary Cooperation

Although the Library Association of El Salvador (Asociación de Bibliotecarios de El Salvador, ABES) had in the past undertaken a few cooperative projects, a growing realization that improvement in library and information service could advance more rapidly through joint efforts led to the formation, in early 1996, of an informal committee on cooperation—undoubtedly influenced by the success of the Committee on University Library Cooperation (Comité de Cooperación entre Bibliotecas Universitarias, CCBU) in neighboring Guatemala.[9] The group in El Salvador consisted of representatives from eight libraries, not all of them in universities. Following a number of meetings, the group issued a document in May 1996 which examines such issues as improving library services, application of information technology, and cooperative cataloging.[10]

In 1997 the group adopted as its name the Committee on Library Cooperation in El Salvador (Comité de Cooperación Bibliotecaria de El Salvador, CCBES) and was able to open a secretariat when the Pan American University (Universidad Panamericana, UP) provided space and USIS donated a small amount of equipment. CCBES worked with UP in establishing the new training course for practicing librarians and in sponsoring a symposium (12 November 1997) on "Library Development in El Salvador"; in the same month it issued the first number of a bulletin.[11]

Future plans call for moving forward on several projects, expanding membership (to be defined as institutional rather than personal), and seeking outside funding. CCBES also hopes to hold joint meetings, at least once a year, with CCBU in Guatemala.

Conclusion

From this review of the improvements in El Salvador's university libraries in recent years, one might cite the following as the most significant on-going trends: (1) a growing awareness of the library's mission and important role in higher education, (2) slowly increasing financial support, (3) progress in improving and expanding library quarters, (4) beginnings of interlibrary cooperation, and (5) more qualified staff.

Yet it is equally clear that much remains to be done. First and foremost, holdings of all types—printed, audiovisual, and electronic—must be greatly expanded and improved in quality, both at individual institutions and through cooperative access. Second, not only are more buildings needed, but better design should lead to easier access to collections. Finally, universities must secure a library staff that is not only greater in numbers and able to utilize the new technology but also trained to provide a high level of service to readers. To move forward on all of these fronts is the challenge as universities in El Salvador enter the twenty-first century.

Notes

1. For a review of and comments on private institutions, see Joaquín Samayoa, "Problemas y Perspectivas de las Universidades Privadas en El Salvador," *ECA, Estudios Centroamericanos*, nos. 547-548 (1994), 469-487.
2. El Salvador, Dirección Nacional de Educación Superior, *Resultados Finales de la Primera Calificación*

a las Instituciones de Educación Superior en El Salvador ([San Salvador, 1997?]), unpaged. Cf. *The World of Learning 1997* (47th ed.; [London] Europa Publications [1997]), pp. 432-433 which lists only 6 universities for El Salvador.

3. William V. Jackson, "La Misión de la Biblioteca Universitaria y su Estado Actual en América Latina" (lecture given at UNESCO Conference, San José, Costa Rica, March 1997).

4. Andrew W. Mellon Foundation, *Report from January 1, 1993 through December 31, 1993* (New York, 1994), p. 63. Neither the Foundation nor UCA has provided further information on this grant.

5. For a history of this program, see Helen Guardado de del Cid, "La Carrera de Bibliotecología en El Salvador: Su Nueva Orientación Curricular," in *Latin American Studies into the Twenty-First Century: New Focus, New Formats, New Challenges* (Albuquerque: SALALM Secretariat, 1991) pp. 441-453. For a current description of the program, see Universidad de El Salvador, *Catalógo Académico, 1998-1999* (San Salvador, 1997), pp. 129-135.

6. William V. Jackson, "Program Report: Association of Librarians of El Salvador, June 30, 1995," *Third World Libraries* VI (Fall 1995), 48-51.

7. Universidad Panamericana, *Diplomado en Bibliotecología y Ciencias de la Información* (San Salvador, 1997) (flyer).

8. For comments on a similar situation in Nicaragua, see Frank J. Lepkowski, "The Closed-Stack Model and the Culture of Librarianship in Nicaraguan Academic Libraries," *Third World Libraries* III (Fall 1992), 62-67.

9. Raquel Flores, "The Importance of Sharing Resources: The Experience of the Committee for Cooperation among University Libraries in Guatemala," *Third World Libraries* III (Fall 1992), 79-84.

10. Comité Interinstitucional de Cooperación Interbibliotecaria, *Plan de Cooperación Interbibliotecaria* (San Salvador, 1996).

11. *Cooperación Bibliotecaria, Boletín Informativo*, 1, no. 1 (Nov. 1997) ([San Salvador] Comité de Cooperación Bibliotecaria de El Salvador [1997]).

5. Academic Libraries in Colombia: Challenges and Cooperation

Charlotte E. Ford and Luz M. Quiroga

Colombia, a country in the northwestern corner of South America with more than thirty-four million inhabitants, has a long tradition of higher education and of librarianship. The first university was founded in the sixteenth century;[1] the National Library was established in 1777.[2] Colombia is also home to the Inter-American Library School, founded in 1956 at the University of Antioquia to provide training in librarianship to students from Colombia as well as other Latin American countries.[3] There are currently around 275 institutions of higher education of varying size and quality, including close to one hundred universities.[4] Institutions of higher education are required by law to provide information services to their students; thus, all universities include some kind of library service.[5]

Traditionally, higher education has been the domain of the elite in Colombia, although educational access boomed in the 1960s and 1970s.[6] It is currently estimated that nearly 15 percent of 18- to 21-year-olds enroll in institutions of higher education in Colombia; however, more than 50 percent drop out, mainly because of a lack of financial resources.[7] Higher education institutions (universities, technological institutes, or intermediate professional institutes) may be public or private; the public/private mix is currently around 30/70.[8] Regardless of their status, all of these institutions are supervised by a government office: the Colombian Institute for the Promotion of Higher Education (ICFES), which regulates the physical structure, budget, costs, and academic activities of educational institutions.

The ICFES has always played a major role in planning and implementing information policies for academic libraries. In 1966, its predecessor (the National University Fund, FUN) created the Working Group for University Libraries as a consulting and advisory body for university library services. Since then, some version of this Working Group has existed within ICFES, although it has evolved and changed its name to reflect new responsibilities. It has been known as the National Council on Library Services (1969), the Regional Committees for University Libraries (1972), the Colombian Network of University Libraries (1977), and Information and Documentation Services for Higher Education, or SIDES (1983). In 1994, ICFES was restructured, and academic projects now fall under an Informatics Unit, as part of the National System of Information for Higher Education, or SNIES.[9]

In the case of the established national and regional universities (such as the Universidad Nacional, Universidad del Valle, and Universidad de Antioquia), academic libraries developed alongside the universities themselves. However, it was not until the 1960s that real professionalization began. During the 1960s, the first graduates of the Inter-American Library School began to assume professional positions. As a result, many existing departmental libraries were merged into centralized library departments under their direction.[10] A number of institutions constructed buildings for these library departments, with the support of the national government and loans from international organizations.[11] Higher education began to expand rapidly during this time, and new universities emerged. Most of these institutions provided library services from the start, in accordance with a requirement for the validation of any new university in the country.

Toward the end of the 1960s, two coordinating agencies were created which were destined to play major roles in the development of Colombian academic libraries: the aforementioned ICFES (in 1969) and the Colombian Fund for Scientific Research & Special Projects, or COLCIENCIAS (in 1968), which was concerned from the very beginning with the creation and transmission of scientific and technological data.[12] COLCIENCIAS quickly began planning a national network of scientific and technical information. The National Council on Library Services, under ICFES, studied the situation of university libraries in the country, determined their basic needs, elaborated guidelines for improvement, and began to provide technical and financial assistance to improve library services and collections.[13] In 1969, ICFES sponsored the First Congress of University Libraries in Bucaramanga. This marked the beginning of many cooperative efforts among academic libraries, inspiring, as one librarian put it, "a common vision oriented toward the future."[14]

The 1970s: Cooperative Efforts Emerge

Cooperative efforts among Colombian academic libraries began in earnest in the 1970s. In 1972, the National Council on Library Services was replaced by Regional Committees on University Libraries, still under ICFES coordination.[15] José Arias Ordoñez, head of the ICFES Division of Bibliographic Resources, emerged at this time as a key figure in the development of Colombian academic libraries. During his tenure at ICFES, a number of important cooperative projects flourished. Among the earliest were the National Union Catalog of Serial Publications and the National Union Catalog of Theses. The first collective catalog efforts were undertaken with minimal technological support, but rather were "labors of love," according to a participant in the process.[16]

Under José Arias's leadership, the Colombian Network of Higher Education Libraries was created at ICFES in 1977. Cooperation and integration were the underlying principles of this network, which strove to reduce the duplication of work in such processes as cataloging, indexing, and abstracting. Policies and procedures were set to insure that tasks would be performed only once and that the resulting products would be made available to all institutional members. The network supported fifteen specific programs. Several of these programs were related to the National Union Catalog of Serial Publications, which by 1978 had grown to include 28,000 titles held in 231 libraries nationwide. In addition to providing a valuable resource for library patrons seeking particular journals, the catalog supported interlibrary loan programs and facilitated the assignment of ISSN numbers for which the ICFES was responsible. Other well-known ICFES programs included the National Analytic Database of Periodical Publications, the National List of Subject Headings, the cooperative cataloging program, and the production of specialized bibliographies.[17]

As the 1970s drew to a close, the Colombian Network of Higher Education Libraries undertook a study of higher education libraries and made some alarming discoveries: that library acquisition funds had diminished while the number of students and professors had increased; that "real information services" were lacking in many institutions because of insufficient collections or inadequate organization, lack of qualified personnel, and lack of continuing education programs; that unnecessary duplications of work still existed; and that libraries were technologically stagnant.[18] These findings led to the creation of the System of Information and Documentation for Higher Education (SIDES) within ICFES, in 1983.

The 1980s: The SIDES Initiative

SIDES was conceived as a coordinated information network that would permit efficient and timely access to national and international information.[19] Funding was procured from the Organization of American States and the American Development Bank to create an X25 network.[20] SIDES consisted of three components:

(1) regional committees through which all libraries in institutions of higher education participated;
(2) nine geographically dispersed specialized nodes (located at universities with strong collections in the area of interest and good infrastructures); and
(3) a central coordinating node at ICFES's National Serials Library.

The specialized nodes were as follows:

- Health Sciences—Universidad de Antioquia, in Medellín
- Engineering—Universidad Industrial de Santander, in Bucaramanga
- Education—Universidad Pedagógica Nacional, in Bogotá
- Basic Sciences—Universidad del Valle, in Cali
- Social Sciences—Universidad Nacional, Bogotá
- Agricultural Sciences—Universidad Nacional, Medellín
- Law and Political Sciences—Universidad Externado de Colombia, in Bogotá
- Economics—Universidad de los Andes, in Bogotá
- Transportation & Telecommunication—Universidad del Cauca, in Popayán[21]

The centralized node, at the ICFES in Bogotá, defined its mission as providing information access, selective dissemination of information, and interlibrary loan, as well as coordinating projects like the National Union Catalog of Serial Publications, national bibliographies, and a directory of Colombian researchers.[22]

The driving idea behind SIDES was to maximize library resources by concentrating acquisitions (especially of scientific journals) in the specialized universities and allowing them to circulate nationally through the network. For various reasons, this project never reached its full potential. One analyst believes it was "doomed to failure" once the funding ended in 1989; others note political problems, hardware and software problems, and lack of clarity in information management, in addition to budgetary troubles.[23] Nevertheless, some of the regional committees continue to offer important services in their areas, and a number of excellent products and services grew out of the SIDES initiative.[24]

For instance, in conjunction with the SIDES project, ICFES pioneered the use of international data bases, such as BRS and DIALOG in Colombia, and developed bibliographic software for use in academic libraries (known as SCIB). The National Serials Library was developed as a part of SIDES; it continues to complement the collections and services of individual academic libraries. The National Union Catalog of Serial Publications (which registers all serial publications in Colombian university libraries, the National Library, and Bogotá's state-of-the-art public library, the Luis Angel Arango Library) was produced on microfiche in 1989 and is now available on the

Internet, facilitating interlibrary loan services. The National Union Catalog of Theses is another significant data base that has outlived SIDES.[25]

Several other national and international projects resulted from SIDES initiatives. For example, a 1985 agreement between ICFES and the Pontificia Universidad Católica in Chile led to the use and updating of the National List of Subject Headings by catalogers in institutions belonging to the Chilean National Information Network. The Colombian Subject Headings provided the basis for the development of the Chilean Database of Subject Headings, which is currently used by Chilean libraries and museums in their cataloging.[26] Educational programs for information users and library personnel developed under SIDES have also had lasting consequences. In the 1980s, SIDES began a program for training information users. The program was aimed at university professors, in the hopes of changing the attitudes of professors and their students toward libraries. Academic librarians were trained in teaching techniques; they then developed seminar workshops in information use for professors, as well as packets for self-instruction.[27] Many academic libraries currently offer bibliographic instruction to their users.[28]

The 1990s: The SNIES Network

In 1994, ICFES was restructured. Academic library projects now fall under an Informatics Unit. Luis Fernando Rodríguez, Assistant Director of the Unit, continues to support and encourage the development of cooperative work among libraries, under the auspices of the National System of Information for Higher Education (SNIES). Several exciting projects are underway that carry the legacy of SIDES one step further. One is the Eratostenes Project, named after the librarian of Alexandria. Eratostenes is an electronic serials library, consisting of 33 SilverPlatter data bases in different subject areas, with full-text service for some (plus an additional 1,500 periodical titles on microfiche for interlibrary loan purposes). The data bases can be consulted over the Internet by multiple users from different platforms; by the end of 1996, twelve different cities (56 institutions) had access to Eratostenes.[29]

SNIES has recently mounted several of its national data bases, such as the National Union Catalog of Serial Publications and the National Catalog of Theses, on the Internet, using ALEPH software and Z39.50 standards. Institutions can use the data bases and then request desired documents through interlibrary loan. Another project involves the use of ARIEL software to provide interlibrary loan. ARIEL is currently being implemented in support of the Eratostenes project. Several cities have now been hooked up to use ARIEL, including Barranquilla , Bogotá, Bucaramanga, Cali, Manizales, Medellín, and Pereira.[30]

In order for ICFES to mount the Eratostenes project, a national network for data transmission first had to be established. This was done in collaboration with COL-CIENCIAS.[31] As noted previously, COLCIENCIAS is the other major government institution affecting the development of academic libraries in Colombia; it has sometimes done so by supporting the efforts of ICFES. In 1973, COLCIENCIAS was empowered to create a National Information System (SNI). SIDES, in addition to being a part of ICFES, was also a subsystem of SNI.[32] During the 1980s, SNI resources were directed toward the creation of data bases among public and private sector groups (including universities). For instance, the Universidad del Tolima participated in developing an agricultural data base that has now grown to include 180,000 references.[33]

COLCIENCIAS's current Strategic Plan for Scientific & Technological Information Systems involves strengthening the SNI, through supporting the consolidation and networking of some of the specialized data bases that have been developed in Colombia (for instance, a statistical database at the University of Los Andes). It is also implementing the construction of networks to connect institutions, information services, and data bases.[34] COLCIENCIAS has been criticized for placing too much emphasis on technology like CD-ROMs and now, on on-line access to remote data bases and networking, with little consideration of access to the primary literature.[35]

Survey Report: Librarians' Perspectives

In fact, the university libraries themselves are still the major sources of primary information.[36] Individual libraries and librarians form the basis for any network; they determine its success or failure, as well as the quality of the information service provided. Librarians in Colombia constitute a fairly large and well-trained group of professionals; four universities offer degrees in library science, and there are six professional associations.[37] In preparing this report, we solicited the opinions of Colombian academic librarians regarding the current state of academic libraries in their country, including achievements, challenges, and examples of outstanding libraries. A short survey and (in some cases) follow-up questions were sent by e-mail to around fifty librarians; sixteen responses were received, some of which combined the ideas of several individuals working in the same setting.

Responses were generally quite optimistic and forward-looking. Several librarians perceived an important process of change: namely, a growing appreciation of the vital role academic libraries play in mediating the production of knowledge that is needed for the country's development. In some instances, this new understanding was leading to larger budgets for collection development, equipment (especially computers, printers, scanners, and multimedia equipment), and telecommunications networks. During the last two years, it was noted, five universities in one city alone (Medellín) had begun the remodeling of their libraries or the construction of new buildings.

Library personnel are working hard to implement new information technologies. As of mid-1997, over fifty Colombian universities had websites on the Internet, and their libraries were represented in most of these, with several libraries making their catalogs available over the Internet. Many libraries have acquired CD-ROM products. However, different levels of development were described, with some libraries being totally automated, others in the process of automation, and many with the desire to automate, but lacking the budget to modernize fully and quickly. Many librarians referred to the sometimes prohibitive expense of the new technologies, which makes strategies of cooperation and integration all the more desirable.

Academic librarians are taking their newly appreciated role and the challenges presented by new technologies very seriously. As one respondent said, they are realizing the need to adapt to the new role the library plays in a world of globalization, technology, and rapid change. Professional organizations and library schools were also striving to respond to new training needs.

The names of several libraries appeared over and over again in the responses of academic librarians. It was not surprising to see the names of the "big five" university libraries repeated (Universidad de los Andes, Universidad de Antioquia, Universidad Javeriana, Universidad Nacional–Bogotá, and Universidad del Valle); these are the largest and best-funded academic libraries, each having a collection of over 100,000 volumes.[38] The Universidad de Antioquia and the Javeriana have been cited as "pioneers in the integration and individual development of technologies" such as the Internet, gophers and the World Wide Web in Colombia; Los Andes provided the first international Bitnet connection for Colombia's National University Network in 1990, and the Universidad Nacional was also involved with international networking early on.[39]

The Universidad del Valle offers an example of how this elite group of libraries has evolved. Like many Colombian libraries, this library began as separate departmental libraries. In 1962, a Rockefeller Foundation adviser evaluated the library situation and made recommendations about the development of collections in services, and in 1963, the Library Department was born, with a centralized administration. A library building was constructed in the 1970s; at the time, it was the largest library building in the country. Support for the library has continued; it is up-to-date and fully automated, with an Oracle Libraries catalog containing 300,000 records that has been on-line since 1995 and is available over the Internet. There are several university branch libraries and documentation centers throughout the city and the region from which the catalog is accessible.[40] The library is fairly well funded, and is "extremely active" and highly professional in its operations.[41]

Other libraries were also considered noteworthy by respondents, including the Universidad EAFIT, the Universidad Industrial de Santander, the Universidad del Norte in Barranquilla, the Universidad Javeriana in Cali. The Universidad Nacional de Medellín exemplifies this type of library, not among the five elite libraries but not far behind. Like the Universidad del Valle, the library at the Universidad Nacional de Medellín uses Oracle Libraries software for its catalog, which is accessible over the Internet. The book collection is barcoded and the automated circulation system was set to come on-line at the end of 1997. The library offers bibliographic instruction in an electronic classroom: orientation sessions for incoming students, higher level classes for students using specific literatures, and Internet training. Their collection includes paper, microfilm, CD-ROMs and multimedia materials. In 1997, the library has acquired fifty microcomputers, shelving, and new furniture, and has created an audiovisual center that seats thirty people; a new library is currently under construction. Librarians are active in academic life; for instance, they participate in a weekly education seminar and on the editorial boards of university publications.[42]

Alongside the achievements of these libraries, areas of need emerge as well. Colombian academic librarians are concerned with the education level of library personnel and with obtaining more continuing education opportunities in order to deal with new technologies. They perceive that some of their colleagues are uncertain, unconfident, and afraid of the information culture. Librarians noted the need to build up local and regional data bases, to establish more cooperative programs, and to improve the telecommunication system in Colombia, described by one respondent as being "summarily deficient."

There are also important concerns about the economic difficulties and economic disparities that exist among academic libraries in Colombia. While a handful of libraries have large, well-funded collections, services and equipment, the average academic library had only four books per enrolled student in the 1980s.[43] Funding is generally inadequate. Even the best funded libraries only receive 1/4 to 1/2 of the funding per student in the United Kingdom; other libraries are so poorly funded as to render such comparisons meaningless.[44]

One librarian wrote that on the threshold of the new millenium Colombian academic libraries offered two possibilities: the developed and the rest. "Those which have not modernized are likely to disappear, because they cannot offer quality services, nor do they have the necessary infrastructure to function in today's world," he wrote. Another librarian, writing from a small provincial university, pointed out that while there has been a lot of development and technological modernization in the last ten years, most of it has been concentrated in the big cities. In the smaller cities, she notes, libraries suffer from inadequate budgets; they sometimes find it difficult to support user needs, are unable to purchase enough technology, and do not always have training opportunities. While the libraries in the big cities appeared to be advancing quickly, those working in provincial libraries felt they were falling behind.

The picture of Colombian academic libraries as drawn by the librarians who know them best is hopeful, though far from perfect. New technologies and exciting opportunities for learning, service and expansion are accompanied by new expenses and a constant struggle by professionals to modernize their libraries and maintain currency. Smaller libraries with small budgets worry about their ability to fit into the changing scene. Cooperation and networking appear to offer some answers, but not a total solution. Some librarians expressed concern that the current governmental focus on telecommunication infrastructures and networking has shifted attention away from some of the important initiatives of the 1970s and 1980s; they note that many of the cooperative projects developed under SIDES have been abandoned. However, they also believe that once the network infrastructure is more firmly in place, it will enhance cooperation among academic libraries and may lead to a renewed interest in such projects.

Colombian academic libraries have made great strides over the past several decades in providing information services to their clientele. The scattered departmental collections of the 1950s and 1960s have become centralized libraries, run by professionals, increasingly automated, and now deeply engaged in the process of connecting to each other and to the rest of the world through telecommunication networks. The challenge for Colombian academic libraries is the same challenge currently facing all libraries: how to combine the successful strategies and achievements of the past with the technology of the future to make these new connections meaningful ones.

Acknowledgment

In gathering information for this chapter, the authors consulted with a number of academic librarians in Colombia and Chile. We thank them for generously sharing their thoughts and information. Without their contributions, this chapter would not exist.

Notes

1. B. Alvarez and A. Alvarez, "Colombia," in *Encyclopedia of Higher Education*, ed. B. R. Clarke and G. Neave (Oxford: Pergamon, 1992), 151.

2. A. Torres, "Biblioteca Nacional de Colombia," *Boletín de la ANABAD* 42 (July-Dec. 1992), 75.

3. William V. Jackson, "Colombia, Libraries in," in *Encyclopedia of Library & Information Science*, ed. A. Kent and H. Lancour (New York: Marcel Dekker, 1968), v.5, p. 305.

4. "Consultas," Instituto Colombiano para el Fomento de la Educación Superior, Sistema Nacional de Información de la Educación Superior (cited November 26, 1997), available from http://moises.icfes.gov. co:8080/snies/consultasies.htm.

5. Anabel Torres, "Colombia," in *World Encyclopedia of Library & Information Science*, ed. R. Wedgeworth, 3d ed. (Chicago: American Library Association, 1993), 219. It is difficult to get a precise figure for the number of university libraries in Colombia, since different publications use different definitions of "university" and "library." Published figures range from 71 college and university libraries affiliated with 48 institutions listed in the *World Guide to Libraries* (12th ed., Saur, 1995) to 74 university libraries affiliated with 66 institutions listed in UNESCO's *Information Services Worldwide* (1997), to 225 higher education libraries listed in the *Statistical Abstract of Latin America* (1996, figure given is for 1985).

6. Alvarez, 154.

7. *Anuario Estadístico de América Latina y el Caribe* (Santiago, Chile: Economic Commission on Latin America, 1997), 63; A. J. Evans, *Colombia Case Study* (London: British Library Research & Development Department, 1996), 2.

8. "Consultas," ICFES.

9. Luz M. Quiroga and Charlotte Ford, "Colombian Academic Libraries" (unpublished survey, Indiana University, 1997), 14.

10. Ibid., 6.

11. José Arias Ordoñez, "Sistema de Información y Documentación para la Educación Superior: Hemeroteca Nacional Universitaria," *Educación Superior y Desarrollo* 1 (1982), 34.

12. Jackson, 286.

13. Arias, "Sistema," 19.

14. Quiroga & Ford, 6.

15. Alfonso Monsalve Solórzano, "Investigación y Servicios de Información en Colombia," *Arbor* 157 (May-June 1997), 137.

16. Quiroga & Ford, 6.

17. José Arias Ordoñez, "Red Colombiana de Bibliotecas Universitarias," *Revista Interamericana de Bibliotecología* 1 (May-Aug. 1978), 8; Quiroga & Ford, 7.

18. Arias, "Sistema," 19-20; Elsa Martínez and Manuel Guerrero, "El Sistema Bibliográfico Colombiano—Catalogación Automatizada—LIBROUNAM," *Revista Interamericana de Bibliotecología* (Jan.-Dec. 1980), 217; José María Serrano Prada, "Bibliotecas Universitarias: Planeamiento, Políticas de Ciencia y Tecnología, Educación y Función en el Contexto Universitario," *Revista Interamericana de Bibliotecología* (Jan.-Dec. 1981), 58.

19. Quiroga & Ford, 10.

20. Evans, 4.

21. Monsalve, 137.

22. Arias, "Sistema," 28-31.

23. Evans, 4; Quiroga & Ford, 10, 15.

24. Monsalve, 138.

25. Ibid.; Quiroga & Ford, 3, 23.

26. Quiroga & Ford, 15.

27. Gloria Lopera Q., "Un Nuevo Enfoque en la Formación de Usuarios: la Experiencia Colombiana," *Revista AIBDA* 9 (1988), 65-71.

28. Torres, "Colombia," 219.

29. Quiroga & Ford, 11.

30. Ibid.

31. Ibid.

32. Monsalve, 137.

33. Sonia Laverde Eastman, "El Sistema Nacional de Información Bibliográfica del Sector Agropecuario Colombiano," *Revista AIBDA* 15 (1994), 67-8.

34. Monsalve, 137, 142.

35. Evans, 5.

36. Ibid.

37. Ibid., 3; Estela Morales Campos, "Latin America and the Caribbean," in *Information Services Worldwide*, ed. Y. Courrier and A. Large (Paris: UNESCO, 1997) (cited October 15, 1997); available from http://www.unesco.org/webworld/wirerpt/wirenglish/chap8.pdf

38. *World Guide to Libraries*, 12th ed., s.v. "Colombia" (Munich: K. G. Saur, 1995), 112.

39. Morales, 110; Monsalve, 136.

40. Quiroga & Ford, 2.

41. Evans, 6.

42. Quiroga & Ford, 1.

43. Torres, "Colombia," 219.

44. Evans, 6.

6. Discovering Treasures in Ecuador

Patricia A. Wand

I was left incredulous and exhilarated by my discoveries. Standing on a stepladder, I stretched to reach the top shelves of the stacks that lined the walls and randomly pulled down an old, dusty leather-bound volume. Gingerly I turned it over in my hands and carefully opened the front cover. The title was written in Latin and the imprint read 1781 in Roman numerals. I blinked and shook my head. Returning it to its place on the shelf, my hand moved to the right five or six volumes. I chose another book, whose leather binding was equally dusty, and carefully took it off the shelf. The imprint on this volume was even earlier, 1650!

I was examining the collection in the library of Colegio Benigno Malo, a secondary school in Cuenca, Ecuador. Yolanda Gallego, the librarian, was attending my in-service training course in July 1989 and had implored me to visit her school library. She knew she had treasures that really did not belong in the working collection of a high school and wanted advice from me about what to do with the gems she inherited from her predecessors.

Both of these volumes, and the several hundred others of their vintage that rested on the top shelves of the collection, were in excellent condition. That fact can be attributed primarily to the dry, cool climate of the Andean highlands in which these books were housed since colonial times and to the attention paid them by their caring curators over the centuries. However, it was true that these rare books did not belong in a high school library. I urged Srta. Gallego to work through her headmaster and contact the Banco Central, which had the resources to store the books properly.

How I Found Them

I was not expecting to find these treasures, nor thousands more like them, as I visited collections in Ecuador. But there they were, nestled in the most unexpected places. As priceless as they were, however, it was the people who worked in the libraries that impressed me the most. All of the 125 working librarians who registered for the "Current Issues in Librarianship" course I taught were bright, enthusiastic and eager to improve their skills and knowledge. They were intrigued with discussions about new ways they could manage their collections and serve their users.

My primary responsibility as a Fulbright Senior Lecturer was to develop a two-week in-service training course and to teach it in Spanish to librarians in five different cities. The classes met from 5:00 P.M.-8:00 P.M. five days per week for two weeks. In Quito, Cuenca and Guayaquil the course was taught in the USIA Lincoln Libraries; in Riobamba, it was hosted by the Escuela Superior Politecnica de Chimborazo (ESPOCH); in Ambato, by the Universidad Tecnica de Ambato.

Students were all practicing librarians who attended classes after working all day. Few people working in libraries in Ecuador have formal training in librarianship; most learn bibliographic skills while on the job. Those who attended my courses were hungry for professional development opportunities. For many it was the first time that they had come together with colleagues from other libraries to discuss issues of mutual concern. Most of them did not know one another before the courses began. The small group projects and class discussions provided opportunities for interaction. Many students ended the courses with a commitment to continue the network of communication in the future.

I felt frustrated at times when I could not quite explain a concept in Spanish. I had written the entire course syllabus in Spanish and, with the expert guidance of Teresa Molineros, Director of the Lincoln Library and of the USIA bicultural library program in Ecuador, I compiled a bilingual glossary of library terms. Still, I found myself stumbling for the right words upon occasion and students had several good laughs at my expense. Like the time I asked them to divide into "pajaros" (birds) when I meant to say "parejas" (pairs)!

The Fulbright Scholar Learns

Visiting fifty libraries in Ecuador was "frosting on the cake" for me. I taught classes in the late afternoon and visited libraries most mornings. The collections were housed in various spaces; several in libraries no bigger than offices and others, like the Biblioteca Nacional in Quito and the Biblioteca Municipal in Guayaquil, occupied entire buildings. With the exception of the USIA libraries, none of the libraries lent books to borrowers and all had closed stacks. In many cases the collections had not been entirely cataloged. Hence, retrieval was extremely difficult and further hampered by lack of reference service. Readers had to rely on the goodwill of the library staff who had varying levels of familiarity with their collections.

Automation of card catalogs was under serious consideration in several libraries in 1989. Automation was already underway in the library of Universidad Catolica in Quito, and the library of ESPOCH in Riobamba had developed an effective in-house system with the help of computer scientists teaching at the university. Other libraries were considering using MICROISIS, a system being promoted to Latin American libraries by the United Nations. Less than two years later, in late 1991, twenty-three university libraries had installed computers and were automating their catalogs. They invited me to address them again, this time via televideo conference, and discuss the components of an electronic network.

The absence of a reliable telecommunications system throughout the country, and particularly within smaller cities and towns, is an example of the infrastructure challenges that librarians face in Ecuador and many other countries.

Another challenge was discussed in several of the small group projects. How could librarians influence legislators to change the national law holding librarians personally and financially responsible if a book were missing from the collections? Until that law were changed, the librarians could not contemplate lending books for use outside the library. The small, often non-existent, acquisitions budgets also mitigated against lending volumes to borrowers who may be so desperate for books that they would keep them. How could due dates be enforced if borrowers were too poor to pay overdue fines?

Although I began teaching each course with the statement: "I have never been in a library in the United States or elsewhere that was adequately funded," my visits to libraries proved that these librarians were truly doing more with less. When we discussed the need to instruct readers about using the catalog, indexes and other basic reference tools, the librarians asked quite frankly how they could justify the time when their collections were uncataloged and they operated the library single-handedly. Although they recognized—some more than others—the value of reference services, most were terribly constrained by lack of adequate staff.

In Ecuador there were two programs offering preparation for librarianship: one in Cuenca and the other in Guayaquil. The former was a series of courses offered by the Universidad Catolica and taught by Rodrigo Abad who received his training in Germany and attentively participated in the course I offered. The latter, offered by the Escuela de Bibliotecologia in the Universidad de Guayaquil, was a four-year degree-granting program with a director, five faculty members and three hundred registered students. Several of the faculty members attended my course and the director invited me to speak to each of the four classes.

Banco Central Invests in Culture

"Why is the Banco Central so interested in libraries?" I initially asked of my Ecuadorean colleagues.

The Banco Central is the government "bank" which functions as the national treasury in the broadest sense of the word. It is responsible for preserving Ecuadorean culture in all its dimensions: indigenous, European, religious, archeological, artistic, intellectual, handcrafts. The Banco Central funds numerous projects to preserve the national heritage and to educate Ecuadoreans about their heritage. I visited pre-Inca sites in Cuenca and Ingapirca, for example, where the Banco sponsors archeological research, reconstruction of buildings, museum exhibits and educational programs.

The Banco's commitment to libraries is commendable and encouraging. In Old Town Quito in a historic bank building, the Banco was opening a Biblioteca de Textos to serve as a backup to all university libraries in the city. The Banco had already opened a large comprehensive public library, national and international newspaper library, music library and other special collections in Quito. In Riobamba the Banco had built a beautiful new facility housing both a cultural museum and a public library. The Banco supports similar libraries in Guayaquil and Cuenca. In all, the Banco has established thirteen public libraries in cities and towns throughout Ecuador.

Thus it was that the Banco Central was the only repository with the financial resources to preserve and protect a collection of colonial era volumes, which is why I recommended it to the secondary school librarian in Cuenca. Through its ongoing projects and as financial resources were available, the Banco established various research level collections, cataloged the books, making them retrievable by scholars. Furthermore, it initiated conservation programs in which librarians are trained to restore and preserve their priceless heritage. Some conservators were sent to Florence, Italy, to study conservation techniques with the masters and, upon their return, were encouraged to train other librarians in Ecuador.

One of these librarians, Nelly Peralta, Chief of Conservation and Document Restoration, Banco Central, worked with me in several cities as a "guest lecturer," sharing her expertise with the classes. She talked about the conservation programs of the Banco Central, including a reclamation project in the public library in Portoviejo, Ecuador, after a devastating flood in 1986. She effectively demonstrated the self-destructive characteristics of acidic paper and shared practical measures the librarians could take to prolong the lives of books.

Whenever video equipment was available, I showed *Slow Fires*, the film made by the Commission on Preservation and Access about the slow but inevitable self-destruction of acid-based paper. The Spanish version of *Slow Fires* was not available so Teresa Molinaros, Director of Lincoln Library in Quito and of the USIA bicultural library program in Ecuador, translated the entire script. When I showed the video one of the students read the Spanish version and we muted the English audio portion, except for the portion where President John F. Kennedy speaks. Everyone wanted to hear Kennedy's voice even if they could not understand his words.

Another video that the students found particularly impressive was about CD-ROMs. The technology was very new at that time, and most of the students had never seen a laser disc used to preserve texts and images. We discussed the advantages of CD-ROM technology in countries such as theirs, where telecommunications might be too unreliable to share information electronically, but the stability of laser discs made them a viable option for sharing bibliographic records.

Random Selections from the Nation's Libraries

I spent one morning visiting several libraries in the Universidad de Cuenca. Two energetic librarians, Alicia Criollo and Teresa Torres, were eager to incorporate what they had learned from the course about reference service into the operation of the Biblioteca de Jurisprudencia where they oversaw an 8,000-volume collection supporting the law school. At the Universidad de Cuenca a total of sixteen employees worked in the nine libraries, including the main library with 62,000 volumes. In this case, as in many others, I was reminded of the scarce resources available to librarians as they attempted to meet the needs of scholars.

In the Universidad Tecnica de Ambato, Elsa Naranjo, director of the Biblioteca General, led me through the main library and four separate branch libraries: science, accounting, education and engineering. The librarians lamented their inability to serve users adequately as long as the collections were divided, but no larger spaces were then available on campus to consolidate the collections and operate more efficiently. A new campus was being planned some years into the future and the librarians were hoping for a single, comprehensive library when that campus became a reality.

Guayaquil, unlike the other Andean cities in which I taught, is located on the coast and has a moist, tropical climate. During the two weeks in Guayaquil I visited the libraries of most of the twenty-four students in the course. Rosa Mantilla, librarian in the Instituto de Higiene y Medicina Tropical, worried about where to shelve new books since the stacks in her library were nearly two stories high with books filling the shelves end-to-end. She risked personal injury when retrieving or shelving a volume.

Biblioteca Municipal, the main public library in Guayaquil, was so filled on the Saturday morning I visited that students and scholars stood in lines outside each of the eight reading rooms waiting for seats to vacate so they could study and consult the collections.

Esperanza Cardenas, the director, took me through stacks housing over 120,000 books that were heavily used, many in desperate need of preservation. She wanted to show me the backlog of unprocessed material in the basement. We opened the door, turned on the light and ducked our heads to descend. My face was struck with stale, hot, humid air. I could hardly breathe. As we reached the bottom step I heard a scurry of activity and saw cockroaches racing in all directions. Even in the dim light I could see that some easily measured five inches long. We walked around the stacks of uncataloged books and unbound periodicals. I wondered which was the more over-whelming challenge—the preservation of the deteriorating items or their bibliographic control. It became harder and harder to breathe. When I thought I might be taking my last breath, we turned to leave. Suddenly, a bat flew over our heads.

In Quito, the Convento de Santo Domingo houses one of the richest collections of colonial art and religious artifacts I saw during my four months in Ecuador. The convent dates back to the early seventeenth century and is next to a huge church, Iglesia de Santo Domingo. A major restoration project was under way in which the buildings and collections (sculptures, paintings, ceremonial robes embroidered with gold and silver, books, furniture) were systematically analyzed and restored by experts. Architects, archeologists, librarians, paper conservationists, furniture makers, jewelers and weavers were all engaged in a five-year effort to save the buildings and collections. It was a joint effort, called Project Ecuabel, undertaken and funded by the Ecuadorean and Belgium governments and private contributions.

Within the building complex, which has three courtyards, was an exquisitely designed library that had fallen into disrepair over the years. The roof leaked directly onto priceless, leather-bound volumes, and books were piled on the floor and tables and even on top of the stacks. Under the supervision of Sonia Perez, library project director, conservationists were scrambling to save the 5,000-volume collection.

The large room had a 25-foot ceiling and a balcony encircling the four walls. The walls on both levels were lined with bookshelves and every three feet a double-sided bookcase was built perpendicular to the wall, creating cozy alcoves. On both ends of the long room were wooden stairways to the balcony. The stairs creaked and were worn in the center by the shuffle of thousands of feet that climbed them over the centuries.

The collection was astonishing. I randomly selected an older volume, opening it to discover an imprint of 1500. Incunabula were shelved next to nineteenth century volumes, most in remarkably good condition. Since the stacks were closed to all but a few, the volumes had seen little use over the centuries. Priests and nuns of the Dominican order had obviously protected the collection for the learned and have treasured the scholarship that it supports.

Real Treasures

I discovered treasures in private homes and in designated special libraries. I recall one collection in a walled monastery in Quito. The director of the library led me through room after room filled with rare books. Most were not cataloged, although they were housed in separate rooms by subject designations. The most precious were kept behind double-locked doors for which only the director held the keys.

Still, it was the commitment of the librarians that made the difference: their candid despair over terribly limited resources, their awareness that so much more could be done, their eager responses to new ideas, and their enthusiasm for trying different approaches. The closing ceremonies of each course brought speeches, certificates, testimonials of lessons learned and exchanges of symbolic gifts.

One class gave me a locally made ceramic, heart-shaped box and proclaimed, "To Patricia, who nearly stole our hearts!" Indeed, theirs were the hearts of librarianship in Ecuador, the real national treasures.

7. When Literacy and Oracy Meet: Public Libraries in the South Pacific

Philip J. Calvert

One of the most powerful ways we represent and interpret the world to ourselves is by our use of language. It is language which provides us with a ready means of classifying the world as we experience it, and by which we convert it into our personal "image," that is, our mental view of the world as only we know it. Words help create the image and they become hooks on which we can hang successive experiences of similar objects, thoughts and sensations. Every language has complex rules of grammar for combining words into continuous speech, and it is grammar which makes structured language possible; without it, real communication as we know it would be impossible. As we all share our lives with people who speak the same language and whose understanding of the world is also formed by the same words and grammar, it is quite easy to make an association between language and culture. Ideally, a language is a storage system for the collective experience of the tribe. Every time a speaker plays back the language he/she releases a whole charge of perceptions and memories. Hohepa, a Papua New Guinean writing about the place of language in the school curriculum in his own country, said "the most sensitive expression of a culture is the language which has evolved it."[1] Looking closely at that statement, it is clear that Hohepa saw language as a major factor in forming and developing a culture. Destroy the language and you destroy the culture, he implied.

The South Pacific region has numerous indigenous languages. Languages are the echo chambers of culture, and their maintenance is vital to the tenuous hold the South Pacific has on its own identity. It is the recently introduced languages of Europe, notably English but also French, which have brought with them an alien culture, and the new and different modes of creating the mental image which are an inevitable result. Yet in many countries of the region English is used in all secondary and tertiary education and even much primary schooling. To preserve the indigenous cultures there is a need to reemphasize the local languages as a means of "storing" the inherited knowledge of the people.

The Impact of English

The first Europeans to take an interest in the languages of the South Pacific were Christian missionaries from the United Kingdom and France. They created an orthography for each local language, translated it into their own language, and then started to print numerous Scriptures, prayer and hymn books, and other religious publications. Their success was quite remarkable. By 1870 there were 200,000 volumes in Fijian produced for local distribution, all of which were exclusively religious or directly linked to the evangelical purpose.[2] In New Zealand the indigenous Maori were, for a time in the early nineteenth century, more literate than the European settlers; nearly all printed materials in Maori were religious. What happened next was very instructive for all those who wish to promote reading and public libraries in the South Pacific region. Government educational policymakers directed that English, and not local languages, be used in schools. They had their reasons, of course, and for some children the acquisition of English opened up opportunities in government, business, education and the Church which they could never have hoped for otherwise, but for many children it was a disaster. They did not respond to the introduced languages even if there was, theoretically, a much greater range of reading materials available to them. They stopped reading. Unfortunately, apart from religious publications, there was no other literature in local languages for the children to read, and if there is an insufficient number of stimulating books then the neo-literate soon loses interest.

Print literacy in English gave people access to the sources of European power. These new sources of power—the central government, plantations, trading companies and the churches—completely undermined traditional structures of authority. Education in English or French became a great leveler in that it allowed men from the lower levels of society to acquire power in the new European organizations, but it also had the effect of generating divisions within society that had never been present before.[3] On the one hand, it is no surprise that young people not born to high rank grasped the opportunity to gain social advancement through their ability in English, even though their education gave no recognition to traditional values. "Conflict with the traditional social structures is likely to arise when an individual transcends it by virtue of these functions and . . . , such mobility is often related to literacy and its corresponding ability to obtain, retain and use information."[4]

The use of introduced languages created divisions in Pacific societies which have still not been closed. Those who speak the introduced language have access to European sources of information, and thus come close to real power; those who can "only" speak their own language remain in the social underclass.

The Rift between Classes

For many years throughout the seventies and eighties, politicians in the South Pacific spoke of divergent cultures coming together around themes common to all nations in the region in a process they called, "The Pacific Way." The only problem with this rather cozy picture is that it only described some of the population and ignored many others. For those who speak English there really is a sense of the "region" because they share a common language, travel regularly between the island groups, watch the same television programmes and films, and (at last we get to libraries) read the same books. These people would not have got where they are without being literate in English. It is those people who are not literate in the introduced language who are the losers. They find it almost impossible to get employment in government or business. Most of them will live in their traditional villages or (undoubtedly a poorer option) hover on the fringes of urban life hoping to some day "make it" in the city.

Even if this is viewed in a positive light by saying that the indigenous working class will undoubtedly be preserving the local culture, there is still cause for concern. The problem with this view is that middle-class control of cultural institutions, including libraries, dictates their purpose even when they are superficially trying to serve cultures on the margins of society.

> It is the privileged who can afford to tell the poor their traditions. But their perceptions of which traits of traditional culture to preserve are increasingly divergent from those of the poor, because in the final analysis it is the poor who have to live out the traditional culture;

the privileged can merely talk about it, and they are in a position to be selective about what trait they use or more correctly urge others to observe; and this is increasingly seen by the poor as part of the ploy by the privileged to secure greater advantages for themselves.[5]

This is the challenge for librarians in the South Pacific. They find it relatively easy to cater to the needs of the English-speaking middle class who have gone through secondary and possibly tertiary education. It is very much harder to cater to the needs of the indigenous working class who speak the local language and who are not information literate.

Oracy

Before going on to discuss the impact of print upon Pacific societies, it is important to make it clear that before the arrival of Europeans in the Pacific the transmission of information was mostly achieved by oral means, backed up by the use of carvings, images on mats, house decorations, and so on, as memory aids. Stories passed on from generation to generation did more than transmit "myths and legends" as they were once viewed, for the stories told by the elders contained within them important social information about acceptable and "tabu" relationships, about the time the fishing was good, and much, much more. There was nothing inherently inferior with this means of transmitting cultural information. The evidence is that it worked. Even though many of the oral traditions are gone forever, the strength of "oracy" as a means of communication is still very strong in the region. Using oracy is one hope for establishing better information services for the poor.

Public Libraries in the South Pacific

During the nineteenth century, European settlers established the first public libraries in the South Pacific.[6] They were intended exclusively for European patrons and thus set the pattern which has been followed ever since. In the 1990s public libraries open their doors to all, but the underlying philosophy and a reliance upon print materials in English results in a service skewed towards the needs of a minority. Statistics for use rates of public libraries show that among the local population the heaviest users are school children. This is often greeted as a measure of success by librarians, but unfortunately it fits into the pattern described above. School children are heavy users of the library because they are trying to learn an introduced language and pass all the exams set as hurdles along the path towards a career in government, business or education. Should they clear all the hurdles they then enter the regional, English-speaking middle class which knows the importance of information and how to go about finding it.

It is perhaps not too surprising that (in Western terms) the most "successful" library in the region is at the University of the South Pacific, for that is where you will find the academics and students.[7] These are the ones who have made it. Other educational libraries, for example those in the theological colleges, will also be regarded by outside observers as successful. School libraries face numerous difficulties but, despite chronic funding problems and difficulties in recruiting and training suitable staff, the demand for school library services is so high that they will always be valued. Special libraries fit the pattern of successful libraries in the region, though in reality there are very few as the largest corporate concerns are multi-nationals which house their information services elsewhere. There are some special libraries, for example the libraries attached to regional government associations, and they are often well funded and recruit well-qualified staff, for the library's customers are educated and information literate people. This leaves public libraries and, as has been made clear, these do not serve the needs of the indigenous working class as well as one would wish. They do, however, cater to the needs of the English-speaking middle class, and that should not be forgotten. Public libraries in the South Pacific are doing what public libraries have always done well in the Western world, that is, provide literature for the reading classes.

Community Libraries

There have been numerous attempts to establish "community libraries" in the South Pacific. The idea seems so good that it ought to work. A qualified librarian starts a library service dedicated to the needs of a local community; materials are selected to suit the supposed information needs of local people; some "user education" is done to promote the service. In the short term all is well, but then the qualified librarian leaves the area. That is when everything starts to collapse, and before long the community library is just a collection of books collecting dust and the good intentions are just a memory. For those wishing to study the impact of libraries on rural areas of the Pacific there is plenty of literature on how to establish a community library. Unfortunately, there is nothing written about sustaining the library after its initial success. Not surprisingly, research has not been done on the reasons for the failure of community libraries after the qualified librarian has departed. Suffice it to say that although community libraries satisfy many criteria for a successful South Pacific library, in practice there are few, if any, success stories to tell.

Governments have long assumed they know what information should be provided for the rural population. The information is usually functional, relating to the government's own development programmes. A study done by a Papua New Guinean librarian shed considerable doubt on this assumption, and his analysis of information flow in two villages suggests that government does not know what the rural people really need and want: "The flow of information was incomplete from district to village level and there was often a complete breakdown." [8] The reasons for the breakdown in information flow included a lack of consultation with the rural people, no involvement of the people in information provision, and the absence of feedback at all levels. His most surprising and worrying conclusion is that there was a deliberate rejection of government information services by the village people. There was a problem, he said, on the part of "the rural people whose perceived needs were not being met, and whose behaviour often tacitly rejected, or failed to accept, the information which reached the village." [9]

The lesson is that governments (which includes the national libraries) cannot adequately understand, and therefore provide for, the information needs of rural people. At the least, librarians must talk to the people directly to get some idea of what their needs are, and then if a service is provided they must seek feedback on its success. Ideally, the government will provide financial support for an information service run by and for the local people. The difficulty is that governments are unlikely to fund an information service unless they can also control it. The conclusion which has to be drawn is that if government attempts to control the information flow, the resulting information service will not deliver what the people actually want and need.

Publishing

There has been a pessimistic tone throughout much of this chapter, and the reality is that public libraries have been largely irrelevant to the indigenous working class people of the region. Are there solutions? Given the undeniable fact that print has largely replaced oracy as a formal means of transmitting information, why not just publish materials in the local languages? This has been done to a limited extent by governments, commercial publishers and the missions, but the South Pacific has so many different languages and often each one is only spoken by a small number of people so this is not a practical solution.

Will information technology be a solution? Perhaps it will. Material can be "published" by almost anyone on the Internet, and the variable costs are lower than they are for print. Perhaps motivated individuals and groups will be prepared to place material in local languages on the Internet so they can be accessed free of charge. If the materials are "spiced up" with graphics and sound they will be attractive to some people who dislike the appearance of printed books. It may be a while before small public libraries are in a position to provide easy access to the Internet for local people, but it will happen. Doubts might remain about the quality of such Internet materials, but then that is also true of some of the print materials currently available.

The African Experience

There is no reason to believe the problems cannot be solved, but they probably will not be solved by being inward-looking, or by a reliance upon the West. There are lessons to be learned from the experience of other "oral" cultures and how they have tried to provide for the information needs of the underclass. An English librarian in Africa, Ronald Benge, first drew attention to this. He recognised distinct social, cultural and economic values in Africa which made western librarianship ineffective. He said librarians should not try to override these identifiable values but should try to draw inspiration from them.[10] Recently there have been some interesting experiments in Africa which could well be tried in the South Pacific. The University of Ibadan started the Rural Development Information System (RUDIS), in which a team traveled to villages taking a variety of materials, such as posters, pamphlets and audio tapes, and attempted to provide an information service geared to the needs of the poor. "The experiment proved quite clearly that rural dwellers will react very favorably to a service which allows them to function as independent information seekers, defining their own needs."[11]

In Mali, a project aimed at harnessing the oral tradition was tried. A headquarters sound library was established and villages could use the center to record their oral heritage. "Thus, instead of being isolated in their illiteracy, they will, by means of recorded items, be able to acquire vivifying information on their own culture."[12]

In Namibia, a series of Community Learning and Development Centres have been established based on very sound principles. The philosophy they are using is that "users should be given the opportunity to choose how they want to learn, whether through observing nature, listening to and speaking with village elders, studying books and journals, using mass media or surfing the web. Further, it remains the right of the individual to decide how to relax, feed the imagination and stimulate creativity. Theatre, art displays, musical performance and storytelling should form part of any community information service."[13] The latter point is interesting because already Papua New Guinea has a successful theater troupe, the Raun Raun Theatre, which has taken its own brand of musical dance-dramas into the villages. Their plays are sometimes based on oral traditions, but they also perform modern plays about nutrition and the avoidance of disease. They work in the local lingua franca, Pidgin English. The theatre has no formal links with local libraries, which is a pity, because this is precisely the way villagers absorb information most easily. Surely

Fiji and other countries with a large tourist industry could use tourist dollars to support such theatre companies (or libraries which will run the theatres) so that they can be used for information dissemination in the off-season.

Summary and Conclusion

Over the course of the last two centuries the oral cultures of the South Pacific have taken a fearful battering. Some oral traditions are gone forever. Local languages remain, though, the most powerful means of storing and transmitting the culture across the generations, and the loss of a local language would, in effect, mean the end of the culture. Introduced languages, particularly English, have introduced Western modes of thought into the region. Young people seeking a career must learn an introduced language or else they will fall back to the fringes of society. Libraries in tertiary education, such as the University of the South Pacific, are effective because they do well what they set out to do. For these libraries the global influence is beneficial, and interaction between expatriate librarians and local staff has been good for all concerned. On the other hand, public libraries as they were bequeathed by Europeans will not satisfy the information needs of the non-English speaking people in the indigenous working class. For these people oracy is still the best way to communicate, and if that is not possible then they want to use materials in local languages. For these libraries it would seem that global reach has been a failure. Yet, looking outwards is still their best hope for the future. Instead of looking towards the West for guidance, public librarians should look closely at the experience of other oral cultures, especially in Africa, to learn what might be done. For the public libraries of the South Pacific global reach was once the problem. Now it is the promise.

Notes

1. A. Hohepa, *Culture and the Curriculum* (Port Moresby, Papau New Guinea, The Author, n.d).
2. J. Clammer, *Literacy and Social Change: A Case Study of Fiji* (Leiden: Brill, 1980), 25.
3. It was almost always men and not women.
4. Clammer, 78.
5. Epeli Hau'ofa, "The New South Pacific Society: Integration and Independence," in *Class and Culture in the South Pacific,* ed. Anthony Hooper et al. (Auckland: Centre for Pacific Studies, University of Auckland and Suva: Institute of Pacific Studies, University of the South Pacific, 1987), 1-12.
6. Philip J. Calvert, "The Levuka Reading Room: Fiji's First Library," *Journal of Library History* 20, no. 3 (Fall 1985), 302-309.
7. The USP Library offers its services to the whole community. See Ann Rizio and Jayshree Mamtora, "Meeting the Library and Information Needs of the South Pacific Region: The Role of the USP Library," *Australian Academic & Research Libraries* 24, no. 2 (June 1993), 105-112.
8. Deveni Temu, "Information Needs of Two Papuan Village Communities (Kapari and Virilo) and Rural Development: A Study Report," in *Rural Libraries and Community Resource Centres,* ed. Roy Sanders and James Henri (Wagga Wagga, N.S.W.: International Association of Rural and Isolated Libraries, 1990), 80.
9. Temu, 80.
10. Ronald Benge, *Cultural Crisis and Libraries in the Third World* (London: Bingley, 1979).
11. Paul Sturges and Richard Neil, *The Quiet Struggle: Libraries and Information for Africa* (London: Mansell, 1990), 113.
12. M. Rahnema, "The Sound Library: A Simple But Revolutionary Tool for Development," *Unesco Journal for Information Science, Librarianship and Archives Administration* 4 (1982), 156-157.
13. Veronica Jacobs, "From Local Village to Global Village: Can the Two Meet?" *Information Development* 13, no. 2 (June 1997), 80.

8. Developing Library and Information Services in Micronesia: Cooperation across Vast Distances

Arlene Cohen, Joanne Tarpley Crotts, and Irene Lovas

Stretched across 4,500,000 square miles of the central and western Pacific Ocean, over 2,200 small volcanic and coral islands make up the region of Micronesia, meaning tiny islands. Lying west of Hawaii, south of Japan, east of the Philippines and north of Australia and the equator, the total land mass of all these tropical islands is less than 1,200 square miles with a total population base estimated at approximately 300,000. Micronesia encompasses an expanse of water almost as big as the contiguous United States, but has a total land mass less than that of Rhode Island.

To make this area ever more complex, not only are the islands of Micronesia spread over a large geographic area, but each island group has its own unique culture, language and government structure. "The inhabited areas vary from idyllic villages with no cars or electricity to the high rise resort developments of Guam and Saipan." [1]

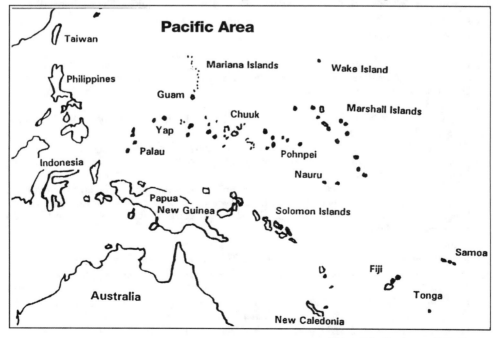

Map created by Joanne T. Crotts

During World War II, most of the Micronesian islands were occupied by Japanese forces. After the war, all the islands except for Guam were placed under the administration of the United States by a United Nations mandate and called the Trust Territory of the Pacific Islands. During the ensuing years, each island group negotiated their political status with the United States and today, Micronesia can be divided into five separate political entities.

The unincorporated United States territory of Guam is the largest and most southerly of the Mariana Islands in the western Pacific Ocean. Originally discovered by Magellan in 1521, the island was ceded by Spain to the United States in 1898. Guam has remained a territory since 1898, except during the thirty months of Japanese occupation in World War II. Within the region, Guam is considered to be the gateway to Micronesia and is the most economically developed of the Micronesian islands. Guam is the largest island geographically (212 square miles) and the most populous; the 1997 midyear population estimate taken from the *Pacific Island Population Data Sheet* cites Guam's population at 145,400.[2]

The United States Commonwealth of the Northern Mariana Islands (CNMI) was established in 1975 and includes the populated islands of Saipan, Tinian and Rota. Held by Spain until 1898, these islands were then sold to Germany at the same time Guam was ceded to the United States. In 1914, with the start of World War I, Japan occupied the islands and at the end of the war, they were officially assigned to Japan under a mandate of the League of Nations. With the close of World War II, they were placed under Trust Territory administration.

The Federated States of Micronesia (FSM), consisting of the island states of Pohnpei, Chuuk, Kosrae, and Yap, are in the Caroline Islands group. Following much the same history as other Micronesian islands, they were also administered as part of the Trust Territory of the Pacific Islands from 1947 to 1986. The island states united under the Federated States of Micronesia and are now an independent country under a compact of free association with the United States.

The Republic of the Marshall Islands is another independent island group in the central Pacific Ocean. First sighted by Spanish explorers in the early sixteenth century, the islands were governed by Spain and then Germany until 1920, when they also were assigned to Japan by the League of Nations. After World War II, they, too, were part of the Trust Territory of the Pacific Islands until 1979 when the Marshalls Constitution was ratified and the Republic of the Marshall Islands was created.

The independent Republic of Palau is another group of volcanic islands and islets in the Western Caroline Islands. As early as 1543, Spanish and Portugese navigators had visited Palau. In 1891, the Spanish sent Capuchin monks to settle on Palau. They were followed by the German occupation around 1900 and then, after World War I, they were under Japanese administration until the end of World War II. The Republic of Palau signed a Compact of Free Association with the United States in 1996 and thus ended all Trust Territory of the United States administration in the region.

Given the varying governmental frameworks and the changing political leadership and status, obtaining consistent and reliable funding for education and library development has been a constant challenge throughout the region. Under the Trust Territory of the Pacific Administration, all the islands qualified for United States federally funded programs. Now, with their change in political status, several island nations have lost various United States federally funded programs, although they now qualify for aid programs from other countries such as Australia and Japan.

Libraries and Other Information Resources in the Region

In the past, little has been published about the libraries, archives and educational institutions in Micronesia. In a 1992 survey used to create the *Directory of Libraries, Archives and Museums in Micronesia,* 106 libraries responded.[3] While not a comprehensive listing of all libraries, this directory included six public libraries, twelve college and university libraries, over forty-five public or private school libraries and a variety of special libraries, including four medical and seven law libraries and five museums.

With over 3,500 students and a one-hundred-acre campus, the University of Guam is the largest educational institution in the region. With a strong undergraduate curriculum in education, nursing and business, it also offers graduate degrees in education, business and public administration, marine sciences and Micronesian studies. There are also seven community college campuses of varying size in the region. These two-year schools provide a variety of programs, including nursing, teacher training, business, tourism and marine science. For example, the Guam Community College is largely devoted to vocational training and includes programs in cosmetology, plumbing and carpentry. The community colleges on the other islands also provide this type of vocational training, as well as liberal arts courses in preparation for obtaining a baccalaureate degree.

There are library collections of varying size and quality to support the curricula of these various campuses. The Robert F. Kennedy Memorial Library at the University of Guam is the major collection within the region with almost 100,000 volumes. The College of Micronesia-FSM in Pohnpei recently completed a beautiful new library building; however, as with all the educational institutions within Micronesia, book, periodical and technology budgets are consistently underfunded.

Each island state or nation has a public library and usually a museum. The size and depth of these collections varies greatly from island to island, as does the use of technology to expand and share resources. These variations generally result again from inadequate funding coupled with the lack of training and expertise among staff. In most cases, only recently has there been an appreciation of the value of the local cultures and the preservation of these heritage materials. This awareness is slowly changing the roles and perception of the libraries, archives, and museums throughout Micronesia.

Every political entity attempts to have a government archives collection. The Republic of Palau and the Federated States of Micronesia each have their own separate national archives collection, while the Commonwealth of the Northern Marianas houses its collection within the community college library. The Republic of the Marshall Islands national archives and museum are combined as one collection. There are also national archives within the different states of the Federated States of Micronesia housed in government agencies on each island state. On Guam, the Guam Public Library has been designated as the official archives. The Micronesian Area Research Center (MARC) has also become the unofficial archives for Guam.

Complementing these established libraries, there are some special collections of note scattered throughout Micronesia. Yap, one of the states of the FSM, houses the Yap Institute of Natural Sciences, which is a private collection of many out-of-print books and materials dealing with the natural history and ecology of Yap, Micronesia and the Pacific Islands. On Pohnpei (FSM), there is the Micronesian Seminar Collection. This is a significant collection, established by the Jesuits, containing material covering Micronesian history, social science, politics and anthropology and includes rare documents such as letters from early missionaries in Micronesia. The Micronesian Area Research Center (University of Guam) also has a substantial collection of materials covering all aspects of Guam, Micronesia and the Pacific. In the Republic of the Marshall Islands, the Nuclear Claims Tribunal Library houses a collection of books, articles and reports on radiation damage to humans and the environment and supports ongoing research. Bikini, an atoll in the Ratak Chain of the Marshall Islands, was the site of U.S. nuclear tests between 1946 and 1958, including the first aerial detonation of a hydrogen bomb on May 21, 1956.

Development of Pacific Islands Association of Libraries and Archives (PIALA)

With the establishment of the Trust Territory of the Pacific after World War II, the United States was instrumental in creating schools and libraries in Micronesia. In the early days of the Trust Territory administration, some few unsuccessful attempts were made to organize librarians throughout the region. A further effort was made in 1978 with the impetus of the United States-supported Governor's Pre–White House Conferences held in several locations in Micronesia. However, there was never enough of a critical mass or easily accessible methods of communication to establish a regional network of people or resources permanently.

In October 1990, new seeds were planted during the CNMI Governor's Conference for Libraries and Information Services, held on Saipan. At the conference, several participants and observers met informally to discuss the formation of a regional association. Thereafter, at another informal meeting held in November 1990 at the Guam Governor's Conference for Libraries and Information Services, more concrete plans for an organizational meeting were developed.

With funding from the United States Office of Territorial and International Affairs (OTIA) available to support a regional archival preservation project, the organizational meeting was held at the University of Guam in February 1991. Two participants each from the Federated States of Micronesia, the Republics of Palau and the Marshall Islands, the Commonwealth of the Northern Mariana Islands and the Territory of Guam attended the meeting. At the meeting, the Pacific Islands Association of Libraries and Archives (PIALA) was established as a regional association committed to fostering awareness and encouraging cooperation and resource sharing among libraries, archives and museums and related institutions of the Pacific Islands.

The participants also adopted PIALA's Bylaws, elected an executive board, established committees, and selected the Republic of Palau as the site for the first conference.[4] To allow for consistent representation from each island entity in Micronesia, the Bylaws state that "the executive board shall consist of the officers, shall represent all locations, and have no fewer than five members. Locations not represented by officers shall elect a representative ... and there cannot be more than two officers from any one location."[5]

Impact of PIALA

With its establishment, PIALA has provided a forum for librarians to network and share resources—both collections and expertise—throughout the region. The greatest strength of PIALA lies in using its local members to identify specific problems and unique needs of the region. PIALA's conferences, publications and activities attempt to respond to these needs. Over the years, PIALA has continued to grow and now attracts international interest and resources.

During PIALA's first year (1991), 29 institutional and 64 individual memberships were accepted. Currently, PIALA's membership is made up of over 75 individuals and 35 institutions, representing countries such as Australia, New Zealand, New Caledonia, Japan, Tonga, Fiji, Papua New Guinea, Finland, the United Kingdom and the United States. Considering the region's small population base, this 20 percent growth is evidence of the association's development and viability, which includes a broadened international membership base.

For seven consecutive years, PIALA annual conferences have been held throughout Micronesia. For the past four years, preconference workshops have provided training and hands-on sessions to area librarians and archivists. Without PIALA, many of those working in remote libraries and archives would never have had the opportunity to travel off their islands or receive any kind of formal training or courses in library skills. Likewise, by moving the conferences each year to a different island, people with no travel budgets have the opportunity to experience a professional conference and attend the training sessions.

PIALA '91, our first annual conference was held on Palau in a traditional bai [6] in the village of Koror, drawing over forty participants from throughout Micronesia, Fiji, Hawaii and the continental United States. With the theme Preserving Knowledge for Tomorrow, presentations were made on topics such as preservation techniques for the tropics and telecommunications in the Pacific, along with discussions on continuing education and resource sharing ideas and opportunities.

In Kolonia, Pohnpei, PIALA '92 carried out the theme, Meeting Information and Conservation Needs Today and Tomorrow, with a variety of workshops and presentations covering areas such basic health science resources, managing small collections, library services for children and local resource sharing activities.

The island of Saipan in the Commonwealth of the Northern Mariana Islands was the venue for PIALA '93, and selected papers from that meeting marked the first publication of the proceedings of a PIALA conference.[7] PIALA '94, held in Guam, drew the largest attendance of any PIALA annual meeting thus far, with over 100 people attending. That meeting marked the first preconference two-day training workshop to be offered at an annual PIALA conference; the workshop was "Collection Development and Management for Small Libraries."

Each year, the conference topics have expanded to include presentations about the cultural heritage of the island hosting the conference. PIALA '95 in Colonia, Yap, with the theme Preservation of Culture Through Archives and Libraries will be remembered for the several important papers presented by local participants and the amazing variety of traditional dances, chants and stories shared by the Yapese people for the enjoyment of the conference attendees.

During the PIALA '96 meeting in Majuro, Marshall Islands, the first PIALA resolution was passed by the membership. The resolution addressed the serious telecommunications problems associated with Internet access and stated that "each Island Government and Nation provide direct cost effective Internet access at a high performance data exchange rate to member libraries and archives in their respective areas." This was a first attempt by local librarians and the association to assert their concerns in a formal way.

When PIALA returned to Pohnpei in 1997, both pre and postconference workshops were part of the program. The post-conference workshop on library advocacy led by

Tuula Haavista, the Executive Director of the Finnish Library Association, clearly illustrates PIALA's impact and demonstrates the growth and viability of the association since its beginnings in 1991. This workshop was funded under a grant awarded by the International Association of Library Associations and Institutions Advancement of Librarianship in the Third World Program (IFLA ALP). The grant covered the entire cost of the workshop, including transportation and accommodations for twelve library association leaders in Micronesia. The training covered political action for libraries, communicating with government agencies and the public, effective lobbying and relating advocacy to funding. It came at a time when PIALA members were working enthusiastically to promote awareness of library services in the region, and provided new advocacy skills to the participants.

PIALA's annual conferences have elevated the awareness of the local populations about librarians and library services they provide in the communities they serve. For instance, in 1995, when sixty librarians descended on Colonia, the tiny capital of Yap in the Federated States of Micronesia, their presence was immediately noticed with television, radio and newspaper coverage. At each of the annual conferences, government officials are invited to conference presentations and dinners and are encouraged to speak on behalf of their governments and their unique cultural heritage. Likewise, officials are able to hear firsthand about the needs and services of libraries and archives directly from the people who work in them. The published *Proceedings* include the comments of invited government officials, providing documentation and tangible evidence of their involvement and support of the association. The *Proceedings* are distributed free of charge to over thirty regional libraries, to the people whose papers are included, and to other key individuals. They are also available for purchase to the world at large. (See note 7.) The sales of the *Proceedings* have almost covered all publication costs and the free distribution copies.

Hosting conferences exacts financial, logistical and human resource burdens on an island. Many islands have fewer than sixty available hotel rooms and no large meeting halls. Even transportation arrangements for conferences can be complicated due to limited flights to many places in Micronesia. To date, Chuuk and Kosrae have never hosted a PIALA conference as these factors make it difficult for them to do so. However, plans are afoot for Kosrae to host PIALA '98, a good indication of the developing interest of local governments as well as the growing enthusiasm and commitment of the members of the association.

Two other PIALA publications, *Directory of Libraries, Archives and Museums in Micronesia* and the *Union List of Serials in Libraries of Guam and Micronesia* focused attention on the region and revealed how many small but unique collections exist.[8] The *Union List* serves as an indication of what resources are available in Micronesia and is a valuable tool for interlibrary loan and collection development. The regional *Union List* includes many local publications that cannot be found in traditional "stateside" produced data bases or collections.

Outside Involvement

PIALA has been a force in implementing information resource sharing through its publications, conferences and training. Several articles about PIALA have been published both locally and also internationally in such periodicals as *National Library of Australia News*, *Third World Libraries*, and the *FID News Bulletin*.[9] As the organization has grown and expanded its membership, PIALA has networked and established relationships with other areas of the world and with other associations. This has increased the awareness of libraries in Micronesia and enabled all involved to share resources to meet the unique information needs of users in Micronesia, as well as in other areas of the globe.

In 1993, a World Wide Web site was established for PIALA through the joint efforts of one of the authors (Arlene Cohen) and Tom Gerhardt, a computer linguist and information scientist working as the Internet manager in the Saarlandes University Library in Saarbrüchen, Germany. Tom heard about PIALA through postings on the Internet and contacted Cohen with an offer to create the Web site. After many e-mail messages, and even some snail mail, the Web site was established. It was moved to the University of Guam in 1996 and can now be found at http://uog2.uog.edu/rfk/piala.html.

Seeing the need for more involvement in international professional associations, Cohen joined the International Federation of Library Associations and Institutions (IFLA) as a personal affiliate member in 1996. Since a one-year association membership in IFLA is almost 25 percent of PIALA's operating budget, there was no possibility that PIALA could afford to join, yet the benefits have been significant.

Soon after joining, Cohen represented PIALA in two sessions at the IFLA '96 conference in Beijing, China.[10] At that conference, she became aware of many funding opportunities, including the Danish International Development Assistance (DANIDA) grants available to librarians in developing countries to attend the IFLA '97 conference in Copenhagen. Both the PIALA president, a librarian from the island of Yap, and Cohen were awarded DANIDA grants and presented a poster session about PIALA at the conference.[11] Cohen was also elected to the Executive Committee of the IFLA Round Table on the Management of Library Associations.

Another funding opportunity that surfaced in Beijing was the International Federation of Library Associations Advancement of Librarianship in the Third World Programme grants. Funding for the PIALA '97 library advocacy workshop was the result of networking with librarians at the IFLA '96 conference in Beijing. Initial plans for that grant proposal were excitedly discussed by Cohen and the Finnish Library Association Executive Director on a tour bus ride to the Great Wall of China.

Another outside organization that has been involved with PIALA is the National Network of Libraries of Medicine (NN/LM). This National Library of Medicine (NLM) program provides access to and the delivery of information to health professionals, especially those in rural areas and those serving minority populations. The Pacific Southwest Regional Medical Library (PSRML), one of eight regional medical libraries, is headquartered at the Louise Darling Biomedical Library at the University of California, Los Angeles, and serves Micronesia. There are a large number of underserved health professionals located in Micronesia. Since 1990, the PSRML Network Coordinator has visited Micronesia several times to survey the hospitals, health services, community colleges and the University of Guam about the availability of health-related materials. The Coordinator has also been actively involved in promoting access to, and the delivery of, information to these health professionals in Micronesia and, like PIALA, to encourage resource sharing of these materials. Included in several presentations given to the National Health Services Corps and the Pacific Islands Health Officers Association (PIHOA) was information about the library services available from NLM and from local libraries.[12]

Another goal of the NN/LM is to foster resource sharing among not only health science libraries but libraries of all types. Therefore, the Network Coordinator from PSRML has been active in PIALA, presenting workshops and sessions on basic healthcare resources, consumer health resources, and resource sharing at four of PIALA's conferences. In 1992, the Robert F. Kennedy Memorial Library at the University of Guam joined DOCLINE, NLM's automated interlibrary loan request and referral system, to expedite document delivery of biomedical information in the Pacific, allowing the library to play a key role in obtaining information resources for health professionals. Shortly thereafter, the U.S. Naval Hospital on Guam joined DOCLINE to expand the availability of healthrelated resources in Micronesia, especially to United States Public Health Service personnel. Recently, with the encouragement of the PSRML, the University of Guam RFK Library was designated as a Resource Library, supporting the delivery of information and local resource sharing to all areas of Micronesia.

In 1995, as the need for updating the 1992 *Directory of Libraries, Archives and Museums in Micronesia* became critical, PIALA updated their listings and was invited to contribute them to a larger regional directory project. In a joint effort with the International Relations Unit of the National Library of Australia in conjunction with the AsiaPacific Special Interest Group of the Australian Library and Information Association, a regional directory has been published and made available free of charge to all participating libraries.

Challenges and Future Directions

Communication from island to island remains the biggest challenge. Without easy, inexpensive access, efforts at networking and resource sharing have been slow to develop and difficult to maintain. It is very expensive to use the commercial telecommunications providers for voice, FAX or Internet access. For example, a phone call from Guam to Palau can cost well over $1 per minute with connections often unreliable. However, this is changing as private Internet service providers are beginning to offer lowcost telecommunication services in the islands. Unfortunately, local governments have been slow to support and fund this new technology.

PEACESAT (PanPacific Educational and Communication Experiments by SATellite), a federally funded telecommunications satellite system spanning Micronesia and the South Pacific, is still the most economical means of communication. With satellite stations on each island, any nonprofit or government agency can use the technology. However, the system has limited channels with very tight scheduling and the stations are prone to frequent breakdowns, with few spare parts and limited expertise available to offer repairs.

The vast distances between islands and between Micronesia and Hawaii also contribute to the challenge of telecommunication access. It is very difficult, even for libraries on Guam and Saipan, which have better connections, to communicate effectively with vendors or libraries not only in a different time zone, but a different day. The slogan on Guam license plates in the early 1990s read "Guam—Where America's Day Begins" in that the International Dateline separates the Pacific Islands from Hawaii and the continental United States.

While vast distances still preclude meeting face-to-face more than once a year, PIALA Executive Board members stay in touch through bimonthly PEACESAT satellite meetings. Members rely on the *PIALA Newsletter*, distributed three to four times a year to an ever-growing mailing list to keep current about what is happening with librarians and archivists throughout the region.[13]

The absence of trained professionals, college-educated or otherwise skilled workers, presents another challenge both for library and information services in Micronesia and for PIALA as a growing association. Currently, a small pool of people have developed leadership skills and experience in maintaining the association. Prior to the establishment of PIALA, only Guam had a local library association. To date, Palau, Pohnpei, and the Marshall Islands have formed local library associations, raising funds for their libraries and providing a local resource for librarians within the community. Since PIALA has created a new awareness of the service that librarians, archivists, and museums curators provide, hopefully, the PIALA '97 library advocacy workshop will enable members to become more proactive in communicating with government officials and the public and in fund-raising efforts.

To compound the problem of the lack of trained professionals, the undergraduate School Librarianship program at the University of Guam has long suffered from a lack of faculty and University support. Few classes have been offered, thus limiting educational opportunities for anyone in Micronesia to locally pursue a career in library and information sciences. The University of Hawaii at Manoa offers the nearest master's program in Library Science within 2,000 miles. To gain the education, knowledge and skills, one needs to travel miles to Guam or to the University of Hawaii. It is a hardship few in the region can afford. This lack of training opportunities makes PIALA an important factor for the librarians in Micronesia, since the preconference workshops and the presentations are sometimes the only training in library skills available to them.

Additionally, the majority of PIALA members receive minimal salaries. Therefore, PIALA's membership fee and conference registration costs are kept as low as possible to ensure maximum participation. Lack of finances prevents underwriting many projects; grant support is actively sought for such projects as additional training or seminars to benefit the membership. However, with the current small leadership pool with limited expertise, regularly pursuing grants has been difficult.

Perhaps the most important impact of PIALA has been the increase of networking and resource sharing among the members. As the association has grown in members, the support among the members has also increased. Through the years, the members have worked together to expand and further develop their association and to organize the annual conferences despite the barriers of vast geographic distances, different languages and cultures, and funding. When one of the libraries considers an expansion or some new service, it is now not uncommon for the librarian to contact someone from another island to seek advice or information.

At the first PIALA conference in 1991, each island's participants tended to stay within their own group, slowly meeting each other by the end of the conference. Today, a conference starts with old friends spontaneously greeting each other and new participants quickly becoming part of the group. Thus, the seeds that were planted in 1990 have begun to be harvested and shared.

Notes

1. G. Bendure and N. Friary, *Micronesia*, 3rd ed. (Australia: Lonely Planet Publications, 1995), 9.

2. Population/Demography Programme, South Pacific Commission, *Pacific Islands Population Data Sheet* (Noumea, New Caldonia: South Pacific Commission, 1997).

3. An updated *Directory of Libraries and Archives in the Pacific Islands*, including all types of libraries in Melanesia, Micronesia and Polynesia is now available. Copies can be purchased for A$12 for Australian Library and Information Association members and A$15 for nonmembers from the

Australian Library and Information Association, P.O. Box E441, Kingston, ACT 2604 Australia. Tel: 61-2-6258-1877; FAX: 61-2-6282-2239 or e-mail: enquiry@alia.org.au.

4. Pacific Islands Association of Libraries and Archives Bylaws. Latest revision November 1996.

5. Ibid.

6. A traditional Palauan men's hut or council house.

7. PIALA *Proceedings* are available from Arlene Cohen, RFK Memorial Library, University of Guam, UOG Station, Mangilao, Guam 96923 or e-mail: acohen@uog9.uog.edu.

8. Copies of the *Union List of Serials in Libraries of Guam and Micronesia* are available from the Guam Public Library, 254 Martyr Street, Agana, Guam 96910. Tel: 671-475-4752; FAX: 671-477-9777. The cost is $14.50.

9. Joanne Tarpley Crotts and I. Rungrad, "Atolls in Association," *National Library of Australia News* 7, no. 7 (April 1977): 9-11; Joanne Tarpley, "Conference Report: Pacific Islands Association of Libraries and Archives (PIALA), 1994 meeting, Tamuning, Guam, November 2-4, 1994," *Third World Libraries* 5, no. 2 (Spring 95): 76-77; Arlene Cohen, "The Pacific Islands Association of Libraries and Archives (PIALA) formed in the Pacific Islands," *FID News Bulletin* 42, no. 12 (December 1992): 285-286.

10. Arlene Cohen, "Library Associations in Underdeveloped Regions and Their Impact on Library Development" (paper presented at the 62nd International Federation of Library Associations (IFLA) Management of Library Associations Workshop, Beijing, China, August 29, 1996); Arlene Cohen and J. Butsch, "Assisting Regional and National Library Associations in Developing Countries" (panel participant at the 62nd International Federation of Library Associations (IFLA) ALP Core Programme Workshop on Aid Agency Information Services Assisting Economic Development, Beijing, China, August 29, 1996).

11. Arlene Cohen and I. Rungrad, "The Pacific Islands Association of Libraries and Archives: A Model for Library Associations in Developing Countries" (poster session presented at the 63rd International Federation of Library Associations (IFLA) Annual Meeting, Copenhagen, Denmark, August 31-September 5, 1997).

12. Irene Lovas, "Accessing the Information Needs of Health Professionals in the Pacific Basin: Final Report" (Los Angeles, Calif.: Pacific Southwest Regional Medical Library, April 1992).

13. Membership to PIALA insures receipt of the *PIALA Newsletter*. Individual membership is $20, and institutional membership is $50 per year. Membership inquiries should be directed to PIALA, University of Guam, RFK Library, UOG Station, Mangilao, Guam 96923 or e-mail: acohen@uog9.uog.edu

9. Library and Information Services in Malaysia

Diljit Singh

Malaysia is a small country that is increasingly attracting the attention of the world. Although this attention has been brought about primarily by the strong economic performance over the past few years, the country has also made significant technological, political, cultural and social achievements, including library and information services. This article describes:

1. the development of library and information services in the country;
2. some of the current issues and challenges faced;
3. the potential of library and information services in two exciting endeavors of the country:
   a. Vision 2020, Malaysia's goal of becoming a developed country, and
   b. the Multimedia Super Corridor (MSC), a bold and innovative step designed to take Malaysia into the Information Age.

Located in the rapidly developing South-East Asian region, Malaysia occupies an area of 329,758 square kilometers (approx. 127,584 square miles, an area slightly larger than the state of New Mexico in the United States). The country is divided into two regions, Peninsular Malaysia on the west, and the two states of Sarawak and Sabah on the east. The two regions are separated by a 540km stretch of the South China Sea.

The strategic position of the country along the maritime trading route between the East and West, coupled with the rich source of spices and other natural resources, attracted the attention and subsequent colonization by the then western powers in the early years. The country was variously colonized by the Portuguese (1511-1641), the Dutch (1641-1786) and the British (1786-1957). Malaya (as the country was known then) finally gained independence from the British in 1957. In 1963, Singapore, Sabah and Sarawak joined the federation to form Malaysia, although Singapore subsequently withdrew in 1965 to become an independent nation.

Malaysia practices a system of parliamentary democracy, where the government is elected every five years. The country has been fortunate to have a stable government, and the same political party has held power for 40 years. This has enabled the leadership to implement long-term development strategies. The official religion of the country is Islam, but the Constitution guarantees freedom of worship for other religions.

The Malaysian economy has undergone great changes since independence. It is now one of the more advanced developing countries, having consistently achieved growth rates of 8 percent or better over the last ten years.

From an agricultural and production economy with rubber, tin, palm oil and timber as its main products, the country is now industrialized and moving rapidly into a service and information economy. This growth of the country has been carefully shaped and guided by the government's strategic five-year development plans. The country is currently in its Seventh Malaysia Plan (1996-2000).

With a culturally diverse population of just over 21 million (1997 estimates) living in harmony, and with impressive socio-economic indicators for a developing nation (e.g., literacy rate: 93 percent; population growth rate: 2.4 percent; life expectancy: 72 years; percentage of cohort completing primary education: 98 percent), the country has seen its nominal per capita GNP increase from RM 1,106 (approx. US$ 442) in 1970 to RM 11,118 (approx. US$ 4,457) in 1996.

History of Library and Information Services

The existence of libraries and information services in Malaysia is a comparatively recent phenomenon. In the early days when most people could not read or write, the main source of information was the *penglipurlara* or storyteller. Publications, if any, and intellectual activities were restricted to palaces, state offices and religious institutions.

The country was in some ways fortunate to have inherited from the British a legacy of basic library services, comprising lending and reference services, which were probably the norm at that time. The first public libraries were set up in Penang (1817), followed by Malacca (1881) and Kuala Lumpur (1925). These were essentially subscription libraries, which charged an entrance fee and a monthly subscription, and were run by volunteers. Among the early special libraries were those attached to research institutions, such as the Institute of Medical Research (1905), Rubber Research Institute (1925) and the Forest Research Institute (1929).

Library development took a major step forward with the formation of the Malayan Library Group (the precursor of the Library Association of Malaysia) in 1955. However, in the early days after independence, little attention was given to libraries, partly because of the priority that needed to be given to the development of basic infrastructure, such as electricity, water, roads and schools. It is only in the last two decades that a balance between basic infrastructure and social growth has been targeted. Library and information services are now given a higher priority, as evidenced by the increasing budget allocations in each five-year development plan.

The origin of the National Library of Malaysia (NLM) can be traced back to 1956 when the Malayan Library Group submitted a memorandum to the government on the need for public library services, including the setting up of a national library in Malaya. The National Library Services Unit was set up within the National Archives in 1966. In 1971, the NLM was formally established in the Federal Department of Archives and National Library of Malaysia. In 1972, the National Library Act was passed, and the library became a federal agency separate from the Archives in 1977. In 1991, the NLM was moved from the Ministry of Culture and Tourism to the Ministry of Education, reflecting the greater educational role expected of it. In 1992, the library moved into its own specially designed building, which itself has become a cultural landmark in Kuala Lumpur.

The University of Malaya Library was the first academic library in Malaya established in 1959, although it existed as part of its parent institution in Singapore earlier. Over the years, the number of university libraries has increased, and the country now has nine public universities. In 1996, the government liberalized the education system, which included allowing the establishment of private universities. The country now has three private universities and plans for at least three more have been announced, including a new on-line virtual university.

Public libraries, although having had an early start, have progressed slowly compared to other libraries. A major turning point in their development was the publication of the *Blueprint for Public Library Development in Malaysia* by the Library Association of Malaysia in 1968. This provided a comprehensive picture of the conditions and laid the groundwork for future development.

School libraries have existed since pre-independence days, although they were well developed in selected schools only. A definitive step in their development was taken in 1962 when the Ministry of Education introduced a one-year full-time course for teacher-librarians. Some of the pioneer group of thirteen teachers later went on to hold key leadership positions in their careers. Other significant developments were:

- the provision of an annual per capita grant by the government for all school libraries beginning in 1974;
- the publication of the *Blueprint for School Library Development* by the Library Association of Malaysia in 1979;
- the amalgamation of educational media services with the print-oriented library services in 1982; and
- the development of State Education Resource Centers and Teachers' Activity Centers over a period from 1982 to 1990.

Present State of Library and Information Services in Malaysia

The present state of development of library and information services can be described as uneven, but promising. The National Library, the academic libraries and a few special libraries are well developed in terms of facilities, staffing, collections, services and information technology. However, public and school libraries are still lagging behind, although they have seen major achievements over the past two decades and continue to hold great potential.

As of the end of 1996, the breakdown of the number of libraries in Malaysia was as shown in Table 1.

National Library

The National Library of Malaysia (NLM) aspires to be a world class library in the provision of information in the realization of Malaysia's vision of becoming an industrialized and developed nation by the year 2020.

The NLM is responsible for coordinating public and government library development in the country. The Director-General of the NLM also acts as an advisor to the Minister of Education on national policy pertaining to libraries. Besides being the designated national bibliographic center for the country, and the coordinating center for ISBN, ISSN and CIP data, it also channels Federal government funds to state libraries. The National Library publishes the *Malaysian National Bibliography*, the *Malaysian Index to Periodicals*, the *Malaysian Newspaper Index* and *the Index to Malaysian Conferences*, in addition to maintaining the Malaysian Bibliographic Database.

Academic Libraries

Academic libraries exist in institutions of higher learning to support the educational and research activities. There are presently nine public universities and three private

TABLE 1
Number of Libraries in Malaysia

Type of Library	Number	
	Sub-totals	Total
National Library		1
Academic Libraries		
University Libraries - Main	12	
University Libraries - Branches	25	
Government Colleges	15	
Private Colleges	38	
Polytechnics	7	
Teacher Training Colleges	31	
Others	15	
Total		143
Public Libraries		
State Public Libraries	14	
Branch Libraries	95	
Town Libraries	54	
Village Libraries	220	
Mobile Libraries	92	
Public Libraries Administered by Local Authorities and Other Government Agencies	676	
Total		1,151
Special Libraries		
Government Departments	203	
Statutory bodies and Private sector	188	
Total		391
School and Teachers' Libraries		
School Resource Centers	8,619	
Teachers' Activity Centers	350	
State Education Resource Centers	14	
Total		8,983
Total		10,669

Source: National Library of Malaysia (for statistics on national, academic, public and special libraries) and Educational Planning and Policy Research Division, Ministry of Education (for statistics on school and teachers' libraries)

universities in the country. In addition, there are also institutions of higher learning which award diplomas and certificates. These libraries are more fortunate as the parent institutions receive comparatively large budgets. There are also private colleges with twining arrangements with foreign universities, and some of them, too, have good libraries.

Public Libraries

Public library services in Peninsular Malaysia are provided by State Public Library Corporations under the respective state governments, while in the East Malaysian states they are provided by the State Library Department (in Sabah), or by the state government and local government authorities (in Sarawak). The National Library does, however, assist in the development of public libraries by providing development grants, training for their personnel, and leadership. The Federal government provides 50 percent of their annual operating budget, which is channeled through the National Library.

Public library services are generally urban-oriented, but rural libraries, village libraries, and mobile libraries help complement the services provided by the state libraries. Other agencies such as Community Development Division (KEMAS) under the Ministry of Rural Development, and the Federal Land Development Authority (FELDA) also provide library facilities, particularly for the rural people.

Special Libraries

Special libraries exist in government ministries and departments, research institutions, commercial organizations, and non-governmental organizations. Special libraries in government departments have benefited from the exchange of staff under the common user scheme of the National Library, while those in the private sector have varying degrees of development, depending on the level of support from the parent organization.

School Libraries

School libraries, or school resource centers as they are officially referred to in Malaysia, exist in all schools. The Educational Technology Division of the Ministry of Education is responsible for their development. The resource centers are administered by teacher-librarians, most of whom have a full complement of teaching duties in the school and manage the library as an administrative responsibility.

While much progress has been made in the development of school resource centers, the concern for most parents is on good results on public examinations. The lack of full-time staff and the remote location of some schools have hindered the development of school resource centers.

Human Resource Development

Four institutions currently provide education leading to a formal qualification in library and/or information science. The School of Library and Information Studies at the MARA Institute of Technology (ITM) has offered a Diploma in Library Science program since its inception in 1968. In 1972, the school also began offering a post-graduate Diploma in Library Science. The National University of Malaysia (Universiti Kebangsaan Malaysia) offers a Bachelor of Information Science degree. The International Islamic University (IIU) has offered a master's degree in Library and Information Science since 1992, and the Master of Library and Information Science at the University of Malaya (UM) was revived in 1995. In addition, the Public Services Department awards scholarships annually to selected individuals to pursue advanced degrees overseas.

Short courses, conferences, seminars and workshops to upgrade the knowledge, competencies, skills and professionalism of librarians are frequently organized by the National Library, the Library Association, and the universities and colleges. Private organizations also keep library professionals informed of new products and services.

Information Technology

The government sincerely believes that information technology has a strategic role in the development of a knowledge-based society and economy. The seriousness is reflected in the establishment of the National Information Technology Council (NITC) as a think-tank and advisor to the government, and it is chaired by the Prime Minister himself. The thrust of information technology development at present is to ensure its widespread diffusion and application in all sectors to stimulate productivity and competitiveness, and further improve the quality of life.

The roots of the use of information technology in libraries go back to the Malaysian MARC (MALMARC) project which started in 1979. Originally intended as a cooperative scheme for shared cataloging between the National Library and academic libraries, it laid the groundwork for a system which today allows libraries to access each other's data bases and to network. Most academic, public and special libraries have either been automated, at least partially, or are in the process of becoming so. Various other IT initiatives involving libraries have also been implemented, such as the Jaringan Ilmu (Knowledge Network) which aims to further increase resource sharing among the National Library, government departments and institutions of higher learning.

The Internet has gained considerable popularity in Malaysia, with the number of users estimated to be 190,000 (in mid-1997), and many libraries making their OPACs accessible through the Internet.

Publications

Among the periodicals produced by libraries are *Sekitar Perpustakaan* (published by the National Library), *Kekal Abadi* (published by the University of Malaya Library) and the *Malaysian Journal of Library and Information Science* (published by the Library and Information Science program, University of Malaya). Book titles are still very few in number because of the limited market.

Library Services for Special Groups

Library services for the visually impaired are available at the National Library and through the Malaysian Association for the Blind (MAB). Facilities for persons handicapped in other ways are still lacking, although there are efforts to make newer buildings accessible to the physically handicapped.

Library Association

Mention has been made earlier of the Library Association of Malaysia. With a membership of 377 (in 1995), it remains the sole association representing library and information professionals in the country, and continues to fight for their betterment.

Global Reach—Local Touch in Malaysian Libraries

Perhaps because of the multicultural population, and to a lesser extent the British colonial influence, Malaysian library services have always had a global outlook while retaining the local elements in many ways. Foreign institutional libraries have been in existence for many years, international experts have been involved in the planning and development of many local programs, and the country plays host to many regional and international conferences. Malaysians reach out globally to share their knowledge and learn from foreign colleagues through formal education programs, conferences and consultancy projects. Interlibrary loans have always been made available by the larger institutional libraries, and the global village through the Internet has practically removed all boundaries.

Historically, the British Council has supported the development of library services in Malaysia. In the early days, staff of the British Council conducted courses to enable Malaysian librarians to sit for the Associateship of the Library Association (ALA) examinations and provided scholarships to selected individuals for further studies in Great Britain. The British Council also runs a public library in Kuala Lumpur, which is still very heavily used today.

Similarly, the United States Information Service (USIS) provides assistance in many ways. It maintains a resource center within the U.S. embassy, although usage is less than in the past because of tight security at the embassy. A number of other foreign organizations and embassies in Kuala Lumpur (e.g., the Goethe Institute, Indonesian Embassy) have reading rooms and these are well patronized by members of the public.

International organizations, such as UNESCO, the British Council, and USIS, have always provided a global touch to Malaysian libraries through the services of experts. John Gray was a key figure in the early stages of the development of National Policy for Library and Information Services. Frank Hogg was closely associated with the establishment of the first library school in Malaysia at the MARA Institute of Technology in 1968. The services of Nella McCalla, Margaret Walker and Marion B. Weise through the Fulbright and Smith-Munat programs were instrumental in the development of school library services in the early 1960s.

Conferences are another area where Malaysian libraries are able to reach out globally while providing the local touch. The country plays host to a number of international and regional conferences. The triennial Conference of Southeast Asian Librarians (CONSAL), which was last hosted by Malaysia in 1996, saw more than 550 delegates from 21 countries. The National Library has just played host, with the support of IFLA, to a Regional Conference of Public Libraries. The neighboring Library Associations of Malaysia and Singapore hold a joint biennial conference, alternating the venues. Many Malaysians also attend international conferences and are able to bring back global experiences to be applied to the local setting.

Education is another area where the country has had a global reach while retaining the local touch. Many of the Malaysian librarians have obtained their advanced degrees overseas and have been able to apply their international experiences with a local touch to their respective institutions. Many local universities retain the practice of appointing external examiners who offer advice on the curricula and resources, including library facilities, for instructional programs, thereby providing a global touch. A large number of private colleges offer twining programs with foreign universities, which allow students to be exposed to foreign curricula while still at home, before proceeding overseas for the final years where they are completely immersed in a foreign culture. Malaysian universities and colleges are also beginning to attract a large number of international students, who again provide elements of a global touch to local institutions.

Library exchange programs are another avenue where Malaysian librarians are able to reach out to other countries and exchange knowledge and experiences.

Malaysia is committed to retaining a global outlook. It is a founding member of ASEAN (Association of South East Asian Nations), an active member of the Commonwealth, and a committed member of the United Nations. The country practices an open policy towards other countries and Malaysian organizations are beginning to make their presence felt abroad.

Current Issues and Challenges

The government is committed to the development of a knowledge society. This is evident from the numerous programs and the incentives that are provided by the government and other organizations.

Since the 1980s, the government has encouraged reading as a means to creating a knowledge society. "The Year of the Reader" was declared in 1988 and the National Reading Campaign has recently been intensified. Each year, the month of August is designated as "National Reading Month." The annual Kuala Lumpur International Book Fair is well attended by the public. The Malaysian Reading Association also continues to receive support. Recent press reports suggest that a blueprint and an action plan to increase the literacy rate and the reading rate of Malaysians are being developed.

Most significantly, in the 1995 budget, the government allowed tax deductions on contributions made by individuals to build or equip public, rural, school and educational libraries. This was a major accomplishment in the efforts to get support for the development of libraries.

However, despite the many attempts by the government and by libraries, the reading habit is still not fully ingrained in the Malaysian public. Many Malaysians do not read beyond newspapers and light magazines, except for those who have to do so for work-related purposes. A recent survey conducted by the National Library indicates that Malaysians, on the average, read only two books per year. Although this is marked improvement from another survey conducted in the early 1980s which indicated that Malaysians, on the average, read only one page per year, the situation is far from satisfactory. The government has launched various programs to increase the amount of materials read by Malaysians, as well as the quality of available materials.

Even then, surveys suggest that the public library is not always the source for reading materials. It is difficult to pinpoint the cause for this, but the roots of it may lie in the overemphasis on paper qualifications, language difficulties and the limited number of books in the local languages, and the ever-increasing competition from the electronic media. There are comparatively few reference books published in the national language. The Language and Literary Bureau (Dewan Bahasa dan Pustaka) is doing a good job, but the logistics of producing or translating works in rapidly changing fields for a small market makes its job difficult.

Another challenge faced is the development of IT literacy among the populace. It was recently reported in the newspapers that only 12 percent of Malaysians aged ten and above were able to operate personal computers. This is surprising considering amount of space that is devoted in local newspapers to IT-related news, the amount of educational and training programs available on IT-related subjects, and the crowds that patronize computer fairs.

However, libraries are among the leaders in this matter. Many libraries are automated, at least partially. Libraries are making their resources available, or at least have plans to do so, through the Internet. At least ten major libraries have their OPACs accessible through the Internet.

Future Developments

Two key developments will have a major impact on library and information service developments in Malaysia, and possibly globally. Vision 2020 aims for the country to become a fully-developed, mature and knowledge-rich society by the year 2020, and the Multimedia Super Corridor (MSC), which is intended to help Malaysia move into the Information Age, and through it, realize Vision 2020.

Vision 2020 represents a national agenda for the long-term development of the nation. First presented by Prime Minister Dr. Mahathir Mohamad at a Malaysian Business Council meeting in 1991 as thoughts about the future course of the nation, the concept caught on rapidly and has today become the cornerstone of many development projects. The vision calls for Malaysia to be a developed nation in its own mold —not only economically, but along all dimensions including socially, spiritually, psychologically and politically. Development is seen not only in terms of economy, but also national unity, social cohesion, quality of life and national pride.

Nine challenges were put forward to the nation, and of particular interest to libraries and information services is the development of a progressive and information-rich society. An often-quoted statement by the Prime Minister, *"it is no accident that there is no wealthy developed country that is information poor, and there is no information-rich country that is poor and undeveloped"* (Prime Minister's Department) has great relevance to libraries and information services. Library and information services have the golden opportunity to advance themselves and to play a vital role in the development of the country. With the mood of the nation towards achieving progress through innovation and development, there are ample opportunities for libraries to provide new services and new approaches in the development of an information-rich society.

The Multimedia Super Corridor (MSC) represents Malaysia's plan for the Information Age where information, ideas, people, goods and services move across borders effectively and effortlessly. As traditional boundaries disappear, Malaysia believes that companies, capital, consumers, communications and cultures will become truly global. As a first step, Malaysia has created a 15km by 50km corridor as a testing ground with unique elements and attributes to create a global multimedia climate.

The MSC, with its seven initial flagship applications—electronic government, national smart cards, smart schools, telemedicine, borderless marketing centers, worldwide manufacturing webs, and R&D clusters—aims to be a vehicle for partnering world-class technology with local industries for the benefit of the global community. Within the corridor, two Smart Cities are being developed. Putrajaya is designed to become the new administrative capital of Malaysia, where the concept of electronic government will be developed, and Cyberjaya, which is planned as an intelligent city with multimedia industries, research and development centers, a multimedia university, and offices of multinational organizations.

The MSC presents a wonderful opportunity for library and information services, both local and international, to explore new forms of information technologies, sources and services, storage and access, as well as policy issues. While local library and information professionals are busy exploring and planning programs within the MSC, Malaysia is open to other countries which may be interested in collaboration and cooperation in the development of a global information-rich society.

Malaysian libraries and information services indeed have an exciting future ahead— reaching out globally while providing a local touch.

References

Kadir, Mariam Abdul. "Library Services in Southeast Asia: An Overview and the Way Forward." *Sekitar Perpustakaan* 21 (1995): 1-6.

Multimedia Development Council. *What Is the MSC?* [cited 1997] Available from http://www.mdc.com.my/msc/index.html.

Prime Minister's Department. *Malaysia—The Way Forward.* [n.d.] Available from http://www.jaring.my/msia/newhp/gov/more-gov.html#projects

Prime Minister's Department. *Seventh Malaysia Plan, 1996-2000.* Kuala Lumpur: Percetakan Nasional Malaysia Bhd., 1996.

Saad, Badilah, Shahar Banun Jaafar, and Chew Wing Foong. "Malaysian Library Services for National Development: A Country Report." Paper presented at the 10th Congress of Southeast Asian Librarians (CONSAL), Kuala Lumpur, 21-25 May 1996.

Yahya, Nor Hayati. "The Library and Information Services in Malaysia: An Overview." *Sekitar Perpustakaan* 18 (1994): 27-30.

10. Libraries and Information Centres in India: A Newly Industrialized Country Scenario

T. N. Kamala

Library Movement in India: A Brief History

Library and information services to the people in India have existed from very ancient times, but the concept of a public library system is relatively modern. It was evolved and developed by Dr. S. R. Ranganathan, the first and only national professor in the field and the Father of Library Science in India. Prior to his coming on the scene, public libraries were considered single independent units, directly controlled by the government. Accordingly, rules and laws framed related to only specific libraries and not to all units. Ranganathan introduced the concept of the public library as a system distinct from unitary libraries. He emphasized that public libraries at different levels, viz., nation, state, city, district, along with lower service units, should be interlinked as to form part of a single large system. According to him, Public Library System meant an integrated nationwide network of public libraries giving free library and information services to one and all of the citizens—literate or illiterate, rich or poor, rural or urban.[1]

There are over 60,000 libraries in India, of which over 10,000 are of considerable size managed by library professionals.[2] But effective membership in the Indian Library Association (ILA) is only 1,800. The role played by the ILA has been in areas of pay scales of librarians and parity with other professions, avenues for promotion, etc. The very first All India Public Library Act was proposed in 1919 by a group of non-professionals. The first ILA conference was held in 1933 with the involvement of professionals, yet the control of the functions of the organization still remained in the hands of non-professionals. Only in 1949, the constitution of ILA was changed to give control to professionals, who were elected as presidents of the association. However, even after sixty years of existence, ILA has not contributed much to the profession.[3] Creating professionalism among librarians and training them to use technology for better services, etc. has not been undertaken by ILA until very recently.

Library Legislation—National Level

The first draft of a model library bill for Indian public libraries was drafted by Ranganathan in 1930, during the All Asia Educational Conference in Benares and later, modified by replacing all clauses with "shall" (compulsory) to ones with "may" (voluntary compliance), so that it would get the then Viceroy's permission. The act was modified further in 1931, 1937 and 1946.[4] Ranganathan tried to get a uniform library bill passed for the different states of India as well as a national library act on several occasions, but his attempts, though appreciated by quite a few, never found fruition. The few landmarks of success during his lifetime, however, include the transformation of the Imperial Library to the National Library of India in 1948, establishment of the Delhi Public Library with assistance from UNESCO in 1951, passing of the Delivery of Books Act in 1954 (amended to include periodical publications and newspapers in 1956), Press and Registration of Books Act in 1967, etc. His last attempt to get library professionals and other public men involved in this process was in 1972 coinciding with the bicentenary of Raja Rammohan Roy, a great social reformer. The government of India set up a large library foundation in his honour, named Raja Rammohan Roy Library Foundation (RRRLF) to promote and support the library movement all over India. This generous and long-overdue financial support by the central government has indeed contributed to the growth and development of public libraries at all levels by providing funds for the purchase of reading materials and for constructing proper buildings to house public libraries.

Library Legislation—State Level

Actually, genuine attempts were made to start a chain of public libraries through five-year plans during 1951-56. In 1957 and in 1963, draft bills were widely circulated among the states in India, but till now, only ten out of the twenty-two states and nine union territories have passed library legislation.[5] The objective was to set up a National Central Library, a State Central Library in each state, and district libraries in each district with a network of circulating libraries consisting of deposit stations and mobile vans in villages with a population of 2,000. Successive five-year plans have tried to include development of public libraries at all levels, but due to lack of firm action, not much progress has been made in many states in this direction. It is only in the seventh five-year plan that a working group came up with a report on modernization of library services and informatics in the country. Funding for such projects both from the central and the state governments have also been increasing steadily since then.

Public Libraries in Different States

Sinha and Gopinath give a detailed account of the status of public libraries in the different states of India and the progress in some states is worth noting.[6] Tamil Nadu, where Ranganathan served as the University Librarian, passed the Public Library Act in 1949, though it came into force only in 1950. Library development in Tamil Nadu enjoys full support of the government and library professionals are treated on par with other state government employees. Recently, the small town and rural libraries have taken on a prominent role, with the adult education programme being given the impetus.

Andhra Pradesh, a southern state, had a glorious past in the library movement due to its origin in the freedom struggle. It also had the support of the state government by way of interest and involvement in library development as well as dedicated and skilled professionals at all levels with a clientele that was highly library conscious. The Hyderabad Library Act passed in 1955 and the current Public Library Act passed in 1960. There are over 4,000 libraries of which only eight are government libraries, but the rest (about 1,750 *zilla* level and over 2,300 aided libraries), run by Granthalaya Samastha or privately, also receive aid from the government. The Delhi Public Library was established in 1949 as a Pilot Project for the spread of fundamental education by UNESCO. However, the Library Bill, despite sincere efforts by Ranganathan and others, was accepted only in 1964.

Karnataka, where Ranganathan spent a number of years and started the prestigious institution called Documentation Research and Training Centre (DRTC), passed the new Karnataka Public Library Act in 1973, though it earlier had a Mysore Public Library Act enacted in 1965. Due to a flexible financial provision incorporated in the Act (3 percent of revenue collected in each district) and by the creation of an independent Department of Public Libraries in the state government, libraries have been opened down to the Mandal level in the state. Funding has been increased during the sixth and seventh five-year plan periods and all libraries receive RRRLF for purchase of books.

Kerala, the first Indian state to claim universal literacy, passed the Public Library Act only in 1991. Sadly, it has yet to be implemented. About 5,000 libraries affiliated with the Kerala Granthasala Sangham get grants from RRRLF but are privately run. The only public library run directly by the government is the state central library in the capital.

West Bengal enacted the Public Library Act in 1979 as an election manifesto of the left-front government. Since then, many new public libraries have been established and funding has been provided for new buildings, new programmes, book fairs, etc. Since 1986-87, even private libraries have been given funds for the purchase of books. Rajasthan has yet to pass the Public Library Act, though the draft bill was presented in 1972. However, it has seen considerable development because of the reorganization of the public libraries by the education department. During 1986-87, three district libraries were established where none existed, and all libraries in the state were made free public libraries, true to Ranganathan's dreams.

Among all, Gujarat stands out in library development though there is no legislation. This is because of its almost century-old library movement started and nurtured by philanthropists and religious institutions. Starting with a 50 percent rate of funding in 1964, the state has increased its funding to 75 percent for grant-in-aid libraries and provides 100 percent funding for government-run libraries. It has set up a network of central and regional libraries for the whole region. Spacious and functional buildings have been provided for district libraries and centrally sponsored and government-funded integrated library services are provided throughout the state, including tribal areas.

Apart from these, many other states have public libraries though development is slow. These and some union territories have small libraries and reading rooms, but they are mostly managed by part-time, unskilled personnel, whether government-owned or run by voluntary organizations. "The present scene of public libraries in India is pathetic. They are still considered to be the storehouses of some newspapers, magazines, novels and short stories, housed in poor buildings without proper furniture, equipment and other physical facilities and staff." [7]

Problems in Implementation of State Legislation in India

One of the main problems in getting the states to implement library legislation is that public libraries come under the purview of state governments. Central government's role is restricted to being only promotional, particularly by providing grants such as RRRLF. Despite several sincere attempts by Ranganathan and by many committees appointed by the central government and their recommendations, not much progress has been made in most states because of the apathy of government officials and lack of motivated and skilled library professionals. Nor has there been any coordination among school, public, college, university and research libraries in different states. Public and state library structure is more or less neglected, and college and universities have developed in isolation, which in fact has virtually hampered the development of a national network in the country.[8] There has also been a good deal of resistance from professionals towards change in the work culture due to fear of technology, lack of training and lack of avenues for advancement in career. No standards for education and training of staff have been followed in most libraries, leading to frustration among trained staff. There is also a negative attitude between staff and users, more so for fee-based services in rural areas where poverty is rampant.

However, there is another major problem that India has—illiteracy. India lives in its villages—98 percent of inhabited land and 74.3 percent of the population are in the rural base.[9] Even after seven successive five-year plans aimed at national development, about 50 percent of the population in the age group 15-35 are illiterate.[10] Not only has universal basic education been neglected, but adult education has also not been provided to most rural folk. The number of registered public library users in India has been very low compared to many other countries, according to successive UNESCO surveys. Use of the library cannot be promoted unless the problem of illiteracy is solved first. Hence, the Government of India took some new steps in this direction in 1988 and declared a massive National Literacy Mission, which reached the length and breadth of the country. A National Adult Education Programme was launched in several states, with both government and voluntary organizations cooperating to make the programme a success. Under this scheme, Kerala, which had over 100 million illiterate people in 1971, claimed the honour of becoming the first state in India to declare universal literacy by 1991. This example has been followed with enthusiasm by Tamil Nadu, which is striving to become the second state to achieve universal literacy. Such success has come, naturally only with the setting up and improvement of public libraries at all levels.

Success Stories

Dilli and Srinath have presented the most encouraging report so far in India on the role of public libraries in the lives of the people and in the overall development of literacy programmes in the country.[11] Ranganathan defined the public library as "an institution for and by the community primarily for the social purpose of providing every opportunity for self-education throughout the life of every person of the community." [12] However, it was only in 1986 that an attempt was made to give shape to his high ideals with the declaration of the National Policy on Education. Objectives of the Policy included wider promotion of books, libraries, Reading Rooms (RRs), media-based learning, distance education, continuing education, and workers' training. With the objective of achieving basic literacy, awareness and functionality among India's masses, several Jana Sikhshan Nilayams (JSNs) and more public libraries that would remain open in the evenings to facilitate adult education were set up throughout the country. Free dissemination of information on developmental programmes, promoting recreation and healthy living, holding evening classes for three to four hours, helping with retention activities for neo-literates and distributing reading material were all made part of the functions of the JSNs. Efforts were also made to motivate and encourage local voluntary libraries to keep them open for longer hours. This has led to the overall social, political and economic development, particularly in the backward regions that were hitherto neglected.

In Tamil Nadu, about 1,175 JSNs were established in various districts under the direct control of the government, universities and voluntary agencies. With funds coming in, literacy rates in the state rose to a significant 63.72 percent in 1991-92, which was higher than the national rate of 52.11 percent.[13] Simultaneously, the state government started a literacy campaign of its own, called "Arivoli Iyakkam," which caught on well with the masses. Under this scheme, 18 district, 1,091 part-time, and 1,542 branch libraries have been set up in the state. In addition, nine mobile units have been provided to reach the remotest of rural areas. The combined efforts of the two programmes have now translated into one library for every four to five villages, but many more are needed to cater to the teeming millions living in remote areas. More resources are needed to keep neo-literate groups from relapsing into illiteracy. However, it is a good model for other states to emulate and for the development of a healthy library movement in the country. It surely augers well for the public libraries of the future, which soon will be networked through satellite technology.

Communication and Information Technologies

There are significant differences between industrialized countries (ICs) such as the United States of America and the United Kingdom and the newly industrializing countries (NICs) like India. The advances in information and communication technologies have been fully exploited and extended to all levels of libraries in the United States, whereas there is no such uniform implementation of modern technologies at different levels of libraries in India. The reasons for this glaring disparity among the libraries which are "haves" and "have-nots" (of technology) are many. Even in the United States, this thorny issue of access to technology or information exists. According to a survey of U.S. households, those with an annual income of over $15,000 are five times more likely to own a PC and ten times more likely to go on-line for information than those with lesser incomes.[14] This results in a wide gap in performance and morale of rich and poor children in schools. Isn't it true that new technology brings with it new problems not anticipated earlier?

The glaring disparity between those "having" and "not having" access to technology is more conspicuous in the Indian context. Ninety percent of the common people do not have even telephones, yet it is some consolation that a small percentage of the people in the country, particularly those involved in academic research, have access to information vital to their research in the same way that people in advanced countries do. Two basic technological infrastructures required to provide access to national and international databases are the communication and information networks. India has made considerable progress in both areas in the last decade. One of the first few to take advantage of these advances is the library and information centres (LICs) in the country.

Communication Infrastructure in India

The Department of Telecommunications (DoT) established a nationwide PSDN, called I-net in 1992, with nodes in eight major cities connected through high-speed channels. I-net supports CCITT standards/protocols and is accessible using dedicated or leased lines with X.28 and X.25 with standard modems and drivers. Database access and e-mail facility on I-Net are of great use to the LICs in India. In fact, the Gateway Packet Switched Services (GPSS) of the Videsh Sanchar Nigam Limited (VSNL —India's overseas communication services) in three major cities made it possible to access international databases and communication across external networks is now a reality. "I-NET and GPSS have ushered in an era of relatively inexpensive and reliable computer communication and it is now up to the library and academic community to take advantage of these facilities." [15]

NICNET—A National Network

National Informatics Centre (NIC) set up a network called NICNET in 1970, almost exclusively with the use of VSAT technology and indigenous satellite, even before the advent of GPSS. Four hundred fifty district nodes in 32 states and union territories could be connected to the central hub at Delhi, without recourse to telephone lines, multiplexers, modems, etc. NICNET was set up for government use—to promote collection, storage, analysis, transmission and exchange of data at different levels of the government to help in planning and management of projects funded by the government. It had also served a very useful purpose during emergency situations like earthquakes and floods, e.g., providing health related and other information. NICNET has also been used for database access—Medline is mounted on one of its minicomputers and is remotely searchable. NLM, Biological Abstracts and SCI are also accessible in CD-ROM format through NICNET services.

INDONET—A Commercial Network

INDONET has been floated by CMC Ltd., a public sector company, to provide access to its sizable computing and software resources to private institutions as well as to the public. It offers somewhat affordable access to sophisticated hardware and costly scientific and business software to those who cannot afford to invest in them on their own. INDONET has its large mainframe computers in Bombay, Calcutta and Madras and two smaller ones in Delhi and Hyderabad. With the Bombay node being connected to GPSS, it has made it possible for its users to connect to computer networks abroad. Database access is also in the cards for the future, but the chances of LICs using INDONET services is bleak, especially since cheaper alternatives have become available.[16]

Data Networks

India has been slow to get on to the information highway, mostly because of its age-old emphasis on indigenous development policy and lack of funds to import know-how as well as a tight bureaucratic structure even in R&D organizations. With the liberalization of investment and economic policies in recent years, much of the basic equipment required to leapfrog in information technology applications had become common in large institutions and government departments in India. Apart from the proliferation of microcomputers from abroad, cheap indigenous ones have flooded the market so much so that many small businesses and individuals have started using PCs. But, more importantly, the successful launching of the multi-purpose satellite INSAT-1B by India has made it possible to provide an incredibly good digital data communication across geographically spread points of the country.

The 1990s have seen great enthusiasm on the part of professionals to embrace technology. Under the auspices of NISSAT (National Information System for Science and Technology) and INSDOC (Indian National Science Documentation Centre), several short- and long-term training programmes have been conducted to train professionals in the use of technology. Continuing education is provided in the form of refresher courses, and there are now library professionals who are at ease with the use of computers and other media for library management and information retrieval.

There have been several efforts to network libraries in the different parts of the country under three levels—national, metropolitan and sectoral. Prominent among these are INFLIBNET (national), DELNET and CALIBNET (metropolitan) and BTISNET (sectoral). Apart from these, there are several networks such as DESINET, CSIRNET, ERNET, VIDYANET, BHELNET, OILNET, etc., established to serve groups of institutions with common research agenda.

INFLIBNET

INFLIBNET was set up by the University Grants Commission (UGC) with a view to network libraries in 184 universities, 23 institutions deemed to be universities, 6,100 colleges and over 200 libraries affiliated to other organizations.[17] It was the first major national effort to improve information access and transfer that would support scholarship, learning, research and academic pursuits. It was also the first attempt to optimize resources scattered all over the country by bringing in the concept of pooling and sharing among libraries, which was till then unheard of. INFLIBNET has been slated to provide catalogue-based services, database access (local and International), e-mail, computer conferencing, bulletin boards, etc. at four levels—national, regional, sectoral and local. INFLIBNET is also expected to evolve standards for uniform adoption throughout the network. Though it is still not in full operation, the fact that the UGC has agreed to foot the entire cost of capital goods and services required while the Government of India would provide the working capital augers well for the success of this pioneering and much needed network. "It is hard to imagine international cooperation with only a local budget," observed Mason.[18] India has at last realized the need for government funding for library networks that would translate into developmental gains in various departments of public life.

DELNET

DELNET is one of the two ventures set up in early 1990s to study the possibility of having a MAN (Metropolitan Area Network) for libraries in the major cities in India. If successful, it would give some hope for networking of public libraries in other parts of the country. Thirty-five libraries in the Delhi area are being linked using packet-switched technology, with all libraries creating databases of their holdings using CDS/ISIS, a database package made available by UNESCO, with records that would conform to the Common Communications Format (CCF). All databases would reside on a central computer in one of the libraries with dial-up access to all others. A union catalogue is also available for search. E-mail, ftp and bulletin boards are the additional facilities provided.[19]

CALIBNET

CALIBNET is the other venture that holds some hope for the public libraries of the future. It was envisaged as a MAN linking Calcutta's thirty-eight science and technology libraries. However, it is dependent on each of the libraries automating its various functions before being networked. MARC records are supported by the software to be used (MAITRAYEE-CMC software), so that import and export of records internationally in the future would pose no problems. Dial-up access to DELNET and GPSS connection to external networks are to be provided.

BTISNET

BTISNET is the first sectoral network set up to serve the needs of researchers in the area of biotechnology in twenty-three centres. Though databases would be produced by each centre, exchange of information would be through NICNET infrastructure.

Pioneering Efforts in the Use of Technology

India's first taste of on-line access for information was in 1972—when DIALOG from the U.S. demonstrated its capabilities. This was followed by a demo by ORBIT in 1973 when information was retrieved from commercial databases. However, it created only very little interest in library professionals, because most lacked the infrastructure to run such services; nor was the need felt by the user community. In 1985, NISSAT conducted two experiments—one in on-line mode and another in off-line mode, using ESA/IRS.[20] However, it was mainly the launch of INSAT-1B that marked the turning point in the field of library and information retrieval. Since then, library networks in the country and even direct links to external networks by institutions have proliferated.

Technology for Dissemination of Information

The National Centre for Science Information (NCSI) is a facility set up at the Indian Institute of Science (IISc), Bangalore, India. It was set up in 1983 by the University Grants Commission (UGC), with a mandate to provide convenient and timely access to scientific information to the researchers in Indian universities and colleges. Starting with Current Awareness Services based on the world's leading bibliographic databases on magnetic tapes, it boasts a wide variety of services based on access to information on a variety of media like CD-ROM, on-line and magnetic tapes, in addition to print. It also has in-house access to over twenty-six million bibliographic records, properties and structural data of about three hundred thousand organic compounds and about two hundred thirty gigabytes of digital storage in the area of biomedicine. Other services include periodicals content page search, numeric data search and document delivery from anywhere in the world. It also extends its services to researchers from all over the world. It has access to all the resources available at the Supercomputer Education and Research Centre. A campus network lets researchers access information on CD-ROM databases loaded on a server from terminals on their desks.

NCSI also runs an e-mail discussion forum called LIS-FORUM for LIS professionals with about two hundred participants from India and abroad. A World Wide Web server is set up to provide information on NCSI as well as to access a few databases and links to key Internet resources in science and engineering such as electronic journals, preprints, patents, software libraries, etc.

INSDOC, the national science documentation centre in Delhi is another institute which has the latest of technologies at its disposal with over three hundred CD-ROM databases and on-line access to several international and national databases. It is the foremost institute providing training to professionals in the use of technology in libraries and information centres in India. Its training programmes cater to the need of other Asian countries, particularly the ASEAN and SAARC. Most of its services are available to the public, but the usage is still not very high because of its far-off location and the lack of communication facilities in remote institutions, not to talk of high costs involved.

Technology for Distance Learning: IGNOU and ETV Programmes

Libraries have a very positive role to play in the overall educational standards in a country. It is often said that education and library services are twin sisters and one cannot live apart from the other. This statement rings more true and appropriate in the information and technology intensive society of today.

IGNOU

Despite delays, two open universities have been set up in India in the last decade to harness the available technology for distance education. One is IGNOU (Indira Gandhi National Open University) run at a national level and the other is B. R. Ambedkar Open University run by the state of Andhra Pradesh. IGNOU is a three-tier system with a main library in Delhi, branch libraries in regional centres and study centres in remote areas.[21] IGNOU offers many courses in different disciplines including a master's degree programme in library and information science. Many working people are able to take advantage of this delivery system and qualify themselves for taking up newer responsibilities. However, the participants from remote areas still have no access to advanced technology and hence are left feeling frustrated. Even the 201 study centres of IGNOU are mostly located in existing educational institutions, which have no space to house the reading materials and have no proper trained staff to help in selecting the right reading material. There is no motivation to promote reading habits and library use and hence a lot of resources are wasted. Yet, it is a good beginning and hopefully, with the proliferation of networked libraries, more and more people will be able to take advantage of this open university system of education.

ETV

For decades, television (TV) has been recognized the world over as a powerful medium of communication. Its use in education has not been fully exploited even now. In the Indian context only in the recent past, the government-owned TV, called Doordarshan, has been willing to devote over 30 percent of telecast for education. The milestone event in the use of media—ETV (Educational TV) in India—took place when a Mass Communication Research Centre (MARC) was set up at Jamia Millia Islamia in Delhi with assistance from the Canadian International Development Agency, over a decade ago.[22] Prior to this, projects to impart social education were produced and distributed by private agencies. With UNESCO's help and the efforts of MARC, three hundred production centres have been established in the last thirty-five years. The advent of video filming has brought down the cost of production considerably, and programmes for primary to university level education are now produced and distributed in video format.

IGNOU and another important institution, viz., Central Institute for Educational Technology (CIET), were also established almost around the same time. Together, the three organizations now provide education to masses in remote areas of the country with the help of INSAT and countrywide classroom of the UGC. Rural primary education has received a shot in the arm and the Consortium for Educational Communication has built a strong base of over 3,500 programmes.[23] Jamia Millia Islamia College introduced computers in its library in 1987 and since then ETV libraries have been automated. A database of programmes has been created and global search through any word known to users is possible. Gradually, the libraries participating in ETV have been networked and the staff trained to use technology, including e-mail.

The National Talkback experiment, where the whole country participated in an interactive classroom began in 1991. "Classroom 2000," which CIET telecast, demonstrated the videoconferencing possibility for distance education programmes in 1993. In all these ventures, library professionals from small and remote libraries are becoming exposed to technology. This is the beginning of the hope for the future.

Libraries with a Difference

Though libraries have not developed in a systematic manner in India, they have existed in many places in different kinds of setups. Temples, both of the Hindu and Jain faiths, Buddhist monasteries and muslim mosques in the country have all had libraries of their own. Among these, the Jain faith has done exceptional work to spread its faith and keep members of its community well informed of its tenets by setting up libraries since the early part of the century. It is the state of Gujarat that the Jain library with the most modern technology is located, which speaks volumes for the generosity of the wealthy among the Jain community.

There is another aspect of Indian society which has defied logic: Through many centuries, somehow women have been denied education and opportunities for self-development, though there have been some exceptions to this general trend. Particularly in the northern parts of India, where the "purdah" system came to be enforced on women (mostly in muslim communities), women were prohibited from going out and mostly confined to their homes. Surprisingly, this very oppression gave birth to the first all-women's library in the country almost a century ago.[24] As mentioned earlier, library development has been remarkable in the state of Gujarat; it is partly due to the fact that it is one of the wealthiest states in the country and, more importantly, because it has been the birthplace of many philanthropists, who were also some of the richest and prosperous industrialists in India. It was in Gujarat that the first women's library was also established.

Public Library with On-line Access: A Unique Achievement

Donald Clay Johnson, Curator, Ames Library of South Asia, University of Minnesota in the United States, has written about the remarkable industrialist-philanthropists of Ahmedabad in establishing three libraries.[25] It is the third one described by him (established because of the concerns of a Jain woman) that has embraced the advances of technology to become one of the leading centres of Jain literature. Though set up as a research centre for Jain studies with a generous donation from Sharadaban Chimanlal Sheth, "it has been at the forefront of scholarly activities that affect libraries and in so doing, is rapidly developing a large collection of books and journals that is turning it into a library."[26] The computer staff at the research centre has to cope with nine different scripts used by fifteen Indian languages; it has begun to compile an on-line index to all literature written about the Jains. Most of the publications have been acquired by the centre, making it a true library collection. Production of a chronology of the Jains and publication of Jain texts are on the cards, both of which need a good deal of bibliographic effort. It is, perhaps, safe to assume that the centre would soon become a unique combination of a special library and a public library, leading the way for others to follow.

Hope for the New Century

If anything should interest a library and information science professional in global librarianship, it should definitely be a combination of scope for work and a challenge. I believe that the state of libraries in India, and the public ones in particular, provide both of these. The field is taking great strides to bridge the gap between the "haves" and "have-nots" of technology within the country as well as outside. Just now, the funds and encouragement from the government as well as the infrastructure are both available. It only needs a band of dedicated and enthusiastic professionals and volunteers to make Ranganathan's dream of a nationwide public library system come true. It may well happen by the turn of the century.

While talking about the future of library and information centres of the new century, one also has to think about the uneven development of resources and services in the field of humanities and social sciences in India vis-á-vis that in the area of science and technology. Due to national policies, the emphasis has so far been on R&D in the various branches of science and technology (S&T). Naturally, the information centres have also developed to cater to the needs of the researchers, academicians and students in those areas. Most of the information centres have actually been set up in research institutions and universities providing training in S&T, as funding and computing resources are available in those places. However, India has a valuable heritage, and large collections of resource materials are scattered in various institutions and remain there without being used, for want of bibliographic control, management, means of access/technology, etc. Kanakachary surveyed humanities libraries in India and found that there were more than five hundred institutions in India dealing with humanities literature, apart from universities that provide education in humanities.[27] They are great storehouses not only of the long and rich Indian thoughts on various aspects of the Indian society, but also of India's great interest in Western thoughts and literature. The author found that the usage of these libraries was quite high and, despite minimal resources, they were providing excellent services to users, who also seemed to appreciate the services. Teachers, students, researchers and even general users seemed to frequent these libraries. Over 87 percent borrowed materials, over 70 percent came for consulting reference materials, about 50 percent used reference and information services and some even asked for interlibrary loan facilities.[28]

The state of social science documentation is slightly better in India because of the existence of a national body, i.e., Indian Council for Social Sciences Research (ICSSR) which includes women's studies, population studies, etc. There is an exclusive international institute for population studies, too. However, it cannot be denied that a greater deal of emphasis is placed on information in S&T than that in social sciences and that there is very little effort to do the same in humanities in the country. This may be justified in some respects, but, as all fields are tending to become interdisciplinary, one has to accept the fact that information access to all areas of human endeavor has to take place at the same pace, so that one is not caught on the wrong foot at a future date. Towards this goal, the committee on National Policy on Library and Information Systems (NPLIS), appointed by the Ministry of Human Resources of the Government of India, recommended in its reports in 1986 that "special libraries in social sciences and the humanities and in language areas should be organized in similar systems to that of science and technology and data banks should be developed in the various subject areas." [29]

Talking of global access, the first step toward international cooperation between large public libraries is to achieve active participation in library networking within each country. As Mason observed, "At present, development is uneven both in the progress of national networks and the participation of public libraries in them." [30] This statement could apply to India as much as to any other country. Thus, one can only conclude that the public library system in India, perhaps, is still in its infancy, but the immediate potential for growth is immense.

Notes

1. S. R. Ranganathan, "Opening Address to the All India Seminar on Public Library System," in *Public Library System: India, Sri Lanka, UK, USA—Comparative Library Legislation*, ed. S. R. Ranaganathan and A. Neelameghan (Bangalore, India: SREFL, 1972): 459.

2. *India: A Reference Annual, 1993*, Research and Reference Division, Ministry of Information & Broadcasting, Govt. of India (New Delhi: Publications Division, 1993).

3. P. S. G. Kumar, "Some Lessons from the Sixty Years History of ILA," in *Library Movement and Library Development: Seminar Papers, Thirty-Ninth All India Library Conference, Bangalore, India, Jan. 7-10, 1994*, ed. C. P. Vashisth (Delhi, India: ILA, 1994): 95-99.

4. V. E. Thillainayagam, "Library Act Based Library Services in Tamil Nadu: A Critical Review," in

Library Movement and Library Development: Seminar Papers, Thirty-Ninth All India Library Conference, Bangalore, India, Jan. 7-10, 1994, ed. C. P. Vashisth (Delhi, India: ILA, 1994): 100-109.

5. Leena Shah and S. Kumar, "Public Libraries of Twenty-First Century," in *Preparing Libraries for the Twenty-First Century Seminar Papers, Fortieth All India Library Conference, Goa, India, Jan. 5-8, 1995,* ed. C. V. Subba Rao et al. (Delhi, India: ILA, 1995): 218-228.

6. Ranjan Sinha and M. A. Gopinath, "Role of State and Central Governments in Public Library Development in India," in *Library Movement and Library Development: Seminar Papers, Thirty-Ninth All India Library Conference, Bangalore, India, Jan. 7-10, 1994,* ed. C. P. Vashisth (Delhi, India: ILA, 1994): 139-155.

7. Shah and Kumar, 218-228.

8. Ibid.

9. *India*, 16.

10. K. T. Dilli and Manorama Srinath, "Role of Public Libraries in Promoting Literacy Programmes in Tamil Nadu: A Comparative Study with Jana Sikshan Nilayam," in *Role of Libraries in National Development: Papers of the 42nd All India Library Conference, Calicut, India, Dec. 21-24, 1996,* ed. R. P. Kumar et al. (Delhi, India: ILA, 1996): 77-85.

11. Ibid.

12. Ranganathan, 459.

13. Dilli and Srinath, 77-85.

14. Roberta Furger, "Unequal Distribution: The Information Haves and Have-Nots," *PC World* (September 1994): 30-37.

15. L. J. Haravu, "Library Automation and Networking in India—An Overview of Recent Developments," *Annals of Library Science and Documentation* 40, no. 1 (1993): 32-40.

16. Ibid.

17. S. S. Pawar, "Impact of New Information Technology in Development of Libraries and Services," in *Library and Information Technology: In Pursuit of Excellence, Seminar Papers: XXXVIII All India Library Conference, Bhubaneshwar, India, Nov. 21-24, 1992,* ed. C. P. Vashisth (Delhi, India: ILA, 1992): 27-31; Haravu, 32-40.

18. Marilyn Gell Mason, "Is There a Global Role for Metropolitan City Libraries?" *American Libraries* (September 1994): 734-738.

19. T. Viswanathan T. et al., "Library Networks in India," *Annals of Library Science and Documentation* 38, no. 2 (1991): 39-52.

20. S. S. Pawar, "Role of Electronic and Communication Media in Networks of Libraries and Information Centres in India," in *Role of Libraries in National Development: Papers of the 42nd All India Library Conference, Calicut, India, Dec. 21-24, 1996,* ed. R. P. Kumar et al. (Delhi, India: ILA, 1996): 373-383.

21. Wooma Sankar Dev Nath, "Resource Sharing among ETV Libraries," in *Preparing Libraries for the Twenty-First Century: Seminar Papers: Fortieth All India Library Conference, Goa, India, Jan. 5-8, 1995,* ed. C. V. Subba Rao et al. (Delhi, India: ILA, 1995): 260-267.

22. Amjad Ali, "Resource Sharing among ETV Libraries," in *Preparing Libraries for the Twenty-First Century: Seminar Papers: Fortieth All India Library Conference, Goa, India, Jan. 5-8, 1995,* ed. C. V. Subba Rao et al. (Delhi, India: ILA, 1995): 302-306.

23. Ibid.

24. K. Sarda, K., "Library Facilities for Women in Andhra Pradesh Public Library System," *Indian Librarian* (June 1976): 34.

25. Donald Clay Johnson, "Ahmedabadi Philanthropy and Libraries," *Libraries & Culture* 31, no. 1 (Winter 1996): 103-112.

26. Ibid.

27. M. Kanakachary, "Assessment of Services of the Humanities Libraries in India: A User Survey," in *Role of Libraries in National Development: Papers of the 42nd All India Library Conference, Calicut, India, Dec. 21-24, 1996,* ed. R. P. Kumar et al. (Delhi, India: ILA, 1996): 184-192.

28. Ibid., 188.

29. Ibid., 189.

30. Mason, 738.

11. Libraries in Azerbaijan: Reaching Forward

Muzhgan Nazarova

Global Reach—Local Touch. It means something very special to me. I perfectly understand what global librarianship can give to my country, Azerbaijan, because actually I myself have experienced the "magic touch" which has allowed me to reach globally to a fascinating world of librarianship. The U.S. librarians (Professor Bob Hayes and Diane Childs from the University of California at Los Angeles and Stephen Mallinger from the U.S. Information Agency), whom I met in my country while working for the U. S. Information Service Library introduced me to U.S. librarianship and helped me to understand the main ideas of it and to realize how far behind Azerbaijan librarianship is compared to the other developing countries. The libraries in Azerbaijan could not meet the lowest requirements of the information society. It is important to find ways to move the libraries of Azerbaijan forward.

A main purpose of this chapter is to speak about global librarianship in relation to my country. I have decided to divide my article into three time lines: the past of the libraries of Azerbaijan, the present and the future. In the latter section, I will speak about my vision on how global librarianship can help libraries in Azerbaijan. I will also include some current information about Azerbaijan and the global changes taking place there because these changes provide a good background for starting to implement changes in Azerbaijani librarianship.

Information about the Country

Azerbaijan is a country lying at the crossroads between Europe, Asia, and the Middle East. It borders Russia and Georgia to the north, Iran and Turkey to the south, Armenia to the west, and the Caspian Sea to the east. The original Republic of Azerbaijan was formed in 1918 in the wake of World War I and was the first nation in the Caucasus to establish an independent, secular, and democratic government. Not long after, the newly formed state of Azerbaijan became a part of the Soviet Union and continued until December 3, 1991, when a new independent Republic of Azerbaijan was formed after more than seventy years of Soviet rule. The 7.9 million people of Azerbaijan live on 86,600 square kilometers, while 20 percent of the territory is occupied by Armenians as a result of the Nagorno-Karabakh conflict. Armenians and Azerbaijanis went to war in the late 1980s over Nagorno Karabakh—a part of Azerbaijani territory inside Azerbaijan's borders mainly populated by Armenians. More than thirty-five thousand people were killed and one million Azerbaijani refugees were created in the process of war. Both sides have generally observed a Russian-mediated cease-fire in place since May 1994, and support the Organization for Cooperation and Security (OCSE)-mediated peace process, now entering its fifth year.

The capital of Azerbaijan is Baku; other principal cities are Gyandzha, Sumgayut and Mingyazevir. The natural resources of the country are petroleum, natural gas, iron ore, nonferrous metals and aluminum. The tremendous energy resources of Azerbaijan serve as a long-term alternative for the Western countries to lessen dependence on the vulnerable supplies of Persian Gulf oil. With potential reserves of two hundred billion barrels of oil, the Caspian region will become the most important new player in world oil markets over the next decade.

The first oil contract was signed between the Azerbaijan State Oil Company and the Azerbaijan International Operating Company (AIOC), a consortium of twelve Western corporations led by Amoco, Unocal, and Exxon of the U.S., British Petroleum, and Norway's Statoil, with British Petroleum and Amoco serving as project operators, in September 1994. This eight billion dollar investment was the first and the largest among the nine other contracts, each worth between one and several billion dollars, signed by Azerbaijan with international oil companies during 1994-1997.

The United States, seeking an alternative to energy sources from the Middle East, has increased diplomatic efforts to expand U.S. interests in the region. In the summer of 1997, Washington hosted Azerbaijan's President Aliyev. The U.S. Energy Secretary Federico Pena, who visited Azerbaijan in November 1997 to participate in a ceremony celebrating the first flow of oil from the Caspian reserves to international markets on November 12, said in his speech: "The celebration of early oil is an important milestone and a symbol for the future. The first flow of Azerbaijani oil will be remembered as a great tuning point for the region and a remarkable turning point in our history."[1]

Past History of the Libraries in Azerbaijan

Library History in Azerbaijan

The earliest library in Azerbaijan appeared in the thirteenth century and belonged to the Maruha Observatory. This observatory was created in the second half of the thirteenth century in the city of Meraga of Eastern Azerbaijan in Iran. The library of more than 400,000 volumes was founded by Nasraddin Tusi—a great scientist, thinker and statesman of that period. In the sixteenth century the biggest library of that time existed at the palace of the Shah Ismail Khatai—a founder of the Safavid dynasty and a famous poet. In the nineteenth century most libraries were private collections. The biggest ones were the personal libraries of Abaskuli bek Bakikhanov and Mirza Fatali Akhundov. Bakikhanov was a prominent Azerbaijani scientist and writer. He is the author of number of works on history, education, philosophy, astronomy and geography. Akhundov was a great Azerbaijani playwright, educator and philosopher. He is considered a founder of Azerbaijani dramatic art and contributed to the development of literary and social thought of the whole Middle East. The first public library was opened in Azerbaijan in 1894.

The most ancient manuscripts of the Azerbaijani language go back to the fourteenth (*Divans* of Gazi Burkhanaddin and Nasimi) and fifteenth centuries (manuscript of the epic *Dede Gorgut*). The epic itself was written in the twelfth-thirteenth centuries. All the manuscripts in the Azerbaijani language created before the middle of the nineteenth century are kept in the Manuscripts Institute of Azerbaijan.[2]

Azerbaijani books published in the eighteenth and nineteenth centuries form part of the Turkic collections of many libraries of the former Soviet Union. The Azerbaijani collection (1845-1931), part of a Turkic collection of the St. Petersburg branch of the Institute of the Asian Nations by number of volumes, occupies the second place among all their collections. These materials mainly cover a period before the 1917 Revolution and are marked by a prevalence of literature on history, art, and folklore. Good examples from this collection include the early works by M. Akhundov (*Hikayat Mulla Ibrahim Xalil Kimiyakira*, Tiflis, 1859), by N. Narimanov *(Shakh- Nadir*, Baku, 1899 and *Shamdan bek*, Baku, 1913), by Fizuli *(Leyla and Medznun*, Baku, 1915), by Molla Nasreddin (*Post Box*, Tiflis, 1912). Early translations of Russian and foreign literature into Azerbaijani are also represented in the collection; for example Tolstoy's *What Men Live By* and *A Captive in the Caucasus* (Baku, 1912), Karamzin's *Poor Lisa* (Baku, 1912), Gorky's *The Children of the Sun*, Shakespeare's *Othello* (Baku, 1893) and also many textbooks and recreational reading. Copies of the following journals, published before the Revolution, are also part of a collection: *Molla Nasreddin* (Tiflis, 1906-1930), *Sedai Kafkaz* (Baku, 1915-1916), *Mektep* (Baku, 1911-1916).[3]

Present Condition of the Libraries in Azerbaijan

The Library System in the Former Soviet Union and Azerbaijan

Even though the libraries all over the world are quite similar and fulfill many of the same basic functions, they differ in that they are integral parts of different societies. Thus, they may take on some completely different functions and tasks in a particular society serving different needs. One factor that affected Azerbaijani libraries is the fact that Azerbaijan has been a part of the Soviet Union for more than seventy years and that libraries in Azerbaijan were a part of a single network belonging to the U.S.S.R. Horecky described this aspect in 1959, "A pattern *sui generis* in the U.S.S.R. is the integration into 'networks' of large numbers of libraries performing identical or analogous tasks or servicing certain strata of the population. Administratively, at the apex of these networks are central governmental or quasi-governmental agencies which are responsible for ministering, staffing, financing their library networks in keeping with current legal regulations and the provisions of the plan."[4]

The functions fulfilled by the libraries in the Soviet Union were described in 1971 as follows:

1. state book store serving the whole Republic;
2. largest public library in each Union Republic;
3. leading bibliographical institution of the Republic; and
4. scientific methods center for the library network of every Union Republic.[5]

Although continuing to be forums for information and ideas, the libraries in the former Soviet Union including Azerbaijan do not exemplify the policies stated in the ALA Library Bill of Rights. A major difference is that citizens do not have easy access to information. Libraries typically have closed stacks and the collections themselves are not selected. The libraries also are rarely automated and make little use of technologies, which would connect them to other libraries around the world. Lack of the necessary technology, computers, reliable telephone systems, effective systems of international communication, prevent the Azerbaijani librarians from accessing the global information network.

The Azerbaijani library system consists of three sectors: public libraries; academic and school libraries; special and technical-scientific libraries. By the beginning of 1990 there were 10, 000 libraries in Azerbaijan having a total number of 140 million volumes.[6] Libraries in Azerbaijan are mainly funded by government and administered by different government departments. Today, when the country is in a transformation period to a market economy and the inflation rate is relatively high, the government has been unable to provide enough funds for libraries and librarians.[7]

Four thousand public libraries are administered by the Ministry of Culture. The Ministry of Education administers another 4,000 academic and school libraries. Two thousand special, scientific and technical libraries are administered by different Ministries as well as by the local authorities and public organizations.

The total number of librarians in Azerbaijan is around 30,000.[8] Unlike the Baltic States and Russia, where independent library associations began to appear in 1988 and have become the driving force for democratic change in the library world, a professional association of librarians has not yet been created in Azerbaijan.[9] Several efforts have been made so far (in 1994 and 1997), but all of them were unsuccessful.

As a result of the Nagorno Karabakh conflict with Armenians, almost two thousand libraries with millions of volumes in their collections located in Nagorno Karabakh and near the Azerbaijani-Armenian border were destroyed and burned by Armenians. The collections contained rare books as well as material on Azerbaijani history, literature and culture. That was a big cultural loss for Azerbaijan.

Library Education in Azerbaijan

A library school for Azerbaijan was first opened in 1947 as a part of the Philological Department of Baku State University. In 1962 the library school became an independent school within the University. The first dean of the school was Professor Halafov. The faculty includes thirty full, associate and assistant professors. Most education at a library school is at an undergraduate level. During the fifty years of its existence 5,000 students have received a diploma from the school. In 1997, 669 students were studying at the school. For the last twenty years eight graduate students got their Kandidat Nauk diplomas. The present dean of the school, Dr. Ismaylov, and a deputy-dean, Dr. Bakhshaliyev, are developing and implementing the U.S. curriculum for the master's degree at the school using the experience of the leading library schools in the United States.[10]

Short Information about the National and Scientific-Technical Libraries of Azerbaijan as a Sample

The libraries listed in Figure 1 are considered the main libraries out of 10,000 functioning all over the Republic.

It is not possible to give a description of each of the mentioned libraries within the limits of this chapter. Information about two of them is given below to give the readers an idea about the libraries in Azerbaijan.

The National Library of Azerbaijan Named after Mirza Fatali Akhundov

The National Library of Azerbaijan serves as a Depository Library for United Nations and World Bank publications in Azerbaijan. It was founded in 1923. Its collection is approximately 4.5 million volumes. This includes a special collection called the "Azerbaijani Books" containing the first publications of famous Azerbaijani authors published in the eighteenth century. Other special collections include translations of

National Library of Azerbaijan (n.a.) M. F. Akhundov

Library of the Academy of Sciences of Azerbaijan Republic

Scientific-Technical Library of Azerbaijan Republic

Academic Affairs Library of Baku State University

State Junior Library of Azerbaijan Republic

State Children Library (n.a.) F. Kozarli

Scientific Pedagogic Library of Azerbaijan Republic

Agricultural Library of Azerbaijan

State Medical Library of Azerbaijan

Figure 1: Main Libraries in Azerbaijan

the works of world famous authors like *Othello* by Shakespeare, published in Baku in 1893. The archives of the library contain 75,000 ancient manuscripts, books, journals and newspapers. It also has two hundred microfilms.

One of the leading departments of the Library is the Department of Foreign Literature having around 100,000 books and 186 journal titles in its collection. The Department had library agreements with twenty-three countries, including the United States, England, Japan and Syria, which allowed the library to receive publications from foreign countries in exchange for Azerbaijani publications. Because of the economic situation in Azerbaijan for the past ten years, the library staff have lost a lot of their contacts with libraries abroad. The Department also has a collection of materials published abroad about Azerbaijan and the works of Azerbaijani authors published in foreign countries. A very important initiative on publicizing Azerbaijan in foreign countries is being conducted by the Department which sends leading journals published in Azerbaijan to different countries of the world on a regular basis.

The administration of the National Library of Azerbaijan is concerned about the Azerbaijani books kept in different libraries of the former Soviet Union and some foreign countries, which have not been returned to Azerbaijan. Lack of funds is cited as a reason.

The Scientific-Technical Library of Azerbaijan

The Scientific-Technical Library was founded in 1930 as a library for the State Oil Company. After the formation of the Ministry for the Oil Industry in Azerbaijan this library provided a service to that Ministry. In 1957 it was transformed into the central scientific-technical library covering the needs of all the industries. The patents collection of the Republic and the collection of standards and industrial catalogs were organized as a part of the library. The collection consists of about seventeen million volumes. The library serves as a depository for technical literature. An exchange collection includes books donated to and from other libraries.

The Republican Scientific Technical Library served as a coordinating center for subscriptions to foreign literature for all the libraries of Azerbaijan through the All-Union Organization *Mezdunarodnaya Kniga* (International Book) and *Soyuzpezat* (Union Press) before a breakdown of the Soviet Union. The library used to receive the literature from fifteen countries of the world. Publicizing of the foreign literature was arranged by organizing exhibits, information days, and open houses. But, again, because of financial problems, everything has stopped now. A Department of Scientific-Technical research was organized in the library in 1976, which conducted the first applied studies in the field of automating library processes.

The Future of the Libraries in Azerbaijan

I am very optimistic about the future of libraries in my country. Global changes are taking place in Azerbaijan and major investments in Azerbaijan's economy are being made by Western businesses. Investments in education and culture have not kept up although everybody agrees that the library system in Azerbaijan needs to be changed. To change the system a lot of librarians must be trained and given an opportunity to see what these changes should look like and learn how necessary they are.

A good example is computer experience, using a PC with Data Trek library automation system software donated to the Department of Foreign Literature of the National Library of Azerbaijan in 1994. The librarians had never used Data Trek and did not have any idea about the software. Instead, a computer was used just for word-processing.

To be able to make global changes the Azerbaijani librarians should be able, if not to see, at least to learn about achievements in librarianship in different countries of the world. The USIA Information Resource Center in Baku, where I have worked, is a sort of demonstration laboratory of the newest technologies in the libraries. It is the place where not only the librarians of the country but also people of different backgrounds, both students and professors, have a chance to see CD-ROMs, library automation systems, multimedia, and other information technology for the first time.

Three U.S. librarians can be considered the first initiators in the history of the development of relations between the Azerbaijan and U.S. librarians. The USIA Regional Library Officer, Stephen Mallinger, is very enthusiastic about conducting workshops and presentations for different groups of the USIA target audience in Azerbaijan including librarians. Mallinger also visited the library school several times, where he gave short talks to the students and the faculty.

Professor Bob Hayes and Diane Childs from UCLA visited Azerbaijan as a part of UCLA-Khazar University Project. They provided support for the creation of a library and computer system in Khazar University. Diane Childs applied for a Fulbright grant to support the development of curriculum and preparation for opening a School of Information and Library Science in Khazar University. If the grant is awarded, then Azerbaijan will be able to have a library school on the U.S. model. This means that, in addition to the task of retraining the older generation of traditional librarians, my country would be able to educate a new generation of young librarians.

Fulbright and other grants in the field of librarianship are extremely important for Azerbaijan now. O. V. Shlykova writes, "The charitable foundations and organizations, the activities of which are aimed at the development of contacts between the specialists of the CIS countries and the U.S., and stimulation of the search of original scientific decisions contribute to the development of library science and practice. The Fulbright Scholarship, Junior Faculty Development Program, and the Freedom Support Act have been carried out in the CIS countries since 1994."[11] The author also mentions that two kinds of Fulbright grants are available for CIS librarians: Exchange for Senior Scholars and the Program for Junior Faculty.

As a recipient of a Freedom Support Act Fellowship (a grant for graduate study in library and information science) I can comment on the programs which are suggested

Libraries	Grant Amount	What the Grant Covered
Western University	$9,500	Book security system; books
Baku Institute of Public Administration and Political Science	6,000	1 PC with CD-ROM drive, 1 photocopier and CD-ROMs
TOMIS	1,850	Collection development proposal
Khazar University	19,650	2 PCs, books, training of librarians

Figure 2: Soros Foundation Matching Grants for Azerbaijani Libraries

by the organization administering my program, the International Research and Exchange Board (IREX). IREX not only brings the librarians from the CIS countries for study and training in the United States, but also offers special projects to support librarians, archivists, and information specialists pursuing projects relating to Central and Eastern Europe and Eurasia. The objective of these grants is to increase access and improve working conditions for American scholars using libraries, archives, and other resources.

Another program, suggested by IREX and the Bureau of Educational and Cultural Affairs of the United States Information Agency (USIA), launched the Internet Access and Training Program (IATP) in December 1995. This program promotes academic and professional exchange in the information age by providing sustainable access to and training in e-mail, Internet, and the World Wide Web for alumni of USIA and U.S. government-sponsored programs and their colleagues in the New Independent States. These activities were planned to start in Azerbaijan in 1997.

Even though there is a long way to go for Azerbaijani libraries to reach the global information highway, there are many exciting changes taking place currently. This is only the beginning. Oil agreements are flourishing and investments are flowing to Azerbaijan. Even though it would be a little more difficult to attract investments in library and information services, some evident changes are taking place.

When I left Azerbaijan in July 1997, full access to the Internet was not available. The Intrans company was able only to provide e-mail and Internet newsgroup access. Today, there are at least seven companies, local and international, which offer full Internet access but their high prices effectively limit the Internet to a narrow range of business users.

The only station providing free access to the World Wide Web is in the Information Resource Center of the USIS in Baku. A new local Dynamic Data company provides Internet access to medical databases and telemedicine. This is only one computer station, which has started to provide the information for the medical scholars and practitioners and to create the conditions for carrying out the worldwide telemedicine consultations since June 1997 on a commercial basis.

Figure 2 shows some projects enabled through the Soros Foundation Regional Library Program Board Matching Funds Award to Azerbaijani Libraries.

I would like to invite U.S. librarians to help Azerbaijani libraries. You will not learn anything new in terms of technology, but you will get the experience of learning about one of the ancient cultures in the world and you will get a chance to get to know the Azerbaijani people.

Your colleagues in Azerbaijan need your advice and support. The first steps towards creating the bridge between the information professionals of the two countries have already been created. I would like to serve as a main foundation stone in its future development.

Notes

1. David Filipov, "In Azerbaijan, at First Gush: Ex-Soviet Republic Taps Promise of Caspian Oil," *Boston Globe*, 13 November 1997.

2. *Azerbaydzhanskaya Sovetskaya Entsiklopediya* (*Azerbaijani Soviet Encyclopedia*) v. 2 (Baku: Azerneshr, 1981).

3. L. B. Medvedeva, "Fondy na tyurskikh yazykakh narodov SSSR," in *Akademiya Nauk SSSR. Institut Narodov Azii. Vostokovednye fondy krupneishikh bibliotek Sovetskogo Soiuza* (Academy of Sciences of SSSR. The Institute of the People of Asia. Oriental Collections of the Largest Libraries of the Soviet Union) (Moscow: Izdatel'stvo Vostoznoy Literatury, 1963), 19.

4. Paul L. Horecky, *Libraries and Bibliographic Centers in the Soviet Union*, Slavic and East European Series, v. 16 (Bloomington: Indiana University Publications, 1959), 15.

5. Simon Francis, ed., *Libraries in the USSR* (Hamden: Linnet Books and Clive Bingley Ltd., 1971), 16.

6. Zokhrab Bahshaliyev, "Yokhsa kitab sakhlanan yer?" ("Library or a book storage?"), Khalg Gazeti, April 1993.

7. Khalil Ismaylov, "Respublikada kitabkhana ishi yenilezekmi," ("Will Librarianship in the Republic Be Updated?") *Khayat*, 21 December 1991.

8. Ibid.

9. Dennis Kimmage, ed., *Russian Libraries in Transition: An Anthology of Glasnost Literature* (Jefferson, N.C.: McFarland, 1992), 149.

10. Azerbaycan Respublikasu Tesil Nazilliyu, M.E. Rasulzade adyna Baku Dovlet Universiteti. Kitabkhanacilig Fakultesi (The Ministry of Education of the Azerbaijan Republic Baku State University, n.a. M. E. Rasulzade. Library School). *Booklet* (Baku, 1994).

11. O. V. Shlykova, "American Programs of the Exchange of Specialists" (Rossisko-Amerikanskiye akademizeskiye programmu obmena spezialistami), *Bibliotekovedeniye* no. 6 (1996): 34.

12. Touching Turkey: The Reach of U.S. Librarianship

Jordan M. Scepanski

Asia Minor long has been recognized as one of the cradles of civilization, an area where learning—and the libraries that fostered and preserved that learning—flourished. Cuneiform tablets uncovered at Bogazköy, the ancient Hittite capital of Hattusas, are said to date to the fifteenth century B.C. or earlier.[1] The library at Pergamum, not far from the Aegean coast, was considered one of the finest of classical times. Indeed, as Pergamum grew in size and reputation it became a competitor of the great library at Alexandria, whereupon the export from Egypt of papyrus, the principal material used for preserving scholarly knowledge, was forbidden. In response, Eumenenes II of Pergamum ordered the refinement of a manufacturing process which used animal skin for writing material and the city began producing it in quantity, thereby giving the world the word "parchment," a corruption of the city's name.[2] With the destruction of the Alexandria library Mark Anthony gifted the impressive collections of rolled parchment at Pergamum—said to have numbered upwards of 200,000—to Cleopatra.[3]

Not far from the acropolis upon which the Pergamum library sat was yet another, that at the Temple of Aesculapius, where it is reported "books" were used to treat patients of the god of health, including those with mental illness, suggesting the origins of the modern medical library. Further south lies Ephesus, city of Roman and biblical renown and home of the magnificent library of Celsus. Built in 135 A.D. its frontal facade is the centerpiece of an extensive excavated ruin. It has been calculated that the Celsus library may have held as many as 9,500 rolls, "or 750 books the length of Homer's Iliad."[4] These libraries in the land now known as Turkey, and those that followed during the Byzantine, Islamic, and Ottoman eras, attest to civilizations that sought to create, collect, and conserve knowledge for ages to come. It is somewhat surprising, therefore, to learn that the profession of librarianship in Turkey is a relatively new one, dating only from the twentieth century.

In 1863 in a suburb of Istanbul an important institution of higher education was founded by Christopher Rheinlander Robert, a U.S. citizen. Robert College soon became an intellectual center of the fading Ottoman Empire and maintained its stature for the better part of the coming century. Here the elite of Turkish society were educated. Robert College graduates made their marks throughout the business, educational, governmental, and military professions. It would be difficult to overstate the influence of its faculty, programs, and alumni on the country. An important Robert College counterpart was the American College for Girls, also in Istanbul. Over the years both institutions developed good, solid libraries modeled after those of U.S. liberal arts schools and in many ways became the standard by which libraries throughout the country were measured. While other U.S.-affiliated institutions could not match the collections at these two colleges, the Y.M.C.A. center in Istanbul, the American School for Boys in Tarsus (in south central Turkey), and the International College in Smyrna (now Izmir) followed U.S. library practice and offered excellent service. The Y.M.C.A. library, for example, is said to have been the only circulating library in Turkey in the late 1920s.[5]

With the founding of the republic by Kemal Atatürk came revolutionary change in every aspect of Turkish society, including the educational sector. Seeking to replace the Ottoman system with a Western one, in 1924 Atatürk invited John Dewey, the distinguished American educator and theorist, to the country to offer his recommendations on improving schooling. Among those recommendations were comments on the library situation. He suggested that students be sent to the United States to learn about library practices there and that librarians be trained at institutions in Turkey. It is uncertain whether Dewey's report to the government had immediate impact, but a Turkish student, Fehmi Edhem Karatay, was sent abroad to study librarianship, though not to the United States. He went to Paris to attend the U.S.-founded "Ecole de Bibliothécaires" and upon his return became director of the Istanbul University library. Karatay proceeded to offer a course in librarianship based upon U.S. practice including modern concepts "such as preparing dictionary catalogs" and "using the Dewey Decimal Classification."[6] But despite this and other attempts to assure a continuing flow of trained personnel into the libraries of Turkey, sustained success in preparing librarians would not be realized for another thirty years.

Arguably the most important event in the development of the modern Turkish library profession was the founding of the Institute of Librarianship at Ankara University in the country's capital city.[7] Turkey's pioneering librarian, Adnan Ötüken, director of the National Library, was well aware of the importance of a well-trained cadre of professional personnel and had initiated classes through which promising library workers could obtain the beginnings of an education in books and bibliography. Others, too, recognized that if progress were to be made in building, organizing, preserving, and making accessible collections of scholarly and leisure reading materials, skilled librarians were essential. Lawrence Thompson, librarian at the University of Kentucky, was sent to Turkey in 1951 "under a Leader Specialist grant to survey the status of libraries ... and to offer a library training course."[8] The report he prepared recommended "the establishment of a school of library science in a Turkish university, in order to fill the need for a 'continuing source of competent young librarians.'"[9]

Notable among the Americans who saw opportunity for the development of the profession, and for the United States to be of assistance in this regard, was Emily Dean (later to become Emily Dean Heilman), at the time director of U.S. library programs in Turkey. A distinguished librarian from the United States with experience in China and South Africa, Ms. Dean was a strong advocate for creation of a formal library education program and her voice joined with those of Turkish and U.S. colleagues to convince the Ford Foundation to fund a four-year grant to Ankara University to found an institute for training librarians.[10] A first for the Ford Foundation (and the first such program to be established anywhere in the Middle East), it turned to the American Library Association (ALA) for assistance. ALA responded by appointing an advisory committee whose initial assignment was to identify an American director for the program.

Robert Downs, director of the library and of the library school at the University of Illinois, was asked to take on this task. Downs arrived in March of 1955, stayed for six months, and set up the institute. He was succeeded by Elmer Grieder of Stanford University who not only taught at Ankara, but conducted courses on school libraries for students at the Gazi Training College for Teachers.[11] Grieder was followed by the University of Southern California's Lewis Stieg (1957-59) and then by Carl White of

Columbia University (1959-61). It became clear during Grieder's term that additional U.S. assistance with the growing effort was necessary and in 1958 the Ford Foundation sent Norris McClellan of the library school at Louisiana State University to work with Stieg. Anne Ethelyn Markley from the University of California at Los Angeles joined White as his associate.

During this time the faculty of Ankara University voted to have the institute become a chair, " a most significant development for the academic status of the school," for it placed "library science on the same footing as other disciplines" at the university. Ford Foundation funding had been extended for an additional two-year period and provided not only for U.S. faculty, but scholarships to enable promising Turkish librarians to attend U.S. library schools. It also permitted purchase of books and equipment and the translation of library texts into Turkish.[12] Among the U.S. institutions that received Turkish students during this period were the Universities of Chicago, Illinois, and Michigan, Columbia and Rutgers Universities, and Simmons College.[13] The individuals who studied at U.S. library schools during this period went on to highly influential positions within the Turkish educational, research, and governmental establishment, beginning a tradition which continues today.

Emily Dean, aware of the importance of promoting good scholarship among the fledgling librarians at the Ankara program and understanding the impact of good publicity for a developing profession, established monetary prizes to be given to the graduates who had written the three best theses in the department each year. A bequest by her to the American Library Association assured ongoing support for this activity or for other purposes related to Turkish librarianship. To this day ALA administers the "Emily Dean Heilman" fund and provides periodic funding for the Ankara Department of Librarianship.

Ford Foundation support ended in 1961 and the Fulbright program was turned to for continued U.S. assistance. Nance O'Neall from the Los Angeles City Schools, Ralph Hopp of the University of Minnesota, and Arthur McAnally from the University of Oklahoma all taught in the early sixties at Ankara as Fulbright lecturers.[14] During this period, Frederick Kuhlman of the Joint University Libraries in Nashville, Tennessee, visited as a UNESCO consultant to advise on the establishment of a central university library for the newly-developing Middle East Technical University in Ankara.[15] Earlier, George Bonn of the Rutgers library school had organized the library of the Turkish Union of Chambers of Commerce, and the University of Nebraska, through funds provided by the U.S. Agency for International Development (USAID), helped Atatürk University with a number of projects including the establishment of a central library.[16]

These early years of Turkish education for librarianship and of modern library development saw the involvement of a veritable who's who of U.S. librarians, men and woman representing some of the United States' most distinguished institutions, who functioned either as teachers in Ankara, as visiting advisors and consultants, or as ALA committee members providing support and assistance. Harvard's Douglas Byrant and Flora Belle Ludington of Mount Holyoke both traveled to Ankara for consultations as members of the original ALA advisory subcommittee, which also included Jack Dalton from Columbia University representing ALA's Board of Education for Librarianship.[17] Lester Asheim visited Turkey in the fall of 1965 in his capacity as director of the association's International Relations Office.

The influence of U.S. librarianship also was significant in the development of a second library science program in Ankara, this one at Hacettepe University, an institution that grew out of the entrepreneurial genius of a U.S.-trained pediatrician, Ihsan Dogramaci. From a clinic which was part of Ankara University to a self-standing medical school to a full-fledged university, Hacettepe became one of Turkey's major educational enterprises. Its secretary-general (the officer with overall responsibility for university operations) during part of this time was Ilhan Kum, previously the university's director of libraries and a graduate of the University of Kentucky. Kum proposed a program in librarianship that would "complement the existing bachelor's level library degree" at Ankara University, one which would be "designed specifically to create library 'professionals' " rather than "to train personnel for the performance of routine library tasks."[18] Thomas Minder of the University of Pittsburgh, assisted by Benjamin Whitten, a Fulbrighter from the University of Southern California (who in the early nineties would become the United States Information Service Cultural Affairs Officer in Ankara), led an effort to establish a master's degree curriculum whose emphasis was on "the application of basic principles of inquiry methodology to the solution of problems" encouraging "continual self-education."[19] The faculty of the program, in addition to Minder and Whitten, consisted of Ilhan Kum, Nilüfer Tuncer, who held a master's degree in library science from the University of Illinois (she later became the director of the documentation center of the Turkish Higher Education Council), and Phyllis Lepon, a U.S. expatriate and a graduate of the University of California at Berkeley library school. In 1976 Morris Gelfand of Queens University of the City University of New York conducted a survey of the Hacettepe program, which ultimately offered bachelor and doctoral degrees as well as the master's.[20] Fulbright and ALA Book Fellow grantees were later to teach Hacettepe's library science students.

As suggested by the work of people like Emily Dean, Lawrence Thompson, George Bonn, and Frederick Kulhman, U.S. activity in Turkey was not limited to education for librarianship. Librarians from the United States were to be found in a number of the schools and colleges set up by U.S. educators, particularly in the major population centers of Ankara, Istanbul, and Izmir. Gertrude Drury, retired from the St. Louis Public library, worked for years as the librarian at the American Collegiate Institute in Izmir.[21] A number of secondary schools, some of which have English as their principal language of instruction, still maintain excellent libraries which were organized by U.S.librarians and in some cases continue to be under the direction of U.S. librarians.

USAID gave major funding for the libraries at Hacettepe and Middle East Technical University (METU) and Robert Downs returned twice to oversee its use.[22] The METU library received signifiant numbers of periodicals from the United States Book Exchange and had the services of various U.S. citizens early in its development including Doris Natelle Isley, William Bennet, Donald John Weber, and even some U.S. Peace Corps volunteers.[23]

The Turkish librarians who succeeded the "Unesco-sponsored 'expert' leadership" were educated in the United States.[24] One of these, Tekin Aybas, later worked for USIS and is now an undersecretary in the ministry of culture. These talented individuals—Turks and U.S. citizens—assured continued advancement of the METU library, one of the finest in the country. Most of the university libraries founded after 1950 were modeled after those at U.S. universities, with collections in a central facility serving all of the faculties as opposed to the vastly distributed approach favored by older institutions such as Ankara and Istanbul universities.[25]

In the mid-eighties Turkey's first private university, Bilkent, was established by Ihsan Dogramaci. Phyllis (Lepon) Erdogan, formerly of Hacettepe and Dogramaci's long-time special assistant, founded the library and remains its director. The Bilkent library is a model of teaching and research support for the liberal arts and professional education. In 1992 the Koç family, head of Turkey's leading business conglomerate, embarked on an enormous educational effort by funding a private university in the

Istanbul environs. Koç University leaders deemed the library to be critical to the founders' ambition that the university would surpass every institution in the country and emulate the best the United States had to offer. The university's rector is Seha Tiniç, a long-time Turkish resident of the United States and a distinguished professor of finance at the University of Texas, who has taken a keen interest in the library program. It was set up with the assistance of U.S. consultants and has been directed by U.S. librarians for all but a few months of its existence.

Throughout the years the United States Information Service has been strongly supportive of library development in the country, working with the Turkish-American Fulbright Commission and the American Library Association to bring to Turkey instructors and consultants, regularly sending Turkish librarians to the United States for professional visits, and sponsoring book donation and other initiatives to help the many universities being established.

In the summer of 1995 in the city of Istanbul, the Turkish library profession played host to the general conference of the International Federation of Library Associations and Institutions. Librarians from throughout the world came to the city straddling two continents, visited its libraries and museums, saw its palaces, and shopped in its famous bazaar. They marveled at its beauty and were treated to its superb hospitality. And they witnessed firsthand how far Turkish librarianship had come in less than fifty years. Progress since Lawrence Thompson first arrived in the country has in many ways been extraordinary. He, Emily Dean Heilman, Robert Downs, and the other librarians from the United States who followed them would be astonished by the state of the profession as the century comes to a close and gratified by the impressive achievements of their Turkish colleagues. They would marvel at the accomplishments of their students and colleagues and most certainly would be proud of the roles they played in helping to advance librarianship in this land of the libraries.

U.S. Involvement with Turkish Librarianship: A Chronology of Selected Events

1924   John Dewey is invited to survey Turkish education and to make recommendations for its improvement.

1939   Dewey's report on education in Turkey is published.

1951/52   Lawrence S. Thompson of the University of Kentucky visits Turkey on a United States Department of State Leader Specialist grant to review the condition of libraries and to provide a training course.

1952   Thompson publishes his report, "A Program for Library Development in Turkey."

1954   At the urging of Emily Dean and others in the Turkish and U.S. library communities, the Ankara University Institute of Library Science is established under a four-year grant from the Ford Foundation.

          Douglas Byrant of Harvard University visits Ankara to consult with university, government, and Ford Foundation officials.

1955   Robert Downs of the University of Illinois arrives in Ankara to set up the institute and to become its first instructor.

          With the support of the United States Agency for International Development (USAID), the University of Nebraska contracts with Ataturk University in Erzurum to provide technical assistance including advice on the establishment of a central library.

George Bonn of the Rutgers University organizes the library of the Union of Chambers of Commerce, Industry, and Commodity Exchanges of Turkey.

1955/57   Elmer Grieder of Stanford University succeeds Downs as director of the institute, teaches in the program, and conducts coursework in school libraries at Gazi Training College for Teachers.

1957   Flora Ludington, Chair of the ALA Advisory Committee on the Ankara University Institute, visits Ankara.

1957/59   Lewis Stieg of the University of Southern California takes over directorship of the institute.

1958/59   Norris McClellan of Louisiana State University teaches on the institute's faculty.

1959/61   Carl White of Columbia University and Anne Ethelyn Markley of the University of California, Los Angeles, join the institute, he as director, she as a faculty member.

1960   The Ankara University Institute of Librarianship becomes the Chair of Library Science.

1961   Ford Foundation support for the Ankara University program ends.

1961/62   Nance O'Neall of the Los Angeles City Schools is a Fulbright lecturer in the department.

1962/63   Ralph Hopp of the University of Minnesota lectures under a Fulbright grant.

1963   Frederick Kuhlman of the Joint University Libraries in Nashville, Tennessee, is sent by UNESCO to serve as a consultant for the central library building at Middle East Technical University (METU) in Ankara.

The METU library is designated a depository for the American Universities Presses Library by USAID.

1963/64   Arthur McAnally of the University of Oklahoma teaches as a Fulbright lecturer.

1967   An Institute of Library Science and Documentation at Hacettepe University is authorized.

The ALA Advisory Committee to the Ankara University program is discharged.

1968   Robert Downs visits Turkey on behalf of the USAID as a consultant on library development grants.
USAID provides $1.5 millon to Middle East Technical University and $650,000 to Hacettepe University for library book purchases over five years.

1970/74   Thomas Minder of the University of Pittsburgh consults on the establishment of the Master's program at the Hacettepe University Department of Librarianship and teaches in the department.

1971   Robert Downs returns to Turkey for USAID.

1973   Benjamin Whitten of the University of Southern California teaches in Hacettepe's Department of Librarianship.

1974/75   Lowell Olson of the University of Minnesota teaches in the Hacettepe Department of Librarianship.

1976   UNESCO sends Morris Gelfand of Queens College of the City University of New York to Hacettepe University to conduct an evaluative survey of the Department of Librarianship and to make recommendations for strengthening of its programs.

1981/82   Jordan Scepanski of Vanderbilt University teaches at the Department of Librarianship at Hacettepe University on a Fulbright grant.

1988/89   Isabel Stirling of the University of Oregon conducts training in on-line services at the library of the Council of Higher Education and lectures at Hacettepe University under the American Library Association's Book Fellow's program.

Notes

1. Leman Çankaya, "Libraries in Turkey," in *Encyclopedia of Library and Information Science*, 31, ed. Allen Kent, Harold Lancour, and Jay E. Daily (New York: Marcel Dekker, 1981), 215; Robert B. Downs, "Librarianship in Turkey," *Stechert-Hafner Book News* 10 (October 1955): 18.

2. John Feather, "Parchment," in *A Dictionary of Book History* (London: Croom Helm, 1986), 198.

3. Edwin M. Yamauchi, "Pergamum Library," in *Encyclopedia of Library History*, ed. Wayne A. Wiegand and Donald E. Davis, Jr. (New York: Garland, 1994), 491.

4. David Ronald Johnson, "The Library of Celsus, An Ephesian Phoenix," *Wilson Library Bulletin* 54 (June 1980): 652.

5. Edna Phillips, "American Book Service in Greece and Turkey," *Library Journal* 53 (March 20, 1928): 219.

6. Osman Ersoy and Berin U. Yurdadog, "Education for Librarianship Abroad: Turkey," *Library Trends* 12 (October 1963): 206.

7. No attempt is made here to provide broad coverage of many important aspects of Turkish libraries and librarianship. For more extensive treatment of historical and current topics the reader is directed to the articles found in the notes and to Lawrence Thompson's "The Libraries of Turkey," in *Library Quarterly* 22 (July 1952): 270-284; "Turkish Libraries: Historical Context" by İrfan Çakin found in *International Library Review* 16 (January 1984): 71-77; the special IFLA issue of *Türk Kütüphaneciliği: (Turkish Librarianship) Eylul* (September) 1995; and a recent piece by Linda Williamson, "Contemporary Turkish Libraries and Librarianship: Gleanings from IFLA '95 in Istanbul," *International Information & Librarianship Review* 28 (1996): 371-381.

8. Beverly J. Brewster, *American Overseas Library Technical Assistance 1940-1970* (Metuchen, N.J.: Scarecrow Press, 1976), 173.

9. Benjamin Whitten, Jr. and Thomas Minder, "Education for Librarianship in Developing Nations: The Hacettepe Experience," *Journal of Education for Librarianship* 14 (Spring 1974): 224.

10. Carl M. White, "The University of Ankara's Institute of Librarianship in 1960," *ALA Bulletin* 54 (September 1960): 666.

11. Ersoy and Yurdadog, 208.

12. "Final Report from Ankara," *ALA Bulletin* 56 (June 1962): 573.

13. Robert B. Downs, "How to Start A Library School," *ALA Bulletin* 52 (June 1958): 402.

14. Brewster, 312.

15. William Bennett, "The Middle East Technical University Library," *UNESCO Bulletin for Libraries* 18 (November 1964): 272.

16. George S. Bonn, "Assignment in Ankara," *Special Libraries* 48 (February 1957): 64-69; Kathleen Kurosman, "The Academic Library in Turkey," *International Library Review* 12 (April 1980): 189-191.

17. Downs, "How to Start A Library School," 402; Flora Belle Ludington, "Kütüphanecilik Bölümü," *Library Journal* 80 (January 15, 1955): 122.

18. Thomas Minder and Benjamin Whitten, Jr., "Basic Undergraduate Education for Librarianship and Information Science," *Journal of Education for Librarianship* 15 (Spring 1975): 264.

19. Whitten and Minder, "Education for Librarianship in Developing Nations: The Hacettepe Experience," 229.

20. M. A. Gelfand, *Library Education in Hacettepe University* (Paris: UNESCO, 1977).

21. Gertrude G. Drury, "Library Service in Turkey," *Library Journal* 84 (November 15, 1959): 3509-3513; Gertrude G. Drury, "Missouri to Izmir via Bookmobile," *Missouri Library Association Quarterly* 21 (June 1960): 65-69.

22. Robert B. Downs, "Library Development in Turkish Universities," *Pakistan Library Bulletin* 4 (September-December 1971): 9; "U.S. Librarians and Books Bolster Turkish Libraries," *Library Journal* 93 (October 15, 1968): 3732.

23. D. A. Redmond and Solmaz Izdemir, "The Library of the Middle East Technical University," *UNESCO Bulletin for Libraries* 14 (September 1960): 202.

24. Donald John Weber, "METU's Library: The First Decade," *UNESCO Bulletin for Libraries* 24 (March-April 1970): 78.

25. Çankaya, 232.

13. Post-Soviet Russian Librarianship in Transition

Michael Neubert and Irina L. Klim

The Soviet Union fell in August of 1991 with the failure of the hard-line communist putsch—coincidentally, this was during the annual conference of the International Federation of Library Associations (IFLA), held that year in Moscow—so many library leaders from around the world witnessed this event first hand.

Since then there have been changes and innovations, both on the national and local level. A few examples:

- LibNet, a national project, is a cooperative effort to coordinate automation and access to the Internet and other resources among the largest Russian libraries, including the Russian State Library (Moscow), the Russian National Library (St. Petersburg) and others. (LibNet has an English-language home page at http://www.libfl.ras.ru/list.html which contains links to the pages of participating libraries (many in English)—an excellent place to look for information via the Internet about Russian libraries.)
- The profile of Russian libraries and librarians has been increased with the discussion and implementation of a national "Law on Libraries" in 1994 and the creation of a "Day of the Librarian" by the Russian National Library (St. Petersburg), starting in 1995.
- In the Russian north, a network of "polar libraries" separated by thousands of miles is cooperating to create and maintain a CD-ROM-based catalog ("PolarPAC") of materials concerning the polar region held by all libraries, with the help of American partners.
- In Ekaterinburg, an "Inter-Nationality Public Library" was created to decrease tensions between different minority nationalities and Russians (the majority population). This novel (and apparently unique) project resulted in a library with collections in dozens of minority languages that organizes programs regularly on a wide range of subjects of interest to its many readers in different minority communities in the Urals region.
- In Novgorod, the previously separate networks of children's and young adult public libraries have united to create a single system called the Children's and Youth Library Center "Reading Town" with 22,000 registered readers and 280,000 books plus a multimedia center.

Even before the failed coup of August 1991, librarians were integrating their *spetskhrany* or special collections into their general collections (*spetskhrany* were collections with access limited to those with the political mindset that would allow them to use these often foreign materials and not be adversely affected). Russian librarians had been much occupied with attempting to direct their readers' interest (and limiting their access to ideologically suspect information)—now they could serve to assist in providing full access to whatever information the reader was seeking. This was a significant change.

On the other hand, the shift to a capitalist economy meant the introduction of many new variables that were unfamiliar to Russian librarians. One, for example, was a chaotic publishing market and the end of a highly disciplined book and periodical distribution system—a situation that is only now beginning to normalize. More importantly, all Russian libraries depended on the state, either directly or indirectly, for their funds, and there were many changes in government priorities in post-Soviet Russia. Some types of libraries, once widespread, have ceased to exist, the largest example being libraries of trade unions. Almost all others have suffered considerable cuts in their budgets, in particular affecting their ability to acquire foreign materials. Despite the fact that no Russian librarian would truly want a return of Soviet power, there are still many who will from time to time become nostalgic about some aspect of the highly ordered world of Soviet libraries that existed.

Russian libraries under the Soviet government existed in disparate universes depending upon which ministry they ultimately reported to—there were libraries under the Ministry of Culture, the Ministry of Higher Education, the libraries of the Academy of Sciences, and so on. Here Russian libraries will be described as much as possible in general terms, because the authors believe that now there is more found in common between Russian libraries and librarians than that which divides them.

Historical Background

Russian librarianship had a developing tradition even before the socialist revolution of 1917. This history goes back to medieval times with the libraries of the Russian princes, religious figures and monasteries. The first university library was in St. Petersburg at the beginning of the eighteenth century. Starting in 1742 there was a law requiring depository copies of new books to the Library of the Academy of Sciences. By the end of the nineteenth century there was a well-developed library system with both public and academic libraries. Centralized cataloging started in 1925 for public libraries and 1927 for academic libraries. In the 1920s and 1930s national conferences on bibliographic control were held. The Ministry of Culture created a department of libraries which gave greater emphasis to library affairs. In fact, until the 1960s in many ways developments in Russian librarianship paralleled those in the United States, except for the ideological control. In the 1970s Russia began to fall behind in technology.

After 1917, the Soviet regime gradually exercised greater and greater ideological control over Russian libraries. Control over information was one of the major control mechanisms of the Soviet regime and librarians were among those charged with controlling the flow of information to the populace and actively participating in their ideological education. For example, access to photocopying was restricted, since this was a kind of printing press (thus, Soviet dissidents were forced to engage in *samizdat*, or self-publishing, using typewriters, onion-skin paper, and carbon copies). Libraries were a source of information for Soviet society but much of this information was by design of a ideological character—in the end, librarians were another source of propaganda about the Communist Party of the Soviet Union. In return for fulfilling this role of information advisors rather than free providers of information, the support for libraries was good. In the late 1980s before the Soviet Union ceased to exist, there were over 335,000 Soviet libraries of all kinds, of which more than one-third were in Russia (one of fifteen republics of the former Soviet Union). About one-half of the Russian libraries were public libraries, organized in an elaborate hierarchy ranging from research-quality institutions at the *oblast* level (of which there are eighty-seven) to small libraries that are nothing more than a single room in a village. In fact, this elaborate hierarchy was part of the system of control. While salaries were not high, they were much closer to the average than today, and more importantly, these salaries were paid regularly. Today many public institutions in post-Soviet Russia are not able to stay current with payment of salaries. Funds for acquisitions are even more difficult to come by, especially hard currency for foreign materials.

The Gorbachev era, marking the beginning of the end of the Soviet Union, was dominated by a sense of cataclysm even in libraries. This is not surprising, since one of the hallmarks was the policy of *glasnost*, or openness—and how were librarians to operate in this new atmosphere? The inability of many public libraries to respond to social change as the Soviet system collapsed meant that they lost three million patrons from 1987 to 1991.

The Post-Soviet Russian Transformation

In August 1991 the Soviet Union became fifteen separate countries, of which Russia was the largest. Russian libraries were exposed to a level of much greater change than under glasnost, one over which they had no control. Russian libraries reacted to these changes in many ways. As noted, some, such as the libraries of trade unions, disappeared altogether as the ability of their sponsoring organizations to support them disappeared. Libraries of all types had to begin charging fees for services as a way to make ends meet. Many staff found that they were interested in taking advantage of the new, higher paying positions that appeared in the new commercial sector, and staff turnover in the late 1980s and early 1990s was extremely high, 40 percent per year. Of course there is now a positive side to this—most staff still working in Russian libraries are very committed to the library profession.

Different kinds of libraries had their own specific problems in the new, post-Soviet world. Public libraries, once in a highly organized hierarchy under the Ministry of Culture in Moscow, were forced to depend on local budgets and resources. Once a visitor to a large public library outside of Moscow could have expected to find much the same services and collections in any city of the same size, but now there was far more differentiation depending on the ability of the library to successfully lobby for funds from the local political authorities and to develop new ways of raising money. Smaller libraries in outlying villages in particular had troubles as their budgets disappeared. On a positive note, recently some of the large public research libraries in the capital cities of different regions have been rebounding.

Many "innovations" that have been implemented have been forced upon libraries because of budget problems. For example, in Ekaterinburg the city had separate systems for children, young adults, and adults (a typical arrangement in the Soviet Union), but in the past year these systems have united to become a single system of forty branch libraries and a central library that offer services to all ages. Although changes were forced upon libraries by budgetary circumstances, for the patrons this is overall an improvement over what existed previously; nonetheless, the city's librarians would have never made this change otherwise.

University libraries as a rule had a much more troubled situation than large public libraries. Since they were part of larger institutions, they had to depend on these parent institutions for funding, and the funding is supposed to come from the Ministry of

Higher Education in Moscow. This funding has declined and seems unlikely to rebound soon. State universities have established new departments that accept only paying students and used other techniques to generate new funds, but it is difficult for the libraries to get the kind of share of their university's budget that they feel they deserve. Soviet university libraries for the most part were expected to have a copy of each textbook for each student that was to use that title—a unenviable responsibility. Given the present budgetary situation and the difficulties in acquiring many titles, this is no longer possible, although most university libraries still feel that in an ideal world this would be one of their fundamental tasks.

Libraries of the Academy of Sciences also experienced difficulties. Many had collections heavy on ever more expensive foreign periodicals, and the funds to acquire these materials disappeared, although George Soros stepped in to help in this critical area. More than other libraries, they continue to operate as a highly centralized system.

In matters related to automation, progress has been slow. Soviet libraries had always been particularly well equipped with card catalogs and thousands of hours were spent preparing bibliographies on many, many topics, but these valuable tools were extremely labor intensive to compile. The move to automate library functions really began only after 1991, and even then, slowly. Today only some of the largest Russian libraries have online public access catalogs (OPACs) and often these are not part of integrated library systems, but simply a database of the books that the library has acquired without item-level access. Few libraries have done significant retrospective work. While programmers in individual institutions labored to create "home grown" systems, no private Russian firms offered effective systems to the library market—even today, many Russian librarians consider that there is no Russian-born automated system worth acquiring.

Some factors are improving significantly. Book publishing was highly disorganized in the early 1990s and the distribution system broke down almost completely. Few libraries, even large ones, were able to acquire many of the titles that were being published in Russia. Some very large libraries were forced to improvise systems for acquiring books even from Moscow and St. Petersburg. Although publishing is still not as organized as might be desirable, there are now book distribution companies that are operating and enable some large research libraries to acquire as much as one half of the titles published in Russia. There are also new *knizhnye salony* (book salons), including several in St. Petersburg alone. In addition there are new regional and subject-oriented book fairs organized with ever greater attendance.

Also of interest, there are significant cooperative efforts on a national level. There is an effort to produce a national Russian "Books in Print," which is considered essential for bringing some order to the publishing world, and Russian libraries are participating in this effort. The State Public Scientific Technical Library in Moscow has been leading efforts to create a Russian "OCLC"—at present, almost all Russian libraries catalog items received by creating records from scratch or by keying in CIP-like records—there is no source of online cataloging copy, resulting in much duplication of effort. This project has many hurdles, not the least of which is the present poor communications infrastructure available to organizations without deep pockets. There is work to create and improve existing national standards, for example, to agree on a version of MARC that will be used in Russian libraries (many libraries use US-MARC) or to update the Russian cataloging code (there is also work being done to harmonize the difference between Russian rules of description and AACR2). These efforts, too, have many problems to overcome, including the fact that many libraries have already decided independently to adopt one or another standard and they must now consider converting to a national standard (or not).

The Russian library literature quickly began to reflect the new realities of Russian librarianship. Books with titles such as *Biblioteka i biznes* (*The Library and Business*) and *Marketing v biblioteke* (*Marketing in the Library*) appeared to help Russian librarians operate in the new environment. Journals contain translations of articles from foreign library periodicals to allow Russian librarians to learn from the experiences of others. One example of the new library journals is the title *Peterburgskaia bibliotechnaia shkola* (*St. Petersburg Library School*).

Nationally, library education for professionals is in turmoil. Many professional librarians under the Soviet Union did not have a professional library education; rather, they were subject specialists (especially in the technical and hard sciences). Most librarians who did have a library education had completed an undergraduate level degree at an "Institute of Culture" and had a background in the humanities or social sciences and work in public libraries. It is now clear that a new model (or models) is needed, but the nature of this new model is only now the subject of intense discussion in the Russian library literature (the U.S. system of professional education is just one model being considered).

To give some direction from the federal level, there is a national "Law on Libraries" passed in 1994 which provides guidance in a number of areas. While for U.S. citizens such a law no doubt seems a bit strange, it is useful in the post-Soviet context in order to systematically include libraries in the new, more open Russian society and to guarantee free access to information through libraries to all citizens. Librarians participated heavily in the drafting of this law and the process of its creation was a useful vehicle nationally to draw attention to librarianship for those outside the field and to give a greater sense of purpose to those within it.

There has been a distinct breaking down of the previous hierarchies at all levels and for the most part this is seen by Russian librarians as a positive development. Although this means that there is now less (or in some cases, no) financial support from central ministries or similar authorities, there is also less standardization of performance required from above. If a city decides to redo its library system to consolidate children's, youth, and adult libraries into one, there is no ministry in Moscow that will say *nyet*.

Conclusion

The first years of this decade were unsettled for Russian librarians, and for the most part they perceived that the negatives far outweighed the positive developments. Conversations with most Russian librarians continually focused on problems and there was a broad sense that they were discouraged and found little reason to be optimistic about their future. Mostly, in fact, they complained. In the second half of this decade there have been many adjustments and the spirit is far more optimistic. There are still many areas that are problematic as discussed above, but those librarians still in the field are far more likely to emphasize positive developments, both existing and potential future ones.

At a recent conference in Seattle, Washington, Russian librarians from large research libraries in the Russian Far East met with North American Pacific Rim colleagues with whom they had also met five years ago and they reflected on the changes that have taken place in their libraries. In particular in the area of automation, they noted that while none had significant automation in 1992, all are now operating local area networks and acquiring new personal computers, software, and doing a variety of automation-related projects. The progress in this area has given them hope for change in other areas.

In short, Russian librarians are becoming a part of the solutions to problems that their libraries face rather than seeing themselves as victims of circumstances beyond their control. This is very pleasant to see, and the next decade will certainly be one of considerable progress for libraries in Russia.

14. Estonia: The Little Country That Could

Eric A. Johnson and Aira Lepik

Once an unwilling member of the Union of Soviet Socialist Republics, Estonia is now widely regarded as a success story in the difficult transition from communist rule to an open, democratic society with a free-market economy. Visiting specialists from the World Bank and other Western organizations were so impressed by the transformations taking place in this small country that they dubbed Estonia "the little country that could," a slogan adopted by former Prime Minister Mart Laar and other Estonian politicians. Indeed, just like Watty Piper's famous Little Engine, Estonia has kept up with its much larger colleagues in the region (Poland, Hungary, and the Czech Republic) to become the first of the former Soviet republic invited to join negotiations for eventual entry into the European Union.

Estonia's libraries and its librarians have played a vital role in their country's recent accomplishments. Opened in 1993 just two years after independence, the impressive new building of the National Library of Estonia (NLE) has become a flagship in the journey towards an open society. The NLE regularly hosts meetings between the president, prime minister, and ministerial council of Estonia and their Baltic counterparts in neighboring Latvia and Lithuania. The NLE has even become a mandatory stop for visiting foreign dignitaries ranging from the Queen of Sweden to Hillary Rodham Clinton. Under the able leadership of Ivi Eenmaa, the NLE has shown that libraries can take a prominent part in the rebirth of a nation. Ms. Eenmaa is currently on leave from her position as general director while she serves as the Mayor of Tallinn, Estonia's capital city and the home to half a million people.

An ancient city founded in the tenth century, Tallinn is located on the Baltic Sea just fifty miles south of Helsinki, the capital of Finland. Estonia, about the size of New Hampshire and Vermont put together, is bordered by Russia to the east and by Latvia to the south. Estonia's numerous islands lie off its northern and especially western shores. While most of the country's twenty-seven research libraries like the Estonian Academic Library are concentrated in Tallinn along with a third of Estonia's population, the university city of Tartu is the site of Estonia's oldest research library with the largest collection (3.7 million items). Tartu University and its library, established originally under Swedish rule in 1632, are two of the most positive legacies that remain from successive waves of Danish, German, Polish, Swedish, Russian, Nazi, and Soviet invaders that have kept Estonia under foreign rule for most of the last 750 years.

Each of Estonia's twenty-one cities and counties has a central library with branches in the surrounding districts, towns, and villages. A network of over six hundred public libraries serves readers everywhere from the industrial city of Narva in the northeast to the island of Saaremaa in the southwest. With its 745 school libraries and close to 100 special libraries, Estonia has a total of 1,284 libraries. As of 1997, these libraries employed approximately 3,200 people of whom close to 2,600 were considered to be librarians (over 1,500 have university degrees in library science).[1] These are rather impressive numbers when considering Estonia's small size. With just under 1.5 million inhabitants, Estonia has roughly the same number of people as the state of Nebraska:

About two-thirds of Estonia's population is ethnically Estonian. The remaining third is predominantly Russian-speaking (a mixture of ethnic Russians, Ukrainians, and Belarusians). While many members of this linguistic minority are not Estonian citizens, Estonian libraries provide equal service to everyone regardless of their actual citizenship status or national origin. The NLE's open-door policy is such that anyone old enough to fill out the application form for a library card is invited to become a reader. Few research libraries in the West provide such limitless access to minors. But from the NLE's point of view, they are simply taking a proactive role in Estonia's future by encouraging the development of its next generation of citizens. As President Lennart Meri said at the opening ceremony of the NLE: "The choice, as always, is made by the people. I hope that they will choose the future of the Estonian Republic from these shelves."[2]

The architecture of the NLE was inspired by various structures in Tallinn's medieval Old Town including several churches (most Estonians are Lutheran). But within the NLE's massive limestone walls, the new co-exists with the old. Thanks to the efforts of nearby Finland and Sweden, Estonia was the first part of the former Soviet Union to get a direct Internet connection back in 1992. By early 1993, the first few staff members at the NLE and the Estonian Academic Library already had full Internet access. In the years that followed, Estonia had one of the fastest Internet growth rates in the world. Today, visitors to the NLE will find public access Internet terminals. Those who have not yet made the trip to Tallinn can visit the library's web page on the Internet (http://www.nlib.ee/i_index.html).

Other Estonian research libraries like the Tallinn Pedagogical University Library provide public access to the Internet while a growing number now have their own web pages. For example, the Estonian Academic Library welcomes virtual visitors (http://www.tatr.ee/index_i.hmtl) as do the Tartu University Library (http://www.ut-lib.ee) and the Estonian Literary Museum Archives Library (http://www.kir-mus.ee/ar/index_en.htm). Those with a particular interest in public libraries can visit the Saaremaa County Library (http://skr.tt.ee/ing/default.htm) to get an idea of what local libraries are doing on the Internet. Because Estonian is such an unusual language, most Estonian libraries have English-language versions of their Internet resources in order to insure maximum global accessibility. Like Finnish, Estonian is a Finno-Ugric language, distantly related to Hungarian. The three are completely unrelated to the Indo-European family of languages which includes English, Russian, and Spanish.

While Tartu University Library was the first Estonian library to make its home-grown OPAC named INGRID available over the Internet, major Estonian research libraries have since adopted a more unified approach to the problem of library automation. In 1995, Tartu University Library joined the NLE, the Estonian Academic Library, and four other research libraries in creating a consortium called ELNET, the Estonian Libraries Network. Together, automation specialists from these seven libraries selected a single integrated library system (INNOPAC) to be used by all Estonian research libraries. Because these libraries were able to come to a consensus, the Andrew Mellon Foundation and the Estonian Government awarded ELNET with matching grants to purchase the necessary software and equipment. The end result of this joint automation project will be a national online union catalog which will be accessible from anywhere in Estonia or from around the world.

As it may be some time before the holdings of every city or county library in Estonia appear in this new online union catalog, George Soros' Open Estonia Foundation is helping public libraries automate. Thanks to a grant, eighteen libraries will use a system developed for Finnish public libraries known as Kirjasto 3000 to get their collections online. The long-term goal is to bring both these separate automation projects for research and public libraries together at some point in the future. The groundwork for this has already been laid because of several efforts at national-level standardization. Estonian librarians recently finished translating the Universal Decimal Classification (UDC) system into Estonian while the finishing touches are being put on a unified system of subject headings known as the Estonian Universal Thesaurus (EUT). On the automation end, USMARC has been chosen as the format for data storage and exchange. USMARC documentation has already been translated into Estonian and is now available over the Internet. The NLE has been the national ISBN agency since 1992 and has been distributing ISSNs to publishers since 1995.[3] Slowly but surely, all the pieces needed for standardization have been falling into place.

The Estonian Librarians Association (ELA) has played a crucial part in coordinating these national-level standardization efforts and mediating between different libraries. Established in 1923 at the original Congress of Estonian Librarians during Estonia's first period of independence (1918-1940), the ELA was banned after Estonia was absorbed into the Soviet Union at the end of World War II. The ELA was then reborn in 1988 during the Fifth Congress of Estonian Librarians when Gorbachev's program of *perestroika* made such things possible. In 1989, ELA rejoined the International Federation of Library Associations (IFLA) after an absence of almost 50 years. The ELA now has over 550 members (about one out of every five Estonian librarians) and publishes a nice, glossy magazine six times a year called *Raamatukogu* (*Library*) with English summaries of all its major articles.

Like IFLA, the American Library Association (ALA) was quick to welcome the ELA back into the fold of international library organizations. With the help of the United States Information Agency (USIA), the ALA has sent four of its Library Fellows to key Estonian research libraries. Two Library Fellows worked on projects at the NLE while the Tartu University Library and the Estonian Academic Library each hosted a Library Fellow of their own. Additionally, an Estonian librarian from Tartu University Library participated in the short-lived Reverse Library Fellows program by completing an internship at the University of Nevada Library, Las Vegas. As it has done elsewhere in the region, the ALA has helped the NLE and other Estonian libraries acquire U.S. works on library science at a large discount. These important contacts and exchanges helped bring an end to 50 years of Soviet-imposed isolation on the development of Estonian librarianship.

In addition to these ALA-sponsored activities, American and Estonian librarians have had several other opportunities to bridge the distance between their two countries since the 1991 collapse of the Soviet Union. Five Estonian librarians have participated in the Library of Congress Soros Fellows Program, spending three months studying and working in Washington, D.C. Three other Estonian librarians have been the guests of the Mortenson Center for International Library Programs at the University of Illinois, Urbana-Champaign, for study periods ranging from two weeks to six months. The Library of Congress' Congressional Research Service trained over a dozen Estonian parliamentary librarians at workshops in Tallinn, Prague, Budapest, and Washington, D.C. USIA and the International Research & Exchanges Board (IREX) have brought several other Estonian librarians to the United States for conferences and study tours.

In addition to helping make many exchanges of librarians possible, USIA has done many other things to help reconnect Estonian libraries to the rest of the world. In 1993, USIA opened an American Information Center and Library in downtown Tallinn (http://www.usislib.ee/usislib). This small library serves as a focal point for accessing information about the United States via the Internet, CD-ROM, and more traditional print media. Thanks to the ongoing efforts of the library's skilled staff, U.S. and Estonian libraries and librarians remain in daily contact.

While U.S. library organizations have helped build their fair share of links across the Atlantic, Estonia's much closer Nordic neighbors have clearly become its most active library partners. Since independence, hardly a day has gone by without a direct connection between librarians in Estonia and their colleagues in Finland, Sweden, Denmark, and Norway. When ELNET chose USMARC as its standard, Finnish librarians were on hand to provide technical guidance. Between 1992 and 1995, Stockholm University Library sponsored a three-year library management development project to help library managers adapt to the brave, new world. The Danish Royal School of Librarianship along with its counterparts in Norway, Finland, and Sweden sponsored a series of workshops on such suddenly important topics as library marketing and public relations.

Dozens of other "training the trainer" programs have taken place throughout the Baltic region as Nordic librarians have done all they can to help Estonia join the information age. Estonian students are attending Nordic library schools while study tours going in both directions have become a regular occurrence. Direct and indirect grants from Nordic governments have helped fund special projects in several Estonian libraries and have subsidized Estonia's Internet connectivity. In the new global village, it helps to have good neighbors. It's even better when they are as generous with their time and money as Finland and Sweden have been.

In addition to all this Nordic library cooperation, Estonian librarians have been strengthening their connections closer to home. The three Baltic states of Estonia, Latvia, and Lithuania are often viewed as a single entity by people in the West. While this perceived unity often falls apart upon closer examination, librarianship in these countries shows a surprising amount of unanimity. Lithuanian, Latvian, and Estonian librarians worked together before World War II and they continued cooperating even during Soviet times when all contacts were supposed to go through Moscow. Every year staff members of the three Baltic national libraries get together for an annual workshop and exchange of information known as LiLaEst. Their colleagues at the academic libraries get together at yearly meetings known as Biliopolis. The library science faculty from Vilnius University in Lithuania, the Latvian University, and Tallinn Pedagogical University also meet on a regular basis. In 1996, the NLE hosted the Fifth Congress of Baltic Librarians. The Fourth Congress took place in Riga in 1991, fifty years after it was originally planned.[4]

While various pan-Baltic consortia like Biblioteca Baltica are at different stages of planning and development, Estonian librarians have been busy cooperating with their Lithuanian and Latvian colleagues through larger regional, European, and international organizations. Estonian libraries and librarians participate in almost thirty such organizations as either institutional or individual members. After five decades of isolation, Estonian libraries can now join their counterparts around the world to discuss common issues and resolve shared problems. The Estonian Academic Library is a member of the Consortium of European Research Libraries. Because it also functions as a parliamentary library, the NLE is a member of the International Association of Law Libraries. The Estonian Children's Library has joined the International Association of School Librarianship. Library science faculty of the Tallinn Pedagogical University are members of the European Association for Library and Information Education (EU-

CLID). From medical to music librarians, connections that were once impossible are now being made.

As Estonia rejoined the international community of nations, it once again became possible to acquire the official publications of foreign governments and international organizations. While the Library of Congress and the NLE began exchanging government documents as early as 1922, the procedure was not formalized until 1938 with the signing of a diplomatic note between the U.S. Department of State and the Estonian Foreign Ministry. While this agreement lay dormant during the fifty years of Soviet occupation, in 1991 the United States was the first country to revive its official exchange of documents with Estonia. When the Estonian Parliament ratified the 1958 UNESCO Convention "Concerning the Exchange of Official Publications and Government Documents between States" in 1993, the NLE began seeking out similar arrangements with other foreign countries. Since 1993, the NLE has also become the official Estonian depository for United Nations documents, European Community documents, as well as the documents of eight other international organizations.

Access to such information is crucial if Estonian legislators and government officials hope to reintegrate Estonia with the rest of the world. One key example of the importance of such exchanges is the opening in 1995 of the Council of Europe's Information and Documentation Center at the NLE (http://www.nlib.ee/ENDIK/). The information provided by this center, along with the depository set of European Community documents, is playing an important role in Estonia's bid to become a member of the European Union. Without these official publications and the librarians to service them, integration into Europe would be all the more difficult.

Estonia's impressive political and economic transition over the last few years has not been without its accompanying problems. Salaries for librarians remain extremely low and noncompetitive. As a result, many libraries are unable to keep qualified staff (especially foreign-language and computer specialists) as they can earn so much more money by working for the private sector. While the NLE, Tartu University Library, and some other Estonian libraries have tried to work around this problem by hiring university students part-time, this is not a long-term solution. Library budgets are also nowhere near as high as they should be. As a result, even libraries like the NLE have been forced to close their doors for the entire month of July the last few years to make ends meet.

In addition to these burdens of the present, Estonian librarians have had to live with several other burdens from the past. One of the major concerns these days of the Estonian Librarians Association (ELA) is that much of the library collections of Estonian libraries are of marginal use. Many of these books are in Russian and were acquired during the fifty years of Soviet rule. These titles were often "pre-selected" in Moscow for Estonian collections. Especially in such fields as politics, economics, and history, the outdated reality described in these books bears little relationship with Estonia's current situation. As many as 60 percent of the books in major research libraries fall into this category of being of questionable value. Because of this, collection development has become one of ELA's new priorities. While the major Estonian research libraries have already developed a cooperative collection development profile by assigning subject-area responsibilities to appropriate institutions, Estonian libraries simply lack the funds to replace or update as much as half of their existing collections.

Another legacy inherited from the Soviet past was a system for training new librarians that was not always adequate. Formal library education at the university level began in Tartu in 1927. By 1944, library science coursework was brought together under a Department of Bibliography. By 1954, the department had grown into the Faculty of

Librarianship. The program at Tartu was phased out in 1968 because library studies were transferred to the Tallinn Teacher Training Institute (now the Tallinn Pedagogical University) in 1965. Although Tartu graduated over 200 accredited librarians and Tallinn has produced over 1,300 to date, those who studied before 1988 were forced to follow a library education model dictated by Moscow and not always suitable to local Estonian conditions.[5]

In 1988, the Department of Information Studies faculty at Tallinn Pedagogical University (http://lin.tpu.ee) began overhauling their instructional program to move away from the Soviet model. Instead of the former rigid program of study that included such mandatory courses as "Scientific Communism" and "Marxist-Leninist Thought," Estonian students can now design their own program of study to focus on their special interests in library science, book science, or information science after completing a series of core courses. New classes in such cutting-edge areas as Internet librarianship have been added to the curriculum. To meet the needs of Estonian libraries, the thirteen full-time faculty members introduced an accredited master's degree program in 1991. Within the larger field of humanities, it is now possible to pursue a Ph.D. in librarianship for the first time in history. Estonian librarians no longer have to go to Moscow or St. Petersburg to study for their doctorates. By 1994, the study of library science had been completely revamped with the help of part-time instructors and other university departments. Several experiments with distance learning, outreach, and professional development courses taught directly at libraries are now underway.[6] The successful transformation of Estonian library science education is a hopeful sign that the other problems still facing Estonian libraries can be overcome as well. With up to fourteen applicants for each available slot, the Tallinn Pedagogical University now has the luxury to select Estonia's next generation of librarians.

Given all the tremendous hardships and handicaps they have faced over the years, Estonian librarians have managed to accomplish an incredible amount in the brief six-year period since independence. By encouraging the Estonian Parliament to pass laws regulating public libraries (1993), the National Library (1994), and a law on elementary and secondary school education which includes provisions for school libraries (1995), there is now a legislative basis for the future development of Estonian libraries. By reaching consensus on national bibliographic standards and on a single system for an online union catalog, the track ahead seems to have been laid out fairly straight. Perhaps it's time for each Estonian librarian to start turning their "I think I can's" into "I know I can's."

Notes

1. *Independence and Libraries: Papers of the 5th Congress of Baltic Librarians, October 21-22, 1996, Tallinn, Estonia* (Tallinn: National Library of Estonia, 1996), 209.

2. *Estonian Libraries* (Tallinn: National Library of Estonia, 1996), 35.

3. *Eesti Rahvusraamatukogu = National Library of Estonia* (Tallinn: National Library of Estonia, 1996), 14.

4. Eric A. Johnson, "Baltic Librarians Group Convenes—After a 50 Year Break," *Library of Congress Information Bulletin* 50, no. 19 (October 7, 1991): 377, 386-387.

5. Aira Lepik, "Librarians in Changing Estonia: Professional Education and Development," *Library Management* 16, no. 8: 27-32.

6. Sirje Virkus, "Distance Education as a New Possibility for Library and Information Science Education in Estonia" (pp. 249-254), in *Human Development: Competencies for the Twenty-First Century: Papers from the IFLA CPERT Third International Conference on Continuing Professional Education for the Library and Information Professions* (Munchen: K. G. Saur, 1997).

15. Romanian Libraries: Past, Present, and Future

Stephen R. Amery

Political and Historical Background

If improving the quality of Romanian librarians was all that was needed to modernize Romanian libraries, the problems would be insignificant and the job would be done in a day. Unfortunately, it is the image of Communism—especially the pale of Nicolae Ceausescu—that casts a long and dark shadow over the recent past. It is this history that determines much that needs to occur for the libraries of Romania to function productively to the standard to which all librarians aspire.

Historical perspective and context help paint a picture of the day-to-day circumstances in which Romanian librarians function. The major turning point during the Ceausescu years came in 1971, when Ceausescu returned from visits to North Korea and China. Impressed by the social engineering and cult of personality that personified the regimes of Kim Il Sung and Mao Zedong, and encouraged by his wife, he began a "cultural revolution" designed to eradicate any signs of undisciplined liberalism and individualism that might pose a threat to his party's monopoly on power.

Despite the cult of personality that Ceausescu created and regardless of an ever worsening human rights record, the West continued to "reward" the regime because of its open defiance of the Soviet Union. Western loans, combined with self-serving policies, led to huge foreign debt ($10,200m in 1981) that crippled the Romanian economy and remains a burden to this day.

Food rationing and restrictions on energy use increased throughout the eighties, while imports were reduced and exports of food and fuel increased in an attempt to meet targets. The result was severe financial and personal suffering wrought on the Romanian people.

Ceausescu's downfall was precipitated by the refusal of the Soviet Union, whom he had so diligently provoked and startled, to prop up his and other threatened Communist regimes. This refusal—combined with the familiar self-serving, back-slapping scene at the Party's Fourteenth Party Congress—proved to be his downfall. Sixty-seven standing ovations at the Congress and a pledge to continue with the uncompromising policies of years gone by were met by a populace who stood up not to praise Ceausescu, but in effect to bury him. In December, 1989 the "Christmas Revolution" began to take hold and on December 21 after being heckled at a rally in Bucharest, Ceausescu realized the precariousness of his position and attempted to flee. Captured and tried by military tribunal, Nicolae Ceausescu and his wife were executed on Christmas Day 1989. Romania's long national nightmare was over, or so the Romanian people thought.

The government that filled the political vacuum and assumed control was the government of the National Salvation Front. Its new president was Ceausescu's former deputy, Ion Iliescu. Therefore, despite the euphoria over Ceausescu's downfall, there was a suspicion amongst the Romanian people that the revolutionary upheaval of

Christmas 1989 was really a charade performed by anti-Ceausescu forces from within the Ceausescu government and that the new government was made up of disenchanted members of the party, army and securitate bureaucracies.

It was not until the elections of November 1996 that Romanians really broke free, dumped these vaguely reform minded ex-Communists, and elected their first free government, thus bringing to an end the revolution that had begun with the overthrow of Nicolae Ceausescu. It was the 1996 election of Emil Constantinescu that afforded Romanians the luxury of looking forward to a future freed from the shackles of central control for the first time in a generation. Citizens and politicians alike now have a golden opportunity to make up for decades of mismanagement and corruption, and move their country forward. It is the purpose of this article to define and describe the role these and past events have played in molding the state of Romanian libraries as well as describing what future is likely to materialize.

From a historical perspective the theme for Romanian libraries is one of peaks and valleys and missed opportunities. The future promises to be much the same. Adverse historical circumstances and governmental interference in the form of hindrance and apathy have served to create a litany of missed opportunities and failure. In general terms, as fast as a significant and plausible library infrastructure developed, an invasion, a war or an ideological movement squandered some, if not all, that had been achieved. While other significant socio-economic and cultural factors have played a role in the life of Romanian libraries, these are useful points of reference to have when thinking of the role of libraries in the life and history of Romania.

Year zero in Romanian library terms appears to have come and gone on a number of occasions. While many libraries have survived Romania's turbulent history, they have not been left unscathed. For the purposes of this discussion, these year zeros can be broken down into four distinct periods: Pre-Communist (pre-1948), Communist—especially the Ceausescu Years (1948-1989), the post-Ceausescu Years of the National Salvation Front (1989-1996) and the Constantinescu Years (1996- present). With regard to the state of Romanian libraries today, it is the shadow of the Communist Years that is felt most. The impact of this period in Romania's history on its libraries past, present and future cannot be underestimated.

For example, after the Communist takeover in 1948, libraries were turned into a propaganda tool as opposed to bastions of intellectual freedom and literary pleasure. Acquisitions from 1948-1989 were limited to books and journals extolling the virtues of official Communist ideologies. Strict censorship prevented access to politically sensitive publications.

Shortly after the end of the Ceausescu regime, Blaine Harden wrote an article in the *Washington Post* on Romanian libraries which clearly described not only the access problem, but served to illustrate the pitiful and deteriorating state of libraries in Romania at that time:

> The National Library stopped receiving hard currency for the purchase of foreign books 10 years ago. The Library's last edition of the major international chemistry journal, *Chemical Abstracts,* is 1972. At Romania's national library, "the knowledge lag is 10 to 15 years" behind what is available outside the country ... A government decree prevented libraries from owning a book published or written by Romanians living abroad. [It was made] difficult and risky for readers to get "sensitive" publications [such as] all books and periodicals dealing with Romanian politics, going back as far as the period between the two world wars ...To get access, application was made to the Cultural Council, a bureaucracy under securitate control and thus ensuring background personal checks would take place, etc. The best place to go was the American Cultural Center library, but as unreported

contact with foreigners was a crime this was not without risk; also university teachers were not allowed to go to embassy libraries. However, they often sent cleaning ladies or grandmothers to check out the necessary books and despite the risk the USIS Bucharest Library averaged 15,000 Romanians per month.[1]

Given such turmoil, it is of little surprise that Romanian libraries today have yet to emerge from the forbidding shadow cast by the pale of Communism. The journey toward a modern, cohesive library system will be a difficult one, but one rich in opportunity. It will mirror historical as well as modern experiences. Hopefully, it will be the final journey marking an arrival at a point of completion rather than an arrival at yet another starting point—as has so often been the case in the past.

The Past

The early history of Romanian libraries followed a pattern similar to that of libraries elsewhere in Europe. In the fourteenth century, monastery libraries flourished, as did those of princely courts within the Romanian territories. While invasions and war took their toll, it was during the sixteenth, seventeenth and eighteenth centuries that important monastery, court, school and private collections developed. This development was fueled by the emergence of printing as an important cultural and political reality.[2] When printed materials began to circulate widely at this time, the need for and consequent foundation of a library system came to fruition.

The founding of the Romanian state in 1859, combined with the accelerated economic, educational and social development of the nineteenth century, coincided with an increase in the need for knowledge and a library infrastructure in Romania. It was during this time that a network of public and academic libraries began to develop.

However, in terms of the creation and development of a national library infrastructure, it is the foundation of the Library of the Romanian Academy in 1867 and the Central State Library in 1955 that is most significant in the course of librarianship in Romania.[3] Both libraries enjoy roles as a legal depository library. The former supports academic and scholarly research with a retrospective focus, while the latter focuses on current materials. As such, access to the Library of the Romanian Academy is restricted to researchers, while access to the Central State Library is general and free.

Founded in 1867, the Library of the Romanian Academy owed much of its initial development to private donations and its legal depository privileges (established in 1885). Its current collection exceeds nine million volumes. It has responsibility for acquiring, preserving and organizing resources needed to support academic and scholarly research and as such, access is restricted to researchers. The academy is responsible for publication of retrospective national bibliographies of monographs and periodicals from the sixteenth century. It has also developed an active exchange and publications program, with publications issued by the Publishing House of the Academy sent to about ten thousand exchange partners in more than one hundred countries. Branch libraries function in major Romanian cities, such as Cluj.

Until 1948 the collection of the academy was focused on the humanities and social sciences, but reorganization at this time initiated the start of a collection of scientific and technical literature. Holdings, now numbering around ten million, include additional stock of manuscripts, rare books, engravings, letters and archives of important personalities.

The National Library of Romania located in Bucharest was founded in 1955 as the

Central State Library (renamed the National Library of Romania in 1990). It has the right of central legal deposit and compiles and publishes the current *National Bibliography*. It offers centralized cataloging, makes up the national union catalog on cards for distribution, and publishes directories and union catalogs of foreign books and serials. In 1993, personal computers were established in the National Library, making automation of bibliographic and cataloging activities at least feasible. The format in use is the CDS/ISIS for monographs.

The National Library is also the national center for gifts and exchanges, and of all the libraries in Romania, it is the only one that has the ability to provide automated systems compatible with foreign systems. Access is general and free. The collections are encyclopedic in character and currently total more than fifteen million volumes. The collection has a nucleus of documentation in librarianship and is a center of methodological guidance for public libraries. It also houses an agency for international exchange of publications and manages international interlibrary loans. It has several reading rooms specializing in various fields of knowledge and categories of publications and media (such as manuscripts and letters, maps, loose sheets and newspapers). Also, housed within its walls is a department for official publications and offices for UNESCO publications and publications of other international bodies. Educational activities include exhibitions, meetings with writers and scholars, musical programs and other events.

Architecturally, Romanians pride themselves on their Roman Empire heritage and have sought to maintain this continuity with the past when it comes to the construction of many of their buildings. The result is buildings that appear at first glance to have been built in the nineteenth century, but in fact turn out to be relics of the 1930s and 1940s. Consequently, both the National Library and many other libraries are housed in ornate buildings pleasing to the eye, but not necessarily suited to the more technical needs of modern librarianship.

Structure

The National Library and the Library of the National Academy are the only libraries in Romania recognized as national in scope. Figures for academic libraries, public libraries, school libraries and a number of special libraries are reproduced in Table 1.

Universal Decimal Classification (UDC) and ISBD standards are used in Romanian libraries. Copyright registration, while centralized at the National Library, is a nonexistent factor in Romania as far as recognition of its significance is concerned. Interlibrary lending exists, but it is essentially an internal phenomenon as international loan requests have to be put through the National Library in Bucharest and the bureaucracy of the procedures makes the service too cumbersome to be used on a regular basis by libraries in the country.

Large libraries traditionally maintain closed stacks and allow only a fixed number of books to be requested at any one time. Copying services are limited; in fact, no Romanian library has self-service photocopying. Automated information retrieval systems are very limited, provided in general terms via the generosity of international benefactors such as the Soros Foundation rather than via a particularly strong commitment on the part of the Romanian government.

The most significant academic libraries are the Central University Library in Iasi, founded in 1841; the Cluj Central University Library, founded in 1872; and the Central

TABLE 1
Libraries in Romania 1990

Type of Library	No. of Libraries	Total Staff	Pop. Served	Volumes
National	2 (2)	570	500,000*	15,820,000*
Academic	44 (43)	2,850	1,500,000*	23,100,000*
Public	6,900** (7,181)	3,200*	7,300,000*	72,200,000*
School	10,987 (10,984)	2,100	13,800,000*	61,000,000*
Special	2,908 (3,158)	3,206*	3,600,000*	2,192,000*
TOTAL	20,841 (21,368)	11,926	26,700,000*[4]	174,312,000

* estimate

**library supported by the public authorities only

Source : *Anuarul statistic al Romaniei 1990*. Figures in parentheses are 1987 figures from
Gheorge-Losif Bercan and Doina Banciu, "An overview of the information network in
Romania," *FID News Bulletin* 40 (10) Oct. 1990, 137-138.

University Library in Bucharest, founded in 1895. Academic libraries report to the Ministry of Education and Science and serve the communities of their individual campuses. The Central University Library in Bucharest acquires domestic books and periodicals for libraries in the academic community network and maintains holdings for the departments of Romanian language, literature, and civilization created abroad.

While the collections of the "big three" academic libraries number more than ten million volumes, there are another forty or more academic libraries with collections averaging around one million. These libraries cover a variety of topics including agriculture, medicine and technical sciences. They have unique responsibilities, for not only do they have to meet the requirements of the educational and research needs of the institution they serve, but they also must fulfill the requirements of study and documentation for the specialists on the university campuses.

Public libraries in Romania are disparate and somewhat disorganized. They are located at the county, city, town and village level, and vary greatly in size, scope and importance, depending upon where they are located and the individual communities they serve. For example, rural areas have few if any library services, while urban centers such as those in Craiova or Sibiu house valuable cultural collections. Libraries at the county level create local bibliographies and provide guidance to other public libraries. While there is little evidence of coordination between the counties, within the counties a semblance of organization does exist. Departmental libraries coordinate the work of the public libraries in each administrative department. Guidance is provided to the various public libraries through, for example, provision of mobile lending centers and development of special sections for children. If this county-level organization were duplicated on a national scale, a huge step could be taken in the progress of librarianship in Romania.

School libraries are sponsored by local educational bodies or by equivalent ministries in the case of technical and vocational schools. Central guidance is available from the Ministry of Education and Science and the Central Pedagogical Library in Bucharest when needed. A useful service in those areas where public libraries are either inadequate or not readily available is the additional provision of adult library materials.

The organization and situation of special libraries are a microcosm of the broader picture of the haphazard structure and organization of libraries throughout Romania. Special libraries form an ill-defined category not encompassed by the academic, public or school networks outlined above. Like special libraries the world over, their collections reflect the character and needs of the community they serve. Many of them can be classed as those libraries run independently of governmental control by international organizations such as the Freedom Forum Library and the Libraries of the Soros Foundation. Domestic examples of special libraries include the Library of the National Institute for Information and Documentation, libraries of research institutes, institutes of higher education, academies, scientific and cultural associations and institutions.

National Library Policy

Ultimately, it is the policy and attitude of the ruling government that molds a nation's library infrastructure and is the final arbiter of its role. Romania is no different, especially when talking of the Communist era of 1948-1989.

In 1970, Ceausescu thrashed out a deal with East Germany for universities to be supplied with books. It was the last such deal. Romanian libraries acquired no new foreign literature for the remaining years of his regime. As a result, libraries could collect and disseminate only information that was either out-of-date or that pandered to the whims of Ceausescu's political ideology.

The unpopularity of the collections—developed as a result of these policies—was demonstrated by the scenes in the National Library and in the History Faculty library at the Central University of Bucharest following the overthrow of the Ceausescu regime. Both examples paint a stark picture of the neglect and the opportunities missed during this period of the history of Romania's libraries:

> The English, Russian, French, German, Italian and Romanian versions of Nicolae Ceausescu's monumental 32-volume opus, entitled *"On the Way of Building Up the Multilaterally Developed Socialist Society*," were themselves on their way ... from the National Library to a recycling plant where they will be boiled into pulp. They will be recycled into paper on which will be printed something that Romanians might be interested in reading, according to Angela Sopescu- Bradiceni, director of the library. When asked ... if anyone had ever come into the library and asked to read anything in the Ceausescu Collection, the director of book acquisitions, Spinu Virgil, replied with one word: "Never."[5]

New political considerations following Ceausescu's demise have also taken a toll, as demonstrated by the situation at the History Faculty library of the Central University of Bucharest. It now contains large gaps in its collections—gaps caused by the removal of multiple copies of Ceausescu's works and the disposal of the many Marxist publications that made up its book stock during the Ceausescu years.

Librarians Today

At the outset of this paper the consensus view concerning the quality of librarians in Romania was stated: if improving the quality of Romanian librarians was all that was needed to modernize Romanian libraries, the problems would be insignificant and the job would be done in a day. To further emphasize this viewpoint, given the perspective of historical and political background thus far portrayed, it can now be stated that the future of Romanian libraries is primarily in the hands of those librarians. It is librarians who share the necessary work skills and the enthusiasm for a vision of a cohesive modern library system who must make their voices heard.

While the need for cohesiveness is the reality, the prevailing Romanian attitude is often one of self-interest. "Cooperation" is a difficult word in Romania, for the legacy of Ceausescu is distrust, jealousy and self-preservation. Libraries and librarians are all competing with each other as old suspicions abound. Working together in harmony, while a necessary long-term goal, appears to be anything but a short-term target. Consequently, it is this lack of a broad consensus within the profession that has precipitated the failure of Romanian librarians as a community to create the solid national infrastructure necessary for their future development and survival. Collective unified cooperation would provide the consensus to enable the profession to overcome the many problems it currently faces.

Working hours and attitudes are a major hindrance to progress. Under Ceausescu, everyone had a job and consequently the work culture was, "we pretend to work while they pretend to pay us." The adjustment away from this attitude has proved to be difficult, especially given the reality of economic conditions that prove a barrier to incentive. Working hours are 8:00 A.M.- 4:00 P.M., but often other chores such as shopping can significantly dent such hours. Inflation is high, wages remain low. Not only is everyone paid the same, but salaries are listed for all to see—diminishing the incentive to excel lest the new salary level be posted, precipitating petty jealousy amongst fellow workers. Jealousy is further perpetuated between young and old, for the young expect enthusiasm to count, while the old think seniority should count.

This picture of self-interest, while an accurate and valid one, does not necessarily translate to a total breakdown of librarianship within the country. As the structure of libraries in Romania bears testament, a degree of national planning and accountability within the library infrastructure certainly does exist. Compounding the basic problems faced by librarians is the reality of day-to-day life within the state of Romania, for it is this reality that makes for a profession preoccupied with having to fight countless daily battles to simply stay functional. As such, the profession is moving forward at a painfully slow pace, at worst it is standing still unable to move forward in the way it would like despite its best and most concerted efforts.

Culturally, Romanians' hospitality to foreign visitors is effusive and they tend to accept and give thanks for everything. The result is out-of-date textbooks discarded from Western shelves and old computers and machinery deemed unacceptable in the West placed in Romanian libraries.

Many libraries talk about automation when they hold one personal computer, often accepting the first offer from the first vendor who comes along, with little consideration given to customer support needs and maintenance costs. Often, the necessary training is rare and computer service departments are unfamiliar with the vagaries and needs of library-related software. The local result is equipment that soon becomes redundant as the cost of the equipment leaves no room in the budget to purchase necessary accessories, paper, toner, maintenance, upgrades etc. The broader consequence is a country littered with idle equipment such as laser printers and photocopy machines and a library profession functioning through manual means with typewriters and handwritten card catalogs. Book stock, funding and technology issues loom large for present and future Romanian libraries.

Issues for the Present and the Future: Technology

The technology most obviously missing from the Romanian library landscape is the computer.[6] It is actually both remarkable and instructive as to the skill level of Romanian librarians to see how a relatively developed and sophisticated culture has coped without the equipment that many libraries in the Western world regard as central to their existence. However, it is also obvious that to move toward and become an integral part of the electronic information revolution, Romania needs to get up to speed with modern-day electronic technologies.

As recently as the mid-1990s information access in Romania consisted of one analogue cellular system in Bucharest and eleven Inmarsat sites run by large national enterprises or by major Western companies for their own private networks, with only ten thousand international telephone lines for the whole country. Internet access was limited. Bucharest University and the Romanian Computer Network for Education and Research, for example, have access to the Internet through a terrestrial leased line.

Funding appears to be the preeminent problem, for given the vast economic problems faced by Romania, funding for the future in the form of a telecommunications network is not compelling enough to gain support from a people and a culture that have more pressing day-to-day concerns. Personal computers are at the end of the fantasy list that backs through photocopiers, microform readers, and electronic typewriters to manual typewriters, photocopying stationery and even typewriting ribbons.

Consequently, the problem of bringing technology up to speed in Romania falls into the lap of international organizations such as Soros and the Freedom Forum and companies such as Microsoft, Sun Microsystems, 3Com and USRobotics. It is through their generosity and sponsorship that the chance for a technological breakthrough for Romanian libraries lies.

The following portrait of a typical technological experience in the Freedom Forum Library at the Center for Independent Journalism in Bucharest is taken from 1996 and illustrates the obstacles faced and the problems that need to be overcome:

> Baud rate for e-mail and for Netscape [in the library] ... is *very* slow. Typing the briefest of e-mail messages takes a long time, lengthy time lapses between each character are the norm rather than the exception. When using Netscape, patience is the key, graphics and images can take 6-10 minutes to load onto the screen.[7]

It seems feasible that the best way for Romanians to receive information at this time is via CD-ROM products, as this would bypass the immediate problem of poor telecommunications. This assumes that there exists the commitment toward the maintenance and upkeep of the equipment required to run CD-ROM technology, and this commitment is neither guaranteed nor widely available.

The lack of technical means in libraries and information centers has meant that no online automated information network has been set up. In effect, a Local Area Network (LAN) in Romanian terms might be a single personal computer hook-up in one room of any given library with no concept of an outside link or a Wide Area Network (WAN). This results in information and documentation activity being carried out under conditions that are difficult and lead to isolation.

Steps toward future technological breakthroughs are slow and at times painful—a forward step is often accompanied by a larger step back. Recent events illustrate this point.

Steps forward have been taken by Carrier Systems—the 3Com/USRobotics business unit, Sun Microsystems and Microsoft. In the summer of 1997, Carrier Systems announced the launch of new technologies in Romania. The company's X2 technology doubled the access speed of the Internet using digital lines and exchanges as opposed to old copper wire technology. ASDL technology that improves the speed of local data transfer by 100 times and—most importantly for Romanian users—functions using the old analogue lines and switchings currently available is now being tested in Romania. With Internet use exploding and the number of connected users increasing at a rate of almost 200 percent a year, such news is a most promising development.

In March of 1996 Sun Microsystems announced a strategic cooperation agreement with the Romanian commission responsible for computer-related activities. In December 1996 Microsoft Romania officially opened. Most significantly, along with eleven other companies, they formed the Romanian branch of the Business Software Alliance, a global watchdog group. This is a development that bodes well for a country rife with computer piracy, copyright infringement and a plethora of poor quality computer software.

Such steps forward are somewhat muted by the direction of the steps taken in regard to the Mateias case, a case illustrative of the prevailing computer culture in Romania. Calin Mateias is a teenage computer hacker who allegedly destroyed public information files and erased free-access hard disks in NASA's computer database because "it was easy." NASA has issued no statement regarding his claims, nor have the Western media covered his alleged "feats." Yet his "feats," which required no particular genius, were cause for the Romanian media to proclaim him as a young computer genius and evidence of Romania's advancement in this field.

The truth is somewhat different. Romania is a country that currently has a low level of computer literacy, and where personal computers are considered by many to be little more than mysterious high-tech gaming devices. What the adventures of Mr. Mateias illustrate is how little accountability there is in the Romanian justice system for this type of crime. He will not be brought to justice for his "feats," as Romania currently does not have any law against computer crimes. The need for a change in the law appears to be an obvious one. His adventures highlight the fact that the Romanian culture has little knowledge of, nor respect for, common computer norms. Exemplifying this further is the level of computer piracy. In 1995, for instance, the local software industry lost around $20 million in revenue due to piracy. The formation of the Business Software Alliance bodes well for the future. Rather than punishing perpetrators of this type of crime, the Alliance seeks to educate them and the average Romanian end user that software piracy is a form of theft.

The first technology requirement, therefore, is an up-to-date modern computer-savvy populace, educated in the norms and practices of their more technologically advanced international counterparts. Once this cultural shift has begun to take place, the issues of equipment, its maintenance and its resulting informational benefits should fall slowly but gradually into place.

Issues for the Present and the Future: Books

The most tangible precedent concerning the book stock in Romania is its quality. Recent publications have been reproduced on paper of such poor quality that the life expectancy for any domestically produced publication is minimal. Such is the scale of book quality deterioration that hardbacks have been unavailable since the beginning of the eighties. Ironically, the books that have survived did so in a rather unusual way, benefiting from the policies of dictatorship and megalomania under Ceausescu. It appears that the preservation of books in some locations benefited from the decree that heating levels must be kept at no more than 8° C and that shops and offices must not be heated at all. Librarians worked under these conditions, wearing multiple layers of clothing including hats and overcoats. It is an irony that this minimalist heating policy was ideal for the preservation of Romanian book stock.

The lack of new foreign literature in Romanian libraries resulting from the policies of the Ceausescu regime meant that research libraries had no choice but to collect and disseminate out-of-date information. For example, the scientific and technical literature that doctors were using was so antiquated that they had no knowledge of how to use many of the modern medical supplies arriving via Western aid. As such, there is a pressing need for many reference and science publications. Generous foreign aid programs, such as the American Library Association Books for Romania Project and the Scottish Books for Romania Appeal, have provided some short-term relief. More work is needed.

A note of caution ought to be voiced here. Although Western aid through such programs is both necessary and warranted, there is no need for book stock that is no longer of use on Western shelves. This only causes Romanian libraries, already struggling under the weight of a decades'-long knowledge gap, to further stagnate. The requirement is for up-to-date literature of the type that will allow Romanian libraries to catch up and move forward into the next century.

While the Western world wrestles with the dilemma of electronic-versus-print access to information, Romania is not quite so *lucky*. There, books are still the stock-in-trade of libraries. The publishing industry and book trade, however, have limited knowledge and experience in the art of commercial publishing. Their printing technology is antiquated. The failure of the publishing industry to manage these dual problems has had a significant impact on the library profession and hence the relationship between the two entities. For instance, the printing technology problem makes for printed materials produced on poor quality paper, making preservation of materials difficult and longevity measured in years rather than decades.

In 1971, 5,000 books were published; by 1989 the total had fallen to 1,000. After 1989 there was an increase in the number of publishing houses. In 1994 the number was 2,300. This editorial boom—in terms of number of publishers and number of printed books—has created several problems for libraries. The main problems stemmed from publishers' ignorance regarding the elementary rules of data presentation of books (unspecified publisher, author or author of translation etc.). The fact that new publishers were unaware of the existence of a legal deposit along with general derailment of the book trade led to a situation in which the National Library of Romania no longer had control over the national editorial production of these years. This affected its own collections and the contents of the *National Bibliography*.

This "literary anarchy" led the National Library to consider the implementation of CIP (Cataloguing-in-Publication). The project in itself was both difficult—in view of publishers' opposition to anything that might seem to them as interference—and ambitious, in terms of how such a program might be achieved at a national level. Essentially publishers new to the trade did not know, or care to know, elementary rules such as those concerning copyright or the established arrangement of data on a title page. As publishers, their main concerns were managerial and financial; the high cost of paper, increased demand for printers' services, lack of modern printing equipment, non-existence of a distribution system for publications, etc. The last thing on their minds was to consider the implications of their growth on the library community. In effect, their rejection and lack of consideration for a CIP program stemmed simply from their ignorance of the practical use of such a program.

The major condition, even on the behalf of those publishers willing to embrace the program, was that someone from the National Library should come to the publisher to fill out the CIP forms as necessary, as the publishers did not have the human resources to do it. Of course, neither does the National Library. So a stalemate was reached.

A modicum of progress is being made, and in the slow ride that is progress in Romanian librarianship right now, this progress must be deemed both significant and noteworthy. An ISBN agency has been established, as has an Association of Private Publishers. Between these two entities, it is hoped that some kind of cooperation between librarians and publishers can be developed. Other helping factors would be the diminishing demand for books on the open market due to higher prices, and the publishers becoming aware of libraries as consistent buyers. This development is slowly affording the libraries a degree of bibliographic control and establishing them as a captive market not only for publishers, but for the public at large—for it seems that in recent years, a significant cultural shift has taken place in Romania's literary habits. Under Ceausescu, the TV and press were basically Ceausescu, his speeches and his propaganda, leading people to turn to live arts and reading for entertainment. Now, with open access to more newspapers, TV channels and radio stations, a shift in social behavior has occurred and people are exploring avenues of cultural entertainment other than those available in libraries.

Legislation

Legislation for libraries in Romania appears to be practically nonexistent. Following the overthrow of Ceausescu and the blossoming freedoms that resulted, it appears that, initially at least, anything that might be construed to be control, censorship or centralization was opposed.

For Ceausescu, legislation for library and information services was quite simply a means of extending the cult of his personality. While not totally prohibited, the opportunities to benefit through foreign contact from worldwide developments were severely limited by an absence of foreign currency and the official policy which discouraged exchanges of personnel and ideas.

Under the government of the National Salvation Front, control remained the key, for the policy of control of library purchasing continued. In many cases this succeeded and has resulted in incomplete periodical runs and little or no foreign book acquisition throughout Romanian libraries.

Of additional significance has been the replacement of library personnel left over from the Ceausescu regime, especially replacement of those who overzealously performed within it. Consequently, the removal of the more experienced but tainted senior librarians and their replacement with less experienced substitutes has resulted in the somewhat chaotic picture that is drawn of current-day librarianship in Romania, mirrored by a government policy facade that has never been clearly defined. It remains to be seen what effect the Constantinescu government will have and whether the replacement of the National Librarian will be a step forward or back for the future direction of Romanian librarianship.

What is necessary and of importance to libraries and their future role in contemporary Romanian society is a clear definition of that role. It would appear that it is necessary to publish a definitive policy statement on Romanian libraries, promote and adopt legislation for Romanian libraries, adopt a statute for librarians, construct and put into action a national program for the building of libraries, plan for the automation of the national library system, and help the professional organization of librarians. For the immediate future, this kind of commitment is far back in the consciousness of Romanian political life.

Summary

Romanian librarianship is a profession made up of talented, hardworking staff who work as isolated pieces of an undefined and all too elusive whole. It is more local touch, less national reach. Symbolic of the lack of cohesiveness is the absence of a national library association. While numerous thriving library associations dedicated to certain facets of the library community, such as public librarians and school librarians, have been established, no national association has been formed.

What is needed in Romania is a cohesiveness that will form these disparate pieces into some kind of single coordinated entity. In so doing, many of the significant problems that the profession faces will be solved by a spirit of cooperation. Such a spirit could realize great savings, for while library budgets and funding are sparse, the expense of forming such a bond will facilitate the kind of communication that is needed but is sadly lacking in current-day Romania. Romanian librarians are professionals working very hard with limited resources to maintain the highest level of service possible. It is probably their greatest achievement that despite the often overwhelming obstacles in their paths, they have still managed to provide service at such admirably high levels. This service could be made even more efficient, if they had a network in which to share ideas and resources.

Goals and needs for the future should include:

- expansion of collections, to make up for previous shortfalls and to bring present day collections up-to-date;
- automation of services, not only to make use of modern day technologies, but also to provide broader networking capabilities both domestically and internationally;
- operational procedures putting internationally recognized methods and techniques in place, to create a greater level of participation and increased feeling of belonging for Romanian librarians with their international counterparts; and
- organization of new activities such as staff training, not locally but nationally to facilitate cohesion and the development of the national library picture that appears most vital for future prospects.

These priorities and goals are many, and given national budgetary constraints and priorities, it would seem that achievement of all of them is a long- rather than a short-term prospect. In sum, automation, replenishment and greater control over the national book stock and greater library community cooperation are the most immediate necessities.

To achieve these priorities and goals, the following commitments are necessary:

- investment in new specialized information centers;
- creation of a modern telecommunications network to facilitate networking between libraries and access to international information sources;
- commitment to equip libraries with modern computers and software, and the means and education to manage and maintain the equipment;

- training efforts to focus more on the present and future and less on the past, supported by the necessary tools through domestic or international sponsorship or both;
- attention to formulating an efficient information and documentation system on a national as opposed to a local scale; and
- development of a system that is neither controlling nor centralized, but is cooperative and beneficial to participants.

The watchword for Romanian librarians should be *cooperation*, especially cooperation amongst themselves. Through cooperation they will be able to share knowledge, share skills and exchange materials in a way that will be beneficial to all and assist the libraries of Romania in moving forward into the next century.

Notes

1. B. Harden, "Romanian Library Topples Ceausescu's Literary Monuments," *Washington Post*, 28 December 1989, sec. A, p. 26.
2. The first book printed in Romania came off the press in 1508.
3. It became known as the National Library of Romania in 1990.
4. The official source for library statistics in Romania is *Anuarul statistic al Romaniei*. It is at best unreliable, at worst not to be trusted. This statistic is a case in point. For libraries to have an estimated population served of 26,700,000 in a country with a population of 22,755,260 is quite an achievement.
5. Harden, p. 26.
6. For example, of 46 libraries listed in the *Libraries and Environmental Information Centers in Central Eastern Europe: A Locator/Directory*, twenty list no automation, while at least half of the remaining twenty-six list either one PC or state that they are simply looking into automation or planning to introduce it.
7. Barbara Semonche, *The Freedom Forum Library*, available from http://sunsite.unc.edu/journalism/freeforumrom.html

References

Banciu, D., M. Bora, and G. Clinca. "Plan director pentru informatizarea bibliotecilor din Romania. Proiect." Guidelines for the use of information technology in Rumanian libraries. A project. *Probleme de Informare si Documentare* 29, 2-3 (1995): 99-116.

Bercan, Gheorge-Losif, and Doina Banciu. "An Overview of the Information Network in Romania." *FID News Bulletin* 40, 10 (1990): 137-138.

Capalneanu, A. M. "Romanian and European Priorities for a Library Integration." British Library, Research and Development Department. *BLRD Report* (1996): 62-66.

Casale, M. "Focus on CIS and Eastern Europe: Appetite for World Information." *Information World Review* 86 (1993): 27.

Clinica, G. "The Functioning of CIP." *IFLA Journal* 20 (1994): 478-487.

Davies, Gill, and Simon Prosser. "Who Will Help Romania?" *Bookseller* (1991): 594-595.

Dragan, M. "American Libraries: Impressions of a Romanian Librarian." *Library Times International* 11, 4 (1995): 45-46.

Guiccione, M. "One Year in Romanian Libraries." *Focus on International & Comparative Librarianship* 26, 1 (1995): 2831.

Harden, B. "Romanian Library Topples Ceausescu's Literary Monuments." *Washington Post*, 28 December 1989.

Johnson, I. "Librarianship and Professional Education in Romania." *Focus on International & Comparative Librarianship*. 24, 2 (1993): 70-74.

Mowat, I. R. M. "Eastern European Libraries: The Worst and Best of Times." In *Bowker Annual*. 38th edition. 1993.

Mowat, I. R. M. "Romanian Library Development : Past, Future and Future." *Library Review* 39, 4: 41-45.

Popa, Opritsa A. "Romania." In *Encyclopedia of Library History,* ed. Wayne Wiegand and Donald G. Davis (New York: Garland, 1994), 553-554.

Prodan, V. "A New Component of the Romanian Information Society: Romanian Society of Information and Documentation." *Probleme de Informare si Documentare* 29, 4 (1995): 236.

Roberts, R. "Eastern Europe's Libraries: Emerging from Isolation." In *Bowker Annual*. 37th edition. 1992.

Stoica, I. "State and Prospects of the University Libraries of Romania." *New Library World,* 96 (1995): 17-22.

Stoica, I. "Problems in the Management of University Education in the Field of Librarianship and Information Science in Romania." *Librarian Career Development* 3, 2 (1995): 17-21.

Stoica, I. "Another Future for the Romanian Libraries." *New Library World,* 95 (1994): 25-27.

Wood-Lamont, S., and I. Robu. "Cluj Medical Library Project: A Model for Romanian Library Automation." *Focus on International and Comparative Librarianship* 24, 3 (1993): 29-37.

Wood, S. "Books for Romania: The Scottish Appeal." *Library Association Record* 92, 2 (1990): 917-919.

"Libraries in Eastern Europe" (pp. 122-128), from D. C. Hausrath. "USIA Bureau of Educational & Cultural Affairs: The Eastern European Challenge." In *Bowker Annual* 1990-1991. 35th edition.

Webliography

"Library—National Foundation Library Programme: Library of the Soros Foundation—Timisoara." available from http://www.sfos.ro/info/progs/96/old/library.html

Semonche, Barbara. "*Dateline Bucharest.*" available from http://sunsite.unc.edu/journalism/buchr.html

E-Mails

E-mails were sent to the following people and organizations, and, while replies were not forthcoming at the time of writing, their help and assistance are gratefully acknowledged.

Barbara P. Semonche, Library Director: UNC-CH School of Journalism and Mass Communication. e-mail: semonch@gibbs.oit.unc.edu

Freedom Forum: e-mail: news@freedomforum.org

Hermina G. B. Anghelescu: Graduate School of Library and Information Science, Austin, TX 78712-1276. e-mail: Hermina@fiat.gslis.utexas.edu.

Jill Martin—International coordinator: The Library Association, 7, Ridgemount Street, London, WC1E 7AE. e-mail: ic@la-hq.org.uk.

Tiberiu Cazacioc: Bucharest Center for Independent Journalism. e-mail: library@cji.centind.ro.

In addition, the help of the staff at the BBC World Service Library, London, and the Christian Science Monitor Library, Boston, is gratefully acknowledged.

16. Genesis of a Library in the Czech Republic: From the Broom Closet to the Book Stacks

Norma J. Hervey

Summer of 1997 brought devastating floods to Central Europe resulting in two hundred deaths and billions of dollars of destruction to personal, public, and business properties in the Czech Republic and other nations. The convergence of three rivers, the Morava, the Oskava and the Bystrice, north of the city of Olomouc in Moravia resulted in damages far beyond my one experience with floods, that of the Allegany River in Upstate New York in 1972.[1] Dr. Karel Konecny, Fulbright scholar, 1997/98 at Luther College, brought a film which eloquently displays the boiling flood waters destroying villages, homes and farms, then racing through the narrow twisting streets of Olomouc, a center of trade and population since the Roman Imperial era, reaching heights of fifty feet which covered the Roman walls upon which medieval fortifications were constructed.[2]

Several viewings of this movie of my second home left me in a state of shocked disbelief: could the park through which I walked to Palackeho University on a daily basis in 1994/95, the city walls which awed me since first seeing them in 1992, the Morava, a slow quiet stream, which winds its way past the university and through the north side of the centrum of Olomouc and serves as a home to countless ducks and other small waterfowl—could any of these familiar places be connected to the devastation represented in the film? Former students and friends shared stories and pictures of their personal losses and the challenges of rebuilding homes, businesses, university buildings. One student from Ostrava, an industrial city hard hit by the flood waters, honored her summer teaching commitment to the Concordia College Language Village due to her good fortune in getting the last seat on the last plane from Ostrava to the international airport in Prague on July 9. An e-mail from Dr. Konecny about the same time stated, "I would take my family to my parents' home if we were able to escape Olomouc." Natural forces had constructed a wall which temporarily divided much of the Czech Republic including Olomouc and Palackeho University, home to the new library upon which this story is based, from the rest of the nation.

The primary intent of this essay is to salute Dr. Josef Jarab and his colleagues at Palackeho University whose visions and leadership achieved one of the miracles of the 1989 Velvet Revolution in Czechoslovakia. They stabilized the university founded by Jesuits in 1573 in a time of financial and community challenges and were successful in reviving faculties removed during the Soviet era. They have now built the first library, celebrating more than four hundred years of a university's history by providing resources available to students and faculty in a modernized building of the eighteenth century. Before beginning that story, a brief history of the Olomouc region and the path which led this librarian/historian from Iowa to the Palackeho University classroom are provided.

The Olomouc Region

Archaeologists trace early man in this region from 80,000 to 10,000 B.C. Regional caves sheltered the remains of Cro-Magnum people and their Aurignacian bone tools. The area shows continuous populations from that time; these stabilized in the Iron Age, beginning in 400 B.C. when Celts colonized the area. The Romans took over about 100 A.D. One local myth describes Julius Caesar addressing his legion near the Town Hall in Upper Square, built in 1378, where today a fountain replica of Caesar on horseback rears up over the very worn cobblestones. Cobblestones are systematically replaced, in streets annually and in the squares as needed, but those surrounding the fountain remain as they were, supporting the myth of Caesar's presence.

Germanic tribes arrived at the end of the Roman period, followed by Slavs in the fifth century. The Slavonic population slowly and peacefully assimilated with the Celts. They fortified Olomouc which would be a primary military base from then until now. Olomouc and its surrounding regions were flourishing feudal estates throughout the era of the Great Moravian Empire. Olomouc, with its strategic location on the rivers, served as a center for defense, commerce, and administrative and ecclesiastical offices which allowed the city to continue to flourish even after the fall of the Empire in the tenth century. From that period until the assassination of the last Premyslid king, Wenceslaus III in 1306, Olomouc was an important center.[3]

Charles IV, elected Holy Roman Emperor in 1355, focused his remarkable energy and intellect on development of his mother's homelands, Moravia and Bohemia. The Golden City of Prague especially mirrors his leadership, an era which ended after his death in the religious wars which began when priest reformer Jan Hus was burned for heresies in 1415. Olomouc, home of the archbishop, strongly supported the Catholic Church and was an early center of anti-Hussite factions. Power shifted between the fifteenth and seventeenth centuries as the wars involved not only religious reformers and the Catholic Church, but the many ethnic groups of central Europe. George of Podebrady, Czech king and moderate Hussite, defeated the Hungarian King Mathias Curviser, bringing a brief period of peace as a result of the Czech victory noted in the Peace of Olomouc in 1478. During the 30-years war which followed, the area was occupied by Polish troops in support of the Austrian emperor, then Swedes who occupied the region from 1642 until 1650. During the latter time, Olomouc suffered physical devastation and loss of population; the royal tribunal and Moravian land records were moved to Brno.

In the eighteenth century, Olomouc was once again primarily a fortress which served the Austrian monarchs. Empress Maria Theresa built an armory there between the Archbishop's palace and the Philosophical Faculty of the University, which is now the university library. When the 30-years war ended, Olomouc once again became the center of Catholicism in Moravia. It also continued to serve as a fortress which led to the early industrialization of the region outside the city walls. The fortress itself housed many unwilling prisoners including the Marquis de Lafayette, considered by Joseph II to be a dangerous revolutionary, and other anti-feudal leaders and revolutionaries from Central Europe. The Olomouc fortress was the headquarters of Tsar Nicholas I during the Napoleonic wars. The Austerlitz Battlefield, one hour to the south, was the site of Napoleon's victory over Austria and Russia in 1805.

The Olomouc legacy during the late eighteenth century was more than military, however. Comenius, the father of education, was from Moravia; there are several museums in villages where he lived near Olomouc. During a childhood tour, Mozart was hospitalized in Olomouc with smallpox. In 1767, while in the city, he wrote *Symphony No. 6 in F Major*. As is true of most cities of Central Europe, Olomouc is a treasure house of monuments and period architecture. Although fires destroyed much of the earliest city on more than one occasion, archaeologists continue to find new opportunities for reconstruction. The romanesque, gothic, and baroque churches, the town hall, the Roman and medieval walls, indeed many of the buildings in the centrum including most of the university, offer a delightful experience in period architectures.

In the twentieth century, the volatility of ethnic issues and international politics had significant impacts on the region. The First World War (1914-1918), the brief years of a new nation, Czechoslovakia (1918-1938), the Nazi invasion and takeover and the Second World War (1939-1945), the transfer of Germans from the region (1945), a short post-war democracy (1945-1948) and the Communist Putsch and resulting Warsaw Pact years (1948-1989) frame the first eighty-nine years.[4] The Velvet Revolution of 1989, a non-violent confrontation, reestablished Czechoslovakia and democratic institutions. In 1992, politicians from both regions divided the federation into two states, the Czech Republic and the Slovak Republic. Political, economic, and social transitions which resulted are still in process.

An immediate result of the Velvet Revolution at Palackeho University was the election of Dr. Josef Jarab as rector. Almost as soon as he was acclaimed, the city fathers selected him as the spokesperson to demand the departure of Soviet troops stationed in Olomouc. Negotiations had gone on for several years as there were missiles and heavy equipment to be removed. In 1991, after a dramatic twenty-four-hour confrontation, the troops departed in such haste that they left behind uniforms and gear. Dr. Jarab's election as rector was approved by the new national government and he served until 1996 when he was elected to the first Czech Senate and invited to serve as rector of Central European University in Budapest.

Personal History

Before moving to developments in the University and Dr. Jarab's tenure there, I will clarify my own involvement with Palackeho. When I came to Luther College in 1988, I was writing a doctoral dissertation in U.S. history. During the seventies, I had earned the MLS and an MA degree in history focusing on the Russian and Soviet empires. As the faculty at Luther College had approved adding a program in the Russian language before I arrived, Dr. A. Thomas Kraabel, Dean and Academic Vice-President, appointed me to chair an ad hoc committee to develop a minor in Russian and Eastern European Studies. By 1992, Luther College had received a National Endowment for the Humanities grant, hired a Russian language professor, and begun the program which also offers study-abroad opportunities for students. This has led to success in professional opportunities and graduate school for a remarkable number of students.

In 1991, the Lutheran Educational Conference of North America, with assistance from the Fulbright Commission, sponsored a faculty seminar in Eastern Europe. Seventeen men and women from various disciplines representing ten institutions embarked on a six-weeks' study of Russia, Ukraine and what was then Czechoslovakia in June, 1992. After orientation sessions at Muhlenberg College in Allentown, Pennsylvania led by Dr. Albert Kipa, the scholar who organized the seminar, we flew to what was then still Leningrad (it has since resumed its original name, St. Petersburg). Our six weeks included time in Moscow, Kiev, Lviv, Bratislava, Trencin, Prague, and Olomouc and smaller villages in each country.

The program was not restricted to meetings with academics. On the contrary, leaders of government, business, social services, religion, and artists and others joined the faculty and student hosts to discuss culture, current problems, goals and needs. From the Moscow City Council to a rural Ukrainian school; from new stock markets to the Gabcikovo Nagymaros Dam on the Danube, site of continuing international legal struggles between Hungary and Slovakia; from Novodevichy Monastir outside Moscow to Palackeho University in Olomouc, we listened, asked questions, and learned. We were not prepared to propose solutions to the problems described to us, a growing source of frustration and guilt for many of us. It seemed the very busy people who gave us so much of their time expected assistance from us.

We offered nothing but short-term attention and concern in return. As a would-be Peace Corps volunteer who stayed home with my children in the 1960s, I resolved in 1992 that I would seek a sabbatical leave opportunity which would allow me to achieve specific goals. These were to teach American history full-time, to contribute to an academic program in Eastern Europe, to enhance my knowledge of the current situations there, to contribute to Luther College's Russian and East European Studies minor, and to seek new opportunities for research and cooperation. I received a one-year sabbatical and Anderson sabbatical leave award from Luther and a modest living stipend from Palackeho. My choice of institution was primarily due to the strong English Studies programs at Palackeho, in place since 1969. American Studies had been added in 1991. There were faculty in other disciplines from many nations.

I was seeking students who would learn by reading multiple interpretations of American history for themselves, who would not be too dependent on their instructor as the sole source of knowledge. I also wished to avoid use of an interpreter in the classroom; I can read several western Europe languages but cannot speak any other language well enough to teach and knew virtually no Czech. I did several guest lectures at Comenius University and the History Institute in Bratislava, using interpreters, and discovered that it was not as big a barrier as I feared, but the value of reading primary and secondary sources was proven again and again. Many works need to be translated if citizens from Eastern Europe are to understand U.S. history and philosophies.

Prior to my departure for Olomouc in September, 1994, I accompanied Luther College's Nordic Choir on tour to Eastern Europe adding to my knowledge of the region by spending time in Hungary, Poland, Lithuania, Russia and the Czech Republic.[5] I stayed in Prague and Olomouc after the choir left to assure myself that I was indeed prepared to live there on my own for a year.[6]

It was a remarkable year which ended much too soon for me. My students wanted more opportunities to study U.S. history. I offered survey courses in U.S. history, the history of U.S. minorities and two seminars in historiography. A surprising number of my students have succeeded in taking more coursework in U.S. universities and colleges. Opportunities to teach the English language and U.S. history in public schools are significant incentives; the interest in this "new" history is there. Since returning to Luther College, I have taken two groups of students to Central Europe during January term and served as the official host for our Fulbright scholar in 1997/98. The founding of the East European Institute by the participants of the 1992 seminar has resulted in two international conferences and further links. One of my Palackeho students wrote an MA thesis on the historiography of the American slave family. Students there discovered many challenges and rewards in studying history which proved to be more than a supplement to their work in linguistics and literature.

Palackeho University

The earliest reference to education in Olomouc is that of a cathedral school in 1253.[7] The Benedictine Monastery, Hradisko, founded in 1078 on the site of a ninth-century Slavonic castle, presently serves as a military hospital. The building of St. Wenceslaus Cathedral, a Romanesque basilica consecrated in 1131, was due to the role of Olomouc as the primary site of the Catholic Church in Moravia, a major factor in the founding of Palackeho University in 1573 by the Jesuit Order. After an irregular history which included service as a gymnasium, the university was opened again after the Second World War and renamed in honor of Frantisek Palacky, a ninth-century historian and politician. There are seven faculties: philosophy, law, natural sciences, medical sciences, pedagogy, physical culture, and, newly rededicated in 1991, the Cyril-Methodius faculty of theology. Theology had been the first faculty; its restoration reflects a strong effort on the part of the church to reestablish and strengthen Catholicism in Moravia and Bohemia, also apparent in the 1995 visit of Pope John Paul II to Olomouc and Prague.

There are presently between 12,000 and 13,000 students in undergraduate, graduate, and professional degree programs. The university, located in the old town, is housed in buildings from many different centuries. The sports arena, dormitories and facilities of the Theological and Philosophical faculties are located on the top of the medieval walls, about three stories above the park and Morava River, which prevented them from suffering flood damages in 1997. Unfortunately, there was extensive flooding in other university buildings. The fortress, a defensive location to protect the militia stationed there and the city, was built on the walls on high ground, which served a different protective role in 1997. Fortunately, Maria Theresa's armory was also on high ground. The library, a full city block in size, was already open for service when the flood waters came.

The older facilities had been modernized, i.e., water, electricity, telephone connections, and past restorations of facade and maintenance. By the Velvet Revolution, they were badly in need of more work. During my tenure, facades were peeling away from primary buildings, hanging down in strips or sheets from the upper levels, revealing the brick structure under the stucco. By 1996, many of these buildings had been restored in celebration of the fiftieth anniversary of the re-opening of the University after the second world war. After reviewing all that is implied in this brief history, the reader must have some scope of the additional challenges confronting the university and builders who modernized and rebuilt an armory unused for the past one hundred years to create a modern library. They are indeed impressive. The cost factor would have fazed most people who could envision what additional learning opportunities a library would offer students. Some were not interested in the development of a library as faculty still had access to materials as they had in the past. Then, the difficulties in replacing the foundations in historic areas protected by national law brought the work to a halt as soon as it began in 1992. Before considering the physical and intellectual achievements necessary to create a major library, it is important to know more about the vision, the previous realities, and the means of achieving such a major transformation.

I have mentioned the rector, Dr. Jarab, earlier in this paper. It is helpful to know more about him and his remarkable life. Six years of his childhood were spent under Nazi rule under war conditions. The Communist government took over Czechoslovakia when he was still a youth. During his student years at Palackeho University, he convinced one faculty member to support him in pursuit of the PhD degree in American literature in a reading/study program typical of European higher education.

However, he was not satisfied to read U.S. authors from Olomouc. In spite of the Cold War, he managed to come to Harlem to study African-American literature and later taught at Earlham College. His academic achievements and his wisdom were recognized by his colleagues who elected him to be rector of Palackeho by acclamation at a public meeting in 1989. Confidence went beyond the University to the city leaders who selected him to represent the community to the Soviet forces stationed in Olomouc. The new national government immediately affirmed his selection in 1990.

Prior to the changes in the Czech Republic, Jarab had been part of the faculty which began a major in English and German philology in 1969. In spite of recognition he received as a recognized scholar of American literature, prior to 1989, Jarab was frozen at the level of senior assistant lecturer in German and English philology. He risked being visible outside the university, a successful balancing act, which made it possible for him to teach, travel, and initiate new programs in the twenty-one years between Prague Spring and the Velvet Revolution. He also paid a price for failing to fit the stereotypical faculty member: no advancement. Yet, he earned the respect of all factions.

Dr. Jarab had a dream to meet the needs of the new Czech realities. An English/American Studies program was quickly established, separate majors from German. These and other languages expanded into interdisciplinary majors based on philology but not restricted to it. He also worked to develop successful, continuing programs with U.S. students from the Associated College of the Midwest, the University of Nebraska, Miami University of Ohio, and Nebraska's Honors Scholars program. He represented the Fulbright Commission in the Czech Republic and welcomed many U.S. academics to teach at Palackeho. Some of these were Czechs who had immigrated, some in 1948, others after the failure of Prague Spring in 1969; but others, Fulbright scholars, new college graduates who taught English, faculty from Germany, England, France, the United States, Russia, Israel, and beyond in fields as diverse as medicine, law, literature, political science, history, etc. were also welcomed to teach at Palackeho.

Dr. Jarab also brought the first professional librarian, Dr. Rostislav Hladky who studied in Canada during 1990-91, to the University in 1990. What challenges did he face in his new position? Olomouc is the site of a regional state library, once the only source of information readily available to students. During the year I lived on Vancurova across the street from the back of the building, at least once a week, often more frequently, dumpsters filled with rotting, decaying materials were carried out. In a brief visit to Vilnius University in 1994, my hosts explained that they had multiple copies of materials, mostly propaganda, which they were required to catalog and retain by the Communist government; they were weeding this material in 1994. Everyone seems to realize it is still important to retain one copy of each text.

One surprising legacy of the Soviet era was the retention and protection of the religious manuscripts of the Middle Ages. While materials were not always available for use, at least they had not been destroyed. This same commitment remains today. The state library in Olomouc did not have materials to help me teach, but it did serve my students. The non-textbook work they were able to do was due to that library and to the cartons of books and journals I brought with me from home. My books and journals were left at Palackeho to support future study of U.S. history there. Were there any resources actually available at the University?

Dr. Jarab spoke in Cedar Rapids at Mt. Mercy College in 1994 sharing the challenges, successes and failures he had experienced in his life, particularly the transitions after the Velvet Revolution. One of his observations was most informative: he wistfully remarked that what Palackeho needed most was a library comparable to the new library of some 80,000 volumes in the collections at Mercy College. His listeners wondered how his university which provides graduate, professional, and undergraduate degree programs could operate without a library or library services. It had never occurred to me that there would not be a library to support my teaching and learning during the year I was to be in Olomouc. My concern had been my inability to read Czech.

I was both right and wrong; there were materials. They were located in every conceivable space and some inconceivable ones as well: the broom closet, the washroom, musty, mildewed collections in dark storage rooms packed to twenty-foot high ceilings, a room here, a hall there, locked cases, faculty seminar rooms, and, thankfully, even two new reading rooms. One of these included new journals and newspapers in many languages filed by title—gift subscriptions. I did not ever discover any backfiles or indices (which does not mean there were not any). The other new room was a large rectangular space intended to serve as a reference room; in addition to tables for users, it housed a few reference-type works and a service desk where one requested use of the titles shelved there. Two of these were very familiar, the *Encyclopedia Americana*, a godsend many times over all year, and *Grove's Encyclopedia of Music*, which represented my primary leisure reading for a year! As there is both an opera house and a symphony orchestra in Olomouc, I was able to attend performances two-four times per week and to learn something about the composers and their works. When added to performances at the Rudolfinium, the Naradoni Divadlo, and the Estates Opera in Prague, I think I have at last earned my undergraduate music appreciation credits. However, the remainder of the reference collection included only a modest number of bound journals and books in Czech. All were outdated as far as I could determine. There was also a photocopy machine, the only one available to students studying in the Philosophical Faculty.

Access to stored materials was much more difficult than the years of closed stacks in U.S. universities. Many of the 800,000 items in the variety of storage areas were damaged. None were classified and many were not in any catalog at all. There were books stacked on floors, window ledges, and all available space in every one of the rooms to which I had keys. Allow a digression here for a few moments: the first physical evidence of serving on the Philosophical Faculty was the massive number of keys given to me my first day in the History Department. It was a trust and a challenge. No one has or needs a key to the main gate which opens into the courtyards from which one can enter the buildings which house the Philosophical Faculty. A gatekeeper, a *vratny*, is there to permit or deny access at all hours throughout the year. The medieval doorway opened to my ring by a person who regarded me with suspicion that first Saturday morning I went to work.

I not only used my office, but also the faculty seminar room and the office which included the e-mail connections to my family, colleagues and friends. E-mail was a godsend, although there was not a printer, which led me to forward materials back to Iowa to be printed there, then mailed back to me. As there were very few people who ever came to the complex during non-public hours, I was obviously a stranger doing strange things. Fortunately, my passport with the long-stay visa was adequate explanation; they soon welcomed me with smiles, a frequent visitor who provided a break to the boredom of gate-sitting. As the majority of the faculty commuted by train from the surrounding areas, it is not surprising that there should be few people present. The rector was often in on week-ends too. One of my Czech colleagues in American Studies also spent an increasing amount of time there as the academic year advanced as he was working on a textbook. Other visiting faculty from many nations occasionally came in as well. It was a bit eerie to pass through the courtyard and climb up three stair levels to enter the darkened building which housed my office.

My key ring required that I number and index each key. Before clarifying those related to library materials, I should explain that two different keys were required to pass through the primary auditorium, the *aula*, where competitive examinations, graduation ceremonies, and ceremonial events took place. A key was required for each door. A few steps after exiting the *aula*, there is a passageway which connected two buildings, again with a door on each end, each with a different key. On the other side was my office. The e-mail and seminar rooms were on the opposite side of the *aula*. I thought at first that I would leave the doors behind me unlocked as I passed back and forth several times, but I quickly learned that the *vratnys* followed behind and locked each carefully so I changed my bad habits. The e-mail room, the seminar, and the History Department, the room housing the most recent materials in history, each had keys too. In addition, there was a box of keys in the hallway which, when one was provided with a key, opened a Pandora's box to storage areas in the basement and throughout the building to other storage areas where books were held.

There were many collections of books in other areas, several of which I used extensively although I lacked keys to access them easily. One of these was a collection of materials in Political Science. An American scholar, Dr. Stephen Baskerville, came to Olomouc after completing his PhD at Cambridge and stayed to develop, then serve as chair of the Political Science Department. He contributed greatly to the development of library collections and services; he was a very active supporter of Dr. Jarab's and Dr. Hladky's efforts to create a central library. The collections in Political Science included massive numbers of new paperback books.[8]

I found many titles critical to my teaching. De Tocqueville's *Travels in America* was my first discovery; having this title and a recent issue of *Natural History* made it possible to introduce students to a course on the History of American Minorities very successfully. The biggest problem was the time the storeroom was scheduled for users. It is likely that I could have requested a key to this collection, but I did not as the lines between departments seemed to me to be significant ones. The room was open for public access one hour per day, Monday-Friday. Some of those hours conflicted with my schedule. As there seemed to be only one person unpacking new boxes of books whenever I got in, that person was not always available when scheduled. This particular room was on the main floor of a building joined to my office building by a courtyard, near the outer gateway and not open on weekends and evenings. The three-story climb down and back up was often a frustrating one, but I used the materials housed there consistently as they were relevant and, within the hour the room was open, I could usually find what I wanted although the books were not organized. Once a book was discovered, I filled out a piece of paper indicating what I was taking, then walked out with the books in my bag. It was another challenge to return them, again during the hours available, and to maintain my own circulation system as I lent some of these titles to my students.

In another situation, that of the Matthew Huggins Library, access was even more difficult. The presentation of this major collection on African-American history, literature, and culture to the University was a major coup for Dr. Jarab. Students in the American Minorities course and in the seminars in historiography benefited greatly once I managed to gain access to the collection. It was housed in a very large, irregularly shaped room at the top of a curving stairway. The door said "Matthew Huggins Library," nothing more. Eventually, I learned that this was also the office of a professor on sabbatical leave who, quite naturally, kept the keys in his possession. It was some time before I learned even this much, and it was a much longer time before the professor picked up his mail which included a note of appeal from me. After negotiation via mail boxes, he informed me that he was meeting with a graduate student in his office and invited me to search for the materials I wanted during that appointment.

The elegant room was a challenge of a different sort. There were many book cases on all of the walls except for the windows which were framed with them; underneath each case was a three-foot-high cupboard. Each door opened revealed stacks of books. There were also stacks of books all over the furniture and the floors. I crawled around seeking specific titles for my student who would eventually complete her master's thesis on the Historiography of the American Slave Family. I found many books of value, for example, Eugene Genovese's *Roll Jordan Roll*. As this was probably going to be the only time I could have access to this collection, I selected massive numbers of titles in spite of the curved stairway going down and then three stories up to my office. Imagine if you will, my crawling around furniture, taking out stacks of books from the cupboards to see the stacks behind them, all while the professor and his student were discussing her thesis. As it became apparent that they would be finished in a short time, I began to ferry the books from his office to mine. He graciously permitted me to send him the bibliography of what I had taken later and then to return these books, as many books as would fit into his mailbox at one time, as we finished using them. Another challenge proved to be worth the effort involved, but dreams of libraries I had worked in haunted my nights as much as did my absent family.

There was also a British Council Library but, not unnaturally, it did not provide materials for my courses. That collection is primarily focused on the English language and linguistics. The collections of materials stored for the University's History Department were often extensive, old, and moldy. The catalog in the storeroom by the department office allowed me to determine whether or not a specific title was held in that collection *and* had been cataloged. Many had not been cataloged, and none were classified. Books were stacked on shelves and the floor according to the date of cataloging. Classification was not planned, although the staff was creating an online catalog using the United Kingdom's TinLib software. When I was there, only new titles were being added. It will be a long time before a truly representative online catalog can be developed. The decision was wise; new titles were often those in demand and it was crucial to begin somewhere. The only professional librarian is the director. The support staff were trained to use the software; there was one person in the History Library who worked several hours each week-day. There was no means of evaluating, rejecting, or weeding titles already owned.

The number of titles was estimated to be 800,000 volumes; of these 10 percent were cataloged on the computer and barcoded. During 1997, classification has begun as experience with the new library has heightened awareness of the impossibilities of satisfactory organization without some coded scheme. In November, 1997, an electronic lending system was introduced. Library hours for the Periodical Room were extended from 8:00 A.M. to 7:00 P.M, Monday through Thursday, 8:00 A.M. until 1:00 P.M. on Friday. When the New Library first opened, it was not possible to use it before 11 A.M. except on Friday. Most importantly, all students and faculty now have access to the materials on a regular basis. Faculty need not rely upon having their own key nor students upon a faculty member to assist or permit them to seek knowledge independently.

The number of books continues to increase as individuals and foundations rise to meet the needs of institutions in Central and Eastern Europe. The Sabre Foundation has provided the greatest support, donating 59.2 million dollars worth of books to six countries and $500,000 for journal subscriptions in the sciences. They respect the need for local selection. The Dialog of East European Partners (DEEP), established by the Budapest Declaration in December, 1995, acknowledges the vital support of Sabre's leadership and emphasizes the ongoing critical need for educational and scientific materials. Textbooks, reference books, journals in all formats in all subject areas at all levels are needed. DEEP provides for mutual assistance between members; it observes laws relating to donations and maintains records of those contributions. Local institutions provide support, develop access, and provide use of the materials; they cooperate to meet customs regulations. The Center for Democracy and Free Enterprise was established by the government in Prague in 1991 to work with DEEP. In addition to working with Sabre, DEEP institutions also cooperate in other areas.

The Ford Foundation funded a Legal Resources Center to meet the need for legal materials; there is an exchange of law faculty and students and opportunities for secondary and university students to travel to England to do research. There are also internship programs provided by Parliament and the new corporations of these nations. The European House provides information on the European Union.

There have been 95,000 books distributed since 1991; there is still a need for English language books and textbooks.[9] My own experience was that there were few books in U.S. history. Literature collections were much stronger. DEEP has a warehouse where books from the Sabre Foundation are sorted after arrival within two weeks. Institutional representatives make their choices from the warehouse and these books are donated to the universities. The U.S. Congress and the Organization of American Historians also worked together to provide basic collections of monographs and journal subscriptions in U.S. History to ten institutions in Central Europe in 1995/96.

Although I tried to assist Palackeho in the selection process, no nation received more than one grant and the university selected in the Czech Republic was the oldest and most well known, Charles University in Prague. Charles should undoubtedly have these materials, but it is unfortunate that it was not possible to extend the opportunity to Palackeho. The first American Studies program was developed at Palackeho and it is the primary American Studies program in the Czech Republic. Another failure of mine was the effort to promote document delivery via UnCover at an affordable price. The UnCover Company made a very attractive offer, but funding and cooperative efforts were such that it was not possible for institutions to accept. Andrew W. Lass, project coordinator of the Czech and Slovak Information Network, says that patience is crucial. There are dividends realized all the time. During the year, I also met American Library Association Fellow, Marie Bednar from Pennsylvania State University who was at Masaryk University in Brno. Ms. Bednar provided invaluable assistance to the University, training staff to create high quality online catalogs. The ALA program has made vital contributions to many institutions.

Earlier in this essay, some of the achievements of Dr. Jarab were described. He was no less successful in seeking and finding funds to develop a library. As stated earlier, the archaeological evaluations required extended the time required to build the New Library.[10] The eighteenth-century armory built by Empress Maria Theresa might be compared to a forty-foot-wide building built, like a thick fence, around a large city block. The center is a massive courtyard which served for review of troops and horse shows. Undaunted by the scope of reconstructing such a perimeter building to support and house one million books and to provide twenty-first-century services, Dr. Jarab successfully sought a grant from the Getty Foundation to do so. The first construction, began in April, 1995, was halted for some months while the archaeologists evaluated and, in some cases, removed valuable artifacts. During this delay, it was not known whether or not it would ever be possible to proceed. I have no pretensions to expertise in the reconstruction, but it seems obvious that a building erected several hundred years ago to house horses and troops did not have adequate foundations to support a three-story library building.

The first building efforts were in the courtyards or the armory center which are now real courtyards. Only after adequate foundations were in place could work on the building's interior proceed. When I was in Olomouc in January, 1996, it was difficult to see progress toward a library as all of the work underway was being done outside. However, the half of the building which is the library was dedicated and opened in 1997 after my January term visit. The newly cataloged materials were moved into the new building; considerable challenges remain in the cataloging and shifting of the remainder of the materials. It is estimated that 100,000 titles will be weeded. As at Vilnius University, it is intended that the library will retain single copies of Soviet-era official publications. The remainder, and many materials which were never part of collection evaluation and development, will now be evaluated and can undoubtedly be removed as was being done in the regional state library. As there remains many specific needs for materials, the collections will also grow. The New Library is essentially a general scholarly collection for the Philosophical Faculty. Separate libraries of the law, medical, theological, and pedagogical faculties remain closed collections.

Approximately 300,000 volumes in the New Library are or will be in closed stacks. The other half of the three-story building is scheduled to be completed by December, 1997. It will house the Archives, the computer center, a-v center, publishing house, bookstore, exhibit area, technical base to manage all of the offices and services, coffee shop, and a club. The library is 3,800 square meters, or 40,736 square feet, slightly more than half of the total space. Of this space, two-thirds is open stacks accessible to both students and faculty. The closed stacks house fragile and rare books. The circulating collection has been barcoded; it is presently organized by "general areas." A security system was in place in the fall of 1997. Handicapped access is provided, a significant accomplishment in an area where medieval buildings usually offer only multiple flights of stairs to reach classrooms, offices, labs. Plans are also being realized for a user-guided interface and interactive media, dependent upon funding from the Mellon Foundation. While it seems unlikely that the square footage available will be able to house the number of titles anticipated, the ceilings are high and Dr. Hladky, Dr. Jarab and others at Palackeho have achieved more amazing feats.[11]

The Classroom

In tribute to the faculty and the students who were in my classes, it seems appropriate to conclude this essay with a description of the students and their aspirations. Now that they have a library, my expectations for them to make significant contributions to their new nation and the next century when they will be the leaders are even higher. My experience in teaching and guiding students reinforces our professional convictions that libraries and access to them are crucial components to education in Eastern and Central Europe. The freedom to learn and to make critical judgments is being greatly enhanced by the New Library and many faculty who are adapting new methodology in teaching. Some may resent this as the traditional role of the faculty as the only source of learning shifts and students are able to discover conflicting interpretations in all disciplines for themselves. Some may reach conclusions which will not always support faculty expertise. The older faculty have lived in a controlled environment for many years. Whether or not they will be open to new learning themselves is a significant question. And there will be legitimate concerns during a time of disorganized and often disreputable information easily accessible on the Internet. Critical assessment is needed by student and faculty alike.

Admission to Palackeho University is very competitive. There are six hundred applicants each year for the American/English Studies program; only forty are accepted. German Studies has a smaller group, about three hundred for the forty available places. The demand is great in non-language programs as well. The History Department admits only a small percentage of those who apply. Each student admitted must be accepted by two programs. Most of my students were in American/English Studies and History. Initially they were to receive only optional, or elective credits, no credit in either major, for my courses. After I returned to the United States, that policy was changed and each of my students received credit toward their majors, those in both disciplines receiving double credits. This was a major step for them and the University. Records for credits are students' responsibility. Each has a credit book which includes signatures of the professor. A lost credit book can result in no credits whatsoever so students treat them with as much care as birth certificates or passports. Exams are both written and oral. The months of January and June are devoted to examinations. These are periods of intense study, not unlike preparations for Graduate Record Examinations or comprehensive exams for graduate degrees.

My classes in Olomouc introduced me to a remarkable number of Czech students, many of whom maintain contact with me. As there is not a formal registration procedure, students just come to classes which have been listed for credit on bulletin boards. I had anticipated twenty students per class, with much smaller numbers interested in the seminars. My expectations were realized for the seminars which were Socratic learning/teaching experiences. It was in them that my students began to do scholarly work which would lead to the first theses in U.S. history. The opportunity of working with them was truly wonderful from the outset; we continued to work via my friend and colleague, Dr. Karel Konecny, e-mail, and the post office since my departure in June, 1995.

The survey courses offered the greatest challenges. In a classroom which could accommodate twenty with ease, I found more than fifty students on the first day of class. Some were seated on the floor, some on the window ledges; as many chairs as could be found outside had been pulled into the crowded room. No one had priority and, as far as I could judge, no one accepted my invitation to take another class. We struggled together in a room which did not even allow freedom of movement at the blackboard, where the level of English ability varied greatly, with students in all five years of higher education. Each had a different textbook so that assignments were given by requesting that each look up the topic in the index and contents of their particular book. Some of the books that I had collected from friends and colleagues as well as my own shelves were collections of essays, not easily adapted to serving as textbooks. They were not intended to be used as such. While many were very good, the primary use was to expand the sources available for research. As I was not prepared for the number of students who enrolled, they had to share texts.[12] Classes lasted ninety minutes and were disrupted by the number of students who had to leave fifteen minutes early to catch the trains back to their villages. Only those who lived outside a certain radius were allowed to live in the crowded dormitories. Worst of all, students were unwilling to speak in class so it was impossible to know if they understood what they were hearing and reading. Second semester I was given larger classrooms and, at that time, I attempted to divide them into discussion groups, each with a specific question to discuss and present to the class. It was not a successful effort so I adapted and provided time in each class for students to write short essays on major issues.

In this way, I discovered many misunderstandings about the materials they were reading and the lectures they were hearing. Many were due to the levels of English language skills; others were my failures to recognize what they did not grasp. So, we began a new routine. Each class began with a clarification of the confusions reflected in the essays written during the previous class. It opened a new world of communication and learning for both the students and me. They were free to express opinions, hopefully one result of the experiences they had had in my classroom. They revealed sensitivity to many issues which bodes well for the future. There were also pockets of confusion and, if such a thing is possible, "naive racism." One student in my American minorities class wrote, "All African-Americans are wealthy and famous; they are not inferior as are the minorities in the Czech Republic." The images of sports heroes, popular musicians, and prominent minorities in every field obviously formed the basis for this person's judgment regarding U.S. citizens. A major challenge to create a healthier Czech society is for many people to confront the ethnic hatreds in their history which remain as significant challenges today.[13]

Ideas expressed by my Czech students presented unique challenges to me. An example: several said that they had believed that any negative information about the United States, i.e., crime, racism, any injustice in our society, was only Soviet propaganda. The challenge was to teach authentic U.S. history without destroying their ideals of the West and democratic government. One angry student complained that he was searching to see if there was "any culture in America." Fast food restaurants, dissonant music, mall-type stores were to be found everywhere; they often seemed to be out-of-place in the medieval centers. Some, such as this young man, obviously fear the loss of their own culture as Czechs embrace the consumer life style denied them so many years. The rapid increase in automobiles and need for roads and parking space are also challenges. I, too, found the presence of some of these entrepreneurial intrusions distressing at times. The fine public transportation, the Metro in Prague, the frequent trains, and the picturesque trams found in most cities are resources which should be maintained. However, even a monument such as the St. Vitus Cathedral includes stained glass windows from every period and architecture, from the original eleventh century gothic to electricity and other amenities of the present. The student eventually decided that many people may not care to dine in fast food places or to shop in supermarkets; those who chose not to do so must allow others to make their own choices. One challenge to citizens everywhere is to establish laws which protect their legacies. Prague represents exciting architectural development from every century including Frank Geary's very modern twentieth-century office building.

The opportunity to speak to students at Comenius University in Bratislava, Slovak Republic in March, 1995 was also instructive. One professor asked me several questions at the end of my presentation on colonial American economic history. The first was, "Pani Professor, will you tell us please what is the official American history on Native Americans?" My reply, "Let me begin by saying, sir, that there is no official American history on anything," brought a traditional Slovak response of approval from the students. These strangers whom I thought knew no English immediately began to stamp the floor and pound on the tables with their fists to indicate their approval. As the struggles to support freedom continue to bring censorship and hardship to Slovakia, I am heartened by that memory and those students. That visit in Bratislava included a demonstration in Freedom Square in support of a group of comedians whose television programs had been cancelled by the state as a result of their parodies of government officials. Over 100,000 people of all ages and groups remained for several hours although it was a bitter cold night.

My U.S. students visiting Central Europe were not always very tolerant either. They were annoyed when they could not find Fruit Loops or Sugar Pops in the hostels which provided us with traditional breakfasts. Some were irritated by the overpowering presence of opera, ballet, and symphonies. As they were strangers during the winter season, some did not discover the discos, and all missed the street music and crowds of tourists of the summer season. Petty crimes modified their views on human rights to some extent. And, above all else, they were displeased with the cultural custom of not making eye contact with strangers, not responding to smiles and greetings. Some very serious problems were evident to them, particularly so, that of air pollution. Economic developments and problems were not so easily grasped. We all have a lot to learn.

A number of my Czech students continue to remain in touch. Forty came to do further study in U.S. history in the United States in 1996/97 so that they would be able to teach it in secondary schools. There is nothing more thrilling than to be addressed by a former student during an intermission in the Rudolfinium several years later who says, "Dr. Hervey, do you remember me?" It is still a gift when postcards or notes arrive from some who had not kept in touch, telling me about their professional experience and their continued interest. Their interest was very evident in the spring of 1995 when they began to come to the office to ask about the courses I would be teaching in the fall. Although I had explained in each course that I was only to be there for one year, their obvious dismay and regret informed me that their interest in U.S. history would not end with my departure. The presence of a major university library now promises the opportunity for my students and all future students at Palackeho University to continue to expand their horizons and knowledge. The book can be a magic carpet. The vision of Dr. Jarab and his colleagues combined with the generous support of foundations and individuals make it available to all who enter the New Library.

Notes

1. The St. Bonaventure University campus was badly flooded but the library escaped the water; others may recall the incredible damage done to the library at the Corning Glassworks in Corning, N.Y. A number of public libraries were also inundated.

2. *Osm dnu moravske apokalypsy* (*Eight Days of the Moravian Apocalypse*) 1997, 17-minute film.

3. This was the "Good King Wenceslaus" known to many of us from the popular Christmas carol which bears his name.

4. There was an interlude of promised reform in Prague in the spring of 1968, when the Communist government eased restrictions and art and life flourished until the Warsaw Pact nations sent troops to remove President Dubcek and his government from power. This legacy remains a significant one. Many intellectuals joined the Communist Party in support of Dubcek's reforms; they have had difficulties since the end of the Soviet Union. The person who symbolizes the hopes and dreams of the people in 1968 is Jan Palach, a student who immolated himself in protest. Jan Palach Square in Prague reminds all who are there of his ongoing legacy.

5. An article on my experiences at Vilnius University in Lithuania appeared in *College Library News* in 1995.

6. My experiences in living and teaching in Olomouc have been described in "East and West: A Conversational Essay on Teaching Overseas," co-authored with Uwe Rudolf, *Lock Haven International Review* 10 (1996), 7-29.

7. My own knowledge of Olomouc and the University has been supplemented by many works but I owe a great deal to one opportunity given to me while I taught there. I was invited to assist scholar and emeritus professor Vladimir Panos prepare his book to be published in English. *Olomouc City*

and Region: Geographical Image and Historical Digest (University of Palackeho, 1995) was the result of our collaboration and has been invaluable to me.

8. Later I will describe the sources of these and other books contributed to the University by many nations and foundations.

9. This is a moving, changing target so these figures cannot be exact.

10. All readers who have had the privilege of visiting Central Europe will be aware of the presence of names like those in Prague—the New Old Stairway, the New Old Synagogue; usually these names refer to buildings from the 12-14th century and reflect the presence of 10-11th century ones, many of which still stand as well.

11. Dr. Jarab was elected to the first Czech Senate in the elections of 1996 and also accepted the position to be rector of the Soros-funded Central European University in Budapest. However, this remarkable man, who was one of the primary speakers at ALA Midwinter in 1998, continues to teach one class in Olomouc and to serve as a leader in many civic enterprises. An example of November, 1997 was his open letter to the Palackeho community calling upon students and faculty to fight racism in the Czech Republic. This was not the first such effort on his part. It was prompted by the tragic murder of an international student from Sudan in Prague.

12. USAid contributed funds to ship these books to Prague. Without this assistance, teaching and learning U.S. history in Olomouc would have been a very different experience.

13. The issue of human rights especially relating to Romany peoples and ethnic minorities in the Czech Republic which includes murder, discrimination, unemployment, inferior educational opportunities, etc., continues to be one of the major concerns of outsiders whom the Czechs aspire to join. The European Union and organizations such as the U.S. Senate, Helsinki Watch, and others have attempted to stimulate resolutions to such crimes and concerns since my initial visit to the region in 1992. In 1997 the world was made aware of the Romany issues when a number of these people attempted to claim asylum in Canada and Britain. The government in Prague and many Czechs, especially the young, are trying to address the problems. I have presented papers, published articles, and spoken on this issue. My friend, Dr. Konecny, and I are working on a monograph to include the history and the challenges inherent in it. My 1994/95 students appeared to have learned a great deal from the United States experience with human rights. Without any pretense of successful resolution of the many challenges we in the United States confront, they learned about the painful realities of U.S. history for Native Americans, African-Americans, and other ethnic groups and discovered a common international need, that of peaceful resolutions to these issues. In their farewell notes to me, this was the primary challenge they want to confront in their own country. I have taught a course at Luther College, "Ethnic Groups of the Former USSR," which continues to teach me and my students the world challenges of the present and the new century: ethnicity, environment, economy.

17. Polish Libraries and Librarianship in a Time of Challenge and Change

George S. Bobinski and Maria Kocojowa

In preface to the main text we are providing some background to our joint authorship since it represents the international cooperation and communication aspect of the "Global Reach, Local Touch" theme.

In 1990 the University at Buffalo and the Jagiellonian University in Krakow, Poland established an Exchange Program. Within that Exchange I went to Krakow in the spring of 1992 as a Visiting Scholar from the School of Information and Library Studies (SILS) and established contact with the Jagiellonian Department of Library and Information Science (DLIS). We at Buffalo then hosted four Jagiellonian DLIS faculty members over a four-year period for one-semester visits. Each of the faculty members focused their studies and observations on a topic of vital importance to Polish librarianship in a new society emerging from the end of Communism in 1989.

Ms. Sabina Arcisz examined business information sources and services in U.S. libraries—in response to the information needs of burgeoning companies being established in Poland's new free-market economy.

Dr. Wanda Pindlowa focused on environmental information sources and on libraries and information centers dealing with environmental information in response to the polluted environment left by the former Communist government.

Dr. Maria Kocojowa examined the role of libraries in the democratic process in response to the democratization of Polish society since 1989.

Mr. Wladyslaw Szczech studied the state of library automation and computerized information retrieval in the United States in response to the need for Polish libraries to catch up in technological developments.

Two SILS faculty members also visited the Jagiellonian DLIS during this period — Mr. Michael Lavin, an expert on business information sources and services, and Dr. William McGrath, an eminent scholar in bibliometrics.

Members of the two faculties also collaborated on a book entitled *The Role of Libraries in the Democratic Process,* co-edited by Maria Kocojowa and myself, published by the Jagiellonian University in 1995.

I was able to return in 1997 to participate in a conference hosted by the DLIS on "Global Strategies in the Education of Libraries and Information Workers."

In summary, our exchange activities have been exciting and rewarding. We have learned much from each other. We plan for these activities to continue. This joint article is a further expression of the exchange. First, we provide a brief overview of the history of Polish librarianship. We then provide an analysis of the problems and challenges facing Polish librarians since the fall of Communism.

Overview of Polish Library History

The earliest books in Poland were manuscript volumes imported for missionary work by Catholic clergy after the country's conversion to Christianity in 966. The first Polish scriptoria, as well as cathedral, chapter, and monastic libraries, appeared at the beginning of the eleventh century at Gniezno, Poznan, and Kracow. The library of the Jagiellonian University in Kracow was founded along with the university itself in 1364. The first printing house was established in Kracow in 1473, and the first printed book in Polish came out in 1513 (most earlier printed works had been in Latin).

Beginning in the sixteenth century, many of the Polish kings and nobles founded their own libraries. Small fragments of these private collections have survived wars and confiscations and can be found in the rare collections of today's Polish libraries. The first city libraries were founded in 1535 (Poznan) and 1596 (Gdansk).

Early in the eighteenth century the Zaluski brothers founded a library that they donated to the nation in 1747, making Poland the first country to possess a true national library. In 1780 a legal deposit law was enacted, and by 1790 the library had become one of the largest in Europe, with approximately 400,000 volumes. The history of this national library reflects the history of libraries in Poland as affected by wars, confiscations, and wanton destruction. After the partition of Poland by its big neighbors, the library was confiscated in 1794 and carried away to Saint Petersburg by order of Empress Catherine II. After World War I, when Poland regained independence, a new National Library was established in 1928. That library sustained great losses (80 percent of the collection) during World War II through deliberate destruction and looting by Nazi occupants—including 2,200 incunabula and 50,000 volumes of pre-1800 Polish books.

During World War II numerous collections and libraries were lost or irreparably damaged. Out of the twenty-two million volumes in Polish libraries only seven million were saved; school libraries lost 93 percent of stock. Only 10 percent of the books taken out of Poland were returned. Librarians were persecuted severely, and many suffered imprisonment, murder, internment camps, and forced labor in Germany and in the Soviet Union. In 1940 the Germans created a central administration for Polish libraries. This administration was given the task of reorganizing all Polish libraries with the view of serving German needs. Their use was restricted to Germans only. After the suppression of the Warsaw Rising in 1944 all of Warsaw's special collections gathered in the Krasinski Estate Library were burned. Polish librarians participated in the resistance movement, organized underground education and unauthorized book lending, professional courses and editorial work. During the 1945-1989 Communist period much reconstruction and rebuilding of Polish library collections occurred under centralized economic, political and social control.

Polish Librarianship in the 1990s

The place of Polish libraries in the 1990s in global librarianship must first be considered in the light of political and economic changes. Poland's major role in the breakup of forty-five years of Soviet domination over Eastern and Central Europe needs to be recognized and emphasized. The Solidarity Movement not only freed Poland but also led to the democratization of the other Soviet bloc countries and, indeed, led to the breakup of the former Soviet Union. A free market economy was also introduced. And libraries have been freed from central autocratic control and from a rigid political philosophy.

Since the tenth century, Poland has played a leading role as a bulwark and defender of Christian Europe, e.g., against invasion of the Tartars, Mongols, Turks, and in 1920 in a war against the Bolsheviks. Poland's recent role against U.S.S.R. domination was therefore not a new one.

Democratic ideals in Poland have always been strong even after long periods of subjugation from 1790 to 1918 and from 1945 to 1989. Previously most Polish kings were elected. And the famous Polish Constitution of 1791 stands out as an early symbol of democratic enlightenment.

Poland in comparison to the United States appears as a small country—the size of the State of New Mexico. But in Europe her almost forty million population and 121,000 square miles place her seventh in population and ninth in size. Among the former Soviet bloc countries freed from Communism, Poland is the largest in population and size. Poland stands in central Europe with the Baltic Sea to the north, with Lithuania, Belorussia and Ukraine to the east, with the Czech Republic and Slovakia on the south and with Germany to the west. Warsaw is the capital while Krakow is the historic capital and center of educational and cultural life—particularly in librarianship. Poland is divided into forty-nine provinces within which are organized the public and school libraries.

During 1989/90 there were 35,000 libraries in Poland—59 percent of them school libraries, 29 percent public libraries, 7 percent special libraries, and 5 percent academic and research libraries. They contained some 370 million volumes, were staffed by about 100,000 library workers, and were used by 7.5 million people. About 21 percent of the adult population used public libraries with 37 percent of the adults reading at least six books yearly and 14 percent reading more than twenty-four books yearly. Forty-one percent of the adult population did not read at least one book per year.

After the economic and political upheaval of 1989 brought on by the end of Communism, the number of libraries had declined to 33,000 by 1995/96 with some of the smaller and less used public, special and government-sponsored libraries being closed. Unfortunately the number of readers did not increase because of the rapid growth of TV programming (many more channels in a free society) and the spread of video rental outlets.

Changes in Polish librarianship during the last eight years have occurred in three directions:

1. growing democratization;
2. movement toward international standardization—particularly in library automation; and
3. growing access to international contacts and cooperation with the European Union.

The first two directions dominated up through the mid-1990s. After the stabilization of the free market economy, priority was given to the third.

It must be noted with gratitude that the changes and advancement in Polish librarianship were made with the assistance (moral and financial) of Western Europe and the United States. For Poland it meant contact and access with countries more advanced in library and information science that formerly had been restricted by the Iron Curtain. Available now were foreign travel, conferences, consultations, joint research projects, and access to formerly forbidden research materials. It also meant foreign professional visitors, visiting scholars, and experts financed by governments and foundations of Western countries.

There have also been LIS conferences organized in the former Soviet bloc to which international participants from the West have been invited as participants. As an example, over 170 librarians, LIS faculty and publishers attended an international conference in Krakow in 1995 entitled, "Libraries in Europe's Post-Community Countries: Their Independent Context." This was organized by the American Association for the Advancement of Slavic Studies, the University of Illinois Mortenson Center, the Stanford University Library, and the DLIS of the Jagiellonian University. Among the sponsors of this important conference were the International Research and Exchange Board (IREX) and the Soros Foundation.

The democratization of Polish librarianship began in 1990 with the end of censorship and of freedom of the press and of publishing. Selection of materials for collections could now be done without political restrictions or indoctrination and from any source —with emphasis on the needs of users. In the past the government-controlled book market was flooded with titles of little interest or use by readers.

Eliminated were the special closed reserved collections with restricted access formerly found in academic and research libraries. Eliminated was the Index of Authors prohibited in public library collections. Lifted also were restrictions on access to obtaining foreign publications beyond the Communist bloc. No longer was it necessary to favor Russian publications or those translated from Russian.

The privatization of book publishing, of newspapers, and of periodicals brought about a flood of new titles in a wide variety of fields—more aesthetically pleasing than in the past, but alas at higher prices. There was also a proliferation of publications dealing with scandal and the sensational as well as romance and pornography.

Polish libraries now faced the problem of dealing with the ideological Marxist literature and political propaganda in their collections. In public libraries this often meant from 30-40 percent of the collection. There was little demand for this material.

Public and school library support and control were decentralized and made primarily a local responsibility. Public and school librarians were now accountable locally. They could no longer seek funding under broad justification like the "enlightenment of society." They had to adopt marketing and good public relations techniques. Political appointments to library positions of communist party members and their relatives came to an end.

New clients and demands were generated for some libraries. Library users appeared who could not afford the purchase of the now much more expensive books or of the foreign publications. Others wanted publications formerly not allowed in open collections. Still others sought information pertinent to the new economy and society— business information, environment concerns, safety and security, self-improvement, etc. Although small in number, the Lithuanian, Russian, Belorussian, German, Czech, Slovak, and Ukrainian minorities wanted publications in their languages.

As noted earlier some libraries were closed—particularly those that were little used. Some libraries, especially public libraries, lost their locations due to the high rent now being demanded by the original owners, to whom formerly confiscated properties were being returned. Some private libraries that had been taken over by the previous government were now returned to their pre-World War II status, e.g., Czartoryski Library in Krakow and the Ossolineum Library in Wroclaw.

Many new private schools were now being established but often without libraries or with very inadequate ones to serve teachers and students.

Libraries sponsored by the Roman Catholic Church were now officially recognized and allowed to grow and develop. The Church has acknowledged their importance, and they have been opened up for wider access and use. New libraries have been established in local parishes and by Catholic organizations. Unfortunately there are no official figures on the number of these libraries, their collections, and users. However, since over 90 percent of Poles are Catholic, their impact must be important.

To meet the new challenges and needs, Polish libraries had to find new sponsors and additional support beyond government funding. Helpful were new organizations like the Committee for Scholarly research (support of journal subscriptions) in Poland, newly formed Polish foundations as well as assistance from the Mellon and Soros Foundations, from the International Research and Exchange Board (IREX), and from the British Council.

Changes have also occurred in library professional associations. The former Association of Polish Librarians was discredited because of its cooperation with the Communist regime. In 1989 a new professional organization was established—the Polish Bibliological Association. Other related organizations established were the Polish Reader's Association in 1991 and the Polish Association of Scientific Information in 1992. New professional journals and newsletters were also begun as well as a series of new monographs published by the schools of library and information science in Poland. All of these expressed new techniques and approaches in librarianship.

Polish library schools also have faced the challenge of training new librarians in the light of the new political and economic conditions with an emphasis on the information needs of people. There has also been a special need for extensive continuing education to upgrade the knowledge and competencies of librarians for the new democratic society and technological age. This is being done by libraries and the thirteen schools of LIS. As a further example of our own exchange program, two master's students from the DLIS at the Jagiellonian will be taking one of our LIS courses which is being offered on the Internet during the spring of 1998.

Another recent development has been the acceptance of international standards by Polish librarians—particularly in library automation. This began during the 1980s but has proceeded at a rapid pace in recent years. In the 1990s Polish software began to appear commercially for use in Polish school and public libraries and smaller academic libraries. Larger libraries began to negotiate with foreign firms for automation systems. Cooperative ventures of these academic libraries were particularly successful, such as the recent Council of Academic Library Directors established in 1997. There is also now a special emphasis on retrospective conversion. Problems with international standards are most evident in small public and school libraries. Unfortunately the staff here is often not trained, nearing retirement or simply not qualified.

There is also the impact of the European Union. Polish librarians and information workers have as their high priority that Poland is able to join the European Union. This would link them even more closely with library advancement in the West.

Digital and virtual libraries, the Internet and world wide web, new distance learning techniques, and other technological progress are advancing the library profession in Poland. Polish librarianship looks forward to continuing interaction with global librarianship.

References

Kocojowa, Maria. *History of Polish Libraries*. Krakow, Poland: Universitas, 1993.

Kocojowa, Maria, and George S. Bobinski. *The Role of Libraries in the Democratic Process*. Krakow, Poland: Jagiellonian Press, 1995.

Libraries in Europe's Post-Communist Countries: Their International Context; Proceedings. Edited by Maria Kocojowa and Wojciech Zalewski. Krakow, Poland: Polish Bibliological Society, 1996.

18. Slavic Book and Serial Exchanges

Bradley L. Schaffner

It is often assumed that the global systematic exchange of information is a recent phenomenon spurred by the availability of inexpensive, but powerful, personal computers and facilitated through the development of the Internet. Surprisingly, the exchange of information between countries around the world has been practiced by libraries and other scholarly institutions for hundreds of years. In an effort to acquire important scholarly materials, regardless of their place of publication, libraries developed and continue to utilize a system of barter to acquire publications. This system is generally referred to as book and serial exchanges.

Some of the earliest exchanges date back to the ninth century.[1] In more recent times, the library of the Hungarian Academy of Sciences established an exchange with the Philosophical Society of Philadelphia in 1832-33.[2] The Smithsonian Institution, while it still had designs on becoming the national library of the United States, established book exchanges in 1846.[3] In Russia, Tsar Alexander II created a Commission of International Publication Exchanges in 1877.[4]

Exchanges were first established so that scholarly institutions could trade their own publications for the publications of other institutions. Over time, many of these exchanges expanded to include local and/or regional materials, rather then simply limiting the program to an institution's own titles. Often, exchanges became such an integral part of a library's collection development activities that independent departments were established to oversee all of the arrangements.

This chapter will summarize the operation of book and serial exchanges and examine the role these agreements play in the collection development activities of academic and research libraries. Given the scope and breadth of many libraries' activities, it would be impossible to describe, in just a few pages, exchange operations between libraries in all of the different countries, or even major regions, of the world. Therefore, this chapter will focus on U.S. library exchanges with Russian and Ukrainian scholarly institutions.

In their most basic form, book and serial exchanges are simple *barter transactions*. No money is used in the operation of exchanges. Publications are traded on an equity basis; page by page, title by title, or by assigned value for each volume. In most exchanges, books are selected title by title from lists of offerings or pre-publication information. Some libraries establish approval or blanket order arrangements to acquire all of the items produced by a publisher or on a specific topic. Exchange books and serials have a monetary value assigned to them by the sending partner. In turn, monographs and serials of equal value are sent as payment. An effort is made to keep the balance of trade equal between partners.

Another form of exchanges operates on the concept of *mutual satisfaction*. This means that each partner continues to send materials, regardless of the equity of receipt, because each participant is receiving important materials for their respective collections. Unfortunately, few libraries are able to operate exchanges based entirely on *mutual satisfaction*, and must maintain an equitable balance of trade and keep records of the transactions.

Mutual satisfaction, however, is the driving force behind all exchanges. Libraries must be willing to make a substantial commitment of money and staff time to operate an exchange program successfully. Therefore, it only makes sense to acquire publications on exchange if these materials will make an important contribution to a library's collection. If a library is not satisfied with the materials sent by its partner, it is not in the best interest of the library to continue the arrangement.

Historically, Slavic exchanges have been complicated by great disparity between the cost of scholarly publications produced in the United States and those produced in the former Soviet Union. The government subsidized and controlled all publishing during the Soviet period. Books usually cost only a few rubles and often cost much less.[5] Subscriptions to periodicals were equally inexpensive. As a result, U.S. publications could cost up to ten times more than their Soviet counterparts. This inequity in price proved to be problematic for both Soviet and U.S. librarians. Because of the inexpensive cost of Soviet publications, most U.S. librarians were not willing to become involved in exchanges on a title by title or page by page basis. Most U.S.-Soviet exchanges were operated on an assigned value per title basis. In general, librarians in the United States would charge their Soviet partners the actual cost of the book. This meant that Soviet libraries would have to send up to ten publications to cover the cost of one U.S. publication. Most Soviet librarians believed this to be an unequal exchange. Therefore, U.S. Slavic librarians regularly negotiated exchange rates that were more favorable to Soviet libraries. As a result, both partners could usually acquire materials in what they considered a fair and cost-effective manner allowing exchanges to operate to the mutual benefit of all partners.

On first thought, most librarians would probably say exchanges were established to save money. Recent studies of Slavic exchanges have shown that these arrangements generally do not save money because their operation is labor-intensive.[6] Exchanges do provide some financial benefits. For example, because no money changes hands, there are no charges for currency conversion or agent's or book vendor fees. Exchanges also allow libraries to acquire materials and develop their collections without expending acquisition funds. This can be accomplished by trading publications produced in-house for similar publications produced at other institutions. Many scholarly publications can only be acquired on exchange because the title is on a specialized topic and printed in limited numbers. These publications are often unavailable from vendors because of their specialized focus and limited commercial appeal. The ability to acquire such publications is one of the real values of exchanges.

Exchange relationships have occasionally served as the framework to provide assistance during periods of natural or man-made disasters. On February 14, 1988, a fire destroyed many valuable collections at the Academy of Sciences Library (BAN) in Leningrad, now St. Petersburg. BAN turned to its exchange partners for assistance in obtaining replacements for some materials originally acquired on exchange, but lost in this fire. Another example today is the assistance being provided to libraries destroyed in Bosnia and Croatia during the recent war. Many foreign exchange librarians are now taking active roles in providing assistance to rebuild collections. Such actions are a major benefit of exchange relationships that cannot be evaluated in the terms of dollars and cents.

The value of exchanges was highlighted during the collapse of communist-led governments in Eastern Europe and the Soviet Union between 1989 and 1991. During this period, most restrictions on publishing and the governments' monopoly on information ended. While the liberalization of East European publishing is a welcome development, the collapse of communist-led governments also resulted in the failure of state-run publishing and book-distribution systems. These events made it very difficult to acquire publications from the region. Thanks to the exchange ties with libraries in Eastern Europe and the Soviet successor states, even in the most chaotic times, libraries continued to acquire Slavic publications.

Another important aspect of exchanges, not immediately evident, is the professional relationships and contacts that develop between exchange librarians usually established through exchange correspondence and by on-site visits. Visits permit librarians to meet their colleagues face-to-face to discuss exchange arrangements and to work out any problems that may exist with the arrangement. Most U.S. Slavic librarians would agree that exchange arrangements between their library and Russian and Ukrainian libraries will improve after a personal visit.

During the Soviet period on-site visits with exchange partners were quite important given the slow and unreliable nature of their postal system. Even today, in the era of electronic mail, it is still beneficial to travel abroad to meet with exchange partners. Most foreign exchange librarians appreciate the fact that their U.S. colleagues are willing to make this effort. While on a trip, the U.S. librarian also has the opportunity to observe the operation of Russian and/or Ukrainian libraries. Such visits allow one to witness the challenges that Russian librarians, along with their colleagues in the other Soviet successor states, face in the daily operation of their institutions. In-country experience also improves the U.S. Slavic librarian's ability to provide first-class reference and research assistance to patrons at his or her home institution.

In addition, the operation of book and serial exchanges has facilitated the continuation of cultural ties even during periods of poor or no political relations between the Soviet Union and the United States. For example, in the 1920s, libraries in the United States and Soviet Russia organized and operated exchanges before most foreign governments, including the United States, officially recognized the Soviet Union. Vladimir Lenin, the founder of the Soviet state, actively supported library development. He instructed libraries to establish international publication exchanges to help facilitate the acquisition of contemporary technical and scientific materials needed to modernize the country.[7] These exchanges also helped to further Soviet cultural and educational ties abroad. Throughout the history of the Soviet Union, exchanges continued to operate regardless of the domestic or international political climate. This was true even at the peak of the Cold War.

Due to limitations placed on publishing and the free exchange of information by the Soviet government, exchanges played a prominent role in the development of Slavic studies collections abroad. During this period, the Soviet Union restricted the export of many publications. While foreign vendors for Slavic materials existed, the Soviet government did not allow the export of most antiquarian, nor many scholarly publications that would be of interest to researchers abroad. However, some Soviet libraries could legally export such materials on exchange. In return, the Soviet government permitted foreign libraries to send normally censored materials to its libraries. Of course, upon receipt, most of these publications were placed in restricted access collections called *spetskhrany,* and not available to the general population.

During Soviet rule, law required publishers to give, at no charge, a certain number of copies of each title produced to most major libraries in the country. Libraries that acquired such materials received sufficient copies of each title so that they could offer some on exchange. In essence, deposit copies became a part of the library's acquisition budget. Current publications were acquired at no charge with additional copies available for exchange. This arrangement provided libraries with a way to obtain foreign publications without having to expend hard (non-Soviet) currency. The government provided another "perk" with the free use of the postal system. Considering all of the support given to libraries for the operation of exchanges, it is obvious that the Soviet government realized the benefits of library exchanges.

A library that participates in book and serial exchanges can provide "value added services" for its partners, making the arrangement more appealing. Exchange partners often establish blanket or approval plans. The sending library selects titles based on a profile describing materials to be sent to the partner. This type of exchange allows libraries to share collection development expertise with one partner, relying on the other's subject specialist to select important scholarly materials. For example, a library in the United States could rely on its exchange partner in Moscow to send significant works of contemporary Russian literature, even if the U.S. library remained unsure what constituted this literature. In return, the U.S. library could provide similar collection development assistance to a Russian library. In addition, exchange partners often provide reference assistance to their partners with electronic mail facilitating this practice.

A short summary of the history of book and serial exchanges utilized by the University of Kansas (KU) Libraries to develop their Slavic collections will illustrate the value of these agreements. Like most other libraries in the United States, the KU Libraries developed many exchanges in the late 1950s.[8] Thanks to the establishment of these exchanges, KU's Slavic collection developed to such a degree that the Library established a Slavic Department with staff to oversee the exchanges and provide reference service in 1967. Even before the department was created, the Slavic librarian and some members of the teaching faculty made several trips to the Soviet Union and Eastern Europe to develop exchanges.

In 1960, the KU Slavic librarian went on an exchange trip and visited the libraries of the University of Helsinki, the University of Leningrad, the Academy of Sciences (BAN), and the University of Moscow. During this trip over 10,000 volumes of nineteenth- and early twentieth-century materials were acquired on exchange. The librarian also observed duplicates of over 100,000 volumes held by some Soviet libraries; KU worked to establish exchange arrangements with these institutions.

By 1967, the University of Kansas Libraries' collections of Slavica numbered 50,000 and was growing at a rate of about 15 percent per year. Much of this growth was due to the numerous exchange programs. Currently, these collections number over 300,000 volumes. Exchanges, while not as productive as in the past, continue to play an integral role for Slavic collection development. KU Slavic librarians continue to travel to Russia and Eastern Europe on a regular basis to cultivate these exchange agreements and to purchase materials in-country.

Recent trips to the region have illustrated that the greatest challenge facing libraries in Russia and Ukraine is the lack of money to finance their operations sufficiently.[9] Current problems with Ukrainian exchanges can be traced back to the collapse of the Soviet Union. Since 1991, the governments of the newly independent states have been responsible for providing funds for the operation of libraries. Given the chaotic situation of the economies of the region, it is not surprising that funding for cultural institutions is limited. Library budgets for acquisitions and daily operations are insufficient, and there is little money for capital improvements and systems modernization.

Ukrainian library administrators are often forced to choose between using their library's limited resources for acquisitions or to pay employees. In 1995, some librarians made as little as 3 million *kupons* per month. (In October 1995 the exchange rate was approximately $1 = 182,000.00 Ukrainian *kupons*, the official currency at the time.) It took about two million *kupons* to pay rent and utilities, leaving only one million *kupons* for other expenses. In addition, many library employees often were not paid for months. In May 1997, numerous librarians had only been paid one month's salary during the past seven to eight months. Making matters worse, many libraries were given no money for their operation in 1997. Yet, these institutions continue to stay open and librarians continue to work.

The privatization of publishing has created many new challenges for Ukrainian libraries. A major problem is the loss of bibliographic control over items that are being published throughout the country. This problem is compounded by the number of new publishing houses in operation. Most librarians have an idea of what is being published in their own region and are fairly confident that they can acquire these materials. Unfortunately, it is more troublesome to keep track of what is being published in the other regions of Ukraine and when titles of interest are identified, it is difficult to acquire those publications. This underscores one reason why exchanges are still important. A foreign library operating exchanges with one or two libraries in each region of Ukraine improves its chance of acquiring most of the important titles published throughout the country.

The financial situation of Russian libraries appears somewhat better than that of Ukrainian libraries. While money is being budgeted to Russian libraries, librarians report that they rarely receive this money in a timely manner. More troublesome is the fact that many libraries now receive their budget on a six-month, or even a monthly, cycle rather than on an annual basis. Monthly budgeting makes it difficult for librarians and administrators to make long-term financial decisions for the institution. Short budget cycles make it difficult to acquire monographs, and almost impossible to subscribe to journals even in Russia, where most journals now offer six-month subscriptions. Short-cycle budgeting means that Russian librarians probably spend much of their time working on budgets and dealing with financial issues.

The poor financial situations of Russian and Ukrainian libraries has made it difficult to continue exchange programs. Resources are limited or unavailable for the acquisition of materials to send on exchange. When materials are available for exchange, it is often difficult to find money to pay for shipping. Despite these financial challenges, libraries work to continue exchanges with foreign partners. Unfortunately, at the present time, the reality is that it is very difficult for libraries to continue these programs on a large scale.[10]

It has been argued by some that exchanges will soon end due to the incredible amount of effort and cost involved. In fact, some libraries have terminated their Slavic exchanges in favor of using vendors and in-country purchasing agents which tend to offer high prices and precarious service. This is unfortunate. Exchanges offer numerous benefits that can not be evaluated in terms of cost. The relationships developed between libraries and librarians have served as the foundation for other cooperative ventures and assistance. Most important, exchanges allow libraries to acquire important scholarly material that would be unavailable by other means.

Notes

1. B. P. Kanevskii, "Bibliografiia i mezhdunarodnyi knigoobmen," *Sovetskaia bibliografiia: sbornik statei i materialov* 3, no. 73 (1962): 110.

2. C. Csapodi, et al., *The Library of the Hungarian Academy of Science: 1826-1961*, ed. G. Rozsa (Budapest: MTA Konyvtara, 1960), 24.

3. B. P. Kanevskii, "Iz istorii mezhdunarodnogo kngoobmena v Rossii 1877-1916" (Komissiia po mezhdunarodnomu obmenu izdanii po chasti nauk i khudozhestov), *Gosudarstvennaia biblioteka SSSR imena V.I. Lenina: Trudy* 8 (1965): 75.

4. Ibid., 72.

5. The exchange rate at the end of Soviet rule was 1 ruble equaled $1.65.

6. Margaret S. Olsen, "The More Things Change, the More They Stay the Same: East-West Exchanges 1960-1993," *Library Resources & Technical Services* 39, no. 1 (January 1995): 5-21.

7. *Istoriia Gosudarstvenoi biblioteki SSSR imeni V.I. Lenina za 100 let, 1862-1962* (Moskva: Izdanie Biblioteki, 1962), 66.

8. Nadia Zilper, "Assessment of Contemporary Research Materials Exchanges Between U.S. and Soviet Libraries," in *Books, Libraries and Information in Slavic and East European Studies: Proceedings of the Second International Conference of Slavic Librarians and Information Specialists*, ed. Marianna Tax Choldin (New York: Russica Publishers, 1986), 469.

9. I have had the opportunity to travel to the region four times since 1990. The last two trips were funded by programs sponsored by the International Research and Exchange Board (IREX). In 1995, I received funding from the IREX Special Projects in Library and Information Science with Central and Eastern Europe and Eurasia program to visit libraries in Kyiv and L'viv, Ukraine. The goal of the trip was to identify and document the specific challenges that libraries in Ukraine face in continuing exchange operations. A copy of my final report is available on the World Wide Web at: www.irex.org/grants/ukralib.htm. In 1997, I received a short-term travel grant from IREX to visit libraries in St. Petersburg and Moscow, Russia; and Kyiv and L'viv, Ukraine.

10. The Library of Congress has had good luck in establishing exchanges with regional libraries in the countries of the former Soviet Union. These libraries were unable to operate exchanges during the Soviet period and are now anxious to establish ties with foreign libraries. Tatjana Lorkovic and Eric A. Johnson, "Serial and Book Exchanges with the Former Soviet Union," *Serials Librarian* 31, no. 4 (1997): 75-76.

19. African Librarianship: Reality or Illusion?

Kingo J. Mchombu

The request to participate in this project was conveyed to me by colleagues from the American Library Association, during the 1997 Zimbabwe International Book Fair at an evening outing. About eight busloads of delegates from all corners of the globe had been shepherded out of Harare, to a lakeside resort for an evening of story telling, African traditional music, professional chitchat and a good meal. We arrived at the location when it was too dark to enjoy the promised beauty of the lake, the weather suddenly turned too cold, with a hint of unwelcome rain, in a drought-stricken country. The evening of idyllic story telling and African music did not fully materialise. The promised reality had turned into a slippery illusion. It was that evening I was asked to write a chapter on African libraries, for a global librarianship project. I accepted. I am forced to recall this incident because it provides a surrealistic backdrop to my discussion.

Libraries in African Society

To appreciate the context and status of libraries in African society, it is useful to realise that the largest percentages of people still belong to an oral system of communication. The largest percentage of people obtain the information they require from kinsfolk, neighbours, village headmen/women, extension services, and other authority figures in the community.[1]

The oral and cultural tapestry holds a rich reservoir of folk tales, legends, wisdom, and unrecorded knowledge, which has belatedly been legitimized under the term, "indigenous knowledge." In some instances, the value of this traditional knowledge has scientific application in solving today's problems in society.[2] When libraries were introduced into Africa, neither the oral context, nor the indigenous knowledge systems were regarded as sufficiently important to influence those who designed library services.

Illiteracy is another significant issue in any discussion of libraries in Africa. The percentage of literacy varies from country to country, ranging from 25 percent in countries like Burundi, to 30 percent in Nigeria, Africa's most populous country, and as high as 85 percent in Tanzania, and almost 100 percent in the island state of Mauritius.[3]

It is of interest that most African public libraries have not been very successful in playing an active part in support of adult literacy education. Tanzania's high literacy rate, for example, was achieved with minimal contribution from Tanzania Library Services.[4] The problem now is that because of lack of rural community information centres, the newly literate villagers have very limited access to materials for the upkeep of their literacy skills, and some may have relapsed back to illiteracy because of lack of reading practice.

In contrast, Malawi and Botswana have both shown that public libraries can be actively involved in the literacy movement.[5] In the case of Malawi, the strategy has resulted in refocusing of public library services to communities in rural areas where 90 percent of the population lives. The Malawi Library Service is an active member of the National Advisory Council on Literacy and Adult Education, a body involved in supervising literacy activities and producing follow-up literature for the newly literate.

The Botswana National Library Service has followed the Malawi model, and there is active collaboration between the public library services and the Department of Non-Formal Education. An innovative project called Village Reading Rooms (VRR) Project was set up as a collaborative venture involving both the Botswana Library Services and the Department of Non-Formal Education, aimed at publishing literacy materials, and taking reading materials to rural communities throughout the country. Botswana is currently moving one step further by introducing community information services into the urban-based public libraries to complement the VRR initiative.[6]

Such a search for new solutions is unfortunately the exception rather than the rule. Many public libraries are not very active in adapting libraries to the socio-cultural realities of their countries, but are content to play a marginalized role in society.[7] Perhaps what is evident in public library services, in most of Africa, is the lack of visionary leadership, strategic thinking, and a pro-active stance to create a public library service in harmony with the realities of Africa.[8]

The thirst for education, from primary school to university level, is very high in Africa. To most parents, the acquisition of formal education is still regarded as a passport to a job and the good life for their children, even though the reality is often the opposite, as the growing number of unemployed secondary school and university graduates testifies. However, this outlook means that the formal education sector provides a target group of dedicated library users throughout Africa.

Many a public library survives only because of the large number of school children using its services, thus providing the only tangible social justification for the existence of such libraries. In some cases, the number of this category of users can be higher than 95 percent which has prompted some writers to question whether the distinction between public libraries and school libraries is a valid one under such circumstances.[9]

In spite of this high demand for library services by school children, the poor state of school libraries in most of Africa comes as an unexpected contradiction. Whereas in the few international schools that cater to the children of embassy staff, donor agencies and the local elite, one finds good school libraries, in most government schools libraries and media centres are lacking. The main culprits appear to be teaching methods which are predominantly teacher dominated rather than learner centred and resource based, and examination-driven education systems, which result in rote learning and cramming.

In addition school principals and teachers who went through their formal education without the benefit of a school library and media centre are resistant to the introduction of school libraries in their schools, which they regard as a luxury.[10]

One solution to the problem of weak school libraries and media centres is the introduction of information literacy as a subject in the curriculum of schools. In Namibia, for example, a new subject has been introduced in the curriculum at primary and secondary school level, called "Basic Information Science."[11]

The official curriculum document offers the following description:

Basic Information Science is a compulsory subject in the school curriculum. Its aims are to help learners:

- gain knowledge of sources of information

- develop the skills needed to retrieve and use information
- generate new information.[12]

To implement this innovative concept, the Ministry of Basic Education and Culture has created a curriculum panel for the Basic Information Science subject, which includes curriculum developers, teacher-librarians, and teachers. At least one textbook to support the teaching of this course has already been published.[13]

African academic libraries, by comparison to public and school libraries are in comparatively better shape. The great demand for higher education in Africa had acted as a catalyst for the development of academic libraries. Much donor funding found its way (and still does, although now reduced to a trickle) to academic libraries. In most countries, academic libraries are among the best organised, and have a better working environment than the other libraries. Perhaps what is most significant, is that the managers of these institutions place high value on their libraries, which is in sharp contrast to the predicament of the other types of libraries. All these factors have combined to ensure that the cream of librarians in any African country is to be found in the university libraries. Indeed, in a few cases, university library staff have won academic status, with conditions of service which are similar to academic staff in the university. One by-product of this has been an increasing volume of professional literature, some of high quality, as the university library staff have become absorbed by the "publish or perish" syndrome.

The Reading Culture, Publishing, and Libraries

That Africans do not have a reading culture is a statement that has been repeated so often that it must surely be true. This conclusion is reached because any casual observation of African society clearly shows that reading for pleasure is not widely established.

The publishing industry in Africa, in an average country, has an annual output of around 300 titles. The partial exceptions to this pattern of low publishing output per country are perhaps Kenya, Zimbabwe, and the Republic of South Africa. Publications are few, expensive, and hardly available outside the capital city because of a weak distribution network.

The non-availability of reading materials is further exacerbated by the skewed distribution of libraries. We have already seen how weak public libraries and school libraries are, but what is perhaps significant is that, in most of Africa, libraries do not exist outside the major urban centres. Even in the towns and cities where libraries "theoretically" exist, they are tucked away in high class neighbourhoods, or business centres, as far away from where the people live as possible.[14]

Given the barren publishing industry already described, it is perhaps not surprising that well over 97 percent of the materials found in libraries are imported (mostly as donations—of course!), in a foreign language, only understood by the highly educated nationals and the expatriate community.

In this context of acute "book hunger," the conclusion that Africans do not have a reading culture is, no doubt, self-evident. To my mind, however, the verdict of "no reading culture" is superficial and based on a failure to explore what has caused the problem, and thus comes up with solutions which are likely to be of little use. My argument is that this is not a cultural problem, but rather a problem that has arisen due to four primary reasons:

1. the materials in libraries and bookshops are too expensive in relation to earnings of the population;
2. these materials are in the wrong languages;
3. the subject matter is often of little concern to potential customers; and
4. for those who live away from the capital city, there is often no bookshop, nor library where they can come into contact with reading materials.

Viewed from this perspective, the problem shifts away from lack of a reading culture, to one of inadequate and irrelevant supply of reading matter.

I am not advocating national self-sufficiency as the goal of local publishing, because no country can or should be self-sufficient in publishing, but a minimum level of publishing in Africa is a requirement if the performance of libraries in providing relevant information is to be achieved. This calls for a partnership between libraries and publishing firms, to form alliances and support each other. It also calls for African publishers to produce books that are within the economic means of their potential customers. As one Namibian publisher put it, "the right book at the right price, and the right place."[15]

India offers the ideal model for Africa with its publication of cheap books, which do not look attractive, but are affordable to the customers. Another major weakness is distribution of African publications, both among African countries and outside Africa. The formation of the African Publishers Network and better bibliographic tools on African publications will help to alleviate this problem. The Zimbabwe International Book Fair, for example, has become an annual marketing event for African publications, which has helped to raise the profile of publishing in Africa and created a significant literary market place.

Information on Science, Technology, and Libraries

Africa now has the dubious distinction of being the most backward continent in the world. Part of the reason why our continent is lagging behind other continents is its inability to exploit to the maximum the scientific and technological advances which are available in other parts of the world.

Access to information on the latest technological advances would help decision makers to reach the right choices on which technologies can be adapted, and this would lead to improved productivity. This calls for an improved information transfer process, both at the international and national levels, covering subjects like agricultural technology—to increase the yield and quality of production; engineering technology—to improve the performance of the construction industry; and medical sciences—to improve the level of health in the population. Information is also essential in the subject of alternative energy sources, including solar, biogas, and hydropower.[16]

Efforts to overcome this information gap in science and technology have included setting up information networks internationally and nationally, from which library and documentation services are offered.

Below are examples of several existing networks with good library and information services:

- International Centre in Agroforestry in Nairobi
- International Institute for Tropical Agriculture in Ibadan
- International Livestock Centre for Africa in Addis Ababa

- Southern African Coordination Centre for Agricultural Research for the Southern Africa Development Community (SADC) based in Gaborone, Botswana
- World Conservation Union, Africa Centre, in Harare, Zimbabwe

These centres represent the best performers among African library and information services because they have access to international funding, the latest information technology, and employ the most competent staff.

Parallel to the above effort, another information-transfer strategy has been the setting up of national focal points, which are part of an international network. The dual mandate of the national focal points is to bring information from the international arena into the country and also to collect local information and feed it into the cooperative international databases. Some national focal points, for example, were started under FAO, called AGRIS focal points, as well as the United Nations Environment Programme (UNEP), based in Nairobi, which has set up infoterra national focal points. By comparison to the regional and international centres described above, this strategy has not worked at all. Most of the national focal points exist only in name, and the only time they come alive is when erstwhile passive staff wake up to attend expensive international and regional donor-funded conferences.

A third strategy to information transfer has been through use of modern information technology to access information held in online databases and the Internet by libraries in Africa. A number of organizations have been active in implementing this strategy including: the Carnegie Corporation of New York, the American Association for the Advancement of Science (USA), International Development Research Centre (Canada), UNESCO, SAREC of Sweden, and many others.

Case studies from recently completed projects supported by the National Research Council (USA) are described in a recent publication titled *Bridge Builders: African Experiences with Information and Communication Technology*.[17] The report describes a complex programme that has the following aspects:

1. projects based on the use of CD-ROM, desktop publishing, and electronic e-mail services;
2. training programs for information providers and organization directors and managers to make them computer literate; and
3. experiments with technologies suitable for communication with rural or distant communities using a variety of technologies.[18]

Conclusion

The title of this paper, "African Librarianship: Reality or Illusion?", was chosen to highlight the tensions and contradictions within African librarianship. Africa, the most backward continent, needs a massive injection of information in science, technology, and the social sciences, to catch up with the rest of the world. The contradiction is that very limited information flows into Africa, and most policy makers do not regard information as a development resource.

The demand for education and literacy skills is quite high, and this demand creates a captive market for libraries of all types. There is, however, tension within African public libraries whether to identify with this market segment and meet its demands fully (for textbooks, literacy materials, and curriculum-related materials) or to continue with the status quo, which is to identify with the "adult users" market segment, which is interested in entertainment and light reading. This segment has not yet fully emerged in Africa. Another contradiction is found within the government and Ministries of Education, that although education is highly regarded, investment in school library and media centres to support meaningful education is minimal.

Academic libraries are more powerful, organized and able to attract scarce donor funding. There is, however, tension within the academic library circles, and between academic libraries and other libraries, whether the former should assume a national role to ensure that the information resources which they house are used optimally. Indeed, in most cases a national vision is lacking, and often competition and not cooperation is the order of the day.

Ultimately, there are two factors that influence library development in Africa. The first is the economic strength of individual countries, to afford, for example, the foreign currency to purchase publications, information technology equipment and create a sound infrastructure. The second factor is strong leadership within the library sector, to guide, plan, and cajole government and donor agencies to support library development. Interestingly, in the Eastern and Southern Africa region (a region with which I am most familiar), when you have strong national economies, good leadership in the library sector seems to be lacking, and where you have strong leadership, the economic situation of the country seems to be very unpromising. This perhaps is yet another contradiction.

The present African library scenario is not bright, but the future is not pre-determined. I feel the situation can be turned around through strategic planning, including clarification of vision and mission statements, consultation with all stakeholders, and setting priorities.

African librarianship, viewed from this perspective, has challenging and exciting possibilities.

Notes

1. K. J. Mchombu, "Information Needs for Rural Development: The Case Study of Malawi," *African Journal of Library, Archives and Information Science* 2 (1992): 17-32.

2. R. Chambers, *Rural Development: Putting the Last First* (London: Longmans, 1983).

3. G. O. Oyelekan, "Promoting Mass Literacy Campaigns through Library Services in Nigeria," *New Library World* 94, no. 1109 (1993): 14-19

4. S. Spaulding, et al., *An Impact Evaluation of the Rural Press and Rural Library Projects in Tanzania* (Paris: UNESCO, 1992); K. J. Mchombu, "Development of Library and Documentation Services in Tanzania: Problems of Strategy and Tactics," *Information Processing and Management* 20 (1984): 559-569.

5. Rodrick Mabomba, "Improving Access to Information in Africa; the Rural Library Service in Malawi" (paper presented at the 59th IFLA General Conference, Barcelona) Booklet 8 (III-AF-RICA-E), 1993.

6. Esther Matenge, "Report on the Francistown Public Library: Users Information Seeking Patterns and Information Needs," August 1996; Margaret Myers (Peace Corps volunteer, Botswana), personal communication, 1997.

7. Paul Sturges and Richard Neill, *The Quiet Struggle: Libraries and Information for Africa* (London: Mansell, 1990); H. K. Raseroka, "Changes in Public Libraries during the Last Twenty Years: An African Perspective," *Libri* 44 (1994): 153-163.

8. K. J. Mchombu, "Which Way African Librarianship?" *International Library Review* 23 (1991): 183-200.

9. Anthony Olden, *Libraries in Africa: Pioneers, Policies, Problems* (Lanham, Md. and London: Scarecrow Press, 1995).

10. P. Havard-Williams, "Education for Library and Information Science in Botswana," *Innovation*, no. 9 (December 1994): 10-15.

11. Namibia Republic, Ministry of Basic Education and Culture, *Basic Information Science Syllabus Grades 4-7* (Okahanja: NIED, 1996).

12. Ibid.

13. I. Goosen, et al., *Adventures into Information: A Manual of Basic Information Science* (Windhoek: Gamsberg Macmillan, 1995).

14. Shirazi Durrani, "Rural Information in Kenya," *Information Development* 1, no. 3 (1985): 149-157; K. J. Mchombu, "On the Librarianship of Poverty," *Libri* 32 (1982): 241-250.

15. Jane Katjavivi, "Books, Learning and Namibian Society" (paper presented at the UNESCO/DANIDA Basic Learning Materials National Book Sector Consultation, Windhoek, 1-5 September 1997), 8p.

16. Leong Kwak Onn, "The Information Factor in the Exploitation of Science and Technology," in *Information for Productivity and Development,* ed. Oli Mohamed and Wong Tuck Cheong (Singapore: Maruzen Asia, 1983), 119-126.

17. National Research Council, *Bridge Builders: African Experiences with Information and Communication Technology* (Washington, D.C.: National Academy Press, 1996).

18. National Research Council, *Science and Technology Information Services and Systems in Africa*, rev. ed. (Washington, D.C.: National Academy Press, 1990).

20. Dreams and Realities: Building a New Information Society in South Africa

Peter G. Underwood and Mary Nassimbeni

A major problem in discussing any aspect of the development of South Africa is whether to treat the country as "developed" or as "developing." In some respects, it has characteristics of a "first-world" culture, with a highly literate group of its population making use of a comprehensive system of telecommunications, information and consumer services. It has, also, a high proportion of its present population who are barely literate, with rates of illiteracy varying from between 27 percent in metropolitan areas to 50 percent in rural areas.[1] In addition, many dwellers in the rural areas can make little direct use of documentary information sources and have little possibility of using information or consumer services because none are available in their locality. The introduction of democratic structures to replace the apartheid state and the need to redress injustices of the past pose a set of stimulating and exciting challenges and opportunities. The development of the "Information Society" offers one possible approach to the need to uplift a large segment of the population of South Africa; however, the design and implementation of appropriate and sustainable systems are problematic within such a damaged culture.

Background: Profile of the Country

Interim results from the first post-apartheid census conducted in 1996 showed that there are 37.9 million people living in South Africa, which is classified as an upper-middle income country of medium-level human development. The human development of the majority, however, is low because the previous regime favoured and implemented policies that privileged whites, who enjoyed high levels of education, consumption, income and access to resources. The majority of citizens are poor in comparison and had minimal access to basic social and economic services. The Human Development Index (HDI) level of development of the country's population based on life expectancy, education and income was 0.716 in 1994.[2] Disaggregation of the figures shows the vast discrepancies in quality of life for different sectors of the society, as the HDI figures in Table 1 demonstrate.[3]

There are also vast differentials between provinces, so that the HDI figure for the Northern Province, the poorest province, is 0.470, while the figure for the Western Cape, the richest, is 0.826. The huge backlog in human resource development, one of the most striking legacies of the apartheid years, is reflected in the 1996 World Competitiveness Report, which placed South Africa 44th out of 46 countries and 46th in the human development category.[4] The World Development Report showed that,

TABLE 1

Population group	Human Development Index
Africans	0.500
Coloureds	0.663
Asians	0.836
Whites	0.897

although South Africa is the country in Africa closest to the developed world, the gap between rich and poor is one of the largest in the world.[5]

Connectivity

Connectivity is one of the keys to the development of the information society in Africa: A year-by-year comparison of connectivity published in map form by Lanweber shows the gradual spread of the Internet across Africa.[6] However, this apparent spread of connectivity masks startling differences in provision, with South Africa being considerably advantaged. The number of Internet hosts in South Africa placed it sixteenth in the world at the start of 1997, but within the African continent it ranks as first, with 96 percent of Africa's hosts. Something of the scale of the disparity can be appreciated by comparing this with the second rank: Egypt occupies this place, with 1.6 percent of the hosts in Africa.[7] Access to telecommunications within South Africa is also very uneven, reflecting the gross inequities inherited from the apartheid state. Although clear commitments to massive expansion of the telecommunications infrastructure have been given in addresses by government ministers, such changes will take a considerable time to have a large-scale effect. In the meantime, access to the Internet and many other features of the "wired" environment could only be available to the majority of the population through institutional access in schools, colleges and tertiary-level education, business and other ventures rather than in their homes.

Library and Information Services in South Africa: A Profile

The library and information sector is characterised by small pockets of excellence and technological sophistication, while the majority of citizens "do not have access to even the most rudimentary library and information services."[8] South Africa's library and information services include two national libraries, 670 public (municipal) libraries, 370 special libraries, 90 government libraries, and 88 university and college libraries. The bookstock consists of 47 million items and there are 1,570 service points.[9] The development has been haphazard and uncoordinated because the apartheid state government abrogated its responsibilities for the provision of library and information services, which it declared would develop adequately in response to market forces.[10] Progressive information workers adopted vigorous protest and lobby actions against the approaches to the conceptualisation and practice of library and information work informed by rigidity, conservatism and alignment with government policies of the period. When it became evident that liberation was imminent, these efforts coalesced into concerted initiatives, in the early 1990s, to start a process of restructuring and transformation in library and information services: This process developed according to an agenda which espoused the principles of non-racialism, non-sexism and redress, promoted by the liberation movement, and which began to move from the mode of critique and opposition to one of engagement with the development of policy options for the new state.[11]

Policy Planning in the Library and Information Services Sector: A New Paradigm

The new Constitution of South Africa, adopted in 1996, confers citizenship and fundamental human rights on all its citizens. Consequently, every aspect of national life is being transformed in the light of the new constitution and democratic dispensation. All public policy, including initiatives to transform library and information services, is formulated within the framework of two over-arching policies for the nation: the Reconstruction and Development Programme (RDP)[12] and the Growth, Employment and Redistribution (GEAR) strategy.[13] The RDP is "an instrument for transforming government and society ... an integrated programme, based on the people that will provide peace and prosperity for all and build a nation."[14] GEAR sets out an integrated economic strategy for rebuilding and restructuring the national economy and meeting the challenges of satisfying basic needs, developing human resources and increasing participation in the democratic institutions of civil society.[15]

The restructuring of library and information services in the country is premised on a number of universal values enshrined in the Constitution and also particular problems of a nascent democracy with a need for "fast tracking" of human resource development and economic growth. Demographic and other characteristics of the country which impact on the provision of library and information services include rapid population growth, a youthful population, low education levels and high illiteracy rates.[16] A government report notes, for example, that although there is a high enrollment of children in primary school, only 40 percent of these currently successfully complete secondary education.[17]

The mission of the library and information services sector has been identified by the Interministerial Working Group on the Library and Information Services (LIS) Function (National Level) as being "to support and stimulate the socio-economic, educational, cultural, scientific and information development of all communities in the country by providing access to relevant information for all, and to raise the information levels and literacy levels" of all citizens.[18] The Report argues that the Information Society should be the framework within which all planning to provide a library and information services infrastructure takes place and that a change in strategic approach is required to lead toward the integration of library and information services policies into broader Information Society policy.[19]

The themes of the Information Society and information literacy resonate in the National Commission on Higher Education Working Group on Libraries and Information Technology (WGLIT) report, which considers policy implications of the role of libraries and information technology in higher education.[20] The WGLIT investigation was framed by a vision of a new national information system capable of integrating its component parts into a seamless whole, rather than one in which individuality is highlighted, and of a transformed higher education system responsive to both the national agenda of reconstruction, and also the demands of globalisation and the new knowledge economy.[21] Graduates of the new system should exit with skills which are attributes of the new information age: the skills to gain access to appropriate information, the ability to evaluate and discriminate between sources, lifelong learning skills, and social skills which promote cooperative work.[22] The library, with adequate levels of information technology and connectivity, is ideally placed through information literacy programmes to participate in preparing graduates to meet the challenges of the knowledge economy.

Education as a Focus for Library and Information Work

There is consensus that the nexus between library and information services and education is a powerful principle in the debate around transformation. Library and information services must be seen as "integral to lifelong learning."[23] The Working Group on National Libraries has considered the educational role of library and information services and summarises the position adopted by most policy statements issued by the library and information services sector:

- Libraries in educational institutions are essential resources for learner-centred, resource-based learning, as distinct from textbook-based rote learning.
- Public and community libraries serve as key resources for pre-school education, literacy work and adult education.
- The above categories of libraries, along with many others, embody and promote the values of a culture of learning, information use, and information literacy.[24]

In spite of high spending on education—nearly 7 percent of the Gross Domestic Product[25]—there are serious backlogs in the education system with respect to plant, facilities, trained person power and other resources. The first nationwide register of school needs, published in August 1997, showed that most of the country's 32,000 schools have no libraries.[26] The cost of provision of basic facilities like classrooms, running water, electricity and adequate toilet facilities is staggeringly high; the short-term prospects of supplying school libraries in the face of such starkly impoverished environmental conditions seem unlikely, particularly, as has been noted, if libraries do not enjoy a higher priority for funding allocations.[27]

Rural Isolation and Neglect

It is widely acknowledged that rural and remote communities suffered the most savage effects under the previous apartheid regime, including extreme poverty.[28] These marginalised communities are the most starved of education, information, employment and other resources. Strategies need to be devised to eliminate the tyranny of distance to avoid the danger that a two-tier society, determined by geography, will manifest itself in the rural/urban divide. Apart from so-called national libraries in the former homeland capitals, none of the schools serving African communities had libraries when the new government came into power in 1994. The only libraries that existed in the Northern Province, for example, were in white schools.[29] The system and network of public libraries are to be transformed from "recreational resources for wealthy whites [into vital resources] for millions of black people who need to fill an educational vacuum" in the words of Meshack Mulaudzi, Director of Library Services in the Province.[30] In the Eastern Cape, which suffers from a similar situation of past neglect and deprivation, the thinking has turned toward clustering schools around service delivery points instead of the impossible task of providing each school with its own library. Unused buildings, such as closed prisons, will be converted into community education centres supplying materials, advice and information to meet community needs ranging from seeds for agriculture to immunisation.[31] The potential for delivery of information and education by way of Information Technology has been considered by the government, and the national telecommunication agency Telkom is committed to extending the infrastructure to the remotest regions of the country.

Information Society and Multi-Purpose Community Centres

The G7 Information Society and Development Conference (ISAD), which took place in May 1996, included a proposal for the establishment of Multi-Purpose Community Centres (MPCCs),[32] but the possible impact of this idea was explored more fully in the complementary conference "Empowering Communities in the Information Society."[33] MPCCs were identified as being one of the best strategic choices for addressing the community needs of previously disadvantaged groups in urban and rural localities. The centres would be an extension, or expression, of the government's concept of the information community, highlighting the need to link communities with information for development. This is an example of the adaptation of the concept of the Information Society to local conditions in a developing country where access to infrastructure is not the most critical problem as many information idealists at the ISAD Conference seemed to suppose. Moreover, it challenges the assumption that the provision of infrastructure and hardware is enough to allow communities to overcome a history of social neglect and to leapfrog into full communion with other members of a potential "information society."[34]

MPCCs will provide a focus for the participation of members of a community, thus beginning to break down the sense of isolation and alienation felt by so many people in urban and rural areas. Community members will be encouraged to build the capacity of their social groups through mutual recognition and transfer of skills and knowledge. Implicit in this is a recognition that literacy can best be inculcated through work at the grassroots level but, also, that oral sources and traditional knowledge form a rich and essential component of the social fabric, needing respect and recognition.

Berlyn notes:

> Community participation provides the main reason for the existence of the MPCCs, which are one of the major initiatives that could be used in the restoration of the social fibre of South African society. The community-at-large is a plethora of contrasts as regards literacy and numeracy, language, opportunities and access to goods and services. This diversity is the most important reason why a common thread is necessary to pull all the disparate threads together.[35]

The delivery and provision of health care, welfare, library and information services will form another important focus for the MPCCs. Also at the heart of the proposals is the recognition that MPCCs could provide the point of delivery for telecommunications service to otherwise-unprovided communities. What is presently unresolved is how the social and direct costs of such provision will be met. The concept of a sharing of national and private sector investment is sometimes raised as an answer. Hall illustrates this point by reference to the development by the company Siemens of "Phone Shops," which can be built as pre-fabricated units and connected to the cellular telephone network. This development was a direct result of the requirement by the

South African government that applicants for government licences for running cellular telephone networks should be able to demonstrate a strong involvement in the enhancement of community telephone facilities.[36] Hall also comments that it may be difficult to ensure that the private sector remains as committed to longer-term policies of social redress as to the more immediate attractions of profits in the short term.

The urban prototype of a one-stop shop multi-purpose community centre is already operational in an urban centre in Gauteng, as the Alexsan Resource Centre. This resource centre, which is not funded by government, incorporates a cluster of facilities, including a well-stocked library with "over 10,000 books in the reference and fiction sections, 6,000 children's books, seven computers, a Braille section and adult education training arm."[37] Other facilities are a career guidance office, a satellite clinic, pension collection points and a computer training centre. The director sees this centre as potentially embodying the government's promotion of the partnership principle between government, private sector, non-governmental organisations (NGOs) and community-based organisations (CBOs).

Technology and the Concept of Community

At the heart of the debate at the G7 Information and Society and Development Conference there was a fundamental difference in perception about the role of information technology. Blake has commented: "ISAD was more a historic confluence of people rather than a meeting of minds. The division being that the interests of the developing world lie in development and the interests of the developed world lie in marketing."[38] This aptly summarises the tension between the views, but the real force of the South African vision is not just about development. The South African society is one which will be wracked by the vestiges of the apartheid history, by the attitudes inculcated in every aspect of society by that history, for many years. Reparation and redress are not merely about giving people goods and services they have formerly been denied: A "Band-Aid" treatment cannot heal the profound divisions which are there. Mbeki notes:

> We are emerging, but only slowly and painfully, out of a deeply fractured society. This is a society which continues to be characterised by deep fissures which separate the black people from the white, the hungry from the prosperous, the urban from the rural, the male from the female, the disabled from the rest.[39]

The free flow of information could have a positive effect if it enables the marginalised and isolated in the populace to begin to recognise themselves as members of communities, to value their own identity but also to see themselves as taking part in the collective rebuilding of our nation.

The global information infrastructure provides a powerful tool for reaching individuals and communities: the challenge for South Africa is to foster the "local touch" through the concept of "ubuntu"—an expression common to many languages in Africa, and meaning "I am, because you are." The South African vision of the Information Society is of empowerment of communities by the use of information technology. Ramphele summarises the need for care in development in these words:

> The African Renaissance has to be driven by collective intellectual energy which draws on the strong historical, cultural, economic and political ties of the region. Africa has to find appropriate solutions to its problems through rigorous self-criticism and courageous lateral thinking.[40]

Notes

1. South Africa, Ministry for Welfare and Population Development, *White Paper for Social Welfare: Principles, Guidelines, Recommendations, Proposed Policies and Programmes for Developmental Social Welfare in South Africa* (Pretoria: Department of Welfare, 1997); Chapter 1 [cited 23 November 1997], available from http://www.polity.org.za/govdocs/white_papers/social971.html#CHAP-TER1.

2. South Africa, Ministry for Welfare and Population Development, *Draft White Paper on Population Policy* (Pretoria: Department of Welfare, August 1997); online [23 November 1997] available from http://www.polity.org.za/govdocs/white_papers/poppol.html.

3. Although non-racialism is enshrined in the new Constitution, because of the imperative for redress it is sometimes necessary to refer to the former categorisation of people according to "population group."

4. "Merely Denting Education Backlogs," *Weekly Mail & Guardian* (South Africa), 22 August–28 August 1997, Supplement on Non-Governmental Organisations: Working in a Changing Society, 3.

5. "While the Rich Get Richer ... ." *Financial Mail* (South Africa), 145, August 1997, 19.

6. Larry Lanweber, *International Connectivity* (1993-1997), online [cited 23 November 1997] available from ftp://ftp.cs.wisc.edu/connectivity_table/.

7. András Salamon, *Internet Statistics* (2 September 1997), online [cited 23 November 1997] available from http://www.dns.net/andras/stats.html.

8. South Africa, Arts and Culture Task Group (ACTAG), Library and Information Services Subcommittee, *Report on Libraries and Information Services: Chapter Six of the Report of the Arts and Culture Task Group, as Presented to the Minister of Arts, Culture, Science and Technology on 31 July 1995: with Supplementary and Background Documents* (Pretoria: State Library for the Department of Arts, Culture, Science and Technology, 1995), 10.

9. Peter J. Lor, "Overview of the Current State of Library and Information Services in South Africa," in South Africa, Arts and Culture Task Group (ACTAG), Library and Information Services Subcommittee, *Report on Libraries and Information Services: Chapter Six of the Report of the Arts and Culture Task Group, as Presented to the Minister of Arts, Culture, Science and Technology on 31 July 1995: with Supplementary and Background Documents* (Pretoria: State Library for the Department of Arts, Culture, Science and Technology, 1995), 135-140.

10. South Africa, Ministry of Arts, Culture, Science and Technology, Arts and Culture Task Group (ACTAG), Subcommittee on Library and Information Services, *Report on Libraries and Information Services*, 10.

11. National Education Coordinating Committee, National Education Policy Investigation (NEPI), *Library and Information Services: Report of the NEPI Library and Information Services Research Group* (Cape Town: Oxford University Press, 1992).

12. African National Congress. *The Reconstruction and Development Programme: A Policy Framework* (Johannesburg: African National Congress, 1994).

13. South Africa, Government, *Growth, Employment and Redistribution: A Macro-Economic Strategy* (14 June 1996), online [cited 23 November 1997] available from http://www.polity.org.za/govdocs/policy/growth.html.

14. South Africa, Minister without Portfolio, *RDP Challenges: An Information Brochure Issued by the Minister without Portfolio* (Cape Town: Government Printer, 1994).

15. South Africa, Ministry for Welfare and Population Development, *Draft White Paper on Population Policy*.

16. South Africa, Department of Arts, Culture, Science and Technology, *Report of the Working Group on the National Libraries of South Africa: Second Draft*, (24 February 1997), online [cited 23 November 1997], available from http://www.polity.org.za/govdocs/reports/library.html.

17. South Africa, Government, *Growth, Employment and Redistribution: A Macro-Economic Strategy*.

18. South Africa, Ministry of Arts Culture, Science and Technology, *Report of the Interministerial Working Group on the LIS (Library and Information Services) Function (National Level): As presented to the Minister of Arts, Culture, Science and Technology and the Minister of Education on 28 February 1997* (Pretoria: Department of Arts, Culture, Science and Technology and the Department of Education, 1997), 18.

19. Ibid., 15.

20. National Commission on Higher Education, Working Group on Libraries and Information Technology (WGLIT), *Policy, Planning and Co-operation: Smart Solutions for Information Provision* (Pretoria: National Commission on Higher Education, 1966).

21. Ibid., 1.

22. Ibid., 3.

23. African National Congress, Education Department, *A Policy Framework for Education and Training* (Johannesburg: African National Congress, 1994), 80.

24. South Africa, Department of Arts, Culture, Science and Technology, *Report of the Working Group on the National Libraries of South Africa. Second draft.*

25. South Africa, Government, *Growth, Employment and Redistribution: A Macro-Economic Strategy.*

26. "R3-billion a Year to Fix Schooling," *Weekly Mail & Guardian* (South Africa), 8 August-14 August 1997, 6.

27. South Africa, Department of Arts, Culture, Science and Technology, *Report of the Working Group on the National Libraries of South Africa. Second draft.*

28. South Africa, Office of the State President, *Rural Development Strategy of the Government of National Unity: A Discussion Document* (1995), online [23 November 1997], available from http://www.polity.org.za/govdocs/rdp/rural1.html.

29. "Growing Up without Books," *Weekly Mail & Guardian* (South Africa), 3 October-9 October 1997, 6.

30. Ibid.

31. Ibid.

32. South Africa, Department of Arts, Culture and Technology and National Information Technology Forum, "The Information Society and the Developing World: A South African Approach," in *Proceedings of the International Society and Development Conference, 13-15 May 1996, South Africa* (Pretoria: Council for Scientific and Industrial Research [CSIR], 1966); Chapter 5.4.1, online [cited 23 November 1997] available from http://www.csir.co.za/isad/chapter5.htm#5.4.1.

33. International Development Research Centre, Regional Office for Southern Africa, *Support for Multi-Purpose Community Centres* (Johannesburg: IDRC, 1966); online [cited 23 November 1997] available from http://idrc.org.za/96890101.htm.

34. "Technology Versus Development," *Weekly Mail & Guardian* (South Africa), 30 August-5 September 1996, B3.

35. J. D. Berlyn, "Empowering Communities in the Information Society," *Meta-Information Bulletin*, 6 (May 1997), 2; online [cited 14 November 1997], available from http://www.librarynet.co.za/Meta-info_bulletin1.htm.

36. Martin Hall, "The Virtual University: Education for All, or a Segregated Highway?" in *Towards Smart Solutions for Information Usage in Higher Education: A Workshop for Organisations Seeking to Invent, Introduce and Replicate Smart Practices, 29-31 October 1997* (n.p.: Centre for Higher Education Transformation and The Ford Foundation, 1997), unpaginated.

37. "New Breed of One-Stop Community Centres," *Weekly Mail & Guardian* (South Africa), 22 August-28 August 1997, 33.

38. Edwin Blake, *Information Society and Development Conference: What Was and Is Happening?* (27 November 1996), online [cited 23 November 1997], available from http://www.cs.uct.ac.za/~edwin/isad-pm/node12.html.

39. Thabo Mbeki, *Deputy President,* Speech at the National Assembly, *Parliamentary Debate on Budget Vote No. 2* (10 June 1997), online [cited 23 November 1997], available from http://www.polity.org.za/govdocs/speeches/1997/sp970610.html.

40. Mamphela Ramphele, "Responsible Citizenship Entails Risk Taking," *Independent Online* (South Africa), 20 October 1996, online [cited 23 November 1997], available from http://www.inc.co.za/online/hero/oct_20/ramphela1020.html.

21. Queens Library: Global Reach to Serve Diverse Communities

Gary E. Strong

The Queens Borough Public Library represents a fundamental public good in our democracy. It assures the right, the privilege, and the ability of individuals to choose and pursue any direction of thought, study, or action they wish. The Library provides the intellectual capital necessary for people to understand the past and plan for the future. It is also our collective memory, since history and human experience are best preserved in writing.

As Queens Library enters its second century, it is dedicated to the needs of its diverse communities; its advocacy and support of appropriate technology; the excellence of its collections; the commitment of its staff to its customers and the very highest ideals of library service. We at the Queens Library believe deeply in equity and that libraries are fundamental in empowering people to take charge of their lives, their governments, and their communities. In this way, Queens Library has an essential role to play in the new millennium. The collections we build, the access we provide, and the technologies we embrace will carry the people of Queens into a productive and creative future.

The Borough of Queens in New York City is the most ethnically diverse area in the United States. One of three Queens residents hails from another country, and nearly half of the borough's residents speak a language other than English at home. Queens is a place in which people of more than one hundred nationalities work toward common goals.

In the 1960s, library materials in languages other than English were few and insignificant. The collections were typically translations of the classics and almost always books. However, the philosophy of customer service at the Queens Library has always been to meet the needs of its customers and to provide the kind of materials and programs that customers want. As a result, the development of non-English language collections shifted significantly in the 1980s after the establishment of the innovative "New Americans Program."

The New Americans Program

Recognizing the tremendous opportunity to serve the new Americans in the burgeoning immigrant neighborhoods in Queens in a unique manner, the Library established the New Americans Program (NAP) in 1977 to provide the special services necessary to welcome and acclimate the area's new communities. Initially funded by the Library Services and Construction Act, the program has been incorporated into the Library structure and now is fully funded from the Library's annual operating budget, offering a variety of enhanced services throughout the entire system. Local branch service is adjusted to meet the community needs and is supported by NAP staff. NAP's talented staff not only represent the communities they serve, but have developed a truly incredible service. The budget for the New Americans Program is currently $950,000 from local funds.

Collections

Say Sí (Spanish Language): 100,000 Items at the Central Library and 20 Branches

In 1985 the Library conducted a Gallup poll which found that, compared to other groups, the large Latino community of Queens was not well aware of the Library and was not using its services. The Library's response was to start a collection development and public relations campaign called *"¡Diga Sí a Su Biblioteca!,"* or "Say *Sí* to Your Library," which came to be known by most Library staff as the *"Say Sí* Project." During the first year of *Say Sí,* comprehensive book collections were placed in seven branches and the Central Library. Since then the number of branches has increased to twenty plus the Central Library. Additionally, musical CDs and recordings, videocassettes and audio books have been added to these collections. At the same time that the collections were being placed in the branches, a public relations campaign was implemented to ensure that the Latino community knew what was being made available. The campaign included the development of Spanish-language brochures, bookmarks, and library card applications, as well as a bilingual manual to be used by non-Spanish-speaking staff when serving Spanish-speaking customers. Translated press releases were sent to the Spanish-language media, and soon the community started to look for the *Say Sí* collections.

The *Say Sí* collections carry a large selection of non-fiction titles, from cooking to politics, from history to parenting, from mysteries of the occult to the newest computer programming books. In fiction, the Library orders both classics and popular fiction, from books by established authors such as Neruda, Garcia Marquez, Sor Juana Ines de la Cruz, and Vargas Llosa, to translations of English-language popular fiction. The collections also include books by many Latino authors living and writing in the U.S., as well as books by emerging new authors from Latin America and Spain. *¡Informé!,* a Spanish-language database, delivers more than sixty periodicals and one hundred information pamphlets to all Library locations electronically.

Ni Hao (Chinese Language): 102,000 Items at the Central Library and 28 Branches

In 1988, the Library launched the *Ni Hao* campaign to meet the community's growing demand for Chinese materials. *"Ni Hao"* means "greetings" in Chinese. The *Ni Hao* program is the largest public library collection development program in the country for general Chinese readers.

During the last nine years the New Americans Program has built a well-rounded Chinese collection with emphasis on publications of modern literature by best-selling authors from the 1920s through the present. In addition to adult and children's books, all *Ni Hao* collections have audiocassettes, CDs, magazines and newspapers. Videotapes are also available in five branches. All materials are selected by staff experienced and knowledgeable in Chinese language and literature. At least 90 percent of adult books and all videotapes purchased are cataloged. NAP has built balanced collections in terms of place of publication (Taiwan, China, and Hong Kong), reading level, and subject matter. NAP also considers the preferences and needs of Mandarin and Cantonese speakers in selecting audio- and videotapes.

Ni Hao has many special features. For example, the "Chinese Periodicals Subscription List," from which branches select newspapers and magazines, is one of the most comprehensive lists of its kind of any public library in the United States. Through standing order plans, NAP places the latest best sellers and other works by popular authors on library shelves as soon as they become available. Based on information learned from regular branch visits, survey findings, and direct communication with customers, materials are transferred between branches to ensure maximum use. *Ni Hao* was developed to meet the changing needs for Chinese materials in Queens and to promote awareness and usage of library facilities, programs, and services of the Queens Library system. Circulation statistics indicate that materials in Chinese are used at a higher rate than materials in English and that all branches with large *Ni Hao* collections have enjoyed a tremendous increase in use.

Hannara (Korean Language): 24,000 Items in 14 Branches

Koreans are the third largest immigrant language community in Queens, after Latinos and Chinese. During the 1980s, the New Americans Program initially purchased some 5,000 volumes of Korean materials as browsing collections for ten branches. Most of the acquisition was popular fiction, and circulation was modest.

In September 1991, NAP received a small federal Library Services and Construction Act (LSCA) grant to conduct a pilot Korean collection development program, based on the models of its successful Spanish and Chinese collection development programs. Collections of adult and children's books, audiocassettes, and periodicals were added to two branches. In September 1992, NAP received a larger LSCA grant to build collections in five additional branches. From 1993 onward, using funds from the Library's materials budget supplemented by small grants and donations, the Korean collection development program has grown to include fourteen branches. Since then, videotapes have been since added to the collections. The *Hannara* is now one of the largest collections of Korean materials outside Korea.

Most of the materials have been purchased off the shelf from local bookstores. Almost all materials have been cataloged to facilitate collection building and bibliographic access. Circulation of materials has increased tremendously, and the collections have become special features of the branches in which they are housed. In 1995, the program was formally designated *Hannara*, a traditional name for the Korean people. The *Hannara* collections are heavily used. In fact, use statistics indicate that in several branches, interest in Korean materials is higher than interest in English materials. Figures also show that all branches with large *Hannara* collections have enjoyed definite increases in use by the Korean community.

Namaste-Adaab (South Asian Languages): 17,000 Items in Bengali, Gujarati, Hindi, Malayalam, Punjabi, and Urdu at 6 Branches

These collections were initiated in 1994 in response to the growing number of immigrants from India, Pakistan, and Bangladesh over the past decade. Materials in the collection include books, periodicals, and audio tapes in six South Asian languages: Bengali, Gujarati, Hindi, Malayalam, Punjabi, and Urdu. A committee of librarians, each with their own language abilities, is in charge of selecting and monitoring usage of the collections.

Privyét (Russian Language): 24,000 Items in Ten Locations

Privyét means "greetings" in Russian. For years NAP had purchased titles in Russian for a select number of branches, but a marked increase in the number of immigrants from the former Soviet Union and a growing demand for new materials have led the Library to establish a formalized collection. Using Library funds in fiscal years 1997 and 1998, over 9,000 new items were purchased, including children's and adult books, audio- and videocassettes and CDs to be placed in nine locations with the largest concentration of Russian speakers. Separately, the Central Library's Russian collection features classic works of literature, biography and history.

Multi-language: Materials to help immigrants learn English; popular books in many immigrant languages available at most libraries

The Library buys materials in more than fifty other languages to meet the needs of the diverse reading public particular to Queens. And, the Library is constantly assessing those requirements as they develop and is continually determining additional areas of concentration. In the past year a small Turkish collection was added to one branch to serve this emerging immigrant enclave.

Educational and Cultural Programming

Creating adequate and innovative collections is but one way the Library serves new Americans. Educational and cultural programs have also been created to assist new populations in acquiring the skills needed to cope in American life. Queens Library offers the largest library-managed English-as-a-Second-Language (ESL) program in the United States. Each year more than 70 ESL classes are taught by specially trained teachers to nearly 3,500 students, representing 82 countries and 51 languages. In addition, there are multi-language materials, including computer programs, which help immigrants learn English, and conversation groups so they can practice. There are popular books in many immigrant languages other than those included in the special collection. The Library's Mail-a-Book program provides materials in Chinese and other immigrant languages that are sent to Queens residents who are not yet acquainted with the Library. Mail-a-Book introduces them to the Queens Borough Public Library, letting them know it is out there for them. The program creates new users and invites them to come to the Library once they have read everything of interest on the Mail-a-Book lists.

Free lectures and workshops on coping skills are offered in the most widely spoken immigrant languages of Queens on topics essential to new immigrants' acculturation, such as citizenship and job training information, advice on helping children learn, and information on available social services. The Library coordinates its programming with many other organizations to maximize the utilization of available resources. Again recognizing the changing composition of the community, the Library offered its first such coping skills programs in Hindi, Urdu, and Turkish this year. Free readings, concerts, and workshops celebrating the literary, performing and folk arts of immigrants from Asia, Africa, Europe, Latin America, and the Caribbean are regularly offered throughout the system. It is the goal of the Queens Library to become a primary provider of services to new populations.

International Resource Center

The International Resource Center will be a focus point for discussing international issues and a crossroads for understanding. Housed in the new Flushing Library, which opens in spring 1998, the Center will be located in the heart of a community where 60 percent of the population was born in another country and 71 percent of the readers speak a language other than English at home. The Center will take as its image the crossroads on which it stands—a place where diverse peoples meet, exchange ideas and are directed onward to their various destinations. Through the training and enthusiasm of its staff and its special combination of community, technology, collections, services, and programs, the Center will provide a venue for a variety of cultural interactions and expressions. Further, the Center will direct customers efficiently to resources within and outside its walls concerning the world's peoples, languages, and cultures.

The International Resource Center has set the following goals to meet its vision:

1. To provide resources, information and referral to customers who wish to know more about the peoples, cultures, and languages of the world.
2. To provide information to customers with a special interest in international business, travel, communication, study, and teaching.
3. To provide customers with a venue for the sharing of cultures and the presentation of old and new cultural ideas and forms.

The manner in which those goals are realized will distinguish the International Resource Center in three ways:

1. The Center's unique combination of collections, services, and programs will offer customers with a variety of international interests comprehensive resources not available elsewhere in one location.
2. The synergy produced by the power of technology, combined with the skill and enthusiasm of a multilingual staff who, by inclination and training are customer- and community-oriented, will create a talent pool which is highly skilled and efficient in helping customers find the international resources they need.
3. The degree to which the Center networks with agencies throughout the system, the city, the nation, and the world will be unprecedented. Through continual reaching out and networking, the Center will identify a host of human, material, and information resources. Through traditional referral and state-of-the-art technology, customers will access these vast resources in their languages of choice. The Center will draw on agencies with which it networks to plan and promote its services and to offer services cooperatively.

The new International Resource Center will not replace the New Americans Program, but will indeed expand and build on the foundation the Program has laid throughout the Queens Library. Collections of popular materials will continue to be built in branches serving new populations, programs will continue to be offered close to new communities, and new customers will be encouraged to use the library resources within their neighborhoods. The International Resource Center will join in the efforts of the New Americans Program but not replace it. A new staff has been recruited to lead the Center and to develop its programs. Appropriate connections are being made within the Queens Library to ensure the success of the Center and this new dimension in international cooperation.

Technological Challenges

The use of technology in serving a community that speaks and reads 120 different languages is no easy challenge. Many of the largest ethnic groups read languages that use non-Roman character sets, presenting a particular problem in the use of the Library's OPAC, in creating bibliographic references, and in accessing Internet sites, such as those in Chinese, Japanese or Korean, since English computer application operating systems do not routinely support the display of those characters on the screen.

To meet this challenge, the Queens Library started with the major languages used by the constituent population. A Spanish version of the Library's home page and OPAC search engine were deemed a necessary first step, since 20 percent of the residents speak Spanish. The goal was to give Spanish speakers the capability of seeing and using Spanish commands, without necessitating the creation of a separate catalog. A team of bilingual librarians/programmers translated the OPAC's function and command screens. Queens Library customers access the catalog through a World Wide Web browser (e.g., Netscape). *Las paginás en español* are accessible by clicking a button on the Library's home page (http://www.queens.lib.ny.us). The catalog system output scripts were altered by in-house programmers wherever possible so search results would come back in Spanish. Certain searches, such as "author" or "title" could not be changed. An index of Spanish keywords, however, was written and scripted so that when a Library customer types "salud" as a keyword, the system relates it to "health," conducts the search as it would in English and returns the results. Customers can choose to search only the Library's Spanish holdings (more than 100,000 items), the Library's total collection, or narrow the search in other ways. The Spanish search engine also provides an interface to other much used information, such as Queens Library's comprehensive Community Services Database, which catalogs and indexes all health, human and social services available in Queens. Links to Spanish web sites are also included and are continually updated.

Serving the growing Chinese- and Korean-speaking populations was more complex. A system-wide search fielded a team of librarians who are also both bilingual and computer savvy. They began by searching the Internet for web sites in those languages that meet the Library's criteria, such as online newspapers. The team is trained in the "html" coding language of the Internet. Team members work five hours per week under the supervision of a full-time librarian/system analyst, translating titles and annotations, and composing the site's pages. Simultaneously, "Asian Suite 97" software has been installed in the Central Library and in the branches so customers can see web sites in Chinese and Korean characters. They access them by clicking on a list of possibilities (the keyboard cannot type in Chinese or Korean). Searches can be done with Asian Suite, which permits the entry of non-Roman characters via pull-down menus and virtual keyboards. The system is dubbed "WorldLinQ™," a variant on the Library's OPAC name, "InfoLinQ." Development is being facilitated by a major grant from AT&T.

Now that the problems of access and cataloging of non-Roman character languages are being dealt with, new possibilities in collection development are opening up. A recent agreement between Queens Library and Shanghai Library to exchange hard-copy library materials and electronic information will make this access particularly valuable, since a wealth of additional information will soon be available to readers of Chinese.

Next steps will be bibliographic references for the Queens Library's 102,000 Chinese- and 24,000 Korean-language holdings in their native character sets, as well as

English transliterations and licensed databases to deliver non-English materials to the Library's multiple locations cost-effectively. (*¡Informé!* in Spanish is, as already described, up and running with full-text of more than sixty periodicals and one hundred pamphlets.) Those steps will be followed by adding other major languages, most likely Russian, Hebrew, and French.

International Cooperation Takes Shape

In July 1996, I met with the director of the Shanghai Library. We began discussions to explore the possibility of a formal agreement of cooperation between the two libraries. We met again at the IFLA meeting in Beijing in August of that year, and Dr. Sherman Tang represented the Queens Library at the dedication of the new Shanghai Library that December. We held friendly and sincere discussions and agreed to cooperate in a wide range of activities, including the exchange of information on library operations, staff training, and other professional activities. We are in full agreement that this type of interlibrary cooperation is highly significant, will promote friendship between the United States and China, and will enhance the development of the library and information profession.

In April 1997, I visited the Shanghai Library to sign the agreements and to set the cooperation in motion. My visit confirmed firsthand that the library, the second largest in China, is committed to opening up its vast resources to a broader public. Its reading rooms and huge collection of rare materials are being organized for public use. The integration of technology will lead public libraries in China. The possibility of bringing an exhibition of rare materials to Queens was discussed. When I met with the Director again at IFLA in Copenhagen, the details of the exhibition were well underway. It is now set to premiere during the summer of 1998 along with an exhibit of children's art. Director Ma will lead a delegation in a two-week visit to Queens in conjunction with the opening of the International Resource Center in July 1998. In August 1997, two staff members from the Shanghai Library arrived in Queens to spend two months working in the United States. That exchange was advanced in December 1997, when two staff members from the Queens Library visited Shanghai. The agreement, with its exchanges, is set to continue through 2001.

I continued my trip in April 1997, leaving Shanghai for Beijing for discussions with officials of the National Library of China. After a fruitful visit with Deputy Director Zhou and Deputy Director Madame Sun, draft agreements were crafted and faxed for consideration. This would be their first such agreement with a public library. In June 1997, Mr. Zhou and the Head of International Cooperation, Ms. Sun (no relation to Madame Sun), visited the Queens Library. It was apparent by the end of the visit that there would be an agreement covering exchanges of information, technology, exhibitions, and materials. In December 1997, I went to Beijing to sign the formal agreements and to further discussions between us.

The Queens Library continues to host visitors under the USIA librarians program from Central and Latin America, and most recently, other locations in China. But that is not all—in 1997 we welcomed for three months our first intern from France. Finishing his graduate library studies, the intern chose the New Americans Program for an in-depth study needed to complete the requirements for his degree. We will seek other such relationships and exchange opportunities that further our understanding and knowledge about library service in other countries. Such a process can only enhance our ability to serve our quickly changing populations in Queens.

As we enter the new millennium, the Queens Library has positioned itself on the global frontier. International Cooperation has been explored by academic librarians and library educators for the past fifty years. It is now time for public libraries to step up and develop programs which go far beyond the "sister city" relationships and visiting dignitary stage. We have all the evidence we need that meeting New Americans on their terms works—people use libraries when there is something there that makes a difference in their daily lives. The Queens Library is making that difference.

22. Global Relevance through Sustained Achievement: Progress and Contributions of the International Association of School Librarianship

Ken Haycock

What constitutes global relevance in librarianship? Is it impacting the improvement of library and information services in both the "developed" and "developing" nations? Is it providing useful tools for professionals in the field? Perhaps it is keeping an international audience informed of progress and problems throughout the world. Surely contributing to the advancement of the profession through systematic and funded research and its widespread dissemination would also be a consideration. By any and all of these measures, and many others, the International Association of School Librarianship (IASL) has an impressive record of achievement and effectiveness in school library development for more than thirty years.

In many states, the school library media community organizes a professional association separately from the general library community to enhance its unique role and qualifications in schools and to enable closer collaboration with the K–12 education community. This local phenomenon is mirrored nationally, for example in Australia, Canada and the United Kingdom, and also internationally through IASL, a unique autonomous organization with members from more than eighty countries, affiliated with international organizations in both the education and library communities.

IASL works to be influential in the establishment and development of school librarianship in every country in the world. Consequently, its mission is to provide "an international forum for those people interested in promoting effective school library programs as viable instruments in the educational process." IASL provides guidance and advice for the development of school library programs and the school library profession and works in cooperation with other professional associations and agencies.

The objectives of the Association are:

- to advocate the development of school libraries throughout all countries;
- to encourage the integration of school library programs into the instructional and curriculum development of the school;
- to promote the professional preparation and continuing education of school library personnel;
- to foster a sense of community among school librarians;

- to foster and extend relationships between school librarians and other professions in connection with children and youth;
- to foster research and the integration of its conclusions with pertinent knowledge from related fields;
- to promote the publication and dissemination of information about successful advocacy and program initiatives;
- to share information about programs and materials for children and youth throughout the international community, and
- to initiate and coordinate activities, conferences and other projects.

When the World Confederation of Organizations of the Teaching Profession (WCOTP), an association of national teacher associations representing millions of teachers, was meeting in Stockholm in 1962, school library leaders recognized the need for an international forum; though the concept was accepted, no action was taken to implement it; an effort was made again in Paris at the 1964 WCOTP meeting when the idea was again shelved. However, in 1967 the American Association of School Librarians, a Division of the American Library Association (ALA), International Relations Committee succeeded in arranging for a small grant from ALA to host a luncheon at the Vancouver WCOTP meeting. Fifty participants representing twenty-two countries met to explore the possibility of organizing an international forum for school librarianship. An invitation to the following year's Dublin meeting was issued through the WCOTP office to all teachers and administrators in school library services as well as people participating in some form of school library work. Following the Dublin conference, a program was planned for 1969 in Abidjan and for 1970 in Sydney. During a brief business meeting, the assembled school librarians and educators agreed that a formal International Association for School Librarianship should be established. At the next conference in Jamaica (1971) action was taken on a constitution.

The association continued to meet with WCOTP until it became evident that the strength of the local school library group did not always coincide with the WCOTP venue, so it was mutually agreed that IASL would arrange its own annual conference beginning in 1978. IASL has since met on all continents (except Antarctica) and tries to meet in different regions so that as many people as possible may be able to attend at least every two or three years.

Governance

IASL is an independent association with individual, institutional and association members. Presidents of IASL have resided in Iceland, Jamaica, the United Kingdom and the United States. Vice-presidents have been citizens of Australia, Canada, Denmark, Iceland, Sweden, the United Kingdom and the United States. Nine regional directors form the core of IASL's international consultative governance model with representation for Asia, East Asia, Australia and Pacific Ocean Islands, the Caribbean, Africa (Sub Sahara), North Africa and the Middle East, North America, Latin America, and Europe. Regional directors have been similarly diverse, and dispersed, coming from Australia, Bolivia, Canada, Chile, Colombia, Denmark, Fiji, Finland, Jamaica, Japan, Kenya, Malaysia, Nigeria, Norway, Palestine/Israel, Philippines, Singapore, South Africa, Swaziland, Sweden, the United Kingdom, the United States, Venezuela and Zimbabwe. Directors represent IASL, relay concerns and propose programs and projects which the organization should undertake, publicize the work of IASL, contribute to and share in world communication and report regularly to the editor of the *IASL Newsletter*.

In order to work closely with educators and librarians on the international level, IASL holds voting membership in the International Federation of Library Associations and Institutions (IFLA) in the Netherlands. It was agreed by IFLA and IASL in 1980 that each should appoint a member to attend the other's conference and executive meetings as an official representative to ensure that each association is fully cognizant of the other's concerns and plans and to avoid duplication of efforts. IASL also has consultative status with the United Nations Education, Science and Cultural Organization (UNESCO) in France and works informally with the International Reading Association (IRA) and the International Board on Books for Young People (IBBY).

The Assembly of Associations came into existence in 1981 when representatives from association members asked to have a forum in which they could discuss association problems and programs. National, provincial and state groups send an official delegate to the Assembly, which meets during the IASL annual conference. The Assembly fosters communication about the organization, policies and programs of these associations and encourages the development of national and international cooperative projects and activities which extend and enhance the impact of information literacy at all levels of education. An Association *Communiqué* is published annually and mailed to all association members.

Special interest groups are coordinated by members, for members and include Advocacy, Children's and Young Adult Literature, Education for School Librarianship, Information Literacy [Skills/Strategies], International Schools, Literacy [Learning How to Read] and Research. Coordinators also manage advertising for publications, electronic communications, the International Book Exhibit, the UNESCO Co-Action Book Project and the International Volunteer Assistance Program.

Publications and Research

IASL has published the quarterly *IASL Newsletter* (ISSN 0085–2015) since its inception. The *Newsletter* has continued to grow from six to sixteen pages and carries reviews, feature articles, news and notes from school library associations, and significant publication notices. It continues to be the only such newsletter for school librarians at the international level and is a perquisite of membership.

IASL maintains contact with its members in a variety of ways in addition to its newsletter and regional directors. IASL-LINK is the official listserv of IASL for communication among members and for the distribution of announcements, discussion papers, articles, news, information about projects, and information from IASL conferences and meetings. IASL-LINK has an important function in making activities of the Association, such as the annual conferences, more accessible to members by enabling those who cannot attend to participate in "virtual conference" activities through the dissemination of papers and summaries and through opportunities for discussion. It is also used to disseminate information from discussion groups and from the decisions of the Annual General Meeting.

In 1995 the Association established *School Libraries Worldwide (SLWW)* (ISSN 1023–9391), a semi-annual refereed journal of research and scholarship in school librarianship, also a perquisite of membership. IASL-LINK carries advance information about each issue and calls for contributions; it also carries a contents listing (with abstracts) for each issue of the journal as it appears. *SLWW* features theme issues such as the potential and difficulties of information technology, useful resources for development and the information searching behaviors of young people.

IASL also maintains a vigorous publications program with 38 titles currently in print. Examples of recent titles include *School Librarianship: International Perspectives and Issues* (ISBN 1-890861-22-7), the best recent conference papers together with an index to the first twenty-five years of conference papers and the *Newsletter*, and *Sustaining the Vision: A Collection of Articles and Papers on Research in School Librarianship* (ISBN 0-931510-65-1). Conference papers are also refereed and published each year. The 1997 papers—*Information Rich but Knowledge Poor? Issues for Schools and Libraries Worldwide* (ISBN 1-890861-21-9)—incorporated the papers presented at the first international forum on research in school librarianship, a refereed program that will be offered each year.

The IASL research program also includes the Takeshi Murofushi Research Award, first awarded in 1997, which provides financial support; the recipient is expected to present the results of the study at a subsequent IASL conference. Preference is given to proposals involving researchers from more than one country to encourage an international perspective. In addition, IASL is involved in collaborative research projects, both jointly funded and implemented, with IFLA.

Awards and Projects

A number of special projects have been an important part of IASL's program. The IASL/UNESCO co-action program collects money for UNESCO unums, an international currency credit, which can be used to purchase books for school libraries in developing countries. Applicants must guarantee shelves, space, personnel and service. Recent school recipients have been in Romania, Jamaica, the Maldives, Bolivia and Swaziland. Also, each year at the annual conference a display of books representing the countries and regions of the IASL membership is donated by members and others and is given to the host country of the conference to be shared with children and youth in that community.

The SIRS Commendation Award recognizes outstanding and innovative projects, plans, publications or programs which could serve as models for replication by individuals and associations in other countries. Examples have included an information technology in education virtual conference, an information skills CD-ROM product, a collection of resource-based units of study developed by teams of teachers and teacher-librarians, a teacher-librarian resource book to support collaboration with teachers, and a national approach to involving children and adults in reading and literacy across the nation.

The Winnebago Progressive School Library Media Awards recognizes the implementation of innovative ideas by school librarians to enhance the lifelong learning skills of students, through two awards, one for developing nations and one for developed nations.

The Leadership Development Grant provides financial support and registration for school library leaders in developing countries to attend the annual conference and thus assists them to share their needs and aspirations, to learn from other conference participants, to develop contacts to further their work and to identify strategies that can be used in their home country. This prestigious award was renamed the Jean Lowrie Leadership Development Grant in 1995 in honor of the first president and first executive secretary of IASL. Recent recipients have traveled from Latvia, Sri Lanka, Antigua and Barbuda, Namibia and Ethiopia.

The Support-A-Member gift program is designed to make it possible for school librarians, library assistants and others interested in school library services who are living in third world countries to belong to IASL.

IASL also acts as a clearinghouse for an International Volunteer Assistance Program. This program is a gesture of professional cooperation and collegiality to permit maximum participation of the membership; IASL neither prejudges requests for assistance nor questions needs; volunteers expect no reimbursement or remuneration.

Conclusion

In her doctoral dissertation, "Convergence and Global Ethics: The International Association of School Librarianship and the Worldwide Promotion of School Libraries" (Ph.D. dissertation, Indiana University, 1995), Rebecca Knuth found that the IASL effectively fosters the worldwide promotion of school libraries. As a voluntary professional association dedicated to the worldwide promotion of school-based libraries, the organization's uniqueness stems from its integration of traditional professional aspects of school librarianship with an international ethos. IASL is value-based and reflects global ethics.

The International Association of School Librarianship is part of an educational movement to promote schools and libraries and of a social movement to promote international literacy. According to Dr. Knuth, its impact is particularly intensified on school librarianship in third world countries. Its progress and contributions reflect both its global relevance and sustained achievement throughout the world.

For Further Information:

President: Dr. Sigrun Klara Hannesdottir, Iceland: grun@rhi.hi.is

Vice-President—Association Relations: Dr. Dianne Oberg, Canada: dianne.oberg@ualberta.ca

Vice-President—Association Operations: Peter Genco, USA: pgenco@iu05trc.trinet.k12.pa.us

Vice-President—Special Interest Groups: Dr. Ross Todd, Australia: rtodd@acs.itd.uts.edu.au

IASL Secretariat, Box 34069, Dept. 300, Seattle, Washington 98124-0266, USA. Voice: 604–925–0266; Fax: 604–925–0566; E–mail: iasl@rockland.com

Home Page: http://www.rhi.hi.is/~anne/iasl.html

Executive Director: Dr. Ken Haycock

Membership is US $50 including the quarterly newsletter and semi-annual journal.

IASL Publications are distributed exclusively by LMC Source, P. O. Box 720400, San Jose, CA 95172–0400. Voice: 800-873-3043; Fax: 408-924-2476; E-mail: lmcs@pacbell.net. Standing orders are available.

Appendix

Policy Statement on School Libraries

Principle 7 of the United Nation's Declaration of the Rights of the Child states: The child is entitled to receive education which shall be free and compulsory, at least in the elementary stages. He shall be given an education which will promote his general culture and enable him on a basis of equal opportunity to develop his abilities, his individual judgment, and his moral sense of a social responsibility and to become a useful member of society.

The existence and utilization of the school library are a vital part of this free and compulsory education. The school library is essential to the development of the human personality as well as the spiritual, moral, social, cultural and economic progress of the community.

The school library is central to the fulfillment of the instructional goals and objectives of the school and promotes this through a planned program of acquisition and organization of information technology and dissemination of materials to expand the learning environment of all students. A planned program of teaching information skills in partnership with classroom teachers and other educators is an essential part of the school library program.

The school library provides a wide range of resources, both print and nonprint, including electronic media and access to data which promote an awareness of the child's own cultural heritage and provide the basis for an understanding of the diversity of other cultures.

Functions

The school library functions as a vital instrument in the educational process, not as a separate entity isolated from the total school program but involved in the teaching and learning process. Its goals could be expressed through the following functions:

Informational: to provide for reliable information, rapid access, retrieval and transfer of information; the school library should be part of regional and national information networks;

Educational: to provide continuous lifelong education through provision of the facilities and atmosphere for learning; guidance in location, selection and use of material and training in information skills, through integration with classroom teaching; promotion of intellectual freedom;

Cultural: to improve the quality of life through the presentation and support of the aesthetic experience, guidance in appreciation of arts, encouragement of creativity and development of positive human relations;

Recreational: to support and enhance a balanced and enriched life and encourage meaningful use of leisure time through provision of recreational information, materials and programs of recreational value and guidance in the use of leisure time.

Materials

Appropriateness implies:

- an awareness of the total range of information and communication technology;
- variety concerning many fields of knowledge and recreational activities;

- material designed to serve children within the range of their cognitive, affective and psychomotor skills;
- relevance to the school's teaching/learning program;
- appeal to children's interests;
- use of the student's primary language;
- reflection of the cultural interests valued by the children's families;
- application of the economic environment.

Facilities

All school libraries, from basic preschool through secondary level, need adequate space in which to exploit the technology available for preparation, processing and storage of all library materials, as well as space to enable students and teachers to utilize fully these materials through reading, viewing, listening and information retrieval and processing skills. The plans should fit functionally into the general architectural design of the school, located near natural centers of traffic with easy accessibility to all users, including the disabled and handicapped. Consideration might also be given to the use of the library outside normal school use. There is a need for flexibility and scope for future expansion and rearrangement of space and use with adequate provision of electrical outlets to allow this. Attention must be given to lighting, acoustical treatment of doors and ceilings, control of temperature and humidity and furniture and shelving suitable to the age of the users.

Personnel

Establishment of the school library requires that all persons who use it learn how it could be used effectively and efficiently. Administrators provide the leadership for such use. Preparation for administrators, as for all teachers, should include information about the role of the school library in the learning process and in the planning and implementation of teaching activities. The administrator should be aware of the unique librarianship skills which the school librarian needs in addition to professional training as a teacher to effectively coordinate the role of the library program in the school, including the preparation of the budget and arranging for a flexible school schedule so the students can make greater use of the library materials and facilities. The administrator should be aware of the educational benefits of a cooperative planning and teaching program within the school.

The International Association of School Librarianship advocates that school librarians be qualified teachers who have, in addition, completed professional studies in librarianship. This type of preparation ensures that teachers receive assistance from, and cooperatively teach with, professional personnel who have an understanding of the principles and practices of effective teaching, the educational program and practices of the child's school. This cooperation with teachers may concern development of the curriculum, the educational activities offered by the school to the child, as well as short- and long-term planning concerning the use of materials, information technology and equipment, and development of information skills for the child's education.

Lifelong Education, Skills, Literacy Development

The skills learned by the student through the school library provide the child with the means of adapting to a wide variety of situations, enabling education to be continued throughout life, even in adverse conditions. The school library promotes literacy through development and encouragement of reading for instruction and recreation.

Reading, viewing and listening activities all stimulate and reinforce the child's interest in reading.

In addition, the student is provided with an insight into the full range of information and communication technology as it is available and with instruction in the utilization of this technology in order to locate and evaluate information to answer educational and recreational needs and interest, thus being able to construct visual, recorded, audiovisual and electronic messages as appropriate for purposes of communication. These skills promote lifelong learning. Acquiring these skills enables the child to continue independent learning even where education is interrupted by natural disasters and social unrest.

All education systems should also be encouraged to extend the learning environment beyond textbook and teacher into the school library. School librarians should cooperate with staff in public libraries and other community information centers to enable sharing of the community's information resources.

Government and Public Support

The establishment of good school libraries demonstrates that public authorities are fulfilling their responsibilities to implement education which will enable children to become useful members of the global society and to develop each child's individual potential. A good school library with a qualified school librarian is a major factor in developing quality education.

The school library may provide materials as sources of information for parents and social agencies to use in serving the needs of children in the home, preschool, school and after-school environments.

For societies and public authorities endeavoring to promote the education of the child, one of the measurable achievements which can be observed is the provision of the tools for education. The society that invests in school libraries for its children invests in its own future. [Developed by the International Association of School Librarianship and approved by the Board in 1984; Adopted by the WCOTP: 1984; Revised: 1993; currently under revision by the IASL.]

Note

For further information on the early history and accomplishments of the International Association of School Librarianship, see Rebecca Knuth, "An International Forum: The History of the International Association of School Librarianship," in *School Libraries Worldwide* 2:2 (1996) : 1-32; and Rebecca Knuth, "Adaptation, Goal Achievement, Integration and Latency: An Analysis of the Projects and Programs of the International Association of School Librarianship," in *School Libraries Worldwide* 2:2 (1996) : 54-98.

23. Quality Library Services to Children and Young Adults for Changing Needs

Barbara Immroth

The International Federation of Library Associations' Standing Committee on Children's Libraries held a pre-seminar satellite meeting coordinated by Barbara Immroth of the University of Texas in Hamburg, Germany, August 26-28, 1997, prior to the IFLA Conference in Copenhagen. The seminar focused on education and training for staff working in library services to children and youth. Speakers addressed the issues, trends and status of education for children and youth librarianship in both developing and developed countries. Four strands were followed: changing needs of children/society/community/world; changing needs in technology; changing needs in financial resources; changing needs in organizations.

Professor Birgit Dankert, Fachbereich Bibliothek und Information der Fachhochschulke Hamburg, presented the welcoming keynote address for the seminar, "Education and Training in Quality Library Services for Children and Young Adults: The German Situation." Germany, a highly industrialized country, has approximately 3,400 public libraries with professional staff and departments for children and young adults. Up to 30 percent of the average budget is for library service for children and young adults, while borrowing by this age group is more than 50 percent of the average library's total circulation. In addition to print materials, the public libraries offer audiovisual media, computers and online information. There are about 5,000 new titles published for children and young adults each year in Germany and only the largest public libraries can afford to purchase all of these titles.

Currently, budget cuts in the cultural field affect the children's libraries, especially the small branch libraries which often provide direct service to children. Politicians try to save money by having volunteers and semi-professionals run the children's libraries. At the same time, the children's libraries are expanding their mission to include developing lifelong readers; imparting media competence; imparting practice in information and cultural skills and using cultural and information resources. Libraries, along with music schools and sports clubs, are the most highly organized cultural institutions for children and young people, serving children from other cultures, handicapped and hospitalized children.

In spite of the positive status of children's libraries, Prof. Dankert asserted that libraries must make the transition to the multimedia future, enlarge their radius of action, and optimize their services. These steps require more staff, more money, better education and continuing education for professionals. Prof. Dankert outlined the curriculum for library services for children and young adults in the German polytechnics. After graduating from high school, the students spend three or four years in elementary studies, practical work in libraries and specialized studies. Stuttgart, Hamburg and Leipzig are the centers for library education for public libraries. Students study management, resources and literature, promotion of the library and storytelling, services for schools and special seminars. In addition, there are general courses that touch on aspects of service to children and young adults.

The specialist/generalist debate continues and schools offer some specialized and some general courses with specialized elements. The question of education in electronic services for children and young adults is not yet resolved. The Public Library in Stuttgart is the leader in electronic information development, as the city is the center of German electronics. The Public Library has a large, well-equipped information center that is heavily used by citizens. The children's department of the Public Library participates in the CHILIAS project, supported by the European Union, a virtual electronic children's library on the Internet (http://www.stuttgart.de/chillas/). In addition to electronic library service for children, the other pressing problems that Prof. Dankert identified are the need for more evaluation of the services to justify the budget for children's libraries and a need for more continuing education for practitioners to survive the rapid changes in technology.

Deborah Denham, University of Central England, presented a paper, "Focus on the Child: Children, Libraries and Literacy into the 21st Century," prepared with Professor Judith Elkin. She considered the place of the child in society and gave examples of the diversity of backgrounds and needs of children, saying that age may be the only thing that children have in common. She described the changing context of public libraries in the United Kingdom and how the Education Reform Act of 1988, with the introduction of a National Curriculum, standard attainment targets and testing, and local budgetary responsibility for schools, has impacted public libraries and the publishing industry. In discussing the role of libraries, Denham noted that while children's public library service has always been a powerful force in promoting books and reading, professionals have been poor at promoting the work which they carry out. She listed and summarized several documents that outline the role of public libraries for children, including the UNESCO Public Library Manifest, the Public Library Research Group; "Guidelines for Children and Young People" from the Library Association; *Children Are People* by Janet Hill; and *Investing in Children*, a report by the Library and Information Services Council for England.[1] A review of *Public Library Service in the United Kingdom in 1995* by Aslib and the government response, "Reading the Future: Public Library Review" in 1997 acknowledge the importance of libraries for young people.

Denham then outlined the knowledge and skills base that needs to be included in the education of children's library professionals as found in the Library Association Guidelines published in 1997. These fourteen elements form a comprehensive list of competencies. Juxtaposed with these specialized elements is the need for library schools to have a general curriculum for information professionals , a situation she also outlined. The balance between specialist and generalist needs can be maintained in part by continuing professional development built on the foundation of core education. Denham concluded that libraries need to adapt and change and embrace new technologies while LIS educators need to keep in touch with the professional world and produce well-rounded professionals who meet the needs of a changing society.

Shirley Fitzgibbons, Indiana University, School of Library and Information Science, wrote a paper titled "Implications of National Movements and Research on Reading and Motivation." Fitzgibbons gave a context for her discussion by outlining the national movements in education and libraries in the United States during the 1980s and 1990s, including the *Goals 2000: Educate America Act* (Public Law 103-227, March 1994); *Kids Need Libraries*, the White House Conference on Library and Information Services, and the current research project of the U.S. Department of Education on the "Role of School and Public Libraries in Support of Educational Reform."[2] She discussed the relationship of school and public libraries in meeting the educational needs of youth in terms of literacy and reading; research on babies and young children; research on reading, motivation and use of libraries; and research on reading attitudes of youth. Fitzgibbons outlined education for youth librarianship, focusing on the two broad competencies of knowledge of materials and services and the various approaches to teaching and learning these competencies. She cites Immroth's paper on competencies, "Education of Children's and Youth Librarians."[3] She also discussed some special issues in education for youth librarians: theory and practice debate, specialist vs. generalist, young adult librarianship as a separate specialist area, and market demand, supply and recruitment of youth librarians. Fitzgibbons concluded her paper with an overview of education for librarianship in the United States and raised questions about the new generation of youth library educators and the balance of traditional and technologist roles.

Adele Fasick, Professor Emeritus, University of Toronto, Faculty of Information Studies, presented "The Effects of Computer Technology on Education for Youth Services Librarians." She discussed the rapid adoption of computers as one of the most profound changes in society ever caused by technology. Fasick sees this change as a "one-way street" with libraries increasing their use of technology. She lists the three stages of change in technology in libraries as (1) new access points to printed information held locally; (2) access to collections in other locations; and (3) electronic storage of text and graphics and new delivery systems. She further said that the changes brought about by the rapid growth of the Internet are the most far-reaching technological changes. Although the media envisions that when access becomes more available, children will access the Internet to find any information they need; the Internet contains a huge amount of information both difficult to locate and evaluate that is inappropriate for children.

Fasick explored the question of how changes in the media affect children and the place of literacy in this technological era. At present, computer users need to be print literate because much online information is textual. She listed six features of online information identified by the University of Michigan's Digital Library Project and discussed them in terms of service to children. *Currency* is usually an advantage for which librarians are responsible because they have cut book budgets to buy electronic resources. *Content from primary resources* can be exciting but, especially for children, primary technical information can be incomprehensible. *Content can be comprehensive,* but often the context is not provided on web sites. *Resources in video and sound clips* can represent information that is difficult to communicate in print. *Students can publish online,* although Fasick questioned the need for so many immature term papers. *Content is readily available;* in order for the advantage to be a reality, each student must have ready access to a computer. She raised questions about children's use and understanding of electronic information to forecast the future of children's library service. The job of selecting materials will be much more complex because of the variety of formats and range of available information sources. The job of making materials accessible will be much more difficult. Librarians will need to understand search engines and how they work, filtering sites and growing commercialism in sources of information. Librarians will need to spend more time teaching information seeking skills and will also need to address the problems of uneven access to information. In addition to the information needs for minority language groups and those with low literacy, geographic isolation presents barriers because of lack of electricity, lack of telephone service, and lack of funds to pay telecommunication charges and buy hardware and software.

Fasick concluded her paper by listing several areas of knowledge necessary for the education of children's librarians: child development, all types of media, means of access, and how to teach children to use information.

Irina Tsaregorodtseva, librarian of the Kamchatka Regional Science Library, described the area of the far northern Russian Pacific Far East as dramatically isolated in her paper, "The Role of Libraries in Children's Leisure Time." She discussed the network of libraries within this area as the cultural centers and the depositories of intellectual heritage and national traditions. The Children's Library Service in Kamchatka includes libraries in Petropavlovsk-Kamchatsky as well as regional, village and school libraries. She reported that the central library has a staff of forty-seven and has over 70,000 visitors annually, 80 percent of whom are children under fourteen years. The central library is open 11 hours daily during the school year. A play area for young children introduces them to the library and books. The librarians would like to have an electronic catalog and databases but are not yet able to because of financial constraints. The library provides traditional reference services.

Ms. Tsaregorodtseva reported the results of a survey of users over age 12 about user needs and how the library answers these needs. Teens want separate space and materials on subjects of personal interest to them such as music, films, sex and drugs.

The library sponsors various clubs for leisure activity for children including ship-modeling, puppet shows, film viewing, Barbie dolls, lacemaking, gardening, safety local ecology, local history (the three hundredth anniversary of Russian annexation of Kamchatka) and old Russian holidays and tradition.

To encourage an interest in literature and reading, the library sponsors several events including a Children's Book Festival featuring the most popular titles, a Fairytale Festival and summer programs for children in day camps for which the librarians plan book-oriented activities. Special attention is given to disabled children and poor children in conjunction with social service agencies. Disabled children are encouraged to use their artistic and literary skills in library contests. Librarians stimulate poor children's interest in reading by encouraging them to participate in library activities. For instance, a Grandparents' Day for children and grandparents was planned in which each age group took turns performing and then shared a tea party and social time. While patriotic and esthetic education is a role of the library, the main role of the children's libraries is introducing reading and literature to children.

Professor Birgit Waning, Royal School of Librarianship, Denmark, presented information about the "Status in Scandinavia" (Norway, Sweden, Denmark, Iceland and Finland). LIS education is at the postsecondary level. The professional training is becoming more academic while retaining the professional image. In the Nordic countries, the public libraries promote knowledge, education and culture by making books and information available free of charge. The public libraries are the responsibility of the local government; there is also a state structure for cooperation and special objectives.

In 1996 in Denmark each child borrowed an average of thirty-five books. Children also use electronic media in many formats. They want the library to provide the software and hardware that they are accustomed to using in their leisure time. In school children use print media and in their leisure time they use a mixture of the new media.

Prof. Waning sees the role of the children's librarian changing to encompass all media and the Internet while retaining the basic skills of librarianship. The Nordic Children and Youth Culture have established an Internet site named for the Nordic God's meeting place, Valhalla.

Genevieve Patte, in her paper, "Education and Training of Children and Young Adult Librarians at the Grassroot Level," stressed the importance of those working directly with young people being the ones who adapt reading to the changing social and cultural contexts. She gives examples from developing countries where innovative practices have satisfied the needs and demands of marginalized communities. Librarians working at the grassroots level know best the habits and reactions of the communities they serve. They can be the spokespersons for national projects and provide expertise to publishers.

Patte described a project carried out by Somboon Singkamanan, Srinakharinwirot University, Bangkok, Thailand. Professor Singkamanan has students in the library training course contribute to the Thai publishing and reading services. Students read and memorize as many books in the University collection as possible so that they can share the stories with children where there aren't any books available. Students often have to translate the books from English to Thai. The students collect traditional folktales and write them down. They encourage children to collect tales from parents and neighbors to learn about their own culture. The books made from these tales are put into portable libraries that can be carried on a bicycle and taken anywhere to share with children. Librarians model behavior for the children with whom they work that says reading and books are important.

Patte reported on two projects that focus on reading, analyzing, reviewing and selecting books. At La Joie par les Livres in France, eight or ten librarians gather monthly to discuss books in relation to the needs of children. The librarians publish their reviews, which are read by publishers and educators. Formal training for librarians and other interested people is organized. Similar reviewing groups for CD-ROMs have been formed. This work has strengthened the development of libraries for young people and generated publications and training sessions.

Another example in French-speaking Africa gives the responsibility for reading and selection of books to those who are in daily contact with the children. Small sets of books are sent out to an informal network of libraries and schools for review by local children and adults. Their reviews are then published in a magazine *Takam Tikou*. This project is creating a demand for training in children's literature.

In each of these instances, close attention to the local population, their cultures and expectations, can help librarians be creative. Patte stated that the training based on doing and making is necessary for facing the changes of society.

Susan Roman, Executive Director, Association for Library Service to Children (ALSC), a division of the American Library Association, discussed "Issues in Continuing Education in Professional Associations." Roman highlighted some of the many ALSC projects that bring children and literature together and promote reading and library service for children. *Kids Can't Wait*, an advocacy paper developed to promote library service; "Born to Read," with Hillary Rodham Clinton as Honorary Chair, focusing on librarians working with health care professionals to reach young children and their parents; outreach such as the Library, Museum, Head Start project with the Library of Congress, Center for the Book and the Association for Youth Museums, "America Reads," with the National Education Association; "Between the Lions," TV for ages 4 to 7; Coalition for America's Children are a few of the projects that ALSC undertakes in partnership with other organizations interested in children and families.[4]

Working on ALSC projects often functions as continuing education for volunteer members who are able to learn from other members and partner organizations. Selecting positive Internet sites for parents to use with their children was a recent, successful project. ALSC has developed and made accessible research and tools for evaluation and measurement. Regional Institutes for leadership and skills development, fund-raising and grant-writing workshops and advocacy training are a part of the

ALSC continuing education for professionals. Publishing a journal and newsletter, promotional materials for programs and outstanding materials, such as the Caldecott and Newbery winners, and professional "how-to" books, as well as production of videos to use with parents and caregivers, is another facet of ALSC continuing education.

The ALSC program also promotes international cooperation; for instance, Roman went to South Korea to talk about high-quality picture books. She visited English language clubs resembling small classrooms that are set up in airports, restaurants and parks. She was able to carry on an exchange of information and ideas that benefits both the United States and Korea. A delegation of U.S. children's literature experts visited South Africa to discuss teaching children's literature at universities, promoting reading in school and public libraries, and educating preschool teachers. In each of these aspects of continuing education, networking and mentoring are important features that enrich those who participate.

Through these projects and activities, ALSC contributes to the purpose of furthering quality library services to children.

· Pauletta Brown Bracy, North Carolina Central University, School of Library and Information Sciences, presented "Services for Children and Young Adults in Library Education: Perceptions of Faculty and Deans," a paper based on research by Susan Steinfirst and Bracy. Five broad areas were studied: teaching, students, content, coverage, doctoral programs and support and status. There was a great deal of agreement between the two groups in answers to the survey. Some of the areas of disagreement were in terms of course loads, summer school teaching, percentage of students enrolled in youth services courses, difficulty in securing jobs and the adequacy with which children's literature and services were addressed in general courses. The paper outlines disagreements between the perceptions of faculty and deans about the decrease in doctoral students concentrating in youth services and in the support and status of faculty in the youth services areas. The two striking trends that Bracy mentioned are a concern that faculty who are not tenured or who retire will not be replaced by faculty who teach in the youth services area and the concern about the increase in technology and the evolving focus on information science that replaces the youth services emphasis.

After hearing all of the presentations, the seminar participants divided into three working groups: administration, materials and services for lively discussion and the formulation of preliminary guidelines for the future education and training for quality library services for children and young adults. Full text of the papers can be accessed at http://www.gslis.utexas.edu/resources/Iflasatellitemeeting.html

---

Notes

1. Janet Hill, *Children Are People; the Library in the Community* (London: Hamilton, 1973).

2. "Kids Need Libraries: School and Public Libraries Preparing the Youth of Today for the World of Tomorrow," in *Issues and Challenges for America's Libraries*. Prepared for the Second White House Conference on Library and Information Services (Chicago: American Library Association, 1991).

3. Barbara Immroth, "Education of Children's and Youth Librarians: Competencies Developed by ALSC," in *US-USSR Colloquium on Library Services to Children*, ed. Susan Roman (Chicago: American Library Association, 1990).

4. Virginia Mathews, "Kids Can't Wait ... Library Advocacy Now!" A President's Paper for Mary R. Somerville, President, 1996-97 (Chicago: American Library Association, 1996); Steven Herb, "Annual Report of the Association for Library Service to Children and Young Adults," *Journal of Youth Services in Libraries* 10 (Spring 1997): 351-359.

24. International Library Women: Identifying Problems, Seeking Solutions

Suzanne Hildenbrand and Mary Biblo

and at my birth my grandmother told my mother she should kill me ...
—panelist, Round Table on Women's Issues program, International
Federation of Library Associations and Institutions, Copenhagen, 1997

Female infanticide and discrimination against women librarians are far apart on the continuum but both are rooted in the ubiquitous devaluation of females. Accordingly, although the Round Table on Women's Issues (RTWI) of the International Federation of Library Associations and Institutions (IFLA) was established to identify common problems faced by women library professionals and to share solutions, we found it impossible to separate professional advancement from the larger cause of women's rights. So the RTWI recognizes both the responsibility of women library professionals to provide information to empower women in their struggle to attain full human rights and the need to promote the advancement of library women. Strategies to promote both of these goals are shared among library women around the world. Activities include meetings and programs, visits to women's libraries and other appropriate sites, publication of a newsletter and sponsorship and dissemination of research.

These activities enjoyed considerable success despite obstacles that include an organizational structure within IFLA that makes focus on populations or demographics difficult, a politically conservative atmosphere worldwide, and cultural difference. Yet the RTWI has established itself and reached a wide audience in scarcely more than five years. This paper will present an overview of the history and activities of the RTWI and conclude with a summary of the ongoing challenges it faces.

Origins

In 1989 IFLA met in Paris, a city celebrating the anniversary of a revolution linked to an unprecedented expansion of human rights. Yet to some women in attendance it seemed that women's rights were not adequately acknowledged at the conference. They noted the secondary role of women at the meeting and in the organization. Few women held important offices and few participated in programs. After the meeting, a letter went out to female attendees to determine if there was interest in forming a women's group within IFLA to address women's needs. The response was gratifying and RTWI was launched with preliminary, informal meetings scheduled for the Stockholm conference the next year. The Moscow meeting in 1991 saw the group listed in the program; two meetings were held, including one of the Executive Committee. The latter worked on objectives and activities for the group and drew up plans for a program to be held the next year in New Delhi.

The 1992 New Delhi conference was crucial in the history of RTWI as it brought the first program meeting and the first issue of the *Newsletter*. Panelists from the United Kingdom and the United States described the status of women librarians in those countries while Indian panelists described resources for women, including those needed for research on women and development. In 1993 the women's group was formally recognized as a Round Table. At the 1994 conference, a brochure describing the history and work of the Round Table was available for the first time. It listed as the two objectives of the Round Table promotion of research on the status of women in librarianship and the promotion of an awareness of women's issues in IFLA. These have evolved into today's broader objectives, including service to women. The fifth anniversary of the Round Table was celebrated in 1996.

During this early period several women emerged with considerable responsibility for the development and growth of the Round Table. Mary Biblo of the Laboratory School of the University of Chicago in the United States, and Pat Darter, then of the Equal Opportunities Commission in Manchester in the United Kingdom, held important offices as co-chairs. Leena Siitonen of Finland, at the Universidad Catholica de Avila in Spain, was Information Officer and Treasurer. Yoko Taguichi of the Kyoto Seika University in Japan has been *Newsletter* editor from the first issue in 1992 to date. Others who offered assistance and support include Eva Trotzig of Sweden, and Suzine Har Nicolescu and Suzanne Hildenbrand, both of the United States.

Programs

Programs provide an occasion for intellectual stimulation, consciousness-raising and sociability within the context of a professional concern for women's issues, both the status of women in the profession and the role of the profession in providing needed information to women. These programs served to highlight the common elements in women's experience and showed that many have faced the same struggles. Where problems are brought to light, solutions that worked in one setting may suggest strategies to listeners from other settings.

Attendance has been good at RTWI programs, averaging over seventy in a crowded conference schedule, but reaching more than one hundred in 1997. These programs have been a major factor in the rapid growth of the Round Table; its mailing list numbers over three hundred names from fifty-nine countries.

Not surprisingly, a major topic on RTWI panels from the outset has been the status of women librarians in a particular country. Data collection is so much easier on this topic than on services to women users. Papers on the status of women librarians often focused on the shortage of women library managers. The countries covered by reports on the status of women librarians include Cuba, Korea, the United Kingdom and the United States. Most of these reports, such as those on women librarians in China and in Finland made a connection between that status and the general condition of women in the larger society.[1] The status of women library workers in Japan was described and FLINT, or the Feminist Library Network of Japan, was introduced.

Some panelists did, however, address service to women users or potential users in their presentations. Both academic communities and the general community of public library users have been considered. The organization and use of collections of materials on women was addressed by U.S. and Indian presenters.[2] Service to community women, stressing the involvement of women librarians with the community, was described in a paper on the libraries in the Ryazan region of Russia.[3] A panelist from

Botswana stressed the need for targeting women in developing countries as a special population to be served, as did an Indian presenter. A panelist from the Netherlands described the emerging network to provide information on women being developed to serve the member countries of the European Union and another from the United States described women as consumers of health information.

In addition to its own programs, RTWI has also jointly sponsored a program with the Government Information and Official Publications Section of IFLA, "Government Information and Publications on Women," at the Havana Conference in 1994.

As a kind of supplement to its programs RTWI invites speakers available at a particular conference with expertise on a topic of relevance to address the program meeting. Monica Ertel of Apple Computers had attended the United Nations Conference on Women held in Beijing in 1995 and spoke to the RTWI the following year about this event of enormous importance to women worldwide. At the Copenhagen Conference Marlise Mensink of the International Information Centre and Archives for the Women's Movement (IIAV) addressed members about the 1998 Conference on the World of Women's Information to be held in Amsterdam under IIAV sponsorship. She also called for greater cooperation between IIAV and the RTWI.

While these programs are important to the RTWI, service to women users is best illustrated by offering librarians the occasion to observe institutions designed to meet the needs of women users. Accordingly, site visits are an important supplement to the programs.

Site Visits

IFLA conference sites are major cities of the world, and the RTWI has taken advantage of the local women's resources these cities have to offer. During the 1995 IFLA Conference in Istanbul, the Women's Library and Information Center was visited. The Center is a true cultural center for women with a small theatre and art gallery. The co-founders, Asli Davaz-Mardin and Jale Baysala, explained the major role of the library in the Turkish women's movement. Similarly, at the 1997 Conference in Copenhagen, RTWI members were encouraged to visit KVINFO, the Danish Center for Information on Women and Gender. Located in its new home, next to the not yet completed national library, the work of the Center was explained by Anne-Marie Erikson, reference librarian. In a talk to a group from the Round Table, she placed the Center's role within the context of the Nordic tradition of gender relations that has historically stressed equality while often falling short of this goal.

But women's libraries are not the only sites that offer Round Table members an opportunity for enrichment. In Havana they visited the headquarters of the Cuban Women's Federation, or FMC, in its elegant colonial style building. Carmen Nora Hernandes, director, and Mercedes Verdeses Vazques, the librarian, addressed the group and explained the organization's pre-revolutionary history and ongoing activities in a state that has vowed gender equality as a national goal.

These visits offer Round Table members an opportunity to see how information services for and about women operate in different national contexts. They may provide ideas about service and collection development that members can carry home and use in their work. Members eagerly look forward to the 1998 visit to the IIAV in Amsterdam. News of these visits is carried to members in issues of the *Newsletter.*

Newsletter

The role of the *Newsletter* for RTWI is crucial. Members are separated by thousands of miles and by differences in language and culture so publication of the twice yearly information sheet is vital. The *Newsletter*, in keeping with the dual objectives of the Round Table, brings members not only information about Round Table activities, including reports on previous programs and visits and calls for papers to be presented at subsequent programs, but also alerts members to information of importance for women generally. For example, recent issues have contained news of the African Gender Institute and of a talk by Marianna Tax Choldin, of the University of Illinois in the United States on "Access to Information and Freedom of Expression," pointing out the relevance of the latter to women's worldwide struggle for information.[4] An added emphasis is on tools of importance such as WomenWatch, an Internet Gateway on the Advancement and Empowerment of Women, launched by United Nations women's organizations on International Women's Day, March 8, 1997.[5] Bibliography and reviews are frequently published so readers have been alerted to relevant titles including *Internet Resources on Women* and *Cuban Women Confront the Future: Three Decades of Revolution.*[6]

Yoko Taguichi, founding editor of the *Newsletter*, has shown considerable editorial and technological skill during her tenure. Her tact in prodding members to contribute and her ability to find items of interest have been most valuable. On the technical side, she has developed strategies for worldwide distribution. After some experimentation, members in different regions receive one "seed" copy which they reproduce and mail, using labels prepared by the Round Table. This will be a transitional year for the *Newsletter* as Beth Stafford of the University of Illinois in the United States takes over the editorship. Wendy Barrett, an Australian at the International Atomic Energy Commission in Vienna, maintains the database for the mailing list. The *Newsletter* has been established on a firm foundation and will continue the twin commitments of informing members about activities and research.

Research

Without research to provide firm data it is impossible to grasp the existence and extent of a problem and to measure future success or failure in solving it. There are currently two aspects to the RTWI research commitment: sponsorship and dissemination. In the former category there is so far only one example. In the latter category writers may draw on their own research or that of others; in either case the content is overwhelmingly on the status of women in librarianship, rather than using the power of information to improve the lot of women more generally since as, noted above, data collection on the former topic is much easier. However, those examining the status of women librarians unfailingly link that status to the social context within which the women librarians, in common with the other women of their culture, find themselves.

IFLA provided the RTWI with funds for a survey of "equal opportunities (EO) work" and Leo Appleton surveyed international library associations for evidence of such work during the summer and fall of 1994. This research served a dual purpose: the collection of data for the RTWI and for Appleton's Honours Degree (BA) from the Department of Information and Library Management of the University of Northumbria. Two RTWI activists from the United Kingdom, Pat Darter and Sandra Parker, the latter Appleton's supervisor, played a major role in the origin and execution of the project. Appleton's thesis, "Equal Opportunities Activity in International Library

Associations," describes the meaning of EO work, his methodology, findings and his recommendations for both IFLA and for national library associations.[7] EO involves both a statement that an organization is committed to equal opportunities and an actual policy describing what will be done to make opportunities more equal for women (and others who face significant barriers including racial minorities, the disabled and so on). Appleton found very few national library associations that had both active policies and provision for monitoring them; only the British Library Association and the U.S. Special Libraries Association met both standards. Only about 60 percent were able to provide a gender analysis of membership. The only evidence of any equal opportunities activity he found within IFLA was the presence of RTWI.

Appleton concluded with recommendations for IFLA and for national library associations. He urged IFLA to become more active in the area, encouraging member associations in EO activities and he further urged that EO be "thoroughly represented within IFLA Divisions, Sections and Round Tables structures."[8] He also urged national associations to formulate policies and establish procedures and bodies for implementation. He recommended that membership monitoring for gender and other EO categories be routinely carried out.

Even acknowledging some weakness in Appleton's methodology—his English-only questionnaire evidently discouraged some participants, and he had no responses from Latin America—it is clear that he has made a major contribution to EO and to the work of the RTWI. He has provided a firm foundation on which others can build, and he has provided a baseline against which future findings can be measured.

Panelists at RTWI programs presented their own research or cited research studies done in their own countries. Among important research papers presented was that by Anne Goulding of Loughborough University in the United Kingdom. Goulding, noting that the impact of information and library studies (ILS) on the position of women in the profession was unstudied, researched the extent to which gender was covered in ILS departments in the United Kingdom. Using literature review, survey methodology and case studies, she examined the overt curriculum, the hidden curriculum and student attitudes. Among her conclusions were that although 93 percent of faculty were supportive or very supportive of presenting gender issues, only 54 percent did so in the classroom. Many students complained that the issue was presented as a marginal add-on. Goulding concludes with specific suggestions to provide better coverage of gender and equity issues in the curriculum to give "female students the intellectual means to challenge the status quo ..."[9]

Sarla Murgai of the University of Tennessee at Chattanooga presented her research on "Motivation to Manage," a comparative study which looked at attitudes of male and female students in India and in the United States. Murgai surveyed students in library and information studies at eleven universities in the southeastern United States and at twenty-three in India, administering a questionnaire designed to measure achievement motivation. Of the 808 students in India, 50 percent were male while of the 665 in the United States only 20 percent were male. The Indian students were as a group younger, unmarried and full-time, while the U.S. students were older, had more library experience and were more likely to be part-time. While motivation to manage is common in both nationalities and in females as well as males, the barriers Indian women face are evident. Forty percent of Indian male respondents "thought it less desirable for women than men to have a job that requires responsibility " compared to only 2 percent of U.S. males.[10] In addition about a third of the Indian male respondents felt that women were insufficiently ambitious to manage while only 2 percent of U.S. males responded thus.

Huang Xin of the Guandong University in China provided some background and brief biographic sketches, as well as data from her own survey, in a paper entitled "Propping Up 'Half the Sky' in the Library."[11]

Even papers that do not report research done by the presenter often cite research efforts by others. For example, Kalpana Dasgupta, former Director of the National Library and currently Director of the Central Secretariat Library in the Department of Culture in New Delhi, in her paper on women managers in Indian libraries drew on an unpublished dissertation entitled "The Problems and Prospects of Women Librarians Working in Indian University Libraries: A Survey."[12]

The collection and dissemination of research on women in the library and information professions can highlight major problems and point the way to solutions. This research can suggest studies that may be emulated by others in different contexts. It is anticipated that the research agenda will expand to include user studies so that both parts of the goals of the Round Table will be served by research. Research is fundamental to facing future challenges with confidence.

Continuing Challenges

In a relatively short time, RTWI has accomplished much, yet it would be irresponsible to overlook the ongoing struggle with familiar obstacles: structural issues, political conservatism, and cultural differences continue to present challenges. IFLA, in common with many library and information science organizations, has a structure that is very traditional, based on types of libraries and library processes. However, today information technology and emerging political realities make such divisions increasingly problematic. Automation makes information networking a reality and the focus shifts increasingly to the user; vendors shape products to end users. Users may not actually enter the library, but opt instead for electronic access. Library organizations will be forced to recognize these new realities and provide structures focused on users.

Politically, library organizations have responded slowly to new or non-traditional constituencies. They responded best to those that expanded the reach of librarianship, without seeking entry into professional ranks. Put bluntly, they responded best to those constituencies that offered no threat to the traditional leadership but afforded significant expansion of professional services.

The growth of a constituency of women demanding services to assist them in non-traditional roles offers a great potential for professional growth. The range and variety of RTWI programs on services to women show the potential for such service. Yet this growth is likely to bring a greater challenge to traditional leadership than children's services, or service to minorities or the disabled has brought. The women practitioners who deliver women's services will undoubtedly share many of the values of their clients. This may make a docile acceptance of the traditional professional hierarchy impossible. (IFLA did not have its first female Honorary President until 1985.)

Not surprisingly traditionalists claim that women's issues aren't truly professional, a claim heard in the past as other subordinated groups demanded library service. Accordingly, women's concerns are usually relegated to temporary or marginal structures within professional organizations. The RTWI has had to pioneer its place in IFLA and both IFLA and the RT continue to work on this issue and continue to negotiate a structure for this vigorous body whose presence represents a structural adjustment to democratic pressures.

These negotiations take place in a time of political conservatism, characterized by a turning away from government solutions and toward market-based ones, in many of the countries with the longest and healthiest traditions of library service. Support for libraries stagnates, making expansion of services geared to women's needs less likely and reduction of personnel, often women, increasingly common. Of particular interest to the RT is the decline of support for professional travel in many countries making attendance by lower-paid librarians—the level at which most of the women are found —more difficult. Political conservatism favors service to the elite, and women rarely find themselves in that category except on the indulgence of men—fathers, husbands and, at work, directors and supervisors.

Cultural differences, poverty, and attitudes toward women, are also a continuing challenge to the RT, defining the excluded and the included. Although the RT actively seeks participation of women from a wide range of countries, this goal is elusive. Whole areas of the world are underrepresented in the RT due to poverty or attitudes toward women, or combinations of both. Only one woman from Africa and a few from the Middle East have participated in RTWI presentations. Also underrepresented are women from Latin America. When IFLA meets in a region, not surprisingly, more librarians from that region attend. So the Havana conference and the Istanbul conference both saw heightened attendance from the region as well as the host country. At both of these conferences the RTWI had participants from the host nation.

Cultural differences are evident in communication and encompass both language and equipment. English has been the working language of RTWI. So those from areas of the world where English is not widely spoken or studied are therefore at a disadvantage. The RT must work harder at translating its materials into the other official languages of IFLA, French, German and Spanish. Modern means of communication, the fax and electronic mail especially, facilitate participation and office-holding duties, but are unavailable in many places or usage may be sharply restricted.

Turning from the excluded to their opposite it is clear that women librarians from wealthier countries with longer traditions of participation by women in public life not only are more likely to attend, but are also more likely to have had some familiarity with English and to have access to modern means of communication. In addition, they are also more likely to have had exposure to feminist activities in their home country, giving them an advantage in suggesting programs and projects. Not surprisingly, the Executive Committee of the RTWI overrepresents women from wealthier countries such as the United Kingdom and the United States.

Despite these problems, the RTWI thrives today and looks forward to a vigorous future built on its traditions of excellent programs and activities. A new group of women will be leading the RT. These include Marta Terry, director of La Bibliteca Nacional Jose Marti, Cuba, who is incoming Chair; Isabelle Stirling of the University of Oregon in the U.S. who is incoming Secretary Treasurer; Beth Stafford who is incoming Information Officer and *Newsletter* editor. They will be assisted by an Executive Committee that includes a good mix of pioneers to ensure continuity, and newcomers to bring fresh ideas and perspectives to the Round Table.

Round Table members recognize that only when societies invest resources in females from birth throughout the life cycle equal to what is invested in males can gender equity be achieved. The status of women librarians is inextricably connected with the status of women, so as we reach out to share our professional expertise with women around the world, we help ourselves *and* our profession.

Notes

Citations are to works available in print or on the RTWI web site. Readers interested in topics mentioned in the text for which no citation is available are urged to contact one of the authors who will refer them to the presenter.

1. Tuula Haavisto, "How Long Do Women Have to Wait?" [cited August 24, 1994], available from http://www.nlc-bnc.ca/ifla/IV/ifla60/60-haat.htm.

2. Jacquelyn Marie, "Setting-up a Women's Studies Library" [cited August 24, 1994], available from http://www.nlc-bnc.ca/ifla/IV/ifla60/60-jacm.htm.

3. Lyudmilla Pronina, "Information Services Provided for Women by the Libraries of the Ryazan Region" [cited August 27, 1996], available from http://www.nlc-bnc.ca/ifla/IV/ifla62/62-prol.htm.

4. "News from Around the World," *Women and Librarianship: Newsletter of the IFLA Round Table on Women's Issues* May/June 1997, 2-3; *Women and Librarianship* ... , October/November 1996, 4.

5. *Women and Librarianship* ... , May/June 1997, 3.

6. Joan Korenman, *Women and Internet Resources: Using Electronic Media in the Curriculum* (Baltimore: National Center for Curriculum Transformation Resources on Women, 1997), cited in *Women and Librarianship* ... , May/June 1997, 4; Vilma Espin de Castro, *Cuban Women Confront the Future: Three Decades of Revolution* (Melbourne: Ocean Press, 1991).

7. Leo Appleton, "Equal Opportunities Activity in International Library Associations" (Thesis, University of Northumbria, 1995).

8. Appleton, 59.

9. Anne Goulding and Marigold Cleeve, "Gender and Equity in the Library and Information Studies Curriculum: Building Confidence for the Future" [cited September 2, 1997], available from http://www.nlc-bnc.ca/ifla/IV/ifla63/63goua.htm.

10. Sarla R. Murgai, "Motivation to Manage: A Comparative Study between Male and Female Library and Information Science Students in the United States of America and India" [cited August 27, 1996], available from http://www.nlc-bnc.ca/ifla/IV/ifla62/62-murs.htm.

11. Huang Xin, "Propping Up 'Half of the Sky' in the Library: Present Situation and Prospects of Chinese Female Librarians" [cited August 27, 1996], available from http://www.nlc-bnc.ca/ifla/IV/ifla62/62-xinh.htm.

12. N. Varalakshmi, "The Problems and Prospects of Women Librarians Working in Indian University Libraries: A Survey" (Dissertation, Gulbarga University, October 1992), cited in Kalpana Dasgupta, "Women as Managers of Libraries: A Developmental Process in India" [cited September 2, 1997], available from http://www.nlc-bnc.ca/ifla/IV/ifla63/63dask.htm.

25. The Influence of Information Technology Infrastructure and Policies on Library Services in Developing Countries

Donald E. Riggs

Notwithstanding gradual improvements in library services and information exchange throughout the world, there are many obstacles to overcome before adequate library services can be provided in the various developing countries. Due to inadequate funding, book collections are insufficient and staffs are too few in number to provide minimal library services. What can be done to improve library services in developing countries? Better local support is a natural immediate response. However, based on economic constraints in some countries, improved local support may not be forthcoming soon. Enabling technology, via national or international cooperatives, may be one of the better solutions for improving local and global library services. Paradoxically, while some countries are making greater use of sophisticated technology, the fact remains that approximately one half of the world's population lives two miles from the nearest telephone. The gap between the "haves" and "have nots" is widening. Since access to information empowers humans in various ways, the growing schism between those who have access to information and those who do not may become one of the world's great calamities. Efforts such as the Global Information Infrastructure (GII) have good intentions toward creating universal access to the world's informational resources, but the journey has not yet seriously begun to eliminate the "information poverty" found throughout much of the world. The information technology infrastructure and policies will have a significant influence on the ways library services are improved globally and locally in developing countries.

Information Infrastructure

"Information infrastructure" is the underlying foundation or basic framework necessary to support an effective information exchange system. Generally, an information infrastructure includes hardware, software, supporting physical and human resources, and data/information/knowledge.[1]

Hardware

The hardware configurations range from the basic high performance microcomputers and telephones to low earth orbiting satellites. Currently, most information is delivered via wireline technologies. The amount of bandwidth accessible is a major factor in the efficiency of an online system. The number of Internet users is expanding daily. In developing countries such as China, Kuwait, and Egypt the use of the Internet is growing dramatically. However, in these particular countries the use of the Internet is still used primarily for business purposes. Outside of the major cities in China, there is little or no opportunity for people to access the Internet due to the lack of telephones. Motorola, however, is building a wireless phone system to serve rural China. In time, satellites will perform an increasingly significant role in building a wireless infrastructure that will work in conjunction with wirelines. Satellites will fill the extensive gaps where terrestrial networks operate poorly or do not exist, but where people will require access to the rest of the world. Satellites are expected to level the playing field for libraries in countries currently without telephones. Both a blessing and a curse may be presented by the use of satellites in the delivering of information. On the one hand they can provide global access to news, entertainment, education, "edutainment," and "infotainment." The concept of a GII includes satellites to provide access in the vast regions of the world that do not qualify for broadband wireline deployment, and in most instances have not even secured narrowband access to "plain old telephone service." On the other hand, several national governments experience great ambivalence when they recognize that satellites make boundaries porous and the citizenry more vulnerable to outside influences.[2] This is particularly true in non-democratic countries.

Nova Southeastern University (NSU) was a pioneer in the distance education arena. It was one of the first universities in the United States to provide academic courses/programs at distance sites. NSU currently offers both undergraduate and graduate courses in several countries. One of the major difficulties it has encountered in its distance education endeavors is that of providing electronic access to library resources. Some locations (e.g., the Bahamas, Jamaica, and Panama) do not have sufficient local library resources to support graduate programs offered by NSU in their respective countries. And the telecommunications are not currently sophisticated enough to allow graduate students in these locations to dial into the NSU electronic library. The phone system in Jamaica is improving and likewise can be said for Panama. Nevertheless, graduate work in these areas is still dependent largely on a paper-based library.

Software

When one thinks of software, the information systems and programs that allow the end user to operate the hardware come to mind. In the multimedia environment, intelligently configured software becomes even more important. One of the greatest failures in the information revolution has been the inability to design and deliver software that is easy to use. One of the primary reasons why more households do not own personal computers is due to the complexities associated with their use. Library systems are frequently criticized by their users because they are not user friendly. Screens will frequently have several icons that tend to confuse the user. Why not have one icon for the older library user who has difficulty with navigating through the various icons or the user who is apprehensive about using computers? The icon could simply be "The Library." Developers of software should include principles of artificial intelligence. Expert systems, a subset of artificial intelligence, could dramatically improve the use of computers, especially by providing a logical and systematic front end. The complexity of software is compounded when citizens (with language/literacy deficiencies) in some developing countries try using online library systems.

Supporting Physical and Human Resources

Libraries will continue to exist for several years. And likewise can be said of librarians. In the most technological advanced society, libraries will be necessary as places where local citizens can go to get assistance/information, and also the socialization factor will remain quite important. The role of librarians will become more significant. Librarians throughout the world, and especially in developing countries, will be necessary to locate, filter, and customize information. The future of the role/importance of librarians depends largely upon librarians themselves. We should become bolder, more aggressive, and reflect more thoughtfulness in the transformation taking place in the information environment. Furthermore, it is difficult to imagine a developing country entering/participating in the information age without librarians/information professionals. Some of the East and South Asia, Eastern Europe, and Latin American countries are in critical need of additional librarians.

Data/Information/Knowledge

The fourth component of the information infrastructure is the actual content (data/information/knowledge) appearing in whatever format: electronic, optical, or hard copy. Content is now appearing in several multimedia forms, including voice, data, video, and graphics. Even though the World Wide Web has been in existence for several years, it remains very useful in permitting the use of hypertext on the Internet. Various interfaces (e.g., Netscape) allow users to select information interactively. The data/information/knowledge dimension is one of the most important parts of the information infrastructure.

In the more developed countries, there will be three types of libraries for several more years. The first type will depend principally on the paper-based collections; the second type will be a hybrid library depending on both the paper collections and online resources; and the third type will become more and more dependent on access to and ownership of electronic resources. In developing countries, the rate of dependence on electronic resources will be much slower. However, if large investments are made in the delivery of information to developing countries via satellites, we could witness a dramatic increase in the use of electronic resources. Getting the right information in the hands of the right user at the right time should be foremost in the minds of the people who are responsible for providing information in the developing countries and elsewhere. This is a high calling, and it certainly should be achieved! Information has truly proven to be "powerful" in so many ways.

Policies

Effective long-range planning and day-to-day operations of library services, regardless of the development stage, depend on well-written and executed policies. A policy is more than a platitude. It should be a helpful guide that serves not only as a "road map," but also ensures consistency and clarity. Policy promotes uniform handling of similar library activities; this is particularly important for libraries in developing countries. Policy acts as an automatic decision maker by formalizing library answers to previously made management decisions about how particular questions and answers should be resolved. Existing policies afford library managers a mechanism for insulating themselves from hasty and ill-conceived requests for a policy change. Policy also serves as a major communication link to a library's constituents.

One of the greatest challenges for a country's government is that of developing an effective information policy. Objectives of information policy include ensuring that:

1. The privacy of individuals and organizations using networked information or the GII is protected. All countries around the world should continually reexamine privacy policies to ensure that they apply comprehensively to the transfer of personal data over global networks. Technologically, it is possible for both governments and the private sector to transmit, process, and store large amounts of information about individuals. The right to privacy must be reflected in policies in order to safeguard this right. Librarians must be more active in protecting the privacy of users. We still hear of horror stories involving national governments examining the reading habits of users.

2. The security and reliability of the networks and the information that passes over them are preserved. Developing countries will have to depend more and more on information infrastructures. Thus, they should be assured that their infrastructure has a security policy that includes integrity, confidentiality, and reliability of the networks and of the information they carry. Otherwise, users will be reluctant to use them, consequently diminishing their value.[3]

3. The intellectual property rights of those who create the information are protected. For inexplicable reasons, some countries fail to honor the intellectual property of others. That is, they will take a copyrighted work produced in another country and make numerous copies for personal, library, or business use without seeking permission or paying any royalty for use of the work. Violation of the intellectual property issues is magnifying as more resources are produced as online multimedia. Policy at the international level has to be enforced to protect authors, creators, and researchers; otherwise, they will become stifled in sharing their creative works with others. The power of new technologies has already transformed the way creators work and how publishers deliver information. There is an urgent need for librarians throughout the world to educate others about the importance of intellectual property protection.

Universal Service

Will we be able to realize universal library service? Maybe, but not for several years. As technology advances and more countries are electronically networked, a "global library" will evolve. The treasures found in the world's libraries will be further developed in a coordinated manner. "Pockets of excellence" in the world's library collections will be identified and electronic mechanisms will be put in place whereby interdependence among these libraries will become commonplace. Libraries in developing countries will benefit tremendously from this interdependency.

With the necessary technology now available, all formats of library holdings can be digitized. Digitized formats make the global library network accessible, open to a large public (world-wide), and virtual. Several digital library initiatives are underway throughout the world; these projects include digitizing older manuscripts (no longer protected by copyright), maps, journals, letters from government officials, and various artifacts. Multimedia format is a prime component of the various digital initiatives. Thus, the intellectual resources appearing in the global library will enable learners to use more of their senses (beyond sight) while perusing/studying the multimedia digital materials. Just thinking about the "global library" is certainly a phenomenon that grabs one's attention and provides room for great expectations!

The electronic capabilities, especially that of digitizing resources, are causing a major transformation in libraries. The following comparison between the traditional library and the 21st century library summarizes the library's metamorphosis:

Traditional library	*21st century library*
Facility-centric	User-centric
Centralized collections	Distributed collection
Just-in-case strategies	Just-in-time strategies
Value = collection size	Value = access to information
Local focus	Global focus

Libraries can no longer rely on their local collection to fulfill the research and information needs of their users. With more books and journals being published each year and more resources appearing in electronic format, libraries have to depend more on one another. The days are over, if they really existed at all, when each library could have its own "crown jewels." Today's effective library has to engage in cooperative resource-sharing consortia that promote interdependence among its members. Due to financial constraints, collection development/management will have to migrate more rapidly toward the "just-in-time" strategy (i.e., acquire the requested item just-in-time for users whether via the local collection or from another library). During the evolving "globalization of knowledge" libraries are certainly moving from a "local focus only" to the "global" reach. The transformation of libraries, as described above, will have a significant influence on the improvement of libraries in developing countries.

Universal library service (or the "global library") will not occur by happenstance. Its development will result from systematic planning and thoughtful implementation. A compelling vision should realize many things, including:

1. Through share planning and action, libraries will broaden the breadth and coverage of global informational resources.
2. There will be ubiquitous access to these information resources, including special efforts to reach the "information poor."
3. The electronic environment will emphasize access to information rather than to the physical carrier of the information. Unlike the conventional library which provides pointers to information that is normally obtained in hard copy, the global library (via digital format) brings the users directly to the content.

Barriers

There are numerous barriers/obstacles standing in the way of the global library/international library networking. They include:

1. Lack of a compelling vision by international leaders. Various governmental leaders from different countries have failed to demonstrate an understanding of and commitment to international information/library networking.
2. National policies that prohibit the exchange of information across binational borders. Some governmental leaders tend to suppress the exchange of information with other countries due to competitive, economical and political reasons.
3. Lack of common standards for interchange codes, cataloging practices, protocols, and character sets.
4. Lack of interoperability between/among hardware and software. This problem will gradually be resolved via Z39.50 and other advanced protocols.

5. The reliability of telecommunications. Users of electronically networked systems do not want to wait 30 minutes before they get an online response.
6. The costs of telecommunications. Some developing countries cannot afford to acquire the expensive hardware, software, and telecommunication systems.
7. Language differences. Some countries have great difficulty with foreign languages. Some Latin American countries, for example, do not fully use the Internet due to the heavy emphasis on the English language. Some European countries have difficulty with the Hungarian language.
8. Library customs/practices. Due to the vast differences in library customs, some countries have difficulty in reaching agreements on cooperative library projects.
9. Lack of a supportive local environment. Despite what some librarians prefer to do in developing library partnerships, their local government may prohibit such.[4]

Let's Not Forget the "Have Nots"

One of the goals of world leaders should be that of equalizing access to the world's informational treasures. Even though the telecommunications systems are becoming more sophisticated and approximately one electronic network is connecting with another network somewhere in the world on a daily basis, much of the world still falls into the information "have not" category. The "have nots" situation is due to the lack of financial resources plus several other issues/factors. Beyond the lack of money, the "information poor" environment is caused and perpetuated by the differences in culture, binational/international competition, lack of democracy in some countries, and mistrust/suspicion among certain governments.

The information "haves" and "have nots" is a major world problem that will get worse before it gets better. We are already witnessing polarization between/among the "have" countries and the "have not" countries. How can we eliminate or greatly reduce the "have nots" situation? If the "information rich" countries become richer and the "information poor" countries become poorer, the world will be headed toward a global problem that may approach the consequences of war. Countries must work together to prevent themselves from becoming further divided on this important issue.

Opportunities

The enabling technology offers many opportunities to assist the "information poor" countries. Now is the time for global leadership in this area! We should not wait until we are in an "information crisis" before taking action. Our international leaders (e.g., participants in the GII and others) must be more active in formulating a strategic plan for helping the information "have nots." Thoughtful strategic directions must be coupled with a dynamic action plan. Technology has made it possible to share information among most parts of the world. If we are to realize the "universal service dream," then access to information will have to be equalized as much as possible throughout the world. Regrettably, we are far from universal access. However, the goal is conquerable! It will be achieved after much thoughtful planning, commitment of resources, and a very strong conviction by the right people to make it happen.

Conclusion

A grand opportunity awaits us to improve electronic access to the world's libraries. Advancing technologies and digital library initiatives are bringing us closer to the "global library" reality. The global human condition will surely improve as a consequence of having access to the rich array of information on health, family, financial, social, political, and educational issues.

There is a huge amount of work to be done before libraries in developing countries become part of the information revolution. First, more local support is required. And resources have to be found for the necessary information technology infrastructure. International leaders must formulate information policies that are recognized, honored, and adhered to by all participants. Policy must precede infrastructure. Librarians in developing countries will require a degree of retooling/training to function effectively in a networked information environment. Inclusion and openness are values that should be givens in the pursuit of enhancing access to information for all, especially for the information "have nots" in developing countries.

Notes

1. Forest Woody Horton Jr., "Viewpoint: A Business Format for the National Information Infrastructure," in *Planning Global Information Infrastructure*, ed. Ching-chih Chen (Norwood, N.J.: Ablex, 1995), 45-56.

2. Robert M. Frieden, "Satellites in the Global Information Infrastructure: Opportunities and Handicaps," *Telecommunications* 30, no. 2 (February 1996): 29-33.

3. Ronald H. Brown, "The Global Information Infrastructure: Agenda for Cooperation," in *Planning Global Information Infrastructure*, ed. Ching-chih Chen (Norwood, N.J.: Ablex Publishing Corporation, 1995), 393-436.

4. Ching-chih Chen, "Information Superhighway and the Digital Global Library: Realities and Challenges," in *Planning Global Information Infrastructure*, ed. Ching-chih Chen (Norwood, N.J.: Ablex, 1995), 176-180.

26. Freedom of Expression: A Comparison of Canada, Mexico, and the United States

Matthew B. Barrett and Beverly P. Lynch

Since 1933, when the American Library Association (ALA) was asked to take some action regarding the book burnings in Nazi Germany—action which the ALA did not take, the U.S. library community has developed its dogmas relating to libraries and freedom of expression. Librarians in the United States have developed mechanisms to resist efforts to remove from libraries books and other materials deemed offensive by some members of the community. There is now in the United States widespread agreement that libraries play an important role in supporting freedom of expression.

The American Library Association has based its intellectual freedom policies on the First Amendment to the U.S. Constitution, which states, "Congress shall make no law... abridging freedom of speech, or of the press."

The ALA also has adopted Article 19 of the United Nations Declaration of Human Rights:

> Everyone has the right to freedom of opinion and expression; this right includes freedom to hold opinions without interference and to seek, receive and impart information and ideas through any medium and regardless of frontiers.

Different societies and different cultures within the same society place various emphases on the rights the individual has vis à vis the community. These differences have important implications for freedom of expression. How libraries are able to respond in such environments depends to a great extent upon the political system, the stage of development and the culture of the library profession, and the confidence librarians have in being able to act within their own professional ideals. While the U.S. library community has worked steadily to affirm its intellectual freedom principles, its definitions and its policies have not transferred to other countries. And while Article 19 of the United Nations Declaration of Human Rights has been adopted worldwide, responses to attempts at censorship and the approaches to matters pertaining to intellectual freedom differ among countries with even great similarities in cultures. A recent comparison of attitudes of librarians in Canada and the United Kingdom— countries with many cultural similarities—shows major differences in attitudes toward censorship and intellectual freedom and variations in policies and approaches to matters pertaining to intellectual freedom and libraries.[1]

At the Initialing Ceremony of the North American Free Trade Agreement (NAFTA) on October 7, 1993, the Prime Minister of Canada, Brian Mulroney, the President of Mexico, Carlos Salinas De Gotari, and the President of the United States, George Bush, made comments inferring that the three countries have common goals of opportunity and freedom for their citizens. An examination of the practices supporting constitu-

TABLE 1
Libraries and Population Per Library

	Canada	Mexico	United States
Public	1,735	25	15,370
Academic	497	326	4,730
Government	402	10	1,875
Special	1,454	33	10,282
Total	4,088	394	32,357
Population per Library	6,667	205,941	7,686

Source: *American Library Directory,* 1996-1997

tional guarantees of freedom of expression show some differences. In this respect, the comment of President Bush: "This accord expresses our confidence in economic freedom and personal freedom, in our peoples' energy and enterprise" suggests some differences between the U.S. and its bordering countries. The U.S., with its culture of personal liberty and economic freedom, has fought to retain and promote its philosophical foundations worldwide, citing its profit margins as proof that liberty and freedom work best. The U.S. has spent a great deal of internal resources on protecting that philosophical base through the judicial process. Canada and Mexico have stronger European cultural and social influences than the U.S., place legislative authority above judicial authority, and find the central role of government more congenial than do many in the U.S. The provision for free expression in the U.S. Constitution, which is largely unassailable given both judicial primacy and an intense respect for the Bill of Rights, provides a foundation for intellectual freedom that other countries lack.

The role of libraries in support of freedom of expression varies among the three countries as does library development. Table 1 compares the countries on libraries and population per library.

The U.S. library community founded the first professional library association in the world in 1876, and professional library education in the United States was established in 1887. The Canadian Library Association was established in 1900. The Canadian library schools are accredited under standards developed and implemented by the Committee on Accreditation of the American Library Association. The Asociacion Mexicana de Bibliotecarios or Association of Mexican Libraries (AMBAC) was established in 1924 and there is now also an Association of Libraries and Institutions of Higher Education and Research. Professional library education in Mexico has not reached the stage of development currently found in Canada, and the U.S. librarians in Mexico have expressed interest in the accreditation process used in the United States and Canada, but nothing comparable to it has been developed for library education in Mexico.

Canada and the U.S. have established libraries in Mexico and have provided technical assistance to Mexican librarians. A number of important cooperative programs are developing between libraries in the U.S. and Mexico, for example, a cross-border interlibrary loan service developed by Daniel Mattes of Universidad Anahuac and Robert A. Seal of Texas Christian University and implemented in 1996.[2] Seven joint conferences have been held between librarians in the U.S. and Mexico, the first Foro Transfronterizo de Bibliotecas or Transborder Library Forum, having been held in 1989. The eighth is planned for spring 1998.

NAFTA not only secures free economic exchange, it also frees the exchange of information. It requires a closer alignment of business regulations and intellectual property protection. Prior to NAFTA, some U.S. printed products such as newspapers, books, and periodicals could enter Mexico duty free, while other commercially printed items carried tariffs as high as 20 percent. After NAFTA, duties on all printed materials dropped to zero.[3] Canada negotiated protection in NAFTA for industries it considers *cultural industries*, such as publishing and media. Mexico, by contrast, opened a more progressive door.

All three nations provide constitutional provisions of freedom of expression. The culture in which those freedoms are based, however, provide different realities.

Constitutional Guarantees of Freedom of Expression

Canada was distinguished as a Dominion within the British Empire by the Constitution Act of 1867, which laid out a form of government for the people inhabiting Canada. All rights and freedoms were assumed to be those existing in English common law tradition. Human rights were assumed, but not specifically mentioned until 1982, when the Constitution was updated. Schedule B, Part 1, guarantees "freedom of thought, belief, opinion and expression, including freedom of the press and other media of communication."

The United Mexican States became a federal republic in 1910 and the Mexican Constitution was adopted in 1917. The Constitution was updated in 1977 when a guarantee of the right to information was added. Article 7 supports freedom of expression:

> Freedom of writing and publishing writings on any subject is inviolable. No law or authority may establish censorship, require bonds from authors or printers, or restrict the freedom of printing, which shall be limited only by the respect due to the right of privacy, morals, and public peace. Under no circumstances may a printing press be sequestered as the instrument of the offence.

Access to Information

Table 2 compares the three countries on a number of indicators related to information access. Mexico differs greatly from Canada and the U.S. on all variables except public expenditure on education.

Each of the countries established libraries early. The first private library in Canada was in Nova Scotia in 1606; the first college library, College des Jesuites de Quebec, was founded in 1635.

The first library in the United States was that of Harvard College, founded in 1636.

Although the first true libraries in Mexico were among the Mesoamerican cultural and religions centers, the first library in Mexico as defined by the Western European colonizers was the library at the Real y Pontificia Universidad de Mexico in 1533. The Mesoamerican cultures left behind a great number of written, pictographic, astronomic and mathematical stone carvings, books, and murals, but most of these materials were destroyed.

As Table 1 shows, Mexico differs significantly from the other two countries in the number of libraries available to the population. Canada, with a ratio of 6,667 people per library, is well positioned to ensure ongoing and adequate library access to information, as is the U.S. with a ratio of 7,686. Mexico's ratio of libraries to population is 205,941.

TABLE 2
Key National Statistics

	Canada	Mexico	United States
Total population from latest national census	27,296,859	81,140,922	248,709,873
Literacy— percent of population illiterate over the age of 15	3.4%	12.5%	0.5%
School life expectancy—number of years	17.6	10.7	15.9
Total public expenditure on education as a percent of GNP	7.6%	5.3%	5.2%
Scientists and engineers per million population	2,322	226	3,873
Book production—number of titles	22,208	2,608	49,276
Periodicals—number of titles	1,627	56	8,855
News circulation per 1000 population	215	116	240
Televisions per 1000 population	640	149	815
Radios per 1000 population	1,030	255	2,118

Source: *1993 United Nations Yearbook* and *UNESCO Statistics on Education*

Mexico's number of libraries per population served, its literacy rate, its school life expectancy, its news circulation per 1,000 population, and its numbers of television sets and radios per population are strong indicators of a low level of access to information available to the population. Constitutional provisions for freedom of expression are one thing; access to information is another.

Censorship Issues

In order to get an overview of the censorship issues in Canada, Mexico, and the United States, the bimonthly *Index on Censorship* was consulted. Each incident cited by the *Index* for the period May 1994 through October 1997 was numerically summarized into general categories (see Table 3). These data provide a rudimentary measure of the current censorship issues faced in each country.

The most common issues for the United States are general freedom of speech issues, obscenity and sex issues, electronic media and artistic expression issues. The obscenity issue is almost unique to the U.S. Obscenity laws are more stringent in Canada and Mexico and less likely to be challenged in court. The organization of government in Canada and Mexico places legislative authority above judicial authority, just the opposite of the U.S. An interpretive legal ruling on obscenity by the U.S. Supreme Court such as the *Miller vs. California* decision (413 U.S. 15 [1973]) is an unlikely occurrence in Canada, and is improbable in Mexico due to Mexico's strict obscenity laws and the supremacy of its legislative authority.

Detention, violence, and death of journalists, authors and dissidents are very high in Mexico as compared to Canada and the United States. Thus, while having constitutional protection for the right to publish, Mexico has had difficulty protecting the human rights of journalists and authors. The Mexican Congress, at the request of President Zedillo, currently is considering issuing visas to foreign journalists for a period of only one year, with four one-year renewal options at the discretion of the State. This

TABLE 3
Overview of Censorship May 1994 - October 1997

	Canada	Mexico	United States	Total
Detention, violence, death of journalists, authors & dissidents	5	47	3	55
Access to, distribution by, and closures of newsstands and bookstores	1	1	5	7
Artistic expression, museums, galleries, exhibitions	2	0	12	14
Obscenity, sex, sexual speech	0	0	25	25
Banned books, speech protests, hate speech, religion	5	0	49	54
Electronic publishing, telecommunications, surveillance	3	4	37	44
Censored trials	2	0	1	3
Total	18	52	132	202

Source: *Index on Censorship*

action may be to mitigate or control media provisions in NAFTA. It is similar, though, to the common practice in many countries of requiring journalists to be licensed in order to control the flow of information.[4]

Current Free Speech Issues in Canada

Under the provisions of NAFTA, the cultural sectors of Canada's economy, including broadcasting, publishing, and book distribution, are protected from foreign investment. It was disclosed on February 8, 1996, that Industry Canada's Investment Review Division, the government arm which protects Canada's cultural industries (broadcasting, publishing and book distribution) from foreign competition, decided to block a joint venture proposed by Borders, a U.S. bookstore chain, to open bookstores in Canada. While the plan structured a board of directors with a majority of Canadian members, the overriding concern was that the company's computerized inventory control and book ordering system would favor U.S. publishers and authors. This was not just an economic concern; it was a cultural one as well.

In March 1994, 16,000 copies of *Wired* magazine were withdrawn from distribution in Canada.[5] *Wired* carried a report of a rape and child abuse trial in Toronto in which the judge had ordered a complete media ban within Canada on any details of the accused Karla Homolka's conviction for manslaughter.[6]

Wired had used the story to illustrate how computer users can circumvent restrictions on information. In Canada, the right to a fair trial for the accused overrode the public's right to information about the trial. Information concerning the crimes committed and the trial itself was removed from the print and the broadcast media. In some cases librarians were forced to clip articles referring to Homolka from non-Canadian newspapers housed in their libraries. The U.S. television show, "A Current Affair," was banned from broadcast in Canada for its coverage of the trial. Canadian cable TV stations blacked out CNN's related news stories. Usenet news group discussions of the case over the Internet also were banned by systems managers and university officials across Canada. The media ban could not control the on-line information; it was impossible to control as alternative computer addresses were used and on-line searches were performed through services such as Compuserve, which revealed that information was culled from many sources. *The Washington Post* published the fullest details from anonymous sources who had witnessed the trial.

In the United States the right of the press to publish information about trials seems to override, in some cases, the right of the accused to a fair trial. Unless it is a matter of national security, a ban similar to the one in the Homolka trial is practically unheard of in the U.S.

The governments of Canada and the U.S. have considered policies and laws to regulate and control the content of the Internet. Librarians in the U.S. are troubled by the issue of filtering Internet content. They support the principle of access to information for all with no censorship or restrictions by the library, yet they are concerned by the possibility of a child's access to pornography over the library's Internet terminals. Mexico has fewer users of the Internet per population and currently is concerned more with expanding its access than it is in controlling the content.

In light of Canada's negotiated exemption for its cultural industries, including book publishing, it appears that its constitutional commitment to free expression is intended to protect only Canadian expression; that emanating from other places will be tightly controlled. In 1987 Canadian customs agents seized and confiscated a shipment of books from the U.S. bound for gay and lesbian bookstores in Toronto and Vancouver; the agents classified the materials as obscene. The confiscation was challenged, and in 1996 the Canadian Supreme Court ruled that while the law governing obscenity itself was not unconstitutional, Custom agents were enforcing it in a discriminatory way. This could have had more to do with the destination of the books—a feminist bookstore, Little Sister's Book and Art Emporium, which had never had any challenges to materials in it before, only when they were coming in from outside of the country— than a judgment based strictly on content. Canadian Customs rarely has seized or confiscated books or magazines bound for mainstream bookstores.

The definition of censorship used by the Canadian Custom's agents came from a controversial Canadian Supreme Court ruling in 1992 that heard arguments from U.S. feminists, Catharine MacKinnon and Andrea Dworkin. The court stated in its opinion "that there was now another more compelling reason to regulate obscenity than mere public prudishness: Pornography harms women."

Current Free Speech Issues in Mexico

Mexico did not exempt cultural industries from the provisions of NAFTA. This may be due to Mexico's more distinctive history, language, and traditions than those of Canada and the U.S. During a recent study of the cultural implications of NAFTA's implementation however, researchers found, unexpectedly, a great deal of concern by Mexican business managers about losing their national identity and culture.[7] The cultural implications of economic integration for Canada, Mexico, and the U.S. never were discussed in the U.S. during public debate, perhaps due to the relative cultural heterogeneity of the U.S. The study, using the European Union as an example of a voluntary economic integration and the former Soviet Union as an example of a forced economic integration, suggests that economic integration does not necessarily decimate national culture. The resilience of cultural heritage was stronger than anticipated.

Perhaps the most famous Mexican president, Benito Juarez, is quoted by former President Adolfo Lopez Mateos as stating, "Nothing justifies attacking the rights of others, for within those rights lies peace." President Mateos, in an address to the press on national press day June 7, 1961, states further:

> You now enjoy, and will continue to enjoy, unrestricted freedom, but that freedom must serve the best causes of the entire Mexican community. Yours is the duty to set forth the truth about the life of the nation, neither belittling, nor exaggerating, nor distorting it. Yours is the duty to conserve national values, to invigorate our traditions, to affirm our way of life, to support historical sequence of our principles.[8]

This provides a conflicting backdrop to the current situation of detainment, torture, disappearance, and murder of journalists covering the Ejercito Zapatista de Liberacion Nacional (EZLN), also known as the Zapatista political movement in the state of Chiapas, and historically, any journalist covering Mexican indigenous people's conferences, attempts to organize new political movements, or reporting on governmental corruption. Judging from the data in Table 2 on the number of incidents reported in the *Index on Censorship*, journalists and authors are free to report and print their findings, but they have paid sometimes for the constitutional privilege of free expression with their lives.

Dissenting voices and the role of public watchdogs by journalists, so prized in the U.S., obviously is curtailed in Mexico. The media (newspapers, radio, television, and film) is regulated by the Mexican Ministry of the Interior, an agency equivalent to the U.S. Department of Justice. A number of these media are dependent on the government for various types of subsides; therefore, they are likely to practice self-censorship in many areas.

The Zapatistas in Chiapas began an "armed rebellion" on the date NAFTA went into effect, January 1, 1994. The leader of the Zapatista movement, Subcommander Marcos, is quoted as saying, "We did not go to war on January 1 to kill or have them kill us. We went to make ourselves heard."[9] The EZLN Zapatista Internet website was established (www.ezln.org), is administered by Swarthmore College in the U.S., and continues to have views on the situation electronically posted in Spanish, English, French, and German. The Zapatistas gave permission for the registration of the nonprofit domain name, but Marcos does not have an e-mail address and does not oversee the site's content. Ironically, Mexico was the host for the Columbian Revolutionary Armed Forces (FARC) website until the Columbian Consul in Mexico convinced FARC's Internet provider to discontinue the service on the grounds it contained messages inciting violence. The incident was characterized as an attack on freedom of expression.

The Aguas Blancas Massacre occurred in June 1995. Seventeen members of an independent trade union on their way to a demonstration were killed by police officers in a poor and rural area in the state of Guerrero. The incident was captured on eighteen minutes of videotape, showing the massacre as cold-blooded killings that culminated in the police officers placing weapons in the hands of the dead peasants in order to stage the incident as an attack on the police. The tape was broadcast on local TV news and the reaction eventually brought down the state governor. During a commemorative event a year after the incident, a new guerrilla movement was formed—"People's Revolutionary Army." Since then, the Mexican army has been hunting down suspected guerrillas and openly violating the constitutional rights and freedoms of Guerrero citizens. The journal, *El Chamuco*, was withdrawn from newsstands at the Mexico City airport for its coverage of the story, and now is banned from sale there for being too "strong."

Conclusion

Canada, Mexico, and the U.S. agree in principle on basic human rights of freedom of information and expression, yet there continues to be distinct cultural conflicts as to the definition of these terms at the local, national, and international levels under agreements such as NAFTA. Canada and Mexico both exert greater direct and indirect governmental control of the freedom of expression than does the U.S., although the U.S. has been under increasing internal pressure to do so. Historically, large concentrations of power in centralized governments have proved to be very dangerous for freedom of expression.

The increased economic exchange among these three countries will have an effect on the future of freedom of information and expression; however, the effect most likely will be quickly outpaced by the issues brought about by the ever-expanding and boundary-less global computer network. Sadly, it is most likely to be Mexico that will suffer from this prospect as access to the technology itself, by virtue of the current level of national poverty, will place it in a continuous technological and social "catch up" pace that will travel faster than the national identity may be willing to accept. This may further alienate the will of the people from its government.

While reconciliation of the freedom of expression practices in Canada, Mexico, and the U.S. may never actually happen under a single North American principle, increased exposure of the citizens of all three countries to the situation and context is important to pursue. Also important to pursue is a common understanding in the three countries of the important role libraries have to play in keeping freedom of expression alive. Keeping freedom of expression before the public as a basic concept and an important right requires constant vigilance and hard work. Libraries and meetings among librarians who hold different beliefs and have different cultural values can assist in the debates on issues of free expression. Libraries are places in which the decisions relating to freedom of expression are acted upon daily. Librarians confront the difficulties raised by freedom of expression decisions regularly and are asked to defend freedom of expression during the course of their work. Libraries can be places in which freedom of expression is taught. Librarians in Canada, Mexico, and the U.S., countries with their economies bound together through NAFTA, must continue to work toward the free flow of information commonly retained in libraries. Librarians must continue to seek ways to eliminate barriers to electronic information. Librarians can bring to others the recognition that freedom of expression extends to all forms of expression, and that the defense of freedom of expression is essential to an open and free society.

Notes

1. Ann Curry, *The Limits of Tolerance; Censorship and Intellectual Freedom in Public Libraries* (Lanham, (Md. and London: Scarecrow Press, 1997).

2. *FORO VII Transborder Library Forum, Ciudad Juarez, Chihuahua, Mexico, February 20-22, 1997. Final Report*, available from http://lib.nmsu.edu/foro/reporten.html.

3. *Business American* 116 (1995): 18-19.

4. Kyu Ho Youm, "Licensing of Journalists under International Law," *Gazette—International Journal for Mass Communication Study* 46 (1990): 115.

5. *Index on Censorship* 24 (1995): 168.

6. Project Censored Canada, *1996 Yearbook*, 8.

7. Mahmood S. Bahaee and Herman A. Theeke, "Cultural Implications of Economic Integration: A Case in NAFTA" *Competitiveness Review* 7 (1997): 16-24.

8. Adolfo Lopez Mateos, "Address Delivered by the President," Annual Freedom of the Press Day, June 7, 1961, Mexico City, Bloque de Obreros Intellectuales, 1961.

9. Joel Simon, "The Marcos Mystery," *Columbia Journalism Review* 33 (1994): 10.

27. The Ethics of Naming and the Discourse of Globalization

Hope A. Olson

"We Control the World by Naming It"

Last spring as I watched my students graduate—watched new librarians being named—I heard some names pronounced and others (especially the Greek, Finnish, and Chinese names of my research assistants) mispronounced. Then professor and poet Rudy Wiebe (pronounced Wēb) quoted the honorary degree recipient, writer Robert Kroetsch (pronounced Krōtch), as having said "we control the world by naming it."[1] Kroetsch had been referring to fiction, but spoke to my perception of authority control. In library and information studies (LIS), authority control is about how we name the intellectual world which we are charged to organize. As we name information for individual libraries, we also name it for the whole world. Through programs such as the International Federation of Library Associations and Institutions' (IFLA) Universal Bibliographic Control Programme (UBC) and networks such as bibliographic utilities, we have a global impact. A record catalogued into OCLC in Edmonton, Canada, one day can be downloaded from the OCLC database into a catalogue in Harbin, China, the next.

In this paper I will address concerns about the authority control aspect of this kind of exchange. Authority control is our mechanism for ensuring that the names we create are used consistently. They may be names of people, of corporate bodies, of titles, or of topics, but each is constructed as a uniform heading. Uniformity has been successful in achieving Cutter's gathering function of the library catalogue by bringing together the records for documents that have some commonality. However, our authority control, while an effective tool when well done, also imposes our uniform headings outside of their intended contexts. With globalization of information retrieval systems, the standards that we create are finding their way into environments where they may marginalize or exclude certain types of information. Because the way we name information reconstructs and recontextualizes it, our authority control practices may turn into an inadvertent form of cultural imperialism with increasing impact in a shrinking world. As Doris Hargrett Clack noted in her classic work on authority control, "cultural biases are difficult to overcome because they are not necessarily obvious or deliberate but rather subtle and unconscious reactions to differing patterns of behavior."[2]

To discuss these patterns and biases I will first explore the general concepts of globalization, naming, and authority. Then I will look at how they come together in our standards for authority control and explore ways to minimize potential cultural imperialism.

Globalization

I have adopted political scientist Caroline Thomas's definition of globalization as "the process whereby power is located in global social formations and expressed through global networks."[3] I suggest that for us the social formations are the discourses of the West/North, that is industrialized North American and European societies, and that the networks are international programs and databases that spread the information standards which reflect these formations.

The intent and results of globalization can be perceived in two nearly opposite ways. The first is cooperation between countries to share information, labour and data for mutual benefit, especially for the benefit of less-developed countries. The second is domination through exploitation of offshore labour and markets, of natural resources, of unregulated environments, and of "exotic" cultures. We generally envision library practices as contributing to the first kind of globalization. I cannot imagine anyone in the library community creating authority records with the idea of exploiting other cultures. However, in a global context the ramifications of what we do as powerful actors in a global context are complex and difficult to predict.

Naming

Kroetsch's assertion that "we control the world by naming it," implies enormous power in naming and the unwitting xenophobia we risk in doing our naming if oblivious to a global context. The following passage from Vietnamese-American film scholar Trinh Minh-Ha discusses representation of other cultures in the context of documentary film, but also gives us insights into the representation of information in library catalogues.

> The imperviousness in the West of the many branches of knowledge to everything that does not fall inside their predetermined scope has been repeatedly challenged by its thinkers throughout the years. They extol the concept of decolonization and continuously invite into their fold "the challenge of the Third World." Yet, they do not seem to realize the difference when they find themselves face to face with it—a difference which does not announce itself, which they do not quite anticipate and cannot fit into any single varying compartment of their catalogued world; a difference they keep on measuring with inadequate sticks designed for their own morbid purpose. When they confront the challenge "in the flesh," they naturally do not recognize it as a challenge. Do not hear, do not see. They promptly reject it as they assign it to their one-place-fits-all "other" category and either warily explain that it is "not quite what we are looking for" and that they are not the right people for it; or they kindly refer it to other "more adequate" whereabouts such as the "counter-culture," "smaller independent," "experimental" margins.[4]

Examining this passage demonstrates the risks we take in a global context. In describing the "imperviousness in the West of the many branches of knowledge to everything that does not fall inside [our] predetermined scope," Trinh suggests that our traditional ways of naming are designed for conventional western knowledge. As I will illustrate below, we have constructed our rules of entry and controlled vocabularies in this conventional manner both in content and in structure. We still fall into this practice even though it has been "repeatedly challenged by [the West's] thinkers throughout the years" and even though we "extol the concept of decolonization and continuously invite into [our] fold 'the challenge of the Third World.'" We generally try to be inclusive, to address the needs of other parts of the world; we try to offer voice to these others "[y]et, [we] do not seem to realize the difference when [we] find

[our]selves face to face with it—a difference which does not announce itself, which [we] do not quite anticipate ... When [we] confront the challenge 'in the flesh,' [we] naturally do not recognize it as a challenge. Do not hear, do not see." That is, we don't really get it. The differences are such that we are not accustomed to looking or listening for them. We cannot perceive them in our usual way of perceiving things which is culturally bound. Each difference "cannot fit into any single varying compartment of [our] catalogued world" so we "assign it to [our] one-place-fits-all 'other' category." What follows from our inability to see is that we cannot fit the "others" of the world into our culturally limited categories for naming knowledge. So although we "invite into [our] fold 'the challenge of the Third World',", we "refer it to other 'more adequate' whereabouts such as the 'counter-culture,' 'smaller independent,' 'experimental' margins." We try to include these others, but end up by suggesting that the burden of naming otherness, of explaining what we do not perceive, must be borne by the very others who are already disadvantaged by being in that category and once borne it is relegated to the margins.

Taking this view of naming places us in a position of power which we are not culturally equipped to handle, no matter how honest our intentions. The mechanism of this power is authority. Authority control in libraries is seen to be aptly named when we look at the broader concept of authority.

Authority

Political scientist Kathleen Jones describes a command-obedience model of the concept of authority as the model typically used in our culture. In the command-obedience model, authority constructs order; enforces obedience and conformity; and silences opposition. "Authority constructs rules with which to organize behavior, to master and control it, to fix it in its (proper) place."[5] Authority control follows this model—we obey the commands to use the names designated as authoritative instead of other possible names. So what happens is that we set up authoritative systems of naming that put us at risk of falling into a globalization that will continue to impose the commands of the West/North on the rest of the world.

What are the sources of these commands? That is, what are the aspects of our practice of authority control that enforce obedience? I suggest that the standards we create are the main source of authority, but that their implementation through automation and our practice of copy cataloguing enable enforcement of obedience.

Standards

Personal Name Authorities

We are all familiar with problems encountered by anyone seeking to standardize catalogue entries. For example, in a global context personal names and their qualifiers (e.g. indications of royalty) in multiple languages, various scripts, various transliterations, abbreviation practices, and cultural practices for multipart family names present challenges to standardization.[6] A more subtle example shows how ingrained our habits are. We impose some of our own structure for names onto names from other cultures in spite of authorization of the vernacular form in the Paris Principles and the *Anglo-American Cataloguing Rules*, 2nd ed., 1988 revision (AACR2R). Rule 22.4B2 of AACR2R makes East Asian names follow western format: "If the first element is a surname, follow it by a comma," even though the comma indicates an inverted form which does not apply to East Asian names.[7] Therefore, the Library of Congress (LC) authoritative heading for Trinh Minh-Ha is *Trinh T. Minh-Ha (Thi Minh-Ha), 1952-* . AACR2R imposes a standardized structure which is here culturally inappropriate.

Other examples come from Muslim names which have numerous parts, far more than just family names and given names. According to Roderic Vassie of the British Library, the part of the name that should come first in a catalogue entry is not always the same part. In some countries and cultures in the Islamic world people will be known by different parts of their names and it is not always consistent between individuals even in the same culture, especially historically.[8]

Tom Delsey has pointed out that in library catalogues the confusion of the "right" way to enter a name in the author's vernacular is complicated by the vernacular of a catalogue's anticipated users. For example, English-reading users will expect a different form of famous names like Confucius than will Chinese-reading users.[9] In these cases the needs of local users are not uniform around the world so privileging the author's choice or the contextually common name may not be universally helpful.

Subject Authorities

Efforts at standardizing subject access are even more problematic. The *Library of Congress Subject Headings* (LCSH) are widely used around the world even though their intended audience is the United States. They are used not only in the wider English-speaking world (e.g., Australia and the United Kingdom), but also in heterogeneous environments that are more or less officially English-speaking such as Canada and South Africa, in countries with diverse languages that use English as a common language such as Singapore and Nigeria, and in countries that use English for its practical external value such as Iceland. Other countries use both LCSH and a translation such as Turkey and Malaysia. Translations are also used alone such as the Spanish versions which are widely used in Latin America (although the North American slant and their high cost sometimes prevents their use). Finally, some countries, such as Portugal, use LCSH-like lists of subject headings.[10]

This widespread use of LCSH creates certain global responsibilities even though LC has never courted such pervasive influence. As Chinua Achebe has said of the English language, "... the price a world language ... must be prepared to pay is submission to many different kinds of use."[11] LCSH's problems representing different cultures affect not only its intended audience, but also audiences in the cultures concerned. As the creators and primary users of LCSH we cannot abdicate the ethical responsibility of a world language.

An example of LCSH's difficulties is the seemingly simple problem of naming people from India. As Usha Bhasker points out, LCSH naming of Indians from India and Indians of North America has resulted in headings unsatisfactory to both.[12] The entry for Indians from India is: *East Indians* with the scope note: "Here are entered works on the inhabitants of India in general. Works on the aboriginal peoples of the Western Hemisphere, including Eskimos, are entered under Indians." And the national characteristics of people from India are entered under:

> National characteristics, East Indian
> UF   East Indian national characteristics
>   Indic national characteristics
>   National characteristics, Indic

From the references to this heading one can see that the adjective *Indic* is also used to describe attributes of Indian culture. Therefore, the heading for Indian philosophy is: *Philosophy, Indic* "UF ... Philosophy, East Indian ... " LC seems to have gone to considerable effort to make its usage consistent using *East Indian* for people and *Indic* for cultural manifestations. It is a problem that comes from the confusion of fifteenth century Europeans that caused us to describe Native Americans as Indians, not a confusion of the two colonized peoples concerned who have no trouble telling themselves apart.

If we search for *colonialism* in LCSH we are commanded to see several different headings one of which is *Colonies*, where we encounter a long scope note that establishes a seemingly neutral approach. However, on closer examination it reflects an imperialist perspective.

Colonies

>Here are entered general works on colonies and colonialism, subdivided further by Africa, America, Asia, or Oceania, if appropriate. Works discussing collectively the colonies ruled by a country or other jurisdiction are entered under the name of the country or other jurisdiction subdivided by *Colonies, e.g., Great Britain—Colonies.* Headings of the type *[country]—Colonies* may be further subdivided by the regions and topics that appear as subdivisions under *Great Britain—Colonies.* Works on the colonial period of individual regions or countries are entered under the name of the region or country with appropriate subdivision, *e.g., India—Politics and government—1919-1947.* Works on the influence of former colonial policies and structures on the existing institutions of former colonies are entered under the current name of the particular region or country with subdivision *Colonial influence.* Topical subjects subdivided by place may also be subdivided further by *Colonies, e.g., Education—Great Britain—Colonies.*
>
>Note under *Colonization.* ...

UF ... Colonialism ...

As a result, there are elaborate ways of representing the perspectives of those doing the colonizing. For colonizers one can specify country of origin, *e.g., Great Britain–Colonies*, subdivide that group of colonies even if they are no longer colonies, *e.g., Great Britain–Colonies–Discovery and exploration* (that is, discovery by the British), and group any geographically subdividable topic by the colonizing activities of a given country, *e.g., Education–Great Britain–Colonies.* However, for colonized peoples one can specify only the postcolonial state of a given region or country, *e.g., Zimbabwe–Colonial influence*, which is the influence on Zimbabwe, not the influence of Zimbabwe; or the relevant time period of the country's history, *e.g., India–Politics and government–1919-1947*, which does not indicate in the heading that it deals with colonialism at all.

Following the note in the heading for *Colonies* we can go to the heading *Colonization* to find:

Colonization

>Here are entered works on the policy of settling immigrants or nationals in colonial areas. Works on migration from one country to another are entered under *Emigration and immigration.* Works on migration within a country are entered under *Migration, Internal.* Works on general colonial policy, including land settlement, are entered under *Colonies.* Note under *Agricultural colonies.*

SA subdivision *Colonization* under names of countries, etc., and under
classes of persons and ethnic groups, *e.g., Africa—Colonization;
Afro-Americans—Colonization; Indians of North America—Colonization;
Mennonites—Colonization*
BT Imperialism
Land settlement
RT Colonies
Decolonization
Emigration and immigration

Here there is a general heading, *Colonization*, to deal with the process of settler peoples moving from the imperial power to the colony as indicated by the scope note and suggested by the broader term *Land settlement* and the related term *Emigration and immigration*. The implication for the subdivision *Colonization* is seemingly at odds with the general heading. It does seem to focus on the place or people colonized. LC's *Subject Cataloging Manual: Subject Headings* does not clarify the meaning of this subdivision though it gives a full explanation of *Great Britain–Colonies* as a pattern for imperial powers.[13] The sum of these references and instructions is a bias toward the view from imperial powers rather than the view from colonized societies.

Syndetic Structure

The syndetic structure—the references that show the relationships between concepts—established by our standards is also reflective of a specific world view. The Paris Principles and IFLA's subsequent efforts, including the *Guidelines for Subject Authority and Reference Entries* and the guidelines currently being developed for subject heading lists, grow out of a European cultural tradition.[14] Our concepts of authorship are drawn from the culture of the European Enlightenment, which is embodied in the equivalence relationships that enforce the duality of names being either the same or different and the primacy of the individual, making an individual's name and how she or he uses it of supreme importance. The syndetic structure prescribed by our standards stresses hierarchical relationships between corporate bodies and topics and reflects the same kind of western philosophy that in the Enlightenment saw the universe as a progression from lower life forms through Man and the angels to God.

In subject headings, both equivalence and hierarchical relationships between concepts are given importance, but not numerous other kinds of relationships which are lumped together as associative relationships represented by related terms (RT's). Other cultures, such as Native North American cultures, have developed a more holistic philosophy that sees people and other entities as part of a circle of life each contributing to and valued as an essential part of that circle, instead of a hierarchical chain of being.[15] The hierarchical structure that we adopt as the framework for our syndetic structures which seems intuitive to us is alien to other cultures.

Mechanisms Enforcing Authority Control

MARC records, automated systems and the economic necessity of copy cataloguing are mechanisms that enforce obedience to authority control. The MARC authority format enforces this syndetic structure which it is built to accommodate. Since the MARC authority format is the standard medium of transfer, its structure affects what can be accommodated and what we expect to put into or find in an authority record—

mainly an authoritative heading enforced by "use" or "see" references and hierarchical relationships.

Automated systems with authority control typically are designed to follow the command-obedience model in their authority mechanisms by flagging headings that do not match or by flipping headings from nonauthoritative references to their authoritative forms. Therefore, the systems enforce the format which enforces the culturally bound syndetic structure.

Finally, the use of copy for both authority and bibliographic records is an economically enforced practice. Following standard practice is essential to the economy of copy cataloguing. Bibliographic records from sources like national libraries will contain standard authoritative headings, enforcing a perspective of the West/North. This problem is especially apparent when bibliographic records are imported into systems without authority control, leaving users with the worst of both worlds—the disadvantages of culture-bound content without possibly ameliorating references.

Augmented Meaning—Another Model of Authority

The word "authority" derives from the Latin, *augere*, which means to augment. This etymology suggests an alternative to the command-obedience model. Authority may be interpreted as the augmentation of meaning. Jones suggests that this interpretation of authority will break down the boundaries between author and reader. It will establish authority as the result of relationships, especially horizontal as opposed to vertical (hierarchical) relationships. Such a view rejects absolute authority and the boundaries it constructs, "reconceptualizing authority in a way that takes boundary transgression as fundamental and gives meaning—since an author/*auctor* is one who gives meaning— to it. This new practice of authority will become a practice of founding community not on identity politics but through diversity ..."[16] To apply this concept of authority to authority control for names and subjects requires that we make space to add regional and local emphasis. Because standards like AACR2R and LCSH are world languages we must, as Achebe said, "be prepared to pay." We are paying for the privilege of being the politically and economically dominant culture. To avoid an exploitative model of globalization in which our standards and therefore our cultural traditions are marketed to all parts of the world, we must make authority locally and affordably augmentable.

At the beginning of this paper I cited Doris Hargrett Clack's warning that cultural biases are difficult to perceive. Our first task is to work toward perception. This exercise is not always a pleasant one as we uncover our very own biases, but our efforts make possible a different model of authority. Clack suggests looking toward technology, and particularly UNIMARC, for solutions.[17] I have described elsewhere some techniques for adapting current technology using theoretical frameworks from other fields to enable an augmentation model.[18]

For example, we need to open up our systems to less rigid relationships. Anna Yeatman proposes a "partnership model" of political representation that is useful in this context. She developed her model in a New Zealand context in which the concerns of a Maori community needed to be taken into consideration by white doctors. The two groups had different expertise, but both were crucial for a productive result. A similar situation occurs between general library standards and local contexts. Some mechanism for accommodating different local needs is required. A wealth of data is contained in the morass of transaction logs. A relevant project that I plan to pursue is to develop a practical way to pull terms out of transaction logs for incorporation into controlled vocabularies on a local basis. In this way, users' voices can be heard in the catalogue's naming of information.

Such uses of technology can be further augmented by standards such as UNIMARC that are less culture bound than other standards. Clack describes UNIMARC as a "neutral" MARC format. She recognizes "the national or cultural orientations of the various national MARC formats" and suggests UNIMARC as a good candidate for bridging them.[19] This type of interface format allows exchange of data while making space for cultural augmentations in local environments. It can address the need for locally augmentable authority control by providing a format that allows integration of variants. UNIMARC also offers some accommodation of parallel headings—headings in different languages—although it still requires that in a given record one version be chosen as authoritative.[20]

A certain degree of local augmentation is, then, possible, but this augmentation also needs to be affordable. Systems capable of using UNIMARC need to be accessible for its widespread use and some means of identifying different intellectual content need to be developed. This analysis is further complicated by the recognition that most countries have heterogeneous populations in which the predominant group is only one part of a diversity of groups or cultures.

Until there is economic support for augmentation at a very local level some of the responsibility still rests with our "world languages," the authority files set up in and for environments of wealth and power. We need to take a serious look at the rigidity of our structures as well as our terminology, to build on our effective tools of authority control while augmenting them for added meaning in diverse contexts.

Notes

1. In speech at convocation ceremony, University of Alberta, Edmonton, Alberta, Canada, 5 June 1997.

2. Doris Hargrett Clack, *Authority Control: Principles, Applications, and Instructions* (Chicago: American Library Association, 1990), 28.

3. Caroline Thomas, "Globalization and the South," in *Globalization and the South*, ed. Caroline Thomas and Peter Wilking (London: Macmillan, 1997), 6.

4. Trinh T. Minh-Ha, *When the Moon Waxes Red: Representation, Gender and Cultural Politics* (New York: Routledge, 1991), 16.

5. Kathleen Jones, *Compassionate Authority: Democracy and the Representation of Women* (New York: Routledge, 1993), 191.

6. Eeva Murtomaa and Eugenie Greig, "Problems and Prospects of Linking Various Single-language and/or Multi-language Name Authority Files," *International Cataloguing & Bibliographic Control* 23, no. 3 (July/September 1994): 55-58.

7. Michael Gorman and Paul W. Winkler, eds., *Anglo-American Cataloguing Rules*, 2nd ed., 1988 revision (Ottawa: Canadian Library Association, 1988), 392.

8. Roderic Vassie, "A Reflection of Reality—Authority Control of Muslim Personal Names," *International Cataloguing & Bibliographic Control* 19, no.1 (January/March 1990): 3-6.

9. Tom Delsey, "Authority Control in an International Context," *Cataloging & Classification Quarterly*, 9, no. 3 (1989): 16-17.

10. The author drew this information from print versions of various national bibliographies and World Wide Web sites regarding national bibliographic agencies such as: Subject Headings Perpustakaan Negara Malaysia, available from: http://www.pnm.my/publication/subjhead.htm, National Bibliographic Database—PORBASE, available from: http://linnea.helsinki.fi/gabriel/en/countries/portugal-union-en.html; The Icelandic National Bibliography, available from: http://konbib.nl/gabriel/en/countries/iceland-natbib-en.html. The author also thanks Maryon McClary for information regarding Latin American use of LCSH.

11. Chinua Achebe quoted in Trinh, *When the Moon Waxes Red*, 170.

12. Usha Bhasker, "Languages in India: Cataloging Issues," in *Languages of the World: Cataloging Issues and Problems*, ed. Martin D. Joachim (New York: Haworth Press, 1993), 159-168.

13. Library of Congress, Cataloging Policy and Support Office, *Subject Cataloging Manual: Subject Headings*, 5th ed. (Washington, D.C.: Library of Congress, Cataloging Distribution Service, 1996), H1140, H1149.5 in v. 2.

14. For a description of work on the *Guidelines for Subject Authority and Reference Entries*, see Maria Inês Lopes, "Principles Underlying Subject Heading Languages: An International Approach," *International Cataloguing and Bibliographic Control*, 25, no. 1 (January/March 1996): 10-12.

15. Paula Gunn Allen, *The Sacred Hoop: Recovering the Feminine in American Indian Traditions* (Boston: Beacon Press, 1992), 59.

16. Jones, *Compassionate Authority*, 230-231.

17. Clack, *Authority Control*, 28.

18. Hope A. Olson, "Between Control and Chaos: An Ethical Perspective on Authority Control," in *Authority Control in the 21st Century: An Invitational Conference, March 31-April 1, 1996, Proceedings* (1996), available from: http://www.oclc.org/oclc/man/authconf/holson.htm.

19. Clack, *Authority Control*, 24.

20. *UNIMARC/Authorities: Universal Format for Authorities* (München: K. G. Saur, 1991).

28. Family Literacy: A Critical Role for Libraries Worldwide

Rebecca Knuth

In the last decades of the twentieth century, libraries worldwide have had to compete for scarce resources by justifying traditional services and taking on new roles, such as the advancement of family literacy. The context for this struggle is a divided world where access to and use of information mark a distinction between two social classes: the "haves" and "have nots." At stake is the preservation of existing libraries in industrialized countries as well as the spread of Western notions of librarianship to developing countries. But complicating the issues are questions about the approaches being taken in the library's new roles, and the political and social implications of, for example, a library's support of literacy initiatives and democratic access to information and knowledge.

During the 1990s, educational trends (towards lifelong learning, expanded definitions of "adult education," less distinction between formal and informal education), social trends (family approaches to change, viewing illiteracy as a social problem), and economic trends (viewing illiteracy as a cause of poverty, the idea of merchandising literacy education) converged to bring to the forefront, as a national and international policy issue, the subject of family literacy. Resources have been mobilized in support of the family literacy movement, but there has not been consensus on a basic definition of "family literacy"; it remains a label that lacks conceptual clarity. As a consequence, library-oriented family literacy programs so far tend to be either fragmented and uncertain in terms of mission or a repackaging of traditional services promoting reading and literature appreciation.

This author contends that family literacy initiatives have the potential to be an organizing and integrating force for revitalizing and expanding the library's roles in promoting lifelong learning and fostering an environment that supports more than a strictly Westernization of literacy. This chapter first offers an introduction to the conceptual basis of "family literacy" and then explores the global historical context of the field of literacy education. An overview of the two dominant perspectives on libraries' adoption of literacy objectives leads to a discussion of various options available to librarians worldwide as they seek to position the library as a dynamic factor in support of literacy, a literate environment, and democratic access and use of information.

The Concept of Family Literacy

A definition of "family literacy" is still under construction by academics and literacy practitioners (who study and design instructional strategies and materials), theoreticians (who view literacy in sociological and political terms), and policymakers and economists (who weigh its contribution to national and global development).[1] Some experts describe it as one of the "new" literacies emerging from a number of related and at times overlapping terms, including parent literacy, intergenerational literacy, and community literacy.[2] Others see family literacy as an "emotive label" that draws the attention of many people (including those involved in workplace literacy, children's literature appreciation, and adult education) and therefore could serve as a mobilization device to bring all literacy workers under a single big tent.[3] But the potential for unifying family literacy initiatives is countered by views of literacy which are based on various implicit or explicit assumptions about illiteracy, poverty, and class. Two camps appear— literacy is either a group of skills to be imparted in replicable programs or a system of socially constructed and embedded practices or literacy behaviors that can be encouraged in local contexts.[4]

Further confusion arises when interested parties such as political, nonprofit, commercial, and professional groups promote family literacy according to their stake (social concern, public affirmation, financial rewards, and professional and educational considerations). Since no clear-cut definition is connected to the label "family literacy," varying operational definitions have been used as necessary, for purposes of defining institutional turf, stealing initiatives from competitive institutions, seeking new resources or opportunities for extending scarce resources, serving the image-building and public relations needs of institutions, or advancing the careers of the organizational elite.[5]

In addition, differences between cultures, structures, and patterns of relationships within families in various regions, classes, and ethnic groups, and thus varying economic, political, social, cultural, and pedagogical ideas about families and literacy, result in difficulties in developing a concrete and universal definition. However, if there is any consensus around some core components, it lies in acknowledgment of these: that the family is an institution for education and learning; that the presence of a literate adult is essential to the family's cognitive and cultural growth; and that family literacy projects should be aimed at maximizing intergenerational transfer of language, knowledge, and values. If the primary purpose of a family literacy program is to enhance literate behavior, including the use of reading in daily situations, then improving the literacy skills of the parent, developing reading as a regular part of family life, and helping children become successful in school should be primary activities of such programming.[6]

Global Historical Context of "Family Literacy"

Global trends in family literacy emerged in the 1990s with three decades of experimentation in literacy development in Third World countries converging with educational and social trends in industrialized countries. Unlike traditional literacy initiatives, which involve formal and nonformal transfer of skills to an individual within a specific age group, family literacy—or at least its rhetoric—springs from contemporary views of literacy acquisition as a lifelong interactive social process rooted in the family and community. Dominant literacy models assume that primary or formal literacy (involving the education of children) is the province of educational institutions, while secondary or informal literacy programs (aimed at adults) are a separate specialization left in the hands of adult literacy specialists. This model was transferred to newly independent nations after World War II when literacy efforts were primarily focused on Third World development and modernization.

In the 1960s, when "development" was considered a primarily economic process, the adult literacy movement became tied to economic requirements, resulting in the professionalization of labor- and work-oriented literacy efforts.[7] However, in the 1970s, awareness of the social components of Third World development increased, and the emphasis on economic functionality was replaced by a new focus on critical literacy, or literacy for personal and social liberation. As historic, cultural, linguistic, religious and ethnic divisions grew "wider and sharper and louder" throughout that decade, concepts of critical literacy and the empowering quality of literacy also gained currency in industrialized countries. [8]

As concepts of literacy evolved and diffused, traditional concepts of the organization and functions of education broadened, and, at least in theory, education became equated with learning, regardless of where, how, or at what age the learning occurred. In 1972, UNESCO's International Commission on the Development of Education issued a report, in which learning was described as a lifelong process. Referred to as the Faure Commission Report, it characterized formal education as inherently limited and unable to meet the full spectrum of important lifetime learning needs.[9] Lifelong learning emerged as an inspirational and comprehensive concept which included "formal, non-formal and informal learning extended throughout the life span of an individual to attain the fullest possible development in personal, social, and professional life."[10] As a result of this reconceptualization of education, "adult education" expanded to include every conceivable activity and extension of education, from adult literacy and post-literacy to farmers' training, family life education, health and nutrition education, cooperative education, vocational education and technical education.[11] And with this expanded view of education, the context of literacy also grew to new proportions.

Western notions of literacy and emerging Third World concepts of the connection between literacy and social justice traveled back and forth between industrialized and developing countries. UNESCO functioned as a global agenda-setting agency, and not only promoted global concepts of lifelong learning but also provided guidance in reassessing literacy education and linking informal education to new strategies calling for integrated and community- based approaches to rural development. Other international agencies adopted and expanded upon UNESCO-sponsored trends and formed a web of support for family-based development efforts and for the coordination of literacy programs with social programs involving health and family education. For example, some USAID-initiated programs took the family as the starting point and promoted family strategies to influence development activities such as income generation and health.[12] UNESCO's "Young Child and the Family Environment Project," which promoted the development of preschool children, included a family literacy component. Global interest in literacy in early childhood education mirrored trends in industrialized countries, where parents were assuming responsibility for cognitive stimulation of young children, governments were funding preschool intervention programs such as Head Start, and "early childhood education" had emerged as a field of academic study.[13]

In 1990 global cross-fertilization of ideas about literacy culminated in the Conference on Education for All in Jomtien, Thailand, as part of the United Nations International Literacy Year. Participants at Jomtien called for a renewed commitment to education for all ages. Early childhood care and development activities were promoted, as were initiatives to increase "the acquisition by individuals and families of the knowledge, skills and values required for better living and sound and sustainable development."[14] Acknowledgment of the importance of educating women highlighted the influence of a mother's literacy on her children's educational attainment.

In 1994 the UN declared the International Year of the Family, a theme chosen because of the perceived disintegration of the family and because of growing concern for social and family development. The official declaration included this statement:

> The family constitutes a context of informal education, a base from which members seek formal education, and should provide a supportive environment for learning. Literacy has a dramatic effect on the dissemination of ideas and the ability of families to adopt new approaches, technologies and forms of organization conducive to positive social change. Often affected by early school leaving or dropping out, literacy is a prime conditioner of the ability of families to adapt, survive and even thrive in rapidly changing circumstances.[15]

As part of the year's special events, UNESCO sponsored the World Symposium on Family Literacy; its purpose was to review the theory and practice of family literacy work to date and consider how this work might be adapted and applied in different regions of the world. The symposium revealed great conceptual confusion. While "family literacy" had been explicitly incorporated in some programs in industrialized countries, "family literacy in its American form has not traveled to the developing world ... [although] programs which involve both families and literacy activities are very common."[16] Thus, many of the participating literacy experts—especially those from Third World countries—basically interpreted "family literacy" as addressing the implicit effect of traditional adult literacy programs on family members. In addition, there was confusion as to the translation of the label itself. For example, in English, the family (in "family literacy") is used as an adjective modifying "literacy"; in French, the words are joined as nouns (l'alphabetisation et la famille).

Those participants that made symposium presentations about programs designed to service the family directly were operating from one of two basic perspectives: a compensatory perspective, which tends to be manifested in replicable literacy programming (often government or commercially supported), or a participatory perspective, which concentrates on the social nature of literacy and focuses on the particular family and community. It is worth noting that most of these speakers emphasized the compensatory perspective and were from industrialized and English-speaking countries. The two perspectives were reflected in the co-sponsorship of the symposium by an international nongovernmental agency (UNESCO) and the commercial group Gateway Educational Products, which distributes educational products under the trade name "Hooked on Phonics." The symposium did not produce consensus on a dominant concept of family literacy or on principles of applicability.

Without consensus and formal direction, such as might have come from a declaration like that produced by the Jomtien Conference, practitioners interested in implementing family literacy programs are especially pressed to weigh all sides of the issues and possibilities and then form their own definition and program. The goal of the next section of this paper is to assist librarians worldwide in understanding the context and premises of these two perspectives on family literacy and their ramifications on libraries' implementation of family literacy programs. Knowledge of this background will aid them in forming alliances with literacy partners, rationalizing and creating viable programs, promoting literacy, and fulfilling professional obligations to make the library a venue for lifelong learning. The two perspectives are not mutually exclusive and a purist stance is not feasible; rather, knowledge of the undercurrents and conflicting conceptual trends can inform choices.

The Compensatory Perspective

Currently the dominant perspective in family literacy efforts in industrialized countries, the policy and money-driven compensatory movement has several major components:

1. programs rationalized by the rhetoric of remedial and compensatory education and an emphasis on the negative effects of illiteracy;
2. influence by public authorities and private bodies interested in creating replicable programs, methods and organizational schemes, including standardized performance measures; and
3. the idea of literacy as a product, as something to be marketed.

Literacy is typically thought of in relation to skills, not its political and ideological contexts, and in terms of its consequences, which include jobs, social mobility and a fuller life. Examples of compensatory-based family literacy programs in the United States would be government-sponsored Even Start programs (which feature early childhood education, adult education for parents, and parenting education) and programs linked to the National Center for Family Literacy (which feature early childhood education, adult education, parent time, and parent and child together time). In Britain, an example is the Adult Literacy and Basic Skills Unit's Family Literacy Scheme, which was funded from 1993 to 1997, and includes basic skills instruction for parents, literacy and language development for children, and time for parents and children to work together on prereading, early reading, and reading skills support.

The compensatory perspective coalesced and gained momentum in the late 1980s and early 1990s, when worldwide interest in literacy (as demonstrated by the Jomtien conference) reached political and policy levels in industrialized countries.[17] Governments recognized literacy as a universal human right and consequently initiated legislation and policy to enforce this right. Increased access to education swelled the number of participants in adult literacy programs; for example, in Germany 5,700 literacy learners in 1985 grew to 20,000 in 1991. In many industrialized countries, illiteracy was blamed for poverty and for inefficiency in the workplace; it was seen as a critical problem threatening the very premise of democratic society.[18] Literacy-as-right became "literacy as a need, and, slowly, literacy as an obligation for the most dependent groups of society."[19]

The United States functions as a pacesetter and exemplar in education among industrialized countries and, ultimately, as an exporter of educational trends. Thus, it is worthwhile to examine the progress of U.S. compensatory literacy efforts for the last decade. These efforts have been significantly affected by legislative and nonprofit actions, and reflect a "context of the overall alarmist concern with the crisis in American education."[20] In 1991, the National Literacy Act sought to eliminate adult illiteracy by the year 2000 and $200 million was allocated for literacy programs. Also in 1991, the U.S. Department of Education sponsored the National Center on Adult Literacy to enhance the knowledge base and improve practice in the adult education field. Family literacy became a significant component in social legislation taking a prominent place in such acts as the Family Support Act of 1988, the Job Training and Partnership Act, the McKinney Homeless Assistance Act, and the Library Services and Construction Act in 1988.[21]

Legislative action was paralleled by action in the nonprofit sector. In 1989, the nonprofit National Center for Family Literacy (NCFL) was founded to serve as a primary source of information, training, and support for the family literacy movement.

The Coors Family Literacy Foundation, the Kenan Charitable Family Trust, and the Barbara Bush Foundation for Family Literacy also emerged to form a network of support for family literacy. A variety of links exist; for example, a Kenan Trust challenge grant provided $500,000 for every $1 million raised annually for NCFL's endowment through 1996. In addition, the nonprofit groups seek corporate support; for example, Kunio Shimazu, President of Toyota Motor Corporate Services of North America, Inc. provides corporate leadership to NCFL.

Infusion of federal money, new nonprofit and corporate partners, and support by commercial interests resulted in a trend toward replicable, skill-based, and standardized literacy programs in the 1990s. Statements such as the following by the NCFL were common and express the compensatory nature of the American approach to promoting literacy:

> Family literacy is a movement that addresses the needs of millions of undereducated families across the United States who are trapped in a cycle of poverty, dependency, and undereducation.

> A more literate, better educated population is unquestionably the best long-term solution to America's poverty problem.

Yet another example: "Illiteracy damages the nation economically, weakening our chances of competing successfully in a global marketplace."[22]

Libraries in the United States were enlisted into the family literacy "movement" through legislation and partnerships. It was a natural step, since libraries had a strong tradition of services and outreach programs for adult and children. Although the division of services according to levels of human development is a distinctive characteristic of the public library as an institution, libraries are in a unique position to blend these traditional organizational divisions, because of common administration.[23] Many libraries already support local adult literacy efforts through providing reader advisory services, tutor workshops, a library-based curriculum, collection development (selection, purchase, labelling of books for new readers), and bibliography preparation.[24] Some libraries provide space for literacy tutors and books for the General Equivalency Diploma.

Libraries' long-term involvement in literacy was substantiated by a 1986 U.S. Department of Education-sponsored study conducted by the University of Wisconsin-Madison School of Library and Information Studies.[25] The history of services to adult learners was traced to the very origin of public libraries in the 1850s; special attention to servicing the illiterate population has been evident since the mid-1960s. The study posits that libraries' literacy activities fall into three general categories—literacy materials, literacy instruction, and literacy support services—and that a library's involvement in promoting literacy may involve more than one of these roles. Because of varying community needs, "it is...not a simple case of a library either being involved or not...libraries will emphasize different roles in literacy education and may select activities from each role."[26] It has been estimated that more than one-half of U.S. public libraries were involved in some form of literacy activity by 1980.[27] Many libraries had expanded their role in literacy education, some through funds from Title II-B of the Higher Education Act and some through state and city grants. For example, the Brooklyn Public Library used money from New York City to open five new learning centers.

What was different about the family literacy movement was its focus on formalizing, refocusing, combining, and extending traditional adult and children's services. To kick-start efforts, in 1990, the American Library Association (ALA) joined forces with Bell Atlantic Charitable Foundation, which provided $300,000 for projects in over twenty urban, suburban, and rural libraries: Libraries in Washington, D.C., Maryland, Virginia, West Virginia, Delaware, New Jersey, and Pennsylvania could apply for $5,000 grants to establish new family literacy initiatives and/or to improve existing programs. Eligible projects involved cooperative efforts by the librarian, the adult basic education specialist or literacy provider, and a community representative from Bell Atlantic.[28] A clearinghouse for family literacy information was established, and particularly effective programs were publicized. ALA developed family literacy "fact sheets," which gave hints on planning and implementing programs.

Compensatory family literacy programs are encouraged (1) to promote children's literature, reading, and a literate environment; and (2) to enhance the parent's literacy and parenting skills (especially those reading-related skills that are tied to children's success in school) and the parent's role as advocate for his or her child's learning, development, and success in school.[29] According to Zapata, there are essentially two lines of action for libraries in the context of family literacy programs: serving as an ally of institutions and organizations whose primary activity is to provide literacy programs, or acting as a service unit that can provide information resources to people participating in literacy endeavors.[30]

A third role—one which is only beginning to be explored—is direct programming. Here, Ruth Nickse's models of family or intergenerational literacy delivery might be useful organizing principles. They are:

1. direct adults/direct children: families are taught to interact around reading with intensive instruction directed at both adults and children; the goal is positive, long-term family intervention.
2. direct adults/indirect children: structured literacy and parenting instruction is directed at the parent; children are secondary beneficiaries; the goal is supplementary, for skill-building and enjoyment.
3. indirect adults/direct children: program helps adults to help their children with homework; adults are secondary beneficiaries; the goal is parent education.
4. indirect adults/indirect children: support of reading for enjoyment; no direct literacy instruction, informal events such as storytelling and read-alongs; adults and children are primary beneficiaries and the goal is supplementary school-related literacy improvement for children.[31]

Nickse's models are helpful in articulating programs in terms of beneficiaries/target groups, activities, and goals.

Reports on existing programs often include categorization according to Nickse's models; they appear to be quite helpful for accountability and evaluative purposes. Reporting and accounting are very important in compensatory-driven programs, where grants and funding are often contingent on the program's inclusion of specific components (for example, instruction on parenting and evaluation provisions).

The compensatory approach has an economic bottom line and involves tremendous amounts of money derived from government funding, donations, and corporate sponsorship. For example, in honor of National Family Literacy Day (November 1, 1994), NCFL sponsored a series of community relations activities nationwide; Turner Network Television presented a tribute to Dr. Seuss and events were held in conjunction with TARGET, Barnes & Noble bookstores, and Random House. With federal and nonprofit funds at stake, family literacy has become a marketing point for commercial educational materials. Librarians are encouraged to buy materials that further the goals of family literacy programs. In fact, such materials are often developed with input from paid specialists and consultants (experts in family literacy), funding agencies, and practitioner consumers. Vendors display at library conferences; they sponsor receptions to build goodwill; and they sometimes put large amounts of money into events such as the UNESCO Symposium on World Literacy. Promoting the dissemination of educational concepts that their products can support is good business. Family literacy merchandising stresses the benefits of acquiring materials that parents can use to foster the child's learning and the concept that an investment in the literacy education of adults is, simultaneously, an investment in improving the educability and school success of the adult's children.[32]

The Participatory Perspective

In a trend counter to the merchandising of family literacy by commercial, governmental, and high-profile nonprofit organizations, activists in the middle part of the 1990s began mobilizing resistance to top-down literacy programs and developing alternative approaches informed by social concepts arriving in the Western world from developing countries. A core of literacy practitioners and theoreticians, informed by research on literacy practices of poor and minority families, are trying to move beyond what they construe as the "deficit perspectives" of the 1980s to a focus on the social implications of literacy—literacy as an expression of social and cultural pluralism, literacy as a function of practices and specific conditions that address the students' and communities' needs, and literacy acquisition as a participatory process.

Those who advocate socially conscious approaches to family literacy repudiate compensatory perspectives, characterizing them as "deficit-driven" and as fostering negative stereotypes. "Illiteracy is not a disease, illiteracy does not breed illiteracy, and a dose of some prepackaged family literacy program will not cure those who are poor...the problem is not so much a lack of literacy, but a lack of social justice."[33] They criticize many family literacy programs as "one- shot, ad hoc and isolated interventions, disconnected from a nation's mainstream education policy"[34] and as products "to be packaged, marketed, and sold as a panacea for family and national problems."[35] From the participatory perspective, community-based and grassroots literacy initiatives are efforts that need to be protected from the increasing influence of public authorities and private bodies and from grants and funding that are "compensatory," a category that traditionally connotes a set of problems to be remediated. Deficit perspectives reinforce an "ideology that blames poor people for their own problems and leaves social inequities intact."[36]

Instead, participatory literacy proponents honor diversity and place the learner and his culture at the center of all literacy practices. There is a distinction between literacy that grows out of the real needs of society and "cosmetic literacy" imposed from outside.[37] Because literacy has very different motivational sources and uses based on one's historical, social, and cultural context,[38] literacy programming and action cannot be forced into universal models, methods, or organizational schemes. The fact that there are multiple roads to literacy makes it unreasonable and even dangerous to expect all families to follow the same path of development.[39]

The participatory perspective stresses the inherent strengths and abilities of families and suggests that literacy begins with positive visions of what learners already know and are capable of: learning experiences relate closely to the learners' lives, and learners have a say in curriculum development.[40] Literacy is a constructed process at once both social and personal, that grows out of local knowledge. Literacy is "critical literacy"—citizens begin to understand, analyze, and reflect on their personal and social situations and to become active participants in promoting change. The primary way in which the participatory perspective differs from the compensatory is in ideology; the compensatory perspective is, in comparison, about enforcing conformity, not independent thought and action.

The Library's Role in Family Literacy

During the middle part of this century, libraries tended to be quite generic; they offered universal traditional services in response to assumed patron expectations. For example, story hours were offered because libraries traditionally offered story hours. Services were vaguely rationalized as supportive of a literate society. Infusions of funding in the sixties, followed by recession in the seventies and eighties, have pushed libraries to develop missions, goals, and strategic plans. To project an image of the library as a dynamic and viable agency capable of supporting societal priorities, librarians adapted or expanded existing service to address new needs. One example is the rapid expansion of information technology and computer support in libraries. Since powerful interests (the government, nonprofit and professional agencies, and commercial agents) validate family literacy while providing funding opportunities, family literacy initiatives have become attractive to libraries.

Implementing family literacy programs offers the potential for varying levels of commitment, ranging from "reframing" existing programs to a revolutionary expansion of the library's roles. It poses an opportunity for librarians to review their services and programs and to examine the library's role as a partner in literacy in light of the library's mission. At the heart of this process is the assumption that a library should serve its community; the difficulty lies in developing operational definitions of that community. Should "community" be defined as current patrons or as the pool of all possible patrons? At this point in the planning process, librarians must grapple with the push-pull of compensatory and participatory perspectives and reexamine arguments in the century-long debate over the role of public libraries in literacy. Should libraries primarily confine themselves to supporting existing patrons and fulfilling traditional roles—promoting children's literature and adult recreational reading, supplying materials for new readers, and, lately, incorporating some computer literacy assistance? Or should libraries "go missionary" with outreach programs to seek out the illiterate and underprivileged, and take an active role in social change and community development?[41] How should libraries' vested interest in literacy express itself? Is it possible for a single institution to serve a truly diverse range of community needs?

Perhaps the answers lie in the nature of the particular local community and whether the needs of that community drive the mission of the library. In implementing family literacy initiatives, options need to be eclectic rather than reflective of an artificial polarity, since all programming and services fall on a continuum of community involvement. Options include creating a family-friendly environment that supports literacy; implementing family-focused programming and support services; reaching out to sponsoring partners (as was done with the Atlantic Bell grants); forming alliances with community programs; or experimenting with combinations of approaches.

A possible way of grouping into categories the many different options for library involvement in family literacy is to think of them in terms of three modes: implicit-to-explicit, compensatory, participatory. These modes accommodate the two major perspectives of family literacy discussed above.

Implicit-to-Explicit Mode

Most libraries are implicitly involved in literacy by providing access to printed materials and supporting a literate environment. Making this involvement explicit by developing programs around specific literacy goals and missions, on principle, is good practice; responding to social and political trends is good public relations—a crucial factor in attracting resources.

By expanding traditional roles and adapting existing services, most libraries can incorporate family literacy efforts and, in fact, may be doing so in a piecemeal way with programs that target specific age groups and, through these individuals, affect the whole family. Libraries can join the family literacy movement on its simplest level, by providing environmental support—making the library a place conducive to family literacy, a place with family-friendly staff members, appealing displays and materials, and areas for families to interact. In addition, existing services may be reframed around family literacy goals. For example, rather than viewing toddler story hour as simply a "fun" experience for young children, implicit benefits could be made explicit goals: toddler story hours expand the children's pre-literacy skills while modeling ways for the parents to interact with their children in ways that promote literacy. Thus, the story hours incorporate goals for the parent's development, goals for the child's development, goals for the parent-child relationship, and long-term goals for the creation of a reading and library "habit" by fostering the connection between reading and pleasure. The librarian's awareness of these goals will improve the success with which a satisfactory experience is created for the family.

Compensatory Mode

Librarians move into a compensatory mode by instituting new services with direct family literacy goals—services that appeal directly to all members of the family and allow for family involvement—in an effort to combat illiteracy. Since the underlying rationale for these services is to respond to a problem—illiteracy and the lack of family support for literacy—librarians are encouraged to reach out to nonusers and fringe users. Outreach programs might be located in public housing areas and childcare facilities.

Canada's National Literacy Secretariat (1994) suggests the following activities:

- encouraging parents to read aloud and to talk, sing, and read to their children from birth;
- providing book bags with children's books and information booklets on family literacy;
- sponsoring family-oriented reading events and recruiting celebrity support of libraries and reading;
- organizing family literacy events that put families in contact with storytellers, illustrators, actors, artists, and musicians;
- sponsoring workshops to train parents as tutors;

- providing reading materials for specific ethno-cultural communities;
- sponsoring information sessions, public forums, workshops, consultations, and support groups;
- developing and publishing family stories; and
- developing materials such as videos, booklets, kits, and newsletters.[42]

Subsidies for such activities may be available through family literacy grants and through partnerships with nonprofit agencies and corporate and local partnerships.

Formal programs may be funded through grants such as those from Bell Atlantic and through support by nonprofit and professional organizations. Support may be contingent upon the librarian's compliance with certain protocols and upon whether the program incorporates explicit goals and demonstrates accountability through documentation and evaluation components. Librarians are encouraged to emulate exemplary programs or to try to develop new programs worthy of widespread use.

Participatory Mode

Supporting family literacy through a participatory mode requires thoughtful consideration of the principles of critical literacy. As identified by the Literacy Support Initiative (undated brochure), these are (1) literacy is defined as the way reading, writing, and numeracy are used in real-life situations; (2) literacy is communication, so it is connected to relationships and interactions between people; and (3) literacy education is a process to help specific groups of people living and working in a specific place to learn the reading, writing, and numeracy skills they need to communicate and interact within their own group and with other groups of people.[43]

The nature of these principles calls for librarians to attend to the local and the particular: first through identifying a need—groups to support in the spread of literacy—and second, through pursuing collaborative local partnerships. The first step involves analyzing community demographics and identifying target groups—particularly ethnic minorities—and determining their use of the library. If a group does not use the library, then librarians should determine whether the environment is "friendly" to this group and whether the collection and current programming support local cultures, interaction, and multiple literacies. Questions they might ask include: Do displays feature topics of interest to particular ethnic groups? Does the collection include brochures and posters providing useful community and health information? Are there areas set aside for interaction, and are these areas being used by community groups? Does the library support the things people do in their lives already and help them increase proficiency with written materials? For example, are there programs and media on reading and understanding job applications, rental agreements, health materials, and welfare forms?

Librarians should ask themselves how they can set up an environment that accommodates cultural differences and adapts to the specific cultural and educational characteristics of the families in their communities. Recent research shows that schools tend to have a cultural mismatch with minority or impoverished families; it seems probable that libraries also are mismatched. While compensatory programs focus on influencing families to adopt school and library practices at home, participatory programs stress making library programs relevant, and making the library a place that fosters confidence, identification, partnership, and a sense of community. Librarians can help transfer mainstream patterns of literacy usage (such as the use of picture books with young children) and support families in adapting to the library as it is (a compensatory approach) and/or they can use a participatory approach and seek a new under-standing among librarians and families alike of each other's specific cultural practices and of the way both define, value and use literacy in daily life. Librarians' responsibility is to accept change, to accept the role of "socializer," and to reflect on this role critically, comparatively, and with a sense of the possibilities for change.

While librarians in a participatory mode play a "supporting" role in literacy (provid-ing books, referring learners to community programs, etc.), they often take a pro-active stance. Rather than reflexively turning outward for models and funding, they seek collaborative relationships locally, join and instigate initiatives with local administra-tions, and adopt self-reliant approaches that use mainly local resources and personnel.[44] Both by supporting and collaborating, libraries can bring valuable assets into literacy programs. By opening the library through inclusive patron-friendly strategies and sharing space and resources, and by reshaping the librarian-patron relationship into a mutual and respectful interaction, they offer a shelter for formal and informal activities and programs.

Particularly powerful as literacy promoters are programs that celebrate minority cultures and facilitate the transition from oral to written culture. Libraries can learn from the success of *Foxfire*, a literary magazine containing stories, songs, recipes, and folklore collected by high school students. *Foxfire* validates community stories by collecting and converting them into print, thus supporting one of the ultimate goals of participatory literacy education—to enable learners to read the heritage of their own culture. [45] The give-and-take aspects of collecting, transcribing, and disseminating oral culture stresses the process of two-way interaction in literacy promotion rather than top-down and one-way approaches.[46]

Family Literacy and Libraries in Developing Countries

Questions about the library's role in promoting literacy—which have largely originated in industrialized countries—intensify when applied to developing countries, where the spread of conventional Western concepts of librarianship (which conceive of libraries as supporting an existing literate population) has been slow. While libraries in indus-trialized countries focus on the need of a core of literate users and are part of a web of literacy support systems (which includes formal and informal educational groups, authors, publishers, booksellers, and book distributors), existing Third World libraries may actually be underutilized because of widespread illiteracy and the lack of a reading and library habit in that particular society. Third World libraries play a crucial role in creating, then maintaining, a literate society[47] and, thus, cannot afford to support literacy in a rhetorical or implicit fashion. Family literacy approaches would provide overt support in forging and maintaining a literate environment if Third World libraries could function well along the continuum with compensatory and, especially, participatory strategies. Promotion of literacy—particularly family literacy in the broadest sense—is an appropriate primary mission that can be supported by adapting models of commu-nity librarianship or developing relevant participatory-mode strategies.

The participatory perspective accommodated notions of "education of the family, for the family and by the family" essential for Third World development, and traditional inclusive meanings of the family.[48] For example, in Indonesia, the family can be a small unit of father, mother, and children, or it can be extended to include close blood relations or even a whole clan or neighborhood. Initiatives aimed at increasing family literacy would involve reconceptualizing the library as a cornerstone of lifelong educa-tion—"a comprehensive concept which includes formal, nonformal and informal learning extended throughout the life span of an individual to attain the fullest possible development in personal, social, and professional life."[49]

Especially in rural areas, the "library" can serve many purposes for family literacy by functioning not only as a storage and access place for materials, a reading room, and a venue for formal literacy-related activities, but as a community resource center and meeting place. Here families can find information about subjects of interest; discuss and share knowledge, information, or concerns with government or nongovernmental organization extension and community workers; organize and work on community projects; use equipment to produce one's own information materials; or enjoy cultural and leisure activities.[50]

In urban and suburban areas, home libraries can support family literacy. Zimbabwe offers a model in which adults (literate, newly literate, and illiterate) and children interact around simple collections of children's books: simple stories are read for pleasure, books are used for information (but not for examinations), and the young and old are linked together through storytelling and the creation and publication of stories. While appreciating vernacular culture, participants also make connections between oral literature and written literature.[51]

Ultimately, libraries might create or sustain a "community of practice," an ongoing community-based situation where families learn new roles and negotiate new identities by sharing learning resources. Libraries could be a place to support the "relationships that center around learning: the relationship of parents and children, of staff and families, of families and communities, of individuals and institutions of learning, and of institutions of learning and the larger society."[52]

When integrated with social life and all aspects of development and modernization, library-centered family literacy can support the family's ability to use multiple literacies to identify and solve personal and community problems and to respond to social change.[53]

Conclusion

Libraries function not in isolation, but as part of complex cultural systems that have a global reach. In the future, libraries may well metamorphose into technological net-works that transcend particular locations and communities; their physical situation may have little to do with the services and information they provide. But for now, a library has a distinctly local character and serves a multitude of functions in supporting its immediate environment. The functions of each local library are determined by choices, which, in turn, are influenced by political, economic, social, and educational trends. Sometimes a particular choice, such as the decision to support family literacy, results in minor adjustments to programming and services or even a complete reframing of the library's mission and organization.

The purpose of this chapter was to provide a background of the issues that influence a librarian's choices about family literacy initiatives by discussing definitions and the conceptual basis of "family literacy," by placing this subject within the global historical context of literacy education, and by exploring the implications of two major perspec-tives on the intersection of literacy effort and library services. In the end, any discussion of library involvement in literacy initiatives raises questions about the library's role as a democratic institution. Does simply providing general access to information discharge the library's responsibility to support democracy? Or is there an underlying mandate to support the act of acquiring reading and writing skills (which, by itself, is an expression of democracy)[54] as well as informed participation. At stake, is the position of libraries either at the heart of literate, democratic societies or relegated to the peripheries.

Notes

1. Thomas G. Sticht, "Family Literacy: A World Movement" (paper delivered at the World Symposium on Family Literacy, UNESCO, 3-5 October 1994).

2. Trevor Cairney, "Family Literacy: Moving towards New Partnerships in Education," *Australian Journal of Language and Literacy* 17, no. 4 (1994).

3. H. S. Bhola, "Family Literacy for Development: Clarifying Conceptions for Appropriate Actions" (paper delivered at the World Symposium on Family Literacy, UNESCO 3-5 October 1994).

4. Glynda Hull, "Hearing Other Voices: A Critical Assessment of Popular Views on Literacy and Work," *Harvard Educational Review* 63, no. 1 (1993): 20-49.

5. H. S. Bhola, "Adult Literacy: From Concepts to Implementation Strategies," in *The Challenge of Illiteracy: From Reflection to Action*, ed. Zaghloul Morsy (New York: Garland Publishing, 1994), 115-126.

6. Debra Wilcox Johnson, "Breaking the Cycle: The Role of Libraries in Family Literacy," *RQ* 32, no. 3 (1993): 318-321.

7. Bhola, "Adult Literacy," 115-126.

8. Phillip H. Coombs, *World Crisis in Education: A Systems Analysis* (Oxford: Oxford University Press, 1985).

9. Ibid.

10. Bhola, "Adult Literacy," 115-126.

11. Ibid.

12. Laurel Puchner, "Early Childhood, Family, and Health Issues in Literacy: International Perspectives," Paper IP93-2 (Philadelphia, Pa.: National Center on Adult Literacy International, 1993).

13. Julia Wrigley, "Do Young Children Need Intellectual Stimulation? Experts' Advice to Parents, 1900-1985," *History of Education Quarterly* 29, no. 1 (1989): 41-75.

14. Rosa Maria Torres, *Literacy for All: Twelve Paths to Move Ahead* [draft] (New York: UNICEF, 1994).

15. Sticht, "Family Literacy."

16. Puchner, "Early Childhood."

17. UIE (UNESCO Institute for Education), "The Future of Literacy and the Literacy of the Future," Report of the Seminar on Adult Literacy in Industrialized Countries (UNESCO Institute for Education, Hamburg, 4-7 December 1991).

18. Shelley Quezada, "Shaping National Library Literacy Policy: A Report from the Alexandria Forum," *Wilson Library Bulletin* 64, no. 3 (1990): 22-24.

19. UIE, "The Future of Literacy."

20. Elsa Roberts Auerback, "Which Way for Family Literacy: Intervention or Empowerment," in *Family Literacy: Connection in Schools and Communities*, ed. L. Morrow (Newark, Del.: International Reading Association, 1995): 11-27.

21. Quezada, "Shaping," 22-24; Carole Talan, "Family Literacy: Libraries Doing What Libraries Do Best," *Wilson Library Bulletin* 65, no. 3 (1990): 30-32.

22. Margaret Monsour, "Librarians and Family Literacy: A Natural Connection," *School Library Journal* 37, no. 2 (1991): 33-37.

23. Johnson, "Breaking the Cycle," 318-321.

24. Marguerite Crowley Weibel, *The Library as Literacy Classroom: A Program for Teaching* (Chicago: American Library Association, 1992).

25. Debra Wilcox Johnson, Jane Robbins, and Douglas L. Zweizig, *Libraries: Partners in Adult Literacy* (Norwood, N.J.: Ablex, 1990).

26. Ibid.

27. Jeffrey L. Salter and Charles A. Salter, *Literacy and the Library* (Englewood, Colo.: Libraries Unlimited, 1991).

28. Monsour, "Librarians and Family Literacy," 33-37.

29. Johnson, "Breaking the Cycle," 318-321.

30. Maria Elena Zapata, "The Role of Public Libraries in Literacy Education," *Libri* 44, no. 2 (1994): 123-129.

31. National Literacy Secretariat (Canada), "Literacy Projects for the Family" (brochure), 1994.

32. Sticht, "Family Literacy."

33. Denny Taylor, ed., *Many Families, Many Literacies: An International Declaration of Principles* (Portsmouth, N.H.: Heinemann Trade, 1997).

34. Torres, *Literacy for All.*

35. Taylor, *Many Families.*

36. Auerback, "Which Way for Family Literacy," 11-27.

37. Alfred Kagan, "Literacy, Libraries, and Underdevelopment—with Special Attention to Tanzania," *Africana Journal* 12, no. 4 (1982): 1-25.

38. Torres, *Literacy for All.*

39. Taylor, *Many Families.*

40. Philip Calvert, "The Cultural Background to School Library Development in Papua New Guinea," *International Library Review* 19, no. 2 (1987): 179-192.

41. Kosi A. Kedam, "Libraries as Partners in the Fight to Eradicate Illiteracy in Sub-Saharan Africa," *IFLA Journal* 16, no. 4 (1990): 447-457.

42. National Literacy Secretariat (Canada), "Literacy Projects for the Family."

43. "Literacy Support Initiative," brochure (Amherst, Mass.: Literacy Support Initiative, Center for International Education, University of Massachusetts, n.d.).

44. John Allen, *Basic Education for All—Afghan Experience—Conceptual Framework and Strategies* (Paris: UNESCO Division of Higher Education, Section for Educational Research and Innovation, 1994).

45. Weibel, *The Library as Literacy Classroom.*

46. Ma Baolan, "Trends of Development in Family Education and Its Research in China" (paper delivered at the World Symposium on Family Literacy, UNESCO, 3-5 October 1994).

47. Rebecca Knuth, "Libraries, Literacy and Development: Combined Libraries as an Option for Developing Countries," *International Information and Library Review* 26 (1994): 77-89.

48. Hasnah Gasim, "Family Literacy in Indonesia" (paper delivered at the World Symposium on Family Literacy, UNESCO, 3-5 October 1994).

49. Bhola, "Adult Literacy," 115-126.

50. Kedam, "Libraries as Partners," 447-457.

51. Genevieve Patte and Alice Geradts, "Home Libraries in Zimbabwe," *IFLA Journal* 11, no. 3 (1985): 223-227.

52. Taylor, *Many Families.*

53. Ibid.

54. Zapata, "The Role of Public Libraries," 123-129.

29. Going Global via the Literature: A Suggested List of Resources

Alma Dawson

In a recent publication, Tony Spybey observed that it has become almost impossible to avoid the influences of the nation-state system, the global economy, the global communication system and the world military order.[1] Similarly, organizations such as the United Nations are studying the "effects of globalization as a result of startling changes taking place in world politics and economics," for the larger community.[2] In addition, other authors such as Cohen are examining contemporary issues, such as global diasporas to provide a deeper understanding of the impacts on world social organizations.[3]

Library leaders and practicing professionals have long recognized the unique role that libraries can play in the sharing of expertise and in the provision of information to a world population. President Barbara J. Ford's presidential year has been devoted to encouraging librarians to provide collection and services to help U.S. citizens better understand our increasingly diverse society and to connect U.S. librarians with colleagues around the world in shaping the global information infrastructure.[4] Cyberspace programs, resources, and activities have all been focused in this regard.

Ford's call for participation has highlighted the need for current and future information professionals to become knowledgeable of the broader technological, social, political and economic areas that underpin and affect local library planning and operations. Reading and examining literature on global issues in other disciplines must be coupled with study of the literature of library and information science that describes library developments in the global library community. This literature is at various stages of complexity, exists in a variety of sources, and in different languages. So, how does the working information professional or student of library and information science learn about the libraries of the world, international organizations, library developments, issues and trends, educational programs and opportunities, and other library activities? They, of course, turn to the literature.

Problem of Definition

Authors have long noted the problem of definition in use of the terms that describe this literature for the field: comparative librarianship and international librarianship.[5] Distinctions have also been made between comparative, international, and world or global librarianship with the notion that international librarianship best describes the approach to study world librarianship.[6] The definition that has largely guided this bibliography is the one offered by Stephen J. Parker. International librarianship includes activities carried out among or between governmental or nongovernmental institutions, organizations, groups or individuals of two or more nations, to promote, establish, maintain and evaluate library, documentation and allied services, and librarianship and the library profession generally, in any part of the world.[7]

Consequently, the purpose of this bibliography is twofold. First, it identifies and provides for the average practicing librarian and student of library and information a beginning point for study and exploration. Second, it is a tool for keeping current on global issues and trends in libraries world over. Although some of the landmark studies on comparative librarianship and single countries have been included for historical purposes, no attempt has been made to be exhaustive in the context due to limited space. Care has been taken to include examples of studies of the literature in various geographic areas and add other bibliographies, such as Huq's *World Librarianship: Its International and Comparative Dimensions: An Annotated Bibliography for Additional Study.* A particular focus of this bibliography is the serial literature and Internet resources as they provide current information and offer opportunities for participation and scholarship.

In summary, this selected bibliography is divided into four parts: serial publications, monographs, articles, and Internet sources. These sources were gathered from a review and examination of all major abstracting services in English (see serial section, abstracting and indexing services for sources used); searches of Internet resources; collections at the Library of Congress; and library catalogs at the University of Pittsburgh, University of Illinois, and Simmons.

Notes

1. Tony Spybey, *Globalization and World Society* (Cambridge, U.K.: Polity Press, 1997), 1.
2. *States of Disarray: Social Effects of Globalization* (London: United Nations Research Institute for Social Development, 1995).
3. Robin Cohen, *Global Diasporas: An Introduction* (Seattle: University of Washington Press, 1997).
4. Barbara Ford, "How to Go Global: Ten Areas Where Libraries Can Lead Communities," *American Libraries* 28 (October 1997): 35.
5. Nonie J. Bliss, "The Emergence of International Librarianship as a Field," *Libri* 43, no. 1 (1993): 39-52.
6. Richard Kryzs and Gaston Litton, *World Librarianship* (New York: Marcel Dekker, 1993), 3-25.
7. Stephen J. Parker, "International Librarianship: A Reconnaissance," *Journal of Librarianship* 6 (1974): 219-232.

Serial Publications

Serial publications are publications issued in successive parts, numbered chronically, and intended to be continued indefinitely. Included in this section are abstracting and indexing services; key journals and newsletters (both print and electronic only) and directories of select international library associations.

Abstracting and Indexing Services

No single service offers comprehensive bibliographic control of the international literature. Each of the abstracting and indexing services covers portions of it in unique ways. For example, (1) *Computer and Control Abstracts or INSPEC* (Section C) provides abstracts of the international technological information; (2) *Current Research in Library & Information Science* (formerly *R A D I A L S Bulletin*) covers the current library and information science research with information on 400 plus research projects annually; (3) *ERIC (Educational Resources Information Center)* provides the full text of many conference proceedings through its document reproduction services and access to those journal titles indexed in *Current Index to Journals in Education*; (4) *Information Science Abstracts* (formerly, *Documentation Abstracts*) covers the science, management, and technology of information in the international literature and includes books, conference proceedings, reports, and patents; (5) *IBZ:Internationale Bibliographie der Zeitschriften-literatur* indexes periodicals from every continent and the Pacific; (6) *L I S A: Library and Information Science Abstracts* provides coverage of 539 periodicals from 68 countries, mainly British and West European; (7) *Library Literature; An Index to Library and Information Science Publications* indexes over 220 periodicals, plus monographs, pamphlets, theses, and some audiovisual materials. Each issue contains a separate list of book monographs indexed and a separate book review section. Subject access to the global literature is through the subject listings, "Librarianship—International Aspects" and "Comparative Librarianship." (8) *Social Sciences Citation Index* (in conjunction with the other abstracting and indexing services and studies) provides an opportunity to identify core journals in the field of international librarianship.

Journals and Newsletters (print and electronic), Directories. The criteria for inclusion of selected titles reflect those whose stated purposes are to provide a global or international focus on libraries and librarianship; those identified by past studies of the library and information science literature; and those indexed by the major abstracting and indexing services. If not a publication of an international library organization, brief descriptions are provided for serials that indicate the international coverage for selected sources.

ASLIB Proceedings [ISSN 0001-253X]. 1949-. ASLIB Publications, London, England. International in scope of coverage, the journal contains papers delivered or contributed at ASLIB Conferences. Indexed: *Library Literature, LISA.*

African Journal of Library, Archives and Information Science [ISSN 0795-4778]. 1991-. Archlib & Information Services Ltd., Ibadan, Nigeria. Reports research findings on empirical investigations and highly theoretical studies on library and archives management and information science. Indexed: *Library Literature, LISA.*

Alexandria: Journal of National and International Library & Information Issues [ISSN 0955-7490]. 1989-. Ashgate Publishing Ltd., Aldershot, England. Covers national library and international policy issues of interest to all in the library and information world. Indexed: *INSPEC, LISA.*

*American Libraries (*formerly *ALA Bulletin)* [ISSN 0002-9669]. 1907-. American Library Association, Chicago. Official organ of the American Library Association. Includes a

"News Fronts International Column" (since July 1995) and periodic articles on library developments worldwide. Indexed: *Current Index to Journals in Education, Information Science Abstracts, Library Literature, Library and Information Science Abstracts* and others.

Archivum: International Review on Archives [ISSN 0066-6793]. 1951-. International Council on Archives, Saur Verlag, Munich. Text in English, French, German, Italian, Spanish. Indexed: *American History and Life; Historical Abstracts.*

Asian Libraries [ISSN 1017-6748]. 1991-. Library Marketing Services, Ltd., Hong Kong. Text in English. Covers Asian information technology trends, information industry and products.

Chinese Librarianship: An International Electronic Journal. http://www.lib.siu.edu/swen/iclc/clej.htm

CONSERLine. Newsletter of the Library of Congress Conser Program (Cooperative Online Serials Cataloging). http://lcweb.loc.gov/acq/conser/consrlin.html

Documentaliste Sciences de l'Information [ISSN 0012-4509]. 1964-. Association Francaise des Documentalistes et des Bibliothecaires Specialises, Paris, France. Text in French, summaries in English. Focus is on European and French-speaking countries. Indexed: *ISA, INSPEC, Library Literature, LISA.*

Education for Library and Information [ISSN 0167-8329]. 1983-. ISO Press, Amsterdam, The Netherlands. Provides international coverage of topics in information science, technology, and librarianship. A useful feature, although it has not appeared since 1995, is its annual bibliography on training and education for information work. Indexed: *Computer Literature Index, ERIC, INSPEC, LISA.*

Focus on International and Comparative Librarianship [ISSN 0395-8468]. 1967-. International Group of the Library Association, Birmingham, England. Each issue contains several pieces about libraries and librarians worldwide, especially developing nations and the former Soviet Union. http://www.fdgroup.co.uk/focus.htm. Indexed: *Information Science Abstracts, Library and Information Science Abstracts.*

Fontes Artis Musicae [ISSN 0015-6191]. 1953-. International Association of Music Libraries, Archives and Documentation Centres. c/o Music Library, Arizona State University, Tempe, Ariz. Text in English, French, German. Indexed: *LISA, Library Literature, Arts and Humanities Index,* others.

Herald of Library Science [ISSN 0018-0521]. 1962-. P. Kaula Endowment for Library and Information Science, Lucknow, India. Articles and reports on library science, with frequent coverage of international issues. Refereed. Indexed: Indian *Library Science Abstracts, INSPEC, Library Literature, LISA.*

IATUL Proceedings. New Series [ISSN 0966-4769]. 1992-. Lyngby, Denmark: IATUL Publications Bureau. Note that the *Quarterly,* published 1987–91, merged with *Proceedings* in 1992. This is the official publication of the International Association of Technological University Libraries. Papers in English. Indexed: *Information Science Abstracts, INSPEC, Library Literature.*

I F L A Journal (International Federation of Library Associations and Institutions) [ISSN: 0340-0352]. 1975-. K. G. Saur Verlag, Munich, Germany. News of the IFLA and its various subdivisions and other articles. Reviews of new publications. Text in English, French and German. http://www.nlc-bnc.ca/ifla/V/iflaj/index.htm. Indexed: *Library Literature, LISA, Social Sciences Citation Index.*

Information Development; the International Journal for Librarians, Archivists and Information Specialists. [ISSN 0266-6669]. 1985-. Bowker-Saur Ltd. Intended to cover developing countries after the demise of *UNESCO Bulletin,* each issue includes four to five feature articles on information provision, information management, or information development worldwide. New publications and reports of current research are useful features for study of international librarianship. Indexed: *ERIC, INSPEC, Library Literature, LISA.*

Information Processing & Management: An International Journal [ISSN 0306-4573]. 1963-. Elsevier Science Ltd., Oxford, England. Covers three broad areas of information science and computer science—basic and applied research, experimental and advanced procedures and their evaluation, and management of information. Refereed journal. Indexed: *ABI Inform, INSPEC, Library Literature, LISA.*

Information Services & Use [ISSN 0019-0217]. 1981-. O S Press, Amsterdam, Netherlands. Scholarly articles on any aspect of information work with an emphasis on technology. Authorship is international; intended audience has no geographic boundaries. Indexed: *CIJE, Information Science Abstracts, Library Literature.*

INSPEL: International Journal of Special Libraries [ISSN 0019-0217]. 1975-. Technische Universitaet Berlin, Universitaetsbibliothek, Berlin, Germany. Text may appear in English, French, German or Russian. Indexed: *INSPEC, Library Literature, LISA.*

International Association of Agricultural Specialists (IAALD). Quarterly Bulletin [ISSN 1019-9926] 1956-. IAALD. Indexed: *Library Literature, INSPEC, LISA,* others.

International Association of School Librarianship. Box 34069, Department 300, Seattle, Washington 98124

Voice: 604-925-0266. E-mail: iasl@rockland.com.

    IASL Conference Proceedings. Annual [ISSN 0257-3229]. 1972-. Indexed: *ERIC.*

    School Libraries Worldwide [ISSN 1023-9391]. Semi-annual refereed journal. 1995-. Indexed: *Children's Literature Abstracts.*

IASL Newsletter. [ISSN 0085-2015] Quarterly newsletter. 1972-.

International Cataloguing and Bibliographic Control [ISSN 1011-8829]. 1972-. International Federation of Library Associations, UBCIM Program, c/o Deutsche Bibliothek, Frankfurt, Germany. Bulletin, refereed. Indexed: *Library Literature, LISA.*

International Forum on Information and Documentation [ISSN 0304-9701]. 1975-. International Federation for Information and Documentation, The Hague, Netherlands. Available in English or Russian. Indexed: *Library Literature, Social Sciences Citation Index, INSPEC,* others.

International Information and Library Review (formerly *International Library Review*) [ISSN 1057-2317]. 1969-. Academic Press Ltd., London, England. Addresses progress and research in international and comparative librarianship, documentation, and information retrieval. Refereed. http://www.hbuk.co.uk/ap/journals/hr.htm. Indexed: *Library Literature, LISA, Science Citation Index, Social Sciences Citation Index.*

International Journal of Legal Information [ISSN 0731-1265]. 1973-. International Association of Law Librarians, Washington, D.C. Indexed: *LISA, Legal Periodicals Index, Foreign Legal Periodicals Index,* others.

International Journal of Special Libraries See *INSPEL*

International Leads [ISSN 0892-4546]. 1957-. American Library Association, International Relations Round Table, Chicago. Quarterly newsletter of the International Relations Round Table. Contains news about international library activities, the international work of ALA and other organizations, and people and publications in the field. Indexed in *Library Literature, LISA.*

International Library Movement [ISSN 0970-0048]. 1974-. Ambala City, India. Text in English. Examines the theory and practice of librarianship and information science with an emphasis on the needs of developing countries.

Journal of Education for Librarianship and Information Science [ISSN 0748-5786]. 1960-. Arlington, Va.: Association for Library and Information Science Education (ALISE). In addition to scholarly articles on the subject, the journal features a regular column,

"International Library Education." Indexed: *INSPEC, Library Literature, LISA, Social Sciences Citation Index.*

Journal of Goverment Information: An International Review of Policy, Issues, and Resources (formerly *Government Publications Review*) [ISSN 1352-0237]. 1974-. Elsevier Science, Inc. Indexed: *Library Literature, LISA.*

Journal of Librarianship and Information Science (formerly *Journal of Librarianship*) [ISSN 0943-7444]. 1969-. Bowker-Saur Ltd. Articles on library and information sciences worldwide. http://www.bowker.saur.com/service/. Indexed: *INSPEC, Library Literature, LISA, Social Sciences Citation Index.*

Knowledge Organization: International Journal Devoted to Concept Theory, Classification, Indexing, and Knowledge Representation [ISSN 0943-7444]. 1974-. International Society for Knowledge Organization, ERGON Verlag, Wuezburg, Germany. Includes both original articles and conference papers. Indexed: *Library Literature, Library and Information Science Abstracts.*

Librarianship and Information Work Worldwide; an Annual Survey. 1991-. Bowker-Saur Ltd., E. Grinstead, W. Sussex, England. Reviews developments in library and information science around the world. Emphasizes issues and events in Europe, Australia, Japan, the U.S. and Canada. To date, six volumes have been published with the next edition scheduled 1997/98.

Libraries and Culture [ISSN 0894-8631]. 1966-. University of Texas Press, Austin, Tex. Explores collections of recorded knowledge in the context of social and cultural history. Formerly *Journal of Library History; Journal of Library History, Philosophy and Comparative Librarianship.* Indexed: *Book Review Index, Library Literature, LISA, Social Sciences Citation Index.*

Library Times International; World News Digest of Library and Information Sciences [ISSN 0743-4839]. 1984-. Future World Publishing Company of Canada, India and the United States. Evansville, Indiana. Newsletter of world news, information science update, special reports on conferences, calendar of national and international conferences. Indexed: *LISA.*

Libri: International Library Review [ISSN 9924-2667]. 1951-. Munksgaard International Publishers Ltd., Copenhagen, Denmark. An international journal with five or six articles per issue on any topic in library science. Articles may be in English, German, or French. Provides international comparative perspectives. Refereed. Indexed: *Information Science Abstracts, Library Literature, LISA, P.A.I.S. International in Print, P.A.I.S. Foreign Language Index, Social Sciences Citation Index.*

Program [ISSN 0033-0337]. 1966-. Aslib, Association for Information Management, London, England. Computer applications to library and information services. Indexed: *INSPEC, Library Literature, LISA, Social Sciences Citation Index.*

Restaurator: International Journal for the Preservation of Library and Archival Material [ISSN 0034-5806]. 1969-. Munksgaard International Publishers Ltd., Copenhagen, Denmark. Text in English, French, and German. Refereed. Indexed in *Chem Abstracts, Current Contents, Library Literature, LISA, Science Citation Index, Social Sciences Citation Index.*

School Libraries Worldwide [ISSN 1023-9391]. 1995-. International Association of School Librarianship, Kalamazoo, Michigan. Indexed: *Children's Literature Abstracts.*

World Guide to Libraries. 1966-. Munich, New York: K. G. Saur. Over 47,000 institutions in 181 countries are listed in the 1998 edition.

World Information Report 1997/98-. United Nations Educational, Scientific and Cultural Organization (UNESCO), Paris, France. http://www.unesco.org/webworld/

wirerpt/report/htm. Presents a "worldwide picture of archive, library and information services" and also reviews issues and trends.

World Libraries (formerly *Third World Libraries*) [ISSN 1092-7441]. 1990-. Dominican University, Graduate School of Library and Information Science, River Forest, Illinois. Coverage of issues relating to libraries and their role in development. Refereed. Indexed in *Library Literature, LISA, C.I.J.E.*

Zeitschrift fur Bibliothekswesen und Bibliographie [ISSN 0044-2380]. 1953-. Verein Deutscher Bibliothekare, Vittorio Klostermann, Frankfurt, Germany. Indexed in *Library Literature, LISA, P.A.I.S. Foreign Language Index, Social Sciences Citation Index.*

Monographs

Bonta, Bruce, and James G. Neal, eds. (1992). *The Role of the American Academic Library in International Programs.* Greenwich, Conn.: JAI Press. ISBN 1-55938-383-6.

Clement, Hope E. A., ed. (1992). *Medium-Term Programme 1992-1997.* The Hague, Netherlands: International Federation of Library Associations and Institutions, 1992.

Clyde, Laurel A., ed. (1996). *Sustaining the Vision: A Collection of Articles and Papers on Research in School Librarianship.* Castle Rock, Colo.: Hi Willow Research and Publishing for the International Association of School Librarianship, 1996. ISBN 0-614-31081-4.

Danton, J. Periam (1973). *Dimensions of Comparative Librarianship.* Chicago: American Library Association.

Evans, John A. (1995). *Planning for Library Development: Third World Perspectives.* Halifax, Nova Scotia: In cooperation with the University of Papua Guinea Press. ISBN 0-7703-9762-X.

Feather, John and Paul Sturges, eds. (1997). *International Encyclopedia of Information and Library Science.* London, New York: Routledge. ISBN 0415-098602.

Gorman, G. E., ed. (1990). *The Education and Training of Information Professionals: Comparative and International Perspectives.* Metuchen, N.J.: Scarecrow Press.

Hajnal, Peter I. (1997). *International Information: Documents, Publications, and Electronic Information of the International Governmental Organizations.* New York: Libraries Unlimited. ISBN 1-56308-1474.

Harrison, K. C. (1989). *International Librarianship.* Metuchen, N.J.: Scarecrow Press. ISBN 0-8108-2213-X.

Haycock, Ken, ed. (1996). *International Association of School Librarianship Worldwide Directory: A Listing of Personal, Institutional and Association Members.* International Association of School Librarianship. ISBN 0-614-30339-7.

Haycock, Ken and Lynne Lighthall, eds. (1997). *Information Rich but Knowledge Poor? Issues for Schools and Libraries Worldwide: Selected Papers from the 26th Annual Conference of the International Association of School Librarianship.* International Association of School Librarianship. ISBN 1-890861-21-9. Annual proceedings are available as ERIC documents and from the International Association of School Librarianship. Exclusive distributor, LMC Source, P.O. Box 266, Castle Rock, CO 80104-0266. (800) 873-3043.

Haycock, Ken and Blanche Woolls, eds. (1997). *School Librarianship: International Issues and Perspectives.* International Association of School Librarianship. ISBN 1-890861-19-7.

Hayword, Trevor (1995). *Info-Rich Info-Poor: Access and Exchange in the Global Information Society.* London: Bowker. ISBN 0-86291-631-3.

Huq, A. M. Abdul (1995). *World Librarianship: Its International and Comparative Dimensions: An Annotated Bibliography, 1976-1992*. Dhaka, Bangladesh: Academic Publishers. ISBN: 984-08-0134-1.

Instituto Tecnologico de Monterrey (Mexico) (1995). *Proceedings of the Trinational Library Forum=Memorias [del] Foro Trinacional de Bibliotecas* (5th, Mexico City, February 23-25, 1995). ERIC ED392460.

International Federation of Library Associations and Institutions (1992). *IFLA's Core Programme for the Advancement of Librarianship in the Third World—ALP.* The Hague, Netherlands: International Federation of Library Associations and Institutions.

Johansson, Eve (1991). *The IFLA ALP (Advancement of Librarianship in Developing Countries) Programme: A Bibliography: 1966-1990*. IFLA Professional Reports, No. 26. The Hague, Netherlands: International Federation of Library Associations and Institutions.

Kaula, P. N., Krishan Kumar, V. Venkatappaiah, and S. R. Gupta, eds. (1996). *International and Comparative Librarianship and Information Systems*. Ranganathan Memorial Volumes 1 and 2. Delhi, India: B. R. Publishing. ISBN 81-7018-870-9 (Set). These volumes contain 93 papers by 91 contributors from 14 countries on the life, work, and impact of S. R. Ranganathan.

Kimmage, Dennis (1992). *Russian Libraries in Transition: An Anthology of Glasnost Literature*. Jefferson, N.C. and London: MacFarland. ISBN 0-89950-718-2.

Kocojowa, Maria and Wojciech Zalewski, eds. (1996). *Libraries in Europe's Post Communist Countries: Their International Context. International Librarian's Conference, Krakow-Przegorzaly*, August 3-5, 1995. Krakow: PTB. ISBN 83-901577-7-2.

Kraske, Gary E. (1985). *Missionaries of the Book: The American Library Profession and the Origin of United States Cultural Diplomacy*. Westport, Conn.: Greenwood Press, ISBN 0-313-24351-4.

Krzys, Richard and Gaston Litton (1983). *World Librarianship: A Comparative Study*. New York: Marcel Dekker. ISBN 0-8247-1731-7.

Line, Maurice and Graham Mackenzie, eds. *Librarianship and Information Work Worldwide 1991-*. London: Bowker-Saur. Annual. 1996/97 available, ISBN 1-85739-169-1.

Lowrie, Jean E. and Mieko Nagakura (1991). *School Libraries: International Developments*. 2nd ed. (1991). Metuchen, N.J.: Scarecrow Press. ISBN 0-8108-2390-X.

Martin, William J. (1995). *Global Information Society*. Aldershot, Eng.: Aslib Gower. ISBN 0-55607715-9.

Olden, Anthony (1995). *Libraries in Africa: Pioneers, Policies, Problems*. Lanham, Md.: Scarecrow Press. ISBN 0-8108-3093-0.

Pisani, Assunta (1992). *Euro-Librarianship: Shared Resources, Shared Responsibilities*. New York: Haworth Press. ISBN 1-56024-266-3. (also available as *Collection Management*, vol. 15, nos. 1-4)

Plumbe, Wilfred J. (1987). *Tropical Librarianship*. Metuchen, N. J.: Scarecrow Press. ISBN 0-8108-2057-9.

Price, Joseph W. and Mary S. Price (1985). *International Librarianship Today and Tomorrow: A Festschrift for William J. Welsh*. New York: K. G. Saur.

Qureshi, Naimuddin and Zahiruddin Khurshid, eds. (1991). *Trends in International Librarianship: A Festschrift Honouring Anis Khurshid*. Karachi, Pakistan: Royal Book Company.

Seldman, Ruth K. (1993). *Building Global Partnerships for Library Cooperation*. Washington, D.C.: Special Libraries Association. ISBN 0-87111-409-7.

Simsova, Sylvia (1982). *Primer on Comparative Librarianship*. London: Clive Bingley.

Swigchem, J. J. van (1985). *IFLA and the Library World: A Review of the Work of IFLA, 1981-1985*. The Hague, Netherlands: International Federation of Library Associations.

Wedgeworth, Robert, ed. (1993). *World Encyclopedia of Library and Information Services*. 3rd ed. Chicago: American Library Association. ISBN 0-8389-0690-7.

Weiss, Joachim W., ed. (1992). *Innovation for Information: International Contributions to Librarianship: Festschrift in Honour of Dr. Ahmed H. Helal*. Essen, Germany: Essen University Library.

Welch, Theodore F. (1997) *Libraries and Librarianship in Japan*. Westport, Conn. and London: Greenwood Press. ISBN 0-313-29668-5.

Wise, Michael and Anthony Olden, eds. (1994). *Information and Libraries in the Arab World*. London: Library Association Publishing. ISBN 0-7201-1780-1.

Zielinska, Marie F. and Frances T. Kirkwood, eds. (1992). *Multicultural Librarianship: An International Handbook*. New York: Saur. ISBN 3-598-21787-0.

Selected Bibliography of Articles

Aina, L. O. (1991). Directions of the Information Professions in Africa as Reflected in the Literature. *International Library Review*, 23, 365-380.

Alemna, Anaba A. (1996). The Periodical Literature of Library and Information in Africa: 1990-1995. *The International Information & Library Review*, 28, 93-103.

Alqudsi-Ghabra, T. (1988). Librarianship in the Arab World. *International Library Review*, 20, 233-245.

Banerjee, Dwarika N. (1996). The Story of Libraries in India. *Daedalus* 125 (4), 353-361.

Bernhard, Paulette (1994). "The School Media/Informations Specialist: A Comparison of Standards and Guidelines about Personnel, Competencies, and Education (International Level, United States of America, France, United Kingdom, and English-Speaking Provinces of Canada." In *School Library Media Annual 1994*. Ed. Carol Collier Kuhlthan. Englewood, Colo.: Libraries Unlimited.

Bliss, Nonie J. (1993). The Emergence of International Librarianship as a Field. *Libri* 43 (1), 39-52.

Bliss, Nonie J. (1993). International Librarianship: A Bibliometric Analysis of the Field. *The International Information & Library Review*, 25, 93-107.

Bourne, Ross (1997). IFLA Section on Bibliography: Report of Activities, 1996/97. *63rd IFLA General Conference—Conference Programme and Proceedings*. http://www.nlc-bnc.ca/ifla/IV/ifla63/63cp.htm

Brogan, Martha L. (May 1990). Trends in International Education: New Imperatives in Academic Librarianship. *College & Research Libraries* 51 (3), 196-206.

Bywater, Margaret A. (1997). Libraries in Cambodia: Rebuilding a Past and a Future. *63rd IFLA General Conference—Conference Programme and Proceedings*. http://www.nlc-bnc.ca/ifla/IV/ifla63/63cp.htm

Calixto, Jose Antonio (1997). Public Libraries and Life-Long Learning—A Southern European Perspective. *63rd IFLA General Conference—Conference Programme and Proceedings*. http://www.nlc-bnc.ca/ifla/IV/ifla63/63cp.htm

Carroll, Frances L. (1982). World Librarianship. *Encyclopedia of Library and Information Science*, 33, 249-254.

Chung, Yeong-Kyong (1995). Characteristics of References in International Classification Systems Literature. *Library Quarterly* 65 (2), 200-215.

Conaway, Charles Wm. (1995). "Impact on the International Development of Librarianship." In *The Impact of Emerging Technologies on Reference Service and Bibliographic Instruction*, ed. Gary M. Pitkin. Westport, Conn.: Greenwood Press, 1995.

Cox, John (1997). The Changing Economic Model of Scholarly Publishing: Uncertainty, Complexity and Multimedia Serials. *63rd IFLA General Conference—Conference Programme and Proceedings*. http://www.nlc-bnc.ca/ifla/IV/ifla63/63cp.htm

Dobroussina, Svetlana (1997). Preservation Strategy in Russian Libraries: Priorities and Realization. *63rd IFLA General Conference—Conference Programme and Proceedings*. http://www.nlc-bnc.ca/ifla/IV/ifla63/63cp.htm

Fang, Josephine Riss and Paul Nauta (1991). IFLA's Contribution to Education for Library and Information Science. *IFLA Journal*, 17, 229-231.

Foglieni, Ornella (1997). How the Library Service Is Changing with Multimedia and the Global Network: A New Librarian for a New Role. *63rd IFLA General Conference—Conference Programme and Proceedings*. http://www.nlc-bnc.ca/ifla/IV/ifla63/63cp.htm

Ford, Barbara (1997). How to Go Global (Ten Areas Where Libraries Can Lead Communities). *American Libraries* 28 (October 1997), 35.

Goyal, S. P. (1987). Seventy Five Years of Indian Periodicals in Library and Information Science (1912-1986): A Survey. *Herald of Library Science*, 26 (1-2), 65-77.

Greguletz, Alexander (1993). Possibilities and Limitations of Adapting the Scandinavian Public Education Model in Germany at the Beginning of the Twentieth Century. *Libraries and Culture*, 28 (1), 55-58.

Guangjun, Meng and Wang Bing (March 1996). The Library and Information System of the Chinese Academy of Sciences. *Libri*, 46 (1), 52-58.

Harley, Bruce (1995). Spanning the Globe: Inter-governmental Organizations (IGO) Information on the Internet. *Database*, 18 (December 1995): 53-57.

Herubel, Jean-Pierre V. M. (1990). Internationality in Journals as Demonstrated in the *International Library Review* and *Libri*. *Collection Management*, 13 (3), 1-10.

IFLA's Conference Proceedings are provided on its world wide web page. For example, 63rd IFLA General Conference, August 31-September 5, 1997. http://www.nlc-bnc.ca/ifla/IV/ifla63/63cp.htm

Jacobs, V. (1997). From Local Village to Global Village: Can the Two Meet? *Information Development* 13 (2), 78-82.

Josey, E. J. (1988). Political Dimensions of International Librarianship. *Urban Academic Librarian* 6 (1), 1-16.

Ke, Du (1996). A Brief Account of Librarianship in China. *IFLA Journal*, 22, 83-90.

Kereszesti, Michael (1981). Prolegomena to the History of International Librarianship. *Journal of Library History* 16 (2) 435-448.

Knuth, Rebecca (1994). Five International Organizations Linking Children and Books. *IFLA Journal* 20 (4), 428-40.

Krzys, Richard and Gaston Litton (1983). "World Study in Librarianship." In *World Librarianship: A Comparative Study*. New York: Marcel Dekker.

Kubow, Stefan (1990). Publications on the History of Books and Libraries in Poland, 1981-1988. *Libraries and Culture* 25 (1), 48-72.

LaBorie, Tim, and others (1985). Library and Information Science Abstracting and Indexing Services: Coverage, Overlap, and Content. *Library & Information Science Research* 7 (April), 183-195.

Leonard, Barbara G. (1994). Collection Management in Australian Academic Libraries: An American Perspective. *Library Acquisitions: Practice & Theory* 18 (2), 147-156.

Lepik, Aira (1997). Library and Information Degrees: Traditions and Development in

Estonia. *63rd IFLA General Conference—Conference Programme and Proceedings.* http://www.nlc-bnc.ca/ifla/IV/ifla63/63cp.htm

Leskien, Hermann (1996). Allocated Parts: The Story of Libraries in Germany. *Daedalus* 125 (4), 331-352.

Liebaers, Herman and Margreet Wijnstroom (1988). "The Art of International Librarianship: The CLR-IFLA (Council on Library Resources—International Federation of Library Associations and Institutions) Style." In *Influencing Change in Research Librarianship: A Festschrift for Warren J. Haas.* Washington, D.C.: Council on Library Resources.

Liu, Ziming (1994). Sensitivity to Foreign Countries: A Comparison of U.S. Library Literature about China and China's about the United States, 1980-1989. *Libraries & Culture* 29 (2), 210-219.

Liu, Ziming (1992). A Comparative Study of Library and Information Science Education: China and the United States. *The International Information & Library Review*, 24, 107-118.

Loe, Mary H. (1990). Book Culture and Book Business: The UK vs. the U.S. *Journal of Academic Librarianship* 16 (1), 4-10.

Lor, Peter Johan (1996). A Distant Mirror: The Story of Libraries in South Africa. *Daedalus*, 125 (4), 235-265.

Ma, Yan, Steven J. Miller, and Yan Quan Liu (1997). Cataloging Nonprint Resources in the United States and China: A Comparative Study of Organization and Access for Selected Electronic and Audiovisual Resources. *International Cataloguing and Bibliographic Control* 26 (2), 46-49.

Marco, Guy A. (1987). Bibliographic Control of Library and Information Science Literature. *Herald of Library Science* 26 (1-2), 3-14.

Matare, Elizabeth (1997). Libraries and Cultural Priorities in Africa. *63rd IFLA General Conference—Conference Programme and Proceedings.* http://www.nlc-bnc.ca/ifla/IV/ifla63/63cp.htm

Miller, Marilyn L. (1989). "Afterword: Ten Years Later." In *US-USSR Colloquium on Library Services to Children, September 12-21, 1989*, ed. Susan Roman. Chicago: American Library Association, 1991.

Miranda, Antonio (1987). Publishing of Library Science Journals in Latin America. *Herald of Library Science* 26 (1-2), 31-34.

Mohlenbrock, Sigurd (1993). Reading as a Means in the Political Process. *Libraries and Culture* 28 (1), 39-43.

Moore, Nicholas Lister (1981). Library Periodicals from Developing Countries: Coverage by Major Abstracting and Indexing Services. *Journal of Librarianship* 13 (1). 37-45.

Mortensen Center for International Librarianship. *International Leads* 7, no. 1 (1993): 6-7.

Nilsen, Sissel and Torny Kjekstad (1997). The Division of Libraries Serving the General Public—A Survey. *63rd IFLA General Conference—Conference Programme and Proceedings.* http://www.nlc-bnc.ca/ifla/IV/ifla63/63cp.htm

Ogundipe, O. O. (1994). International and Comparative Librarianship in Developing Countries. *Journal of Education for Library and Information Science* 35 (3), 236-248.

O'Neill, M. (July 1994). British Cultural Exchange. *Library Association Record* 96 (7), 370-371.

Pacey, Philip (1994). "A Grapevine around the World": The Development, through 25 Years, of the International Role of ARLIS/UK & Ireland. *Art Libraries Journal* 19 (3), 53-60.

Penchansky, Mimi B., and Adam Halicki-Conrad, comps. (1986). *International and Comparative Librarianship: An Annotated Selective Bibliography on the Theme of the LACUNY 1986 Institute. Shrinking World/Exploding Information: Developments in International Librarianship.* The Library Association of the City University of New York.

Postlethwaite, B. (1992). The Global Library: The Impact of High-Speed Networks on Libraries. *Proceedings of the 14th International Essen Symposium: Libraries and Electronic Publishing: Promises and Challenges for the 90s: 14-17 October 1991.* Edited by Ahmed H. Helal and Joachim W. Weiss. Essen, Germany: Universitatsbibliothek Essen, 1992, p. 55-71.

Prytherch, Raymond John (1987). "Major Sources of Information: Abstracting and Indexing Services." In *Sources of Information in Librarianship and Information Science,* 2d ed., by R. J. Prytherch, 39-75. Brookfield, Vt.: Gower.

Prytherch, Ray and Mohinder Partap Satija (1986). Indian Library and Information Science Literature: A Guide to Its Coverage and Control. *Libri* 36 (2), 163-186.

Qureshi, Naimuddin (1980). Comparative and International Librarianship: An Analytical Approach. *Unesco Journal of Information Science, Librarianship and Archives Administration* 2 (1), 22-28.

Rader, Hannelore B. (1994). "International Role of U.S. Librarians." In *Bowker Annual Library and Book Trade Almanac.* 39th ed. New Providence, N.J.: R. R. Bowker, 1994.

Raptis, Paschalis (1992). Authorship Characteristics in Five International Library Science Journals. *Libri* 42 (1) 35-52.

Raseroka, H. K. (1997). Public Libraries and Life Long Learning—African Perspectives. *63rd IFLA General Conference—Conference Programme and Proceedings.* http://www.nlc-bnc.ca/ifla/IV/ifla63/63cp.htm

Reviller, Dominique (1992). IFLA-UNESCO: leurs relations et le developpement de la cooperation bibliotheconomique internationale. *Bulletin des Bibliotheques de France* 37 (6), 62-67.

Riedlmayer, A. (1996). Libraries Are Not for Burning: International Librarianship and the Recovery of the Destroyed Heritage of Bosnia-Herzegovina. *Art Libraries Journal* 21 (2), 19-23.

Roberts, B. (1993). Librarians in the New Europe: Training and Education Needs of Librarians Working in National Libraries. *Education for Information* 11 (4), 283-288.

Romano de Sant'Anna (1996). Libraries, Social Inequality, and the Challenge of the Twenty First Century. *Daedalus* 125 (4), 267-281.

Rooke, A. (1983). Assessment of Some Major Journals of International/Comparative Librarianship. *International Library Review,* 15, 245-255.

Rovelstad, Mathilde V. (1978). A New International Librarianship: A Challenge to the Profession. *Unesco Bulletin for Libraries* 32 (3), 136-143.

Rusch-Feja, Diann (1996). International Librarianship and Its Impact on the Profession. *Education Libraries* 20 (1/2), 13-24.

Schmidmaier, Dieter (1989). International Library Co-operation: A Summary. *IATUL Quarterly* 3 (3), 146-152.

Schurek, Antje (1994). UNESCO Network of Associated Libraries. *Herald of Library Science,* 33, 221-233.

Segal, JoAn S. (1990). Global Librarianship: The Role of American Academic Librarianship and ACRL. *College & Research Libraries News* 51 (6), 543-546.

Seidman, R. K. (1994). Building Global Partnerships for Library Cooperation. *Australian Library Review* 11 (1), 104-105.

"Select Bibliography on Soviet Librarianship in English." In *Russian Libraries in Transition.* Jefferson, N.C.: McFarland, 1992, 205-207.

Shyu, Jin-fen (1989). Selected Periodicals on Comparative and International Librarianship [in Chinese]. *Journal of Library and Information Science* 15 (2), 215-220.

Shyu, Jin-fen (1990). A Study of Research Methodology in Comparative and International Librarianship [in Chinese]. *Journal of Library and Information Science* 16 (1), 60-79.

Siddiqui, Moid A. (1994). Saudi Arabian Librarianship: An Annotated Bibliography (1987-1993). *International Information & Library Review*, 26, 243-255.

Singh, Sewa (1987). Literature Survey of Library and Information Science Publications in India. *Herald of Library Science* 26 (12), 48-61.

Spain, Victoria (1996). Russian Libraries, an Indestructible Part of National Memory: A Study Guide for Librarians. *Reference Services Review* 24 (1), 73-96.

Srikantaiah, Kanti and Xiaoying Dong (1997). Internet and Its Impact on Developing Countries: Examples from China and India. *63rd IFLA General Conference—Conference Programme and Proceedings.* http://www.nlc-bnc.ca/ifla/IV/ifla63/63cp.htm

Stueart, Robert D. (1997). International Librarianship: An Agenda for Research: The Asian Perspective. *IFLA Journal*, 23, 130-135.

Suttie, M-L. (1990). Libraries and Academic Support Strategies in South African Universities. *South African Journal of Library and Information Science* 58 (1), 98-107.

Torstensson, Magnus (1993). Is There a Nordic Public Library Model? *Libraries and Culture* 28 (1), 59-76.

Tzeng, S-s (1995). Exploration on the International Cooperation among National Libraries [in Chinese]. *Journal of Library and Information Science* 21 (1), 71-92.

Unesco Public Library Manifesto 1994. *Herald of Library Science*, 34 (3-4), July-October 1995, 252-253.

Valauskas, Edward T. (1997). International Federation of Library Associations and Institutions. In *Bowker Annual Library and Book Trade Almanac.* New Providence, N.J.: R. R. Bowker, 197-204.

Vosper, Robert (1984). IFLA and the Recent Growth of Organized International Librarianship. *Advances in Librarianship*, 13, 129-150.

Walker, M. (1996). A View from the Bridge. *Focus on International & Comparative Librarianship* 27 (3), 140-143.

Waneck, Kirsten (1997). Relations Entre le Secteur Public et le Secteur Prive Dans la Production des Bibliographies Nationales: Le Modele Danois. *63rd IFLA General Conference—Conference Programme and Proceedings.* http://www.ncl-bnc.ca/ifla/iv/ifla63/63 cp.htm

Ward, D. M. (1996). Promoting Global Resource Sharing and Cooperation: Recent Activities of IFLA's UAP, UBCIM, and UDT Core Programmes. *Resource Sharing and Information Networks* 11 (1/2), 193-201.

Wedgeworth, R. (1995). Toward a Global Library Community. *American Libraries* 26 (10), 1012, 10-14.

Williams, Sinead (1996). Library Services to the Blind in the United Kingdom and Ireland: A Comparative Study Five Years on. *Journal of Librarianship and Information Science* 28 (3), 133-140.

Wuest, R. (1993). From National Libraries to the Global Village Library: Networks Offer New Opportunities for Traditional Libraries. *IFLA Journal* 10 (4), 385-390.

Zaitsev, Vladimir (1996). Problems of Russian Libraries in an Age of Social Change. *Daedalus* 125 (4), 293-306.

Internet Resources

Organizational Web Sites

American Library Association
 http://www.ala.org/GoGlobal
 Tips for promoting libraries and librarians; selected resources.

 http://library.uiuc.edu/ahx/intala/rglist.htm.
 ALA Archives materials relating to international librarianship at the University of Illinois.

> *WESSWEB* Western European Specialists Section, Association of College and Research Libraries
> http://www.lib.virginia.edu/wess/

British Library. Library Development Office for Developmental Studies
 http://nt.1.ids.ac.uk/eldis/libr/lbr_lele.htm
 A selective list of sources on library and information work and lists of recent publications.

FID (International Federation for Information and Documentation)
 http://fid.conicyt.cl:8000/store1.htm
 Source for current FID publications, programmes, activities.

Global Information Alliance (GIA)
 http://fid.conicyt.cl:8000/giaopen.htm
 Nongovernmental organizations in information, communication, and knowledge to serve the world community.

International Association of School Librarians
 http://www.rhi.hi.is/~anne/iasl.html

International Federation of Library Associations and Institutions (IFLA)
 Worldwide independent organization devoted to library development, headquarted in The Hague, Netherlands.

> *IFLANET*
> IFLA's International Office for Universal Data Flow (UDT) at the
> National Library of Canada, maintains a web site and three listservs:
>> http://www.nlc-bnc.ca/ifla/
>> Includes Conferences and Proceedings; Core Programmes
> IFLA-L (listserv for communication with professionals worldwide)
> DIGLIB (development of digital libraries)
> LIBJOBS (posts jobs worldwide for librarians)

International Organization for Information Specialists (IOIS)
 http://www.rec.hu/iois
 International individual membership organization dealing with digital libraries, networks, libraries, and information management.

International Organization for Standards (ISO)
 http://www.iso.ch

International Research and Exchanges Board (IREX)
 http://www.irex.org/grants/us/libsproj.htm

Library of Congress Country Studies
 http://lcweb2.gov/frd/cshome.html

National Libraries of the World: An Address List
   http://www.nlc-bnc.ca/ifla/VI/2p2/natlib.htm

United Nations Educational, Scientific & Cultural Exchange
   http://www.unesco.org
   Under its General Information Programme (PGI), UNESCO assists its Member
   States in strengthening library infrastructures, promotes international interlibrary
    cooperation, and contributes to the restoration of selected libraries.
   http://www.unesco.org.webworld/library/library.htm

UNESCO Network of Associated Libraries (UNAL)
   http://www.unesco.org/web/unal/unalpg.htm
   Organized in 1990, UNAL promotes library cooperation for international
   understanding and encourages public libraries to undertake activities related to
   UNESCO's major goals. It publishes *UNAL INFO*, a quarterly in French, English, and
   Spanish.

International and Comparative Librarianship Web site
   http://www.shore.net/~amery/intindex.htm
   The author describes the purpose of this site as a starting point for those
   interested in researching international and comparative librarianship, and learning
   more about library development in a particular country. The site is divided into six
   categories: country information, foundations and organizations, sources, education,
   journals, and listservs.

   National libraries are included in country information, but users can connect to other
   types of libraries within the countries, including public and academic libraries.
   Charitable institutions, the United Nations, and selected international library
   organizations comprise the foundations and organizations category. The sources
   section links to library catalogs and library networks among other things. The education
   section links to schools and departments of library and information science and
   courses in international and comparative librarianship in US library schools. The
   journals category includes international journals with country notations and includes
   homepages of library journals. The listserv section provides connections to scholarly
   and professional listservs and selected library and information science listservs.

Contributors

Stephen R. Amery works as an information services assistant for a leading biotechnology company. Formerly a researcher in the news library of the BBC World Service and a deputy editor for Reuters, interested primarily in news research and the humanities, he has designed web pages on Romanian libraries and international and corporate librarianship. M.L.S. Simmons College, Boston, Massachusetts.

Matthew B. Barrett is Senior Analyst to the CFO at the Los Angeles Metropolitan Transportation Authority. He is in his second year of study toward a Master's of Library and Information Science. He received his B.A. in History and Art History in 1989 from University of California at Los Angeles with an emphasis in Latin American History and pre-Columbian art history.

Mary Biblo is a Master Teacher and school librarian at the University of Chicago Laboratory Schools, Illinois. She is a member of the Standing Committee on School Libraries of the International Federation of Library Associations (IFLA) and chair of the Round Table on Women's Issues (IFLA). She serves as a member of the Council of the American Library Association (ALA) and has been a member of several ALA committees including International Relations, Organization, Intellectual Freedom, Status of Women in Librarianship, and chair of the Minority Concerns Committee. She is a member of the Association for Library Service to Children and the American Association of School Librarians. She has served as treasurer and executive board member of the Black Caucus of the American Library Association.

George S. Bobinski is professor and dean of the School of Information and Library Studies at the State University of New York at Buffalo. He has been a visiting scholar at the Jagiellonian University in Krakow, Poland, and has had a longtime interest in Polish libraries and Polish librarianship. Ph.D. University of Michigan.

Philip J. Calvert is currently a visiting teaching fellow in the Division of Information Studies, Nanyang Technological University, Singapore; normally senior lecturer in the School of Communications and Information Management, Victoria University of Wellington, New Zealand. He was editor of *New Zealand Libraries* 1992-1996, and convenor of the Research SIG of the New Zealand Library and Information Association for the same period.

Arlene Cohen is assistant professor and systems librarian at the Robert F. Kennedy Memorial Library at the University of Guam. Before coming to Micronesia from Seattle, Washington, in 1987, she worked in academic settings as a library systems specialist, bibliographer and educator, and in the private sector as a technical editor and systems analyst. Prof. Cohen's work in Micronesia has focused on the areas of library automation, development of regional resource sharing networks, and telecommunications. A founding member of the Pacific Islands Association of Libraries and Archives (PIALA), she has also served as president, vice-president and executive secretary. Currently, she is the Guam representative on the PIALA Executive Board; secretary and executive committee member of the IFLA Round Table for the Management of Library Associations; treasurer of the Guam Library Association; and editor of the

PIALA annual conference *Proceedings*. Master's of librarianship, University of Washington, Seattle.

Joanne Tarpley Crotts, a resident of Guam for eleven years, is assistant professor and reference librarian at the Robert F. Kennedy Library at the University of Guam. A founding member and past treasurer of the Pacific Islands Association of Libraries and Archives, Prof. Crotts currently serves as its *Newsletter* editor and is the editor and compiler of the *Union List of Serials for Guam and Micronesia*. Her interests include resource sharing, interlibrary loan, Internet training and web page development. Joanne is married to Guam Symphony director Milton Crotts and has a nine-year-old son Miguet. M.L.S. Catholic University, Washington, D.C., in 1983.

Alma Dawson is assistant professor at the School of Library and Information Science at Louisiana State University, Baton Rouge. She has over twenty years' experience as a practicing professional librarian, including serving as bibliographer and librarian of the Library and Information Science Library at Louisiana State University. Dr. Dawson holds membership in the American Library Association, the Association for Library and Information Science Education, and Phi Delta Kappa. Ph.D. Texas Woman's University, Denton, Texas.

Barbara J. Ford is executive director of the Virginia Commonwealth University Libraries, Richmond and the 1997-1998 president of the American Library Association (ALA). A librarian for more than 20 years, she served as a Peace Corps volunteer in Panama and Nicaragua. Ms. Ford is a member of the Virginia State Council of Higher Education Library Advisory Committee and Virtual Library of Virginia Steering Committee. She serves on the boards of the Fund for America's Libraries and the Freedom to Read Foundation. The author of many publications and presentations, Ms. Ford has traveled around the world to address such topics as information literacy, the future of academic libraries, international cooperation among libraries, and virtual libraries. She earned a bachelor's degree in history from Illinois Wesleyan University, Bloomington, a master's degree in international relations from Tufts University, Medford, Massachusetts, and a master's degree in library science from the University of Illinois at Urbana-Champaign.

Charlotte E. Ford is a doctoral student at the Indiana University School of Library and Information Science, Bloomington. She has worked as a reference librarian, government documents librarian, and cataloger in various academic libraries in the United States and Colombia. M.L.S. 1986 Indiana University.

Ken Haycock is professor and director at the University of British Columbia School of Library, Archival and Information Studies in Vancouver, Canada, and executive director of the International Association of School Librarianship. Dr. Haycock is also currently president of the American Association of School Librarians, the Council for Canadian Learning Resources and the West Vancouver School Board and a member of the ALA Council. He is a past president of the Canadian Library Association and the Canadian School Library Association. Honored by several associations, Dr. Haycock is editor of *Emergency Librarian* and *Resource Links*.

Norma J. Hervey is head librarian, 1988-1997, and professor of history, 1997- at Luther College, Decorah, Iowa. She also served Luther College as chair of an ad hoc Russian Studies Committee and then as chair of the resulting Russian Studies Minor from 1992-1997. Dr. Hervey served on the *Choice* editorial board and several committees of the College Libraries Section of the Association of College and Research Libraries. Her sabbatical year, 1994/95, was spent teaching history at Palackeho University. In addition to serving as an NEH grant coordinator, she is the official host for the current Fulbright scholar at Luther College. She has led several study abroad courses in Eastern Europe. M.L.S. State University of New York, Ph.D. history, University of Minnesota, Minneapolis.

Suzanne Hildenbrand is associate professor at the School of Information and Library Studies of the State University of New York at Buffalo where she teaches cataloging and online bibliographic retrieval. She is the editor of *Reclaiming the American Library Past: Writing the Women In* (1996). She has served on the Committee on the Status of Women of the American Library Association. Her M.S. in Library Service is from Columbia University and her doctorate is from the University of California at Berkeley.

Barbara Immroth is professor at the University of Texas at Austin, Graduate School of Library and Information Science. She is vice-president of Beta Phi Mu and is currently serving as president of the Texas Library Association and the ALA representative to the IFLA Standing Committee on Children's Libraries. She is on the ALA research team for the National Assessment of the role of public and school libraries in educational reform and a past president of the Association for Library Service to Children.

William V. Jackson, Professor Emeritus at the University of Texas, Austin, is currently Senior Fellow at Dominican University and Visiting Lecturer at Pratt Institute. He has long specialized in library development in Latin America, as well as on Latin American resources in U.S. institutions, and has undertaken numerous assignments in all parts of the region—as consultant to the U.S. Information Service (USIS) in many countries and to Agency for International Development (AID) on the national textbook program in Brazil. He has been visiting professor at the library schools of the University of Antioquia and University of Buenos Aires. Among individual institutions with which he has worked are the University of San Marcos, University del Norte, Francisco Marroquín University, and Universidade Federal de Santa Maria. He has written numerous books, reports, articles, and reviews, including *Aspects of Librarianship in Latin America* (1962, 2nd ser., 1992). He is past president of the Seminar on the Acquisition of Latin American Library Materials (SALALM) and past chair of ALA's International Relations Round Table (IRRT). In addition to his work in Latin America, he has spoken in Europe, Australia, Singapore, Turkey and Egypt. Recently, he undertook two missions to Bolivia, and for the past five years has served as continuing advisor on library development to USIS in El Salvador and to a number of individual institutions in that country. Ph.D. Harvard University; M.S. (in L.S.) University of Illinois.

Eric A. Johnson is the senior exchange specialist at the Library of Congress responsible for book and serial exchanges with libraries in Estonia, Latvia, Lithuania, and Russia. In 1993, he worked at the National Library of Estonia as an ALA Library Fellow. Estonia was the inspiration for his first two books for children: *The Stone-Dragons of Metsamaa* (1994) and *The Color Thieves* (1996). M.L.S. University of Maryland, College Park.

T. N. Kamala is currently working on a compendium on user studies that cover both theoretical and experimental aspects of human-computer interaction, with special reference to information retrieval. She served as information scientist and as a member of the INIS (International data base of the International Atomic Energy Association) Group, Bhabha Atomic Research Centre, India, for several years. She is the recipient of the AAUW International Education Foundation Fellowship (Centennial Year Award), the ACRL/ISI Doctoral Dissertation Award, the Sigma Xi, the Scientific Research Society Grant, and the Ralph Shaw Professional Award. Dr. Kamala began her career as an experimental physicist and moved on to information science and has extensive research experience in special libraries. She was the founding editor of the Indian Women Scientists Association (IWSA) *Newsletter* and also served on the editorial committee of the Indian Vacuum Society. She won the Virginia Grant for IWSA for training women on computers. She has a M.Sc. in physics and B.Lib.Sc. from India and has M.L.I.S. and Ph.D. in CIS from the U.S.

Irina L. Klim is a director of the Information Resources Center at USIS, St. Petersburg, Russia, and a visiting professor at the St. Petersburg Academy of Culture, Department of Library and Information Science. She was dean of the Department of Library Science at St. Petersburg Academy of Culture from 1989 to 1993. From 1993 to 1995 she studied (Pratt Institute, SLIS) and worked in the United States of America (Brooklyn Public Library) under the auspices of NAFSA/USIA. She is a member of Beta Phi Mu, ALA and the St. Petersburg Library Association, and editor of the section "Translations" in a Russian professional journal *Petersburg Library School*. Dr. Klim has two master's of library science from Russia and the United States, and a Ph.D. in library science (cataloging and classification) from St. Petersburg Academy of Culture, Russia.

Rebecca Knuth is assistant professor at the University of Hawaii, Department of Information and Computer Sciences, Honolulu. Her areas of research interest include international and comparative librarianship, libraries and literacy in developing countries, school libraries, and information policy. Ph.D. Indiana University, Bloomington.

Maria Kocojowa is professor and head of the Department of Library and Information Science at the Jagiellonian University in Krakow, Poland. She also serves as associate dean of the faculty of Management in which DLIS is located and is president of the Research Council of the LIS Institute. Dr. Kocojowa is on the editorial board of *Knigotyra* and *Krakowski Rocznik Archiwalny* (Krakow Archives Annual). She is a prolific author of many scholarly works dealing with Polish librarianship. Ph.D. Warsaw University, Poland.

Aira Lepik is professor of librarianship at the Tallinn Pedagogical University, Department of Information Studies, Estonia. She is a member of the Standing Committee/Section on Education and Training, IFLA (1995-99); corresponding member of the Executive Committee of Round Table on Research in Reading/Section of Reading (1991-1997); member of the International Development in Europe Committee of the International Reading Association (since 1992); president of the Estonian Reading Association (since 1992); and board member of the Estonian Librarians' Association (1994-1998). She is an editorial board member of *Journal of Research in Reading* (United Kingdom) and the electronic journal *Infofoorum* (Estonia). Ph.D. State Institute of Culture of St. Petersburg, Russia.

Kate Lippincott is reference and government documents librarian at the Selby Public Library in Sarasota, Florida. She has published an ERIC Digest on diversity in the library profession and compiled *OLOS: Twenty-Five Years of Outreach—A Bibliographic Timeline.* She has worked in academic libraries in Georgia and Alabama and worked on the PALS Across Georgia Union Catalog Project. M.A. University of South Florida, School of Library and Information Science, Tampa, Florida.

Irene Lovas is currently the librarian at Long Beach Community Medical Center. She was formerly the network coordinator at the Pacific Southwest Regional Medical Library, one of the eight regional offices of the National Network of Libraries of Medicine (NN/LM). She has served on various local and national committees and task forces for the Medical Library Association, as well as California State Library task forces.

Beverly P. Lynch is professor in the Graduate School of Education & Information Studies, University of California, Los Angeles. She has been president of the American Library Association, chair of the Association's International Relations Committee, chair of its International Relations Round Table, and serves on various national and international professional boards and committees. She was dean of the Graduate School of Library and Information Science, UCLA, 1989-1994, and university librarian, University of Illinois at Chicago, 1977-1989. She was executive secretary of the Association of College & Research Libraries, 1972-1976. Ph.D. University of Wisconsin-Madison.

Daniel Mattes is university librarian at the Universidad Anahuac, a major private university on the outskirts of Mexico City, Mexico. He was previously director of library services at the University of the Americas (Mexico City Campus) and served as National Library Fellow in Mexico from 1984-1986. He has also worked at medical and public libraries in the United States, as well as the Institute of Latin American Studies at the University of Texas at Austin. He has presented papers on topics related to Mexican librarianship at meetings of the Mexican Library Association (AMBAC), Texas Library Association, American Library Association. He has also frequently presented papers at the Mexico City Association of Medical Librarians. He is an active member of the Mexican Library Association, ALA's subcommittee on Latin America and the Caribbean and the Transborder Library Forum. Prof. Mattes has a B.A. in philosophy, psychology and Spanish from the University of Texas at Austin, where he received his M.L.I.S. He has also done graduate studies in Latin American Studies.

Kathleen de la Peña McCook is professor and director at the University of South Florida, School of Library and Information Science, Tampa, Florida. She has been president of the Association for Library and Information Science Education; chair of the American Library Association Office for Literacy and Outreach Services Advisory Committee; Office for Library Personnel Resources Advisory Committee and Status of Women in Librarianship Committee; editor of *RQ* and *Public Libraries*; and currently serves on the Board of Directors of REFORMA. Ph.D. University of Wisconsin-Madison.

Kingo J. Mchombu is professor at the University of Namibia, Department of Information and Communication Studies, Windhoek, Namibia, southern Africa. He was training officer of Tanzania Library Services and a senior lecturer, University of Botswana, Department of Library and Information Studies. He currently serves on the editorial board of the *International Information Library Review* and the *African Journal of Library, Archives and Information Science*. He is the founding editor of *Namibian Development Journal*. Ph.D. University of Loughborough, United Kingdom.

Margaret Myers joined the Peace Corps to work in libraries in rural Botswana in 1995. Before the Peace Corps, Myers was director of the American Library Association Office for Library Personnel Resources for nearly twenty years. In this capacity she was involved with helping prospective librarians learn about careers in librarianship, educational programs, and scholarships. She was responsible for developing conference programs and workshops and publications on a variety of personnel-related topics to assist library employers and staff with such issues as collective bargaining, salaries, affirmative action, performance appraisal, staff welfare, job placement, and career development. Myers received a master's degree in librarianship from Rutgers University and also holds a master's degree in social work from the University of Illinois. Prior to coming to the ALA Myers taught and was placement director at the Rutgers University library school.

Mary Nassimbeni, associate professor in the School of Librarianship of the University of Cape Town, South Africa, has taught library and information studies since 1981. Her research interests focus on the development of the information society and national library and information policy. She has numerous publications and has served on a number of national commissions in South Africa dealing with these topics. Ph.D. University of Cape Town, South Africa 1988.

Muzhgan Nazarova, a citizen of Azerbaijan, is currently participating in the Freedom Support Act Fellowship Program as a graduate student in library and information science at the University of North Carolina at Chapel Hill. IREX administers her fellowship. She received a Certificate in Management from the Nottingham Trent University Business School, England. She works as director of the Information Resource Center for the USIA in Baku, a capital of Azerbaijan. She was awarded a Danida Grant to attend the IFLA Conference in Copenhagen, Denmark, this year. She is the first Azerbaijanian to receive an M.L.S. from an ALA-accredited institution and to be a member of ALA.

Michael Neubert is a senior reference librarian working in the European Reading Room of the Library of Congress, specializing in Russia. He is active in the American Association for the Advancement of Slavic Studies. During the 1990s he has visited many libraries in the former Soviet Union, presenting seminars on American librarianship. He was selected as an ALA Library Fellow to spend eight months in Ekaterinburg, Russia, during 1997-1998.

Hope A. Olson is assistant professor at the School of Library and Information Studies, University of Alberta, Edmonton, Alberta, Canada, where she teaches cataloguing, classification, indexing, and feminism and LIS. Her current research is developing a prototype to make the Dewey Decimal Classification useable for interdisciplinary areas and disadvantaged groups. She uses feminist poststructural and postcolonial theory in practical application. Ph.D. University of Wisconsin-Madison.

Luz Marina Quiroga is a Ph.D. candidate at Indiana University in the School of

Library and Information Science, Bloomington, Indiana. In her work as a systems designer, she has collaborated on such projects as the Serial Union Catalog in Colombia and Mexico, and the National Mexican Bibliography. M.S. in Computer Science 1980, Universidad Nacional Autonoma de Mexico, Specialist in Library and Information Science 1994, Indiana University.

Donald E. Riggs is vice-president for information services and university librarian at Nova Southeastern University, Fort Lauderdale, Florida. Prior to his current position, Riggs was dean of University Library and professor of information at the University of Michigan, Ann Arbor. He has served as president of the Library Administration and Management Association; an American Library Association Councilor; a member of the Library and Information Technology Association Board of Directors; founding editor of Library Administration & Management; and is currently editing *College & Research Libraries*. In 1991, Riggs received the Hugh C. Atkinson Memorial Award for his innovation and leadership in library technology.

Jordan M. Scepanski is executive director of the Triangle Research Libraries Network, a consortium of Duke, North Carolina Central, and North Carolina State Universities and the University of North Carolina at Chapel Hill. From 1984 to 1996 he was director of library and learning resources at California State University, Long Beach. He is past chair of the American Library Association's International Relations Round Table, has taught as a Fulbright Lecturer in library science at Hacettepe University in Ankara, and was a U.S. Peace Corps volunteer in Turkey where he has lectured and consulted widely. M.Ln. Emory University, Atlanta, Georgia, and M.B.A. University of Tennessee at Nashville.

Bradley L. Schaffner is the head of the Slavic Department and coordinator for international programs at the University of Kansas Libraries, Lawrence, Kansas. He serves as librarian for Russian and East Slavic studies. He is chair of the Slavic and East European Section of the Association of College & Research Libraries and a member of the Bibliographic and Documentation Committee of the American Association for the Advancement of Slavic Studies. He holds an M.A. in Russian and Soviet history and an M.L.S., both from Indiana University, Bloomington.

Diljit Singh is coordinator of the Library and Information Science Program at the University of Malaya, Kuala Lumpur. He previously taught in two secondary schools, worked with the Pahang State Department of Education and the Aminuddin Baki Institute, Ministry of Education. Currently he also serves as director for Asia in the International Association of School Librarianship (IASL) and is the chairperson of the School Resource Center Committee, Library Association of Malaysia. Dr. Singh serves on the editorial board of the *Malaysian Journal of Library and Information Science*. Ph.D. Florida State University, Tallahassee.

Gary E. Strong is director of the Queens Borough Public Library in New York City. He was the state librarian of California from 1980-1994. He has served as president of the Library Administration and Management Association, Pacific Northwest and Oregon Library Associations, Western Council of State Libraries and Chief Officers of State Library Agencies and currently co-chairs the National Organizing Committee for the IFLA 2001 Conference to be held in Boston, Massachusetts. He holds degrees from the University of Idaho and the University of Michigan, where he was named Distinguished Alumnus in 1984.

Peter G. Underwood is professor of librarianship at the University of Cape Town, South Africa, having occupied this position since 1992. Formerly he was at the College of Librarianship Wales, living through its growth and eventual amalgamation with the University College of Wales, Aberystwyth. He is author of *Managing Change in Libraries and Information Services: A Systems Approach* (Library Association, 1990) and *Soft Systems Analysis and the Management of Libraries, Information Services and Resource Centres* (Library Association, 1996) and, with R. J. Hartley, of *Basics of Data Management for Information Services* (Library Association, 1993).

Patricia A. Wand is university librarian at the American University in Washington, D.C. She has held library positions at the University of Oregon and Columbia University Libraries. She earned degrees at Seattle University, Washington, Antioch University, Ohio, and the University of Michigan. Ms. Wand served as a Peace Corps volunteer in Colombia and as a Fulbright senior lecturer in library science in Ecuador. Besides library administration, Ms. Wand has focused on the delivery of information to users and teaching users to be information literate. Active in the American Library Association, she has worked extensively on library legislative issues on the state and national levels. She recently served as president of the District of Columbia Library Association. Ms. Wand has published numerous articles and made presentations on library issues related to electronic delivery of information and copyright concerns.

Robert Wedgeworth is university librarian and professor of library administration at the University of Illinois at Urbana-Champaign. He was the 1997 recipient of the American Library Association Melvil Dewey Award. Prof. Wedgeworth was dean of the School of Library Service at Columbia University of New York from 1985-1992 and executive director of the American Library Association from 1972-1985. He serves as a trustee for the Newberry Library in Chicago and chairs ALA's Advisory Committee for the Office of Information Technology. Prof. Wedgeworth is the author of *The Starvation of Young Black Minds: The Effects of the Book Boycotts in South Africa* 1989 and *Issues Affecting the Development of Digital Libraries in Science and Technology* 1996. He is the recipient of the International Council of Archives Medal of Honor, the Most Distinguished Alumnus Award from the University of Illinois and the 1989 ALA Joseph Lippincott Award. He received a bachelor's degree from Wabash College in Crawfordsville, Indiana, and a master's degree from the University of Illinois at Urbana-Champaign.